Ceramics

A POTTER'S HANDBOOK

fifth edition

Ceramics

A POTTER'S HANDBOOK

Glenn C. Nelson

Harcourt Brace College Publishers
Fort Worth   Philadelphia   San Diego
New York   Orlando   Austin   San Antonio
Toronto   Montreal   London   Sydney   Tokyo

Publisher   Susan Katz
Managing editor   Edward B. Cone
Acquisition editor   Karen Dubno
Senior project editor   H. L. Kirk
Picture editor   Joan Scafarello
Manuscript editor   Susan Converse Winslow
Production manager   Nancy J. Myers
Art director   Lou Scardino
Text design   Caliber Design Planning
Cover design   Lou Scardino

Library of Congress Cataloging in Publication Data

Nelson, Glenn C.
   Ceramics: a potter's handbook.

   Bibliography: p.
   Includes index.
   1. Ceramics. I. Title.
TP807.N363   1984   738.1′4   83-12633

ISBN 0-03-063227-7 College softcover edition
ISBN 0-03-064163-2 General Book hardcover edition

Printed in the United States of America.

5 6 7 8 9 0   032   15 14 13 12 11 10

Composition and camera work by York Graphic Services, Inc., Pennsylvania
Color separation and printing by Lehigh Press Lithographers, New Jersey
Printing and binding by Von Hoffmann Press, Inc., St. Louis

Preface

Twenty-five years ago I began working on the first edition of *Ceramics: A Potter's Handbook*. Previously I had written two small reference manuals, primarily for my own students, for during the 1950s there was little published to serve as a classroom aid to the beginning pottery student. At that time, I looked forward to working with my new publisher, Henry Holt, to expand and turn my original manuals into a more useful and complete work. I never expected that today I would be completing a fifth edition of a basic how-to manual for the beginning and intermediate potter as well as a reference source for the more sophisticated craftsperson. A large part of the success of the book is due to the kindness of fellow potters whose work has illustrated the various editions and whose valuable criticism and suggestions have resulted in improvements over the years.

The book begins with a discussion of clays—their origin, composition, and types. Following this are two chapters that briefly survey the ten-thousand-year history of work in clay and provide a context for viewing the contemporary ceramic pieces that illustrate other chapters. The next two chapters cover, respectively, hand-building and wheel techniques, with step-by-step photos to illustrate each process. A general chapter on decorating and glazing techniques shows the complete range of possibilities, from simple dip-glazing to complex figural work combining many methods, followed by two detailed chapters on glaze formulation and glaze calculations and chemicals. Because the ultimate firing is so crucial to any ceramic work, I devote an extensive chapter to contemporary kilns, kiln materials, kiln construction, and the various processes for oxidation, reduction, salt-glaze, and raku firings. The book concludes with an analysis of the role played by the professional potter, whether in the classroom, the studio, or industry. There are also several appendices of practical and technical information and a bibliography and glossary of ceramic terms.

There are several important changes in this fifth edition of *Ceramics*. For one thing, by request I have restored the historical survey of ceramics, omitted in the fourth edition. The concept of integrating examples of historical works with each forming and decorating technique had seemed logical then, but in practice many instructors had difficulty locating works from a particular period or culture as they needed them.

As always there are numerous new works by contemporary potters, but fewer pieces are from areas outside North America. Thirty or forty years ago regional characteristics were easily observed in the world of ceramics; today, the ease of communication between countries has fostered an eclectic style in which the ceramics of one country can hardly be distinguished from the ceramics of other countries. In a way this is to be regretted, but perhaps it cannot be helped. In the past, generations of potters combined to develop and refine a form, glaze, or decoration slowly over time. Our quest for the new and different is more impatient; in the end, however, it may prove just as frustrating as the thought of working in an evolving style.

Several additional features are new to this edition. One is an increased attention to safety and health in the ceramic studio. In all chapters where use of equipment and materials requires caution, the relevant information has been boxed off from the text and highlighted in a distinctive manner. Another is the setting off for easy reference as photo essays the step-by-step procedures for various forming and throwing techniques. Many of the standard procedures are illustrated by new photographs, and there are some new and unusual techniques as well. A unique feature is the inclusion of personal statements by several professional potters about their careers. The serious student who contemplates making a living in this field should find these particularly interesting.

Acknowledgments

I thank the many potters who have allowed me to use examples of their work in this edition. Without their new and exciting pieces the text would be very dull indeed. I am also indebted to the many museums both here and abroad who have furnished photos of work from their collections. For the new throwing and forming shots I am most grateful to potter Jay Lindsay and the help of photographer Pete Dommermuth. I am especially grateful to the potters who allowed me to use their personal statements in the Professional Potter chapter. It is kind of them to "go public" in matters of their personal careers. I am also appreciative for process shots furnished by Carol Jeanne Abraham, Nino Caruso, William Daley, Dick Evans, John Glick, Marilyn Levine, Jane Peiser, Don Reitz, and Peter A. Slusarski.

I must also express thanks to the following potters and teachers who made constructive suggestions for the new edition and read the manuscript: Richard Buckman (St. Louis Community College at Florissant Valley, Missouri), Val Cushing (Alfred University, New York), Art Haney (East Carolina University, North Carolina), Wayne Hauxhurst (Florida Keys Community College, Florida), Richard Mower (Montgomery College, Maryland), Polly Myhrum (New Hamburg, New York), Myra Toth (Ventura College, California), Ann Tsubota (Somerset County College, New Jersey), John Wantz (College of Du Page, Illinois), Helen Weisz (Bucks County Community College, Pennsylvania), and Warren Wilson (Brigham Young University, Utah). Particular thanks go to Walter Hyleck, who in his overall criticism of the old text and in suggestions for improvements was of great assistance to me.

The staff of Holt, Rinehart and Winston, new to this edition, were helpful in many ways throughout the development and production of this complex project. They are cited on the copyright page along with the roles they played.

My final debt is to my wife, Edith, who in a noncritical way may be even more excited about ceramics than I am. She has buoyed me up when discouraged, deciphered my scrawl, retyped endless manuscript pages, and will equally enjoy seeing the new edition in print.

G. C. N.

Garrison, New York
September 1983

Contents

10 ● The Professional Potter   297

Appendices   319

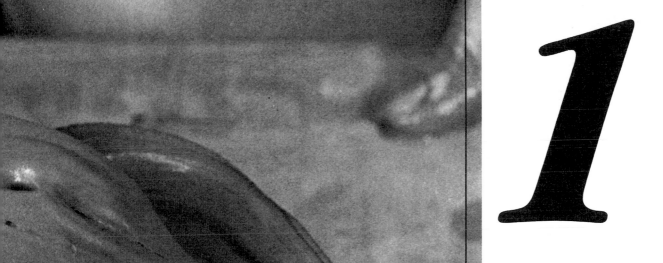

1

Clay and Clay Bodies

Clay is the very common but unique material that makes ceramics possible. It should not be confused with soil—a combination of clay, sand, humus (partially decayed vegetable matter), and various other minerals. Compared with other materials in the earth, soil forms an extremely thin outermost layer—varying from several inches to a foot (about 7 to 11 cm to .33 m) thick. There are, of course, large areas without soil, such as most desert and mountain regions. Between the soil proper and the rocky core of the earth rests a thicker layer of subsoil composed of clay mixed with sand and gravelly mineral deposits. Within this layer large beds of clay are found. In order to explain better the variety and nature of clay types, a brief description of the formation of this layer of subsoil is necessary.

Formation of Clay

As the earth cooled very slowly from its fiery origins, a rocky outer crust hardened, while internal pressures and volcanic eruptions pushed up mountainous areas. Gradually, water vapor formed, and an atmosphere was created. The resulting rains and winds caused erosion, while extremes of heat and freezing temperatures led to expansion and contraction of the earth's surface. These combined forces fractured and crumbled the exposed rock. The initial composition of this rock varied greatly from place to place, so that the process of erosion had different effects and occurred in different manners over the surface of the earth. For the formation of clay beds, the two most important forces were the melting and movement of the ice cover during the glacial ages and the organic acids released by the decay of vegetation.

1 Electron micrograph of Georgia kaolinite (magnified 52,000 times) showing platelike particles. Courtesy Kenneth M. Towe, Smithsonian Institution, Washington, D.C.

CLAY AND CLAY BODIES

Clay derives from the disintegration of granite and other feldspathic rocks that, as they decompose, deposit alumina and silica particles. The most valuable clays for the potter consist mainly of the mineral kaolinite, which has an ideal formula of $Al_2O_3 \cdot 2SiO_2 \cdot 2H_2O$. Kaolinite particles (Fig. 1) are shaped like very thin plates less than 2 microns in size (1 micron is 0.001 millimeter or 0.00004 inch). Fine grains of sand are huge in comparison— 0.02 inch (0.05 cm) in diameter. Unlike the granular structure of sand, kaolinite particles are flat and cling together like a deck of wet playing cards. These particles slide and support one another in both wet and dry states, giving clay its most valuable quality, *plasticity* (Fig. 2).

Most clay found in the earth does not contain sufficient amounts of kaolinite to make it plastic, and nearly all clay has some impurities. These impurities and variations of the basic formula account for the different characteristics of the numerous clay types.

2 Dora De Larios, U.S.A. Wall sculpture showing the intricate plastic effects possible in clay, length 20″ (50.8 cm).

Clay Types

As they are mined, clays can be classified as either residual or sedimentary. *Residual* clays have remained more or less at the site of the decomposed rock. They are less plastic than sedimentary clays, and because they have been subject to fewer erosive forces, their particle size is much larger. *Sedimentary* clays are those that, by the action of wind or running water, have been transported far from the site of the parent rock. This action had considerable effect on the mixture and breakdown of the minerals, and therefore the particles are very fine and the clay more plastic.

Kaolin

Kaolin is a very pure form of clay that is white in color and *vitrifies* (becomes nonporous and glasslike) only at very high temperatures. For these reasons, kaolin is seldom used alone but makes an important ingredient in all high-fire whiteware and porcelain bodies (Fig. 3). Kaolin also provides a source of alumina and silica for glazes.

The wide variety of kaolin types available illustrates the difficulty of classifying clays. In the United States the major commercial deposits are in the Southeast. North Carolina produces a residual kaolin with many coarse rock particles, while the deposits in South Carolina and Georgia are sedimentary. Florida deposits are even more plastic and are often termed ball kaolin or EPK (Edgar Plastic Kaolin from Edgar, Florida). No kaolin, however, is truly plastic in comparison with ball clay.

The kaolin beds in England are among the largest in the world. They are mined by hydraulic methods and require a complicated system of separating out the finer particles in huge settling tanks. Clays from the various mines are blended to produce kaolin of several consistent types. The fineness of particle size makes these clays suitable for casting or throwing bodies. The type called *grolleg* is the best kaolin addition for a plastic porcelain throwing body.

Ball Clay

Ball clay is chemically similar to kaolin after firing. In its unfired state, however, the color ranges from a light tan to a dark gray because of the organic material present. Although weathered from a granite rock much like

3 Jo Kirschenbaum, U.S.A. Tea set. Porcelain with a brown (high iron) temmoku glaze. Decoration in rutile, iron, and Albany slip, height of teapot 9″ (22.8 cm).

CLAY AND CLAY BODIES

that which produced kaolin, the ball clay particles were deposited in swampy areas. Organic acids and gaseous compounds released from decaying vegetation served to break down the clay particles into even finer sizes than those of the sedimentary kaolins.

Ball clay imparts increased plasticity and dry strength when used as a body component. If a clay body contains 10 to 20 percent ball clay, it has greatly improved throwing qualities. Like kaolin, ball clay matures at a high temperature and can serve as a source of alumina and silica in recipes for *glaze* (a liquid suspension of ground minerals applied to fired ceramic ware) as well as a binding agent. However, when stored for long periods of time, such glazes tend to form gas that can lead to glaze defects. In this event the glaze can be dried out and reused, or a few drops of formaldehyde can be added to discourage fermentation.

Stoneware Clays

Stoneware clays are of particular interest to the potter because they are generally very plastic and fire in the middle range of temperatures, from about cone 5 to cone 10.* (See Fig. 4.) Stoneware bodies are almost completely vitreous. Depending upon the atmospheric conditions of the firing, the color will vary from buff to gray. In the United States stoneware clays occur in scattered deposits from New York and New Jersey westward to Illinois and Missouri, as well as on the Pacific coast. The clays differ in composition. Compared with kaolin they contain many more impurities, such as calcium, feldspar, and iron—all of which lower the maturing temperature and impart color to the clay.

Fireclay

Fireclay is a high-firing clay commonly used for insulating brick, hard firebrick, and kiln furniture (the shelves and posts that hold pots inside a kiln). Its physical characteristics vary. Some fireclays have a fine plastic quality, while others are coarse and granular and more suitable for handbuilding than for throwing. Fireclays generally contain some iron but seldom have calcium or feldspar. The more plastic varieties, like some stoneware clays, often occur close to coal veins. They can be high in either flint or alumina and therefore have special industrial uses. Fireclays of one type or another are found throughout the United States, absent only from a few mountainous regions and the southeast and northeast coasts. Its availability and plasticity make fireclay a component of stoneware bodies.

Earthenware Clays

Earthenware clays comprise a group of low-firing clays that mature at comparatively low temperatures ranging from cone 08 to cone 02. (See Fig. 5.) They contain a relatively high percentage of iron oxide, which serves as a *flux* (a substance that lowers the maturing temperature of the clay), so that

---

*See temperature chart in the Appendix giving cone equivalents in degrees Fahrenheit and Centigrade. Cones indicated in text refer to the Orton series. Note that Seger cones have a slightly different range.

4 Bill Read, England. Teapot. Stoneware with carved decoration. Talc-glaze-fired to cone 8 in reduction.

5 Tom Kerrigan, U.S.A. *Repeated Fours*. Lidded container of burnished earthenware with slip-trailed designs in terra sigillata, reduction fired, height 14.5″ (36.25 cm).

when fired they are rather fragile and quite porous. The iron also gives fired earthenware its deep red-brown color. Unlike stoneware bodies, the usual earthenware body, after firing, has a porosity between 5 and 15 percent. Because of the various fluxes it contains, earthenware cannot be made vitreous, for it deforms and often blisters at temperatures above 2100°F (1150°C). All of these factors limit its commercial use to such things as building bricks, flowerpots, and tiles. Many potters, however, have done considerable work in earthenware. Some find its red-brown color attractive; others use it as a base for bright, low-fire glazes.

Earthenware clays of one type or another can be found in every part of the United States, although commercial deposits are abundant in the lower Great Lakes region. Many such clays, available commercially, are of a shale type. Shale deposits are clays laid down in prehistoric lake beds. Time, chemical reactions, and pressure from overlying material have served to cement these clay particles into shale—a hard, stratified material halfway between a clay and a rock. Shale clays are mined and ground into a powdered form similar to ordinary clay. The small lumps that remain can be troublesome if not screened out, for, like plaster, they will absorb moisture, expand, and rupture after firing.

Some earthenware clays are of glacial origin and therefore vary greatly in composition. They frequently contain soluble sulfates that are drawn to the surface during drying. When the clay is fired, a whitish film appears on the surface. This defect can be eliminated by an addition to the clay body of 2 percent barium carbonate.

Slip Clay

Slip clays naturally contain sufficient fluxes to function as glazes without further addition. (See Fig. 3.) Although white and even blue slip clays exist, the most common are tan, brick red, or brown-black. Most slip clays fire in a middle range from cone 6 to cone 10. The best-known commercial slip clay is Albany, mined in pits near Albany, New York. There are many small deposits of glacial clays scattered throughout the northern United States that will make satisfactory slip glazes with little or no addition. Slip glazes are easy to apply; they usually have a long firing range and few surface defects. (By contrast, casting slips are special bodies compounded for such production methods as jiggering and casting; see Chap. 10.)

Bentonite

Bentonite is an unusual clay. In small amounts it functions as a plasticizer. Deposits are found in most of the western mountain states, the Dakotas, and in several Gulf states. It has the finest particle size of any clay known.

Bentonite was formed in prehistoric ages from the airborne dust of volcanic eruptions. Compared to kaolin, it is slightly higher in silica and lower in alumina, with a small amount of iron. A nonclay glaze may include up to 3 percent bentonite for an adhesive without noticeably changing the glaze. When used in nonplastic (short) clays, 1 part bentonite is equal to 5 parts ball clay. The body should be mixed dry, since bentonite becomes quite gummy when mixed alone with water.

Clay Bodies

An earthenware, stoneware, or porcelain body that is completely satisfactory for the potter seldom occurs in nature. The clay may not be plastic enough, may have an unattractive color, or may not fire at the desired temperature. Even clays from the same bed will vary slightly in chemical and physical qualities. Thus, it is usually necessary to mix clays in order to achieve a workable body.

In making up a clay body, you will generally begin with a clay that is available at a reasonable price and has no major faults, such as an excessive amount of sand or grit. No clay should be considered unless it is moderately plastic. The plasticity can be improved by additions of ball clay or bentonite. In rare cases, a clay may be so fine that it will not dry easily without cracking. In this event, you can add a less plastic clay—silica sand or a fine grog (crushed, fired clay)—to *open up* the clay body and make it more porous so it will dry uniformly. This treatment is often necessary to make an extremely fine, or *fat,* clay throw and stand up better. Some potters add coarse grog to a clay body for the rough, textured effects it creates.

Occasionally, a clay will lack sufficient fluxes to fire hard enough at the desired temperature. When this occurs, inexpensive materials containing fluxes—such as feldspar, talc, dolomite, nepheline syenite, or bone ash—are usually added. If the color is not important, you can use iron oxide. In some cases a small amount of lower-firing clay can be added, which has the advantage of not cutting down on plasticity. If, on the other hand, there is too large

6 Allester Dillon, U.S.A. Openware vase of hand-rolled coils. Sculpture clay body fired to cone 9 with a thin mat glaze, height 10″ (25.4 cm).

7   Kazuko K. Matthews, U.S.A. Wall form. Raku with slips and oxides. Strong, smoky reduction fire, 17″ × 17″ (43 × 43 cm). Collection Mr. and Mrs. William Klages.

a proportion of fluxes and the clay body deforms at a relatively low temperature, you must either begin again with a different clay or add clays that are higher in alumina or in silica and alumina. Either a Florida kaolin or a plastic fireclay of high maturity will work for this purpose.

Basic Clay Bodies

Raku Bodies   The composition of raku bodies must be quite different from those for normal firing, because of the raku firing process (Fig. 7). The ware is placed in a hot kiln, and, when the glaze becomes molten, it is removed and cooled very quickly. In order to withstand these radical temperature changes, the ware must be thick walled. The body is generally a stoneware clay containing at least 20 percent grog. Raku pottery remains rather porous after the final glaze firing. (See Chap. 9 for firing techniques and the Appendix for a raku body formula.)

Earthenware Bodies   Earthenware bodies are characterized by their deep reddish brown color (caused by the high iron content) and a high porosity that results from their lower firing range. These qualities make earthenware popular with sculptors and hand builders. White earthenware clay rarely occurs in nature. Low-fire white bodies contain large amounts of talc along with kaolin and feldspar to reduce their firing temperatures to between cone 08 and cone 04. The bright and even color of these bodies provides a good base for high-contrast, low-fire decorative effects, such as decals, lusters, and bright, primary colors. Because of the rising cost of fuel, many ceramists are also adapting traditional stoneware and porcelain techniques to low-fire bodies.

Stoneware Bodies There is little chemical difference between a stoneware and a porcelain body, except for the presence of small quantities of iron and other impurities that color the stoneware and reduce its firing range to between cone 6 and cone 10. Stoneware bodies, however, are generally much more plastic than porcelain and are better suited for throwing and hand-building techniques (Fig. 8). Many hand potters are attracted to stoneware for the range of color that can be obtained in a gas kiln under *reducing* conditions (firing without oxygen) from a very light buff to tan to a dark brown. Most stoneware bodies contain grog to make the clay stronger and more versatile in its plastic state.

8 Alan Peascod, Australia. Jar. Stoneware with incised decoration and mat iron glaze, height 33.75″ (53 cm).

9

9 Robin Hopper, Canada. Shallow bowl. Porcelain with neriage (colored clay) inlay, diameter 12″ (30 cm).

China Bodies Bone china resembles porcelain, except that bone ash has been added to the body as a flux to increase translucency and to reduce the temperature needed for maturity to about cone 6. Like porcelain, bone china is very hard, white, and translucent when thin. Its greatest faults are a tendency to warp in firing and the lack of sufficient plasticity for throwing.

The term *chinaware* is used rather loosely to designate a white body usually fired between cones 4 and 8. Some types, such as restaurant china, are very hard and durable. They should not, however, be confused with the even harder and more translucent porcelain bodies fired at cone 10 to cone 16.

Porcelain Bodies The highest-firing category of ceramic wares, porcelain bodies are characterized by a smooth texture, uniform white color, and the ability to accept fine detail (Fig. 9). They are relatively nonplastic and fire, between cone 8 and cone 12, to an extremely hard, vitreous ware. These qualities make porcelain ideal for commercial products shaped mechanically by casting or jiggering (see Chap. 10). Many hand potters have become interested in exploiting these same effects, and therefore porcelain bodies with greater plasticity and slightly lower maturing temperatures (cone 6 to cone 10) have been developed. Porcelain bodies are compounded principally from kaolin, feldspar, and flint. For increased plasticity some ball clay is generally added, resulting in a higher shrinkage rate. In a throwing body, the ball clay may be as much as 25 percent of the body. (See Appendix for suggested clay bodies.)

Special Clay Bodies

Sculpture Bodies Problems often arise in constructing large, thick-walled sculptural forms in clay (Fig. 10). The most serious of these are a tendency for vertical walls or horizontal spans to sag and the danger that thick areas will

left: 10 **Dora De Larios**, U.S.A. Head. Thrown stoneware sections and paddled clay with additions, fired to cone 10, temmoku glaze, life size.

above: 11 Fragments of fiberglass cut and placed on the clay prior to edging. This increases the clay's strength in the moist state.

crack during drying. The addition of grog to a sculpture body will help the clay to *stand up,* or support itself without collapsing. If grog is wedged into the clay in amounts of 20 to 30 percent of the body, it will reduce shrinkage strains placed upon thicknesses of clay. In drying, the clay pulls away slightly from the grog. This opens air channels, causes a more even exposure of the clay to the air, and lessens the danger of cracks occurring.

Another possible addition to the sculpture body is *fiberglass,* which is actually glass in fibrous form (Fig. 11). Shredded fiberglass can be wedged into the clay to increase its plastic strength. When slabs of unusual stability are needed, some potters sandwich a mesh of fiberglass between layers of clay. Since fiberglass consists mainly of silica, it melts into the body during firing.

Ovenware and Flameware Bodies   Most earthenware and stoneware can be heated at 400°F (204.44°C) in an oven, provided the walls and bottom are of uniform thickness and that the glaze, if any, coats both inside and outside (Fig. 12). This helps the pot to heat and cool evenly. Another general precaution with ovenware is to place it in a cool oven and let it heat up slowly; once it is hot, never expose it to rapid cooling.

A ceramic body can be formulated to control the effects of quartz inversion (see section on quartz inversion in Chap. 9) and make it more resistant to heat shock. The body should be stoneware or fireclay and should first be tested to determine its chemical composition. Depending upon the alumina-silica ratio and fluxes present, a 15 to 20 percent addition of spodumene, wollastonite, or petalite will reduce the possibility of cracking. (Because of the difficulty in obtaining petalite, 3 parts spodumene and 1 part feldspar can be substituted for 4 parts petalite.) A combination of pyrophyllite and talc to replace part of the feldspar in the body will also cut down on thermal expansion.

A direct flameware body is similar to ovenware except that the petalite may comprise as much as 50 percent of the body, the balance being ball clay,

12 **Stig Lindberg** for Aktielologet Gustavsberg Fabriker, Sweden. Set of utensils suitable for either table or oven. Flameproof ovenware.

stoneware, or fireclay. A small amount of feldspar will combine with any free silica that may remain. Firing temperatures should be to cone 10 or above, but the body should retain a porosity of 3 to 4 percent.

Colorants Depending upon firing conditions, most earthenware and stoneware bodies range in color from a light tan through buff and orange-red to a deep reddish brown. The warm, earthy tones result from the different amounts of iron oxide present in the clay. These hues can be made darker by adding either red or black iron oxide and/or manganese dioxide. If the colorants are finely ground, they will create an even tone; colorants with a coarse particle size yield a more speckled effect. Always make tests when adding colorants, for too much iron oxide will lower the melting temperature of the body, and a large quantity of red iron will cause the clay to stain whatever comes in contact with it during the forming process.

Pure white bodies are characteristic of porcelain in the high-firing range and white earthenware in the lower temperatures. It is possible to add oxides to these bodies to produce green, blue, yellow, or even lavender clays. The oxides should be added to clay in its dry state, and the mixture sieved before adding water. See Chapter 6 for decorating techniques with colored clays and the Appendix for colorants and their properties.

left: **13 Georgette Cournoyer**, Canada. Tool bag. Black clay slabs imitative of a leather surface, 16″ × 15″ × 6″ (40.6 × 38.1 × 15.2 cm).

right: **14 Mayer Shacter**, U.S.A. *Reflections on a Marine Venus*. Covered vase. An unusual porcelain piece with thrown and altered additions. Copperred trailed decoration under a celedon glaze, height 9″ (22.8 cm).

Tests for Clay Bodies

Before a new clay or clay body is purchased or used, a few simple tests should be made to determine its various characteristics.

Plasticity

Plasticity is essential to any clay body. A standard, simple test for plasticity is to loop a pencil-size roll of clay around your finger. If the coil cracks excessively, the clay is probably not very plastic. The ultimate test,

however, is to work with the clay to determine if it throws without sagging and joins without cracking. In comparing bodies, make sure that all samples have been aged for equal lengths of time. Three weeks in a plastic state is usually adequate for a clay to improve appreciably. In this time the finest particles become thoroughly moist, making possible the slight chemical breakdown caused by the organic matter contained in all clays. (According to legend, ancient Chinese potters prepared huge quantities of clay that were stored in pits and covered with moist straw. Each generation of potters used the clay prepared by the previous one.)

Wedging, a process by which the clay is kneaded by hand to remove air pockets, has considerable effect in increasing plasticity. In a coarse clay, the realignment of particles by wedging can also prove beneficial (see the section on wedging in Chap. 4).

Water of plasticity refers to the amount of water needed to bring a dry, powdered clay into a plastic state. The finer the particle size, the more plastic a clay will be and the more water it will absorb.

Porosity

The porosity of a fired clay body is directly related to the hardness and vitrification of the clay. To make a porosity test, weigh an unglazed fired-clay sample. After an overnight soak in water, wipe the sample clean of surface water and weigh it a second time. The percentage gain in weight will be the porosity of the clay body.

Most bodies used by the hand potter can be fired with a variation of at least 50°F (10°C) from the optimum firing temperature without proving unsuitable. As a general rule, fired clay bodies fall within the following porosity ranges: earthenware, 4 to 10 percent; stoneware, 1 to 6 percent; porcelain, 0 to 3 percent. A higher firing will reduce the porosity, but normally a specific firing temperature will have been chosen. Adjustments in the flux ratio will affect the firing temperature and relative porosity.

Shrinkage

Shrinkage of the clay body occurs first as the clay form dries in the air and then again as the form is *bisque* fired (low fired but not glazed) and finally when glaze fired. The more plastic clays will always shrink the most. The test for shrinkage is quite simple.

○ First, roll out a plastic clay slab, and either cut or mark it to a measure.
○ When the slab is totally dry, take a second measurement.
○ Make a final measurement after firing.

Clay shrinkage rates generally range from 5 to 12 percent in the drying stage, with an additional 8 to 12 percent shrinkage during firings. Thus, you can expect a total shrinkage of at least 13 percent and an extreme of 24 percent, with a median of 15 to 20 percent between the wet clay and the final glazed ware. These normal shrinkage rates apply to plastic throwing clays. Special whiteware bodies using spodumene in place of feldspar and only small amounts of clay have a greatly reduced shrinkage and can even be compounded to develop a slight expansion in firing. Wollastonite as a replacement for silica and flux in a body will also decrease firing shrinkage.

Clay Prospecting and Preparation

There are few sections of the United States in which a suitable pottery clay cannot be found. Digging and preparing your own clay is seldom an economic proposition, but it can be rewarding in other ways (Fig. 15). If you are teaching in a summer camp, for example, a hike can easily be turned into a prospecting trip. For the few hundred pounds (about 90 to 180 kg) of clay you may want to obtain, you must depend upon the accidents of nature to reveal the clay bed. A riverbank, a road cut, or even a building excavation will often expose a deep bed of clay that is free of surface contamination. If the clay contains too much sand or gravel it may not be worth the trouble. A few tree roots will not disqualify a clay, but any admixture of surface soil or humus will make it unusable.

On the first prospecting trip take samples of a few pounds (about 0.90 to 2 kg) of clay from several locations. Dry the samples, pound them into a coarse powder, and then soak them in water. Passing the resultant clay slip (liquid clay) thrugh a 30-mesh sieve is usually sufficient to remove coarse impurities. If the clay proves too sandy, let the heavier particles settle for a few minutes after stirring, and then pour off the thinner slip. Pour this slip into drying bats until a wedging consistency is reached, and then test for plasticity, porosity, and shrinkage.

In most localities, surface clay is likely to be of an earthenware type. The samples should also be tested as possible slip glazes. It is surprising how many pockets of glacial clay work nicely as glazes, either alone or with a small amount of flux added. In some areas, the riverbank clay may be of a stoneware or fireclay type. All in all, clay prospecting can be profitable, but it is mostly fun. In this day of the super-processed item, starting out from "scratch" gives a rare feeling of satisfaction.

 SAFETY CAUTION

Fine clay dust can be a health hazard. Quarry workers have traditionally been subject to silicosis, a deadly lung disease caused by breathing in fine rock particles. When preparing bagged clay, therefore, be sure to wear a protective mask. Use an oily sweeping compound to keep clay dust from flying when sweeping up dusty studio floors. Dermatitis, an inflammation of the skin, occurs in rare instances from handling wet clay. It is an allergic reaction. If it occurs, unfortunately you have no choice but to give up potting.

Various glaze chemicals are also toxic, as are the gases given off during firing. For specific cautions concerning these and other health problems related to ceramic materials see the chapters on decorating, glazing, and firing (Chaps. 6–9). Also consult W. C. Alexander, "Ceramic Toxology" in Gerry Williams, Peter Sabin, and Sarah Bodine, eds., *Studio Potter's Book* (Warner, N.H.: Daniel Clark Books, 1978); Michael McCann, *Artist Beware* (New York: Watson-Guptill, 1979); "The Impact of Hazards in the Arts on Female Workers," *Preventive Medecine* 6 (1979): 338–348; and *Art Hazards Newsletter* (Center for Occupational Hazards, 5 Beekman St., New York, N.Y. 10030).

right: **15**   Digging clay in the hills near Mashiko, Japan.

below: **16**   Kaolin mining at Sandersville, Georgia. Courtesy Amoco Minerals Company, Englewood, Colorado.

The commercial mining of clay is worth mentioning briefly, even though the production of clay for the potter represents only a very small fraction of the clay mining business. Millions of tons of clay are mined each year for a great variety of industrial purposes—building bricks, refractory liners for steel furnaces, insulating materials, and bathroom fixtures. Especially fine kaolin clays are used for coating printing papers, while other clays serve as extenders or fillers in paint and insecticides.

Depending upon how close to the earth's surface a clay is located, there are basically three different methods for mining clay. High-iron-content clays, primarily for tiles and bricks, occur close to the surface and are usually extracted with a power shovel. Impurities are sieved out after drying and a coarse grinding. Shale clays, found at deeper levels, require blasting techniques, followed by grinding and sieving. Fireclay is often close to coal beds and is mined either in an open pit or in a traditional shaft. The coarsely ground particles are mixed with water, causing the larger particles to settle. After drying, a fine dust is produced by *air-floating*—separating particles by air pressure.

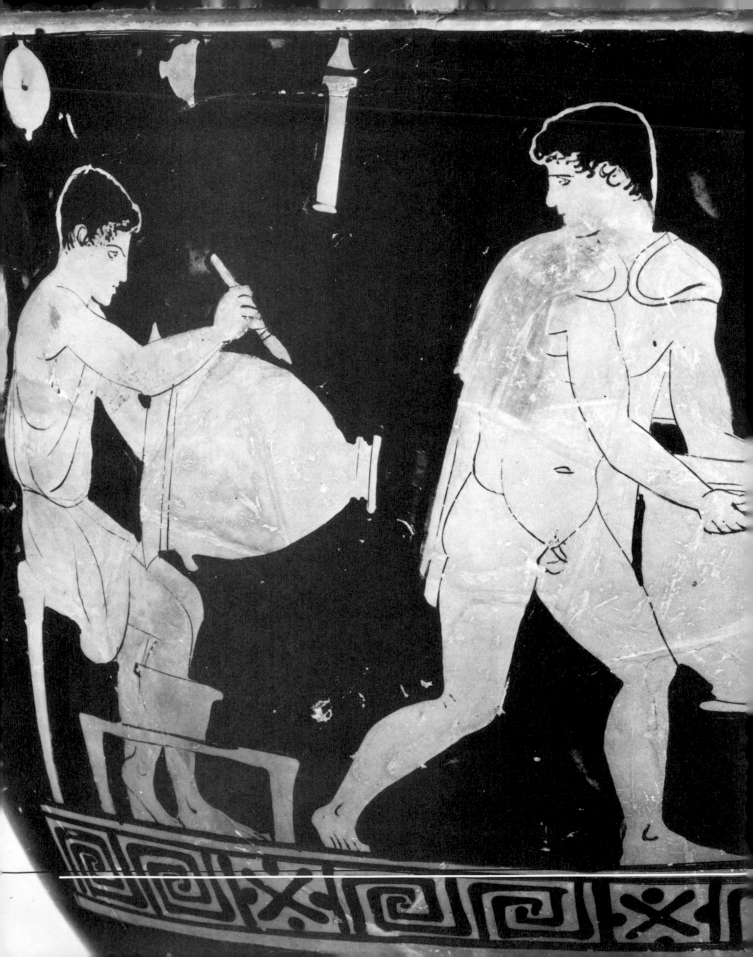

2

Early Ceramic
History

Of all the remains left by ancient cultures, perhaps none have proved as valuable to the archaeologist and the student of history as the numerous artifacts made of fired clay. Except in unusual and fortuitous circumstances, items of wood, leather, and fabric, however carefully fashioned, that have survived more than a thousand years are rare. Even bronze and iron are prone to disintegrate, and exposed stone weathers nearly as rapidly. Clay, which is usually abundant everywhere, has the unique property of being easily fashioned into a variety of forms. When fired in a kiln or even in a bonfire, it fuses into a hard and durable material.

This almost indestructible nature of fired clay has allowed us to surmise the existence of cultures that otherwise would be completely unknown. Birth, puberty, and death are the great traumatic experiences of human life. Although we in the twentieth century tend to be a bit blasé about these events, our ancestors celebrated them with elaborate ritual. Death in particular was a frightening and mysterious event that required the propitiation of unknown forces. Belief in some sort of existence in the hereafter dates from the furthest reaches of time, for we find that Paleolithic peoples sprinkled their dead with red ochre as a symbol of life and buried them with their stone weapons and a supply of food. As early peoples developed the skill of pottery making, we find pottery included in these funerary offerings. A large portion of the ancient ceramics illustrated in this chapter comes from such grave sites and, for the most part, they were made especially for that purpose. The forms were often those in common use at that time but with a thinner and a more carefully finished body and elaborate decoration. Reflecting the conservative nature of religious customs, the grave ware might also resemble an older style and could, for example, still be hand built although the ware made for daily use was wheel thrown. Often the grave offerings were overly elaborate and nonfunctional in design and were even decorated with fugitive colors, reflecting their one-time use.

Through changes in these pottery styles we can often trace the rise of ancient cultures, the beginnings of early trade routes, the dislocations caused by war, and the restless migrations of peoples seeking a better land. Regardless of the initial development of a form or decoration, we find that if it is accepted by the populace at large it acquires, as it were, a life of its own and continues to be transmitted from parent to child as in most traditional crafts. Thus in various parts of the world we can see echos of ancient forms and decorations that have survived for millennia.

As far as can be determined, the potter has been historically conservative in outlook and working habits. Throughout the ages the potter has been an artisan of low social status, producing ware in direct response to the needs of the community. The pressures for individuality and the desire to be different, so prevalent among potters today, have no historical precedent, for the technical nature of ceramics is such that a small change in methods or materials can well produce disastrous results. Therefore, for most of history, the craft of ceramics has changed slowly, even in the face of an improved technique. For example, although the potter's wheel was introduced into southern Germany, France, and England during the period of the Roman occupation and local potters learned to use it, they seem to have forgotten the technique after the Romans retreated to the Mediterranean area. We find no more wheel-thrown pottery until the seventh century in England. It gradually reappeared elsewhere as trade between northern and southern Europe increased during the Middle Ages.

17 Bison, Tuc d'Audoubert, Ariège, France. After 15,000 B.C. Modeled clay, 25 and 24″ (63.5 and 61 cm) long. Photo Yan, Toulouse, France.

Social and economic conditions have had a controlling influence on whether the potter's work was rigidly traditional or modified by outside influences. Early small, self-contained communities generally had a conservative tradition. Even as population grew, the first urban centers arose, and trade among communities expanded, an occasional imported jar doubtless had little effect on local potters. If competing trade among communities developed to any extent, however, then the local potters were forced to adapt the new shapes and/or decorations. It is likely that trade has had as an important an effect on changing ceramic styles as have the dislocations caused by migrations, war, or the overthrow of established ruling classes.

Origins of Pottery

Although early people were using crude stone tools in East Africa in the early Paleolithic period, as long as 2.6 million years ago, most of human cultural development has occurred much more recently, since the beginning of the Neolithic period after 10,000 B.C.

Paleolithic and Neolithic Cultures

The peoples of the Paleolithic period were wandering hunters. They also gathered wild seeds, tubers, and fruits. At the end of the Paleolithic period, about 10,000 B.C., the icecap covering most of nothern Europe, Asia, and North America receded, and much of northern Africa and western Asia became hot and dry. During the early Neolithic period, after about 7000 B.C., early communities began to settle down in fertile and temperate river valleys, first in western Asia and eastern Europe, later in Egypt, India, China, and Mexico. They deliberately planted seeds to produce a more dependable yield. Wild emmer and einkorn wheat from the upland valleys of Anatolia (now Turkey) and Iran are the source from which modern varieties of wheat are descended. These early farmers also domesticated wild goats and cattle. Dogs, of course, had long been hunting companions.

Long before these Neolithic developments of sedentary life, agriculture, and animal husbandry, Paleolithic cave paintings in Altamira, Spain, and the Dordogne Valley, France, about 25,000 to 15,000 B.C., reveal on the part of their creators a critical observation and graphic skill we can envy today. Numerous bone carvings also exist from Paleolithic times. Rock outcroppings in the caves were modeled with clay and painted to resemble animal forms (Fig. 17). Because of the plastic nature of moist clay it is also likely that figurines, probably fertility fetishes, were made, although they have long since perished. In any event, such figurines, both fired and (more rarely) unfired, are found in all later, Neolithic cultures. The Syrian votive statue in Figure 18 is representative of this type of cult image. From these early artistic achievements we can speculate that perhaps the economic changes of the Neolithic period were due less to an innate improvement in human capacity than to the effects of a changing climate.

The First Pottery

The women of Neolithic families gathered wild and cultivated seeds and stored them in tightly woven baskets. Often the baskets were coated on the inside with clay to form a more effective container. Because the oldest

18 Votive figure, Syria. 1400 B.C. Terra-cotta. Metropolitan Museum of Art, New York (gift of George D. Pratt, 1933).

pots in most Neolithic cultures have a basketlike or a corded texture (Fig. 19), many scholars have speculated that pottery making was first discovered by the accidental burning of a basket and the subsequent hardening of its clay lining. This is only theory, since the oldest known pots (the early Japanese *Jomon* ware discussed later in the chapter) were made by a fishing and shellfish-gathering culture that had not yet reached the agricultural stage.

It is true, however, that the first pottery in all cultures was probably made by women as part of their household chores. Only as settlements grew and a market developed where a skilled worker could trade wares for grain, leather, and other goods, did pottery become a craft practiced largely by men and their households.

Although the discovery of pottery by early Neolithic cultures seems to have taken place independently in many areas of the world, the discovery of glassy ceramic glaze, which had both practical and decorative value, was not universal. Glaze was first used on beads and decorative tiles in Egypt about 2700 B.C., but its adoption in the Middle East was slow. Neither glazes nor the potter's wheel developed in sub-Sahara Africa, Oceania, or the New World. Although high-fired stoneware and porcelain developed early in the Orient, because of the continued use of low-fire kilns and lack of interest in higher-firing clays, these wares never developed in the Middle East and appeared in Europe only in relatively recent times. Thus ceramic development worldwide was very uneven; neglected in some areas, it made tremendous advances in others, as this chapter and the next, which trace the history of pottery form and decoration, will show.

19   Pot, found in the Thames near Mortlake, England. Fired clay with cord impressions, height 5.25″ (13 cm). British Museum, London.

Early Kilns

To understand the development of ceramic form and decoration it is useful to know something about early kiln design, for the two are directly related.

Pit Firing

The first pots and figurines were fired in what was little more than a bonfire (Fig. 20). Usually a shallow pit was dug and filled with a layer of dry twigs or even coarse grass. On this bed the sun-dried ware was placed and covered with more twigs and dry wood. After the pile was lit and burning, more small pieces of wood were added until the ware was covered with a glowing layer of red-hot coals. After a couple of hours the fire bed was covered with a layer of ash, broken pottery shards, and earth to contain the heat and allow the ware to cool slowly.

Only a low-firing clay could be used in such a procedure. The ware, fired to only about 1500°F (800°C) was not really mature but was able to serve a useful purpose. Since the body was porous, it was often rubbed with the leaves of gummy plants while still hot, which gave it a slight waterproof coating. Most low-firing clays have a high iron content. When smothered with ashes, the normal red iron (Fe_2O_3) in the clay body is converted by the lack of oxygen into the black oxide form (FeO). Carbon impregnated in the surface of the ware also contributes to the dark color of pit-fired pottery. Long after proper kilns capable of oxidization were developed, many cultures continued to make black ware by firing with a nearly oxygen-free atmosphere. These pieces were first coated with a fine decanted slip and burnished to produce a glossy surface. The Chinese *Lung-Shan* ware and the Etruscan *bucchero* ware, discussed later, are examples of the advanced black-ware tradition.

Bank Kilns

In an effort to fire clay at a higher temperature in order to produce a more durable ware, early potters developed the bank kiln (Fig. 21). Dug into the side of a bank or hill, it provided a fuel port for the fire at the bottom, an enclosed heat-retaining chamber next to it, and a ventlike chimney opening

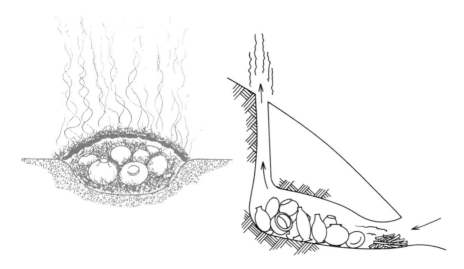

left: 20   A primitive bonfire firing in a shallow pit.

right: 21   An early bank kiln, showing firebox and chimney.

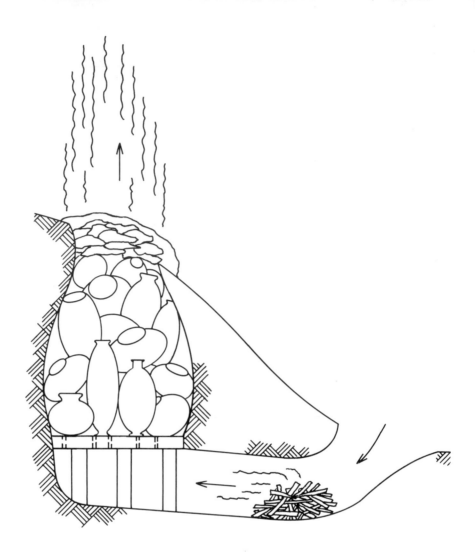

above: **22** Top-loading bank kiln with firebox construction.

left: **23** Rectangular Rennaissance updraft kiln.

below: **24** Large single-chamber climbing-bank kiln similar to those used at Ching-Te-Chên.

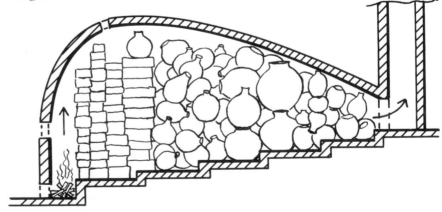

farther up the hill. This arrangement created an updraft that contributed to higher temperatures. In time a slotted kiln floor was added and the chamber enlarged (Fig. 22). In addition to the higher temperatures, the bank kiln made it possible for the potter to control the firing atmosphere at either a reducing or an oxidizing state.

Freestanding Kilns

Eventually potters evolved a freestanding kiln made of clay bricks with a firebox on the bottom separated by a slotted floor from a kiln chamber above. The change from pit-fired ware to kiln-fired ware can be distinguished by the appearance of wares with red bodies, often decorated with brushed slip decorations. This shift occurred as early as 5700 B.C. in southeast Anatolia and slightly later in Iraq and China. It is likely that there was much cooperation between the early metalsmith and the potter because both depended upon obtaining high temperatures to make their product. There is no record or metal casting in a culture without a developed pottery tradition.

During the Classical Greek and Roman periods (fifth century B.C.–fifth century A.D.) the typical kiln in the Mediterranean region was shaped like a beehive about 6 feet (1.8 m) in diameter. Beehive kilns were also common in northern China. By the eighth century A.D., kilns in the Islamic Middle East were often built with an upper and a lower chamber. The cooler upper level was used either to fire ware to the bisque state or to give it a *luster* (metallic) glaze. By the fifteenth century in Renaissance Italy, a larger, rectangular updraft kiln had evolved in order to fire the greater quantities of pottery then being produced (Fig. 23).

All this Greco-Roman and Islamic pottery and most pottery in medieval and Renaissance Europe was earthenware, fired at a temperature seldom exceeding 2000°F (1093°C). Only in the Rhine Valley, where stoneware clays were discovered and there was plenty of wood to keep up a hot fire, did potters, about the fourteenth century, begin to make higher-fired stoneware in rectangular downdraft kilns.

Bank-Climbing Kilns

As early as 1000 B.C. potters in southern China were producing a few high-fired proto-stoneware pieces. Stoneware became fairly common by the Han Dynasty (206 B.C.–A.D. 220) and porcelains during the Sung Dynasty (960–1279). This early development of higher-fired ware is explained partly by the fact that China had plentiful supplies of stoneware clays and of kaolin and feldspathic rock for porcelain. Equally important was the bank-climbing, or sloping, kiln, which was constructed up a bank or hillside in mountainous southern China (Fig. 24).

By the Sung period the sloping kiln had developed from a single large chamber often 15 feet (4.57 m) high into a series of large chambers rising in steps up the hillside from the firebox at the base. Heat from a wood fire rose from chamber to chamber and escaped through a vent higher up the slope. Separate fuel ports allowed extra wood to be added to keep the heat even in the upper chambers. The wares were enclosed in *saggars,* round containers of fireclay serving to protect the glazed surface from kiln fumes and the falling ash that had accidentally glazed unprotected Han stoneware. The kiln construction and the saggars created a downdraft, in which the heat was deflected up one side of the lowest chamber by the wall of stacked saggars

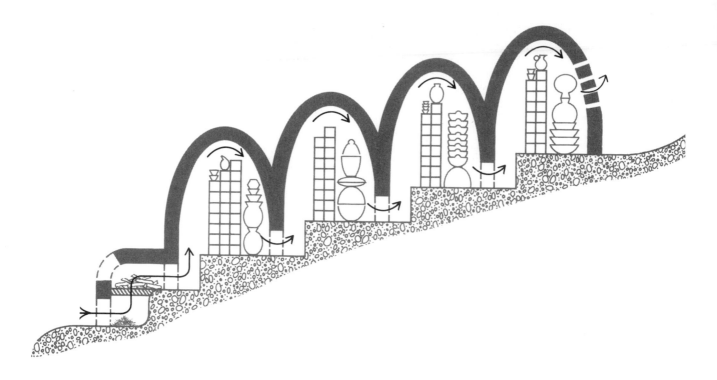

25 Japanese multiple-chamber climbing kiln.

and was drawn down through the ware by the suction of the draft at the opening at the bottom of the chamber wall to pass into the next higher chamber. This design permitted an efficient use of fuel to achieve high temperatures for more ware because the heat that would be lost out the vent in a single-chamber kiln was used to heat the upper chambers.

Korean kilns, or *anagama,* were similar to Chinese sloping kilns but with more numerous auxiliary fuel ports to obtain better control of the heat in the single long chambers. Japanese kilns were based on Chinese and Korean models. By the seventeenth century they consisted of as many as twenty connecting small chambers about 6 feet high and 8 feet wide (1.83 by 2.44 m), an arrangement that greatly improved efficiency (Figs. 25 and 26).

Thus we find that kiln design played as important a role in the development of ceramics as innovations in form, decoration, and glaze. The next sections of this chapter and the following chapter will discuss characteristic pottery in various areas of the world.

The Ancient Orient

The Far East has a long ceramic tradition, dominated by China. The oldest known pottery, Japanese Jomon ware, dates prior to 10,000 B.C. Recently discovered ware in northern Thailand has a tentative date of 7000 B.C. In China itself the earliest known pottery fragments date from before 4500 B.C.

China

Neolithic Period As elsewhere in the Neolithic period, the earliest Chinese pottery was black and round-bottomed and had an impressed-cord

26 Detail of a climbing kiln, showing chamber doorways and saggers.

27 Yang-Shao ware bowl, Peihsien, Kiangsu Province, China. Neolithic (4000–3000 B.C.). Red-brown earthenware, painted; height 3.9″ (10 cm), diameter 7″ (18 cm).

decoration. This ware gave way to a polished ware. As early as 4000 B.C., a highly developed, slip-decorated pottery appeared in the Yang-Shao cultures of Kansu Province in central China. The tall, rounded jars and graceful, flaring bowls of this ware were decorated with curvilinear plant and fish motifs in a black manganese or iron-red slip (Fig. 27). The sophisticated appearance of this early painted ware has baffled many archaeologists. The thin, light red, burnished vessels were baked in an oxidizing fire to at least 1832°F (1000°C) and skillfully decorated. Normally one would expect to fine an intermediate ware, between the polished ware and the Yang-Shao ware, that was more crudely made and decorated, but none has been discovered. Since slip-decorated ware appeared much earlier in the Middle East than in China, some authorities have claimed a diffusion from the Middle East. But in view of the immense distances involved, diffusion seems unlikely.

THE ANCIENT ORIENT

28 Yang-Shao ware oval jar, Pan Shan cemeteries. Neolithic (3000–2000 B.C.). Buff earthenware painted in black and red slip, height 15.25″ (38.73 cm). Victoria & Albert Museum, London (Crown Copyright).

Slightly later examples of Yang-Shao ware, about 2200 B.C. are oval jars with black and red double spirals from the Pan Shan cemeteries (Fig. 28). Typically they are oval with a small base, a large opening with a collar, and loops for tieing down a cover. The Lung-Shan culture to the east in Shantung Province (2600–1700 B.C.) produced thin-walled, black, polished ware with grooved and banded decoration and tall, flaring stems, which reveals the first use of the potter's wheel.

Shang Dynasty   Later, in the Shang Period (c. 1523–1028 B.C.), white clay vases from An-Yang in Honan Province have intricate incised and stamped decorations similar to those on bronze funerary vessels made during the same period (Fig. 29). The smelting and casting of bronze was closely related to the development of higher-firing kilns and clay bodies. Although not common, some gray proto-stoneware was made. At first it was glazed accidentally with falling wood ash during firing. Later it was intentionally covered with a thin, yellow-green glaze.

Chou and Chin Dynasties   The pottery of the Chou Dynasty (1027–256 B.C.) continued to have pressed and incised designs. The turmoil of the Warring States Period (481–221 B.C.) led to the rise of the first Chinese emperor, Ch'in Shih Huang-ti, who united northern and central China in 221 B.C. The earlier practice of burying the dead ruler with his attendants gave way to the more humane practice of providing him with ceramic figures of attendants, such as the thousands of life-size guardian warriors found near Shih Huang-ti's tomb in Hsi-An, Shensi Province, in 1974 (Fig. 30).

right: **29** Cylindrical vase, Anyang, Honan Province, China. Shang Dynasty (1766–1122 B.C.). Thrown earthenware with banded and incised decorations of metallic character, height 10″ (25 cm). Metropolitan Museum of Art, New York (Harris Brisband Dick Fund, 1950).

below: **30** Warrior with his horse from Tomb of Ch'in Shi'n Huang-ti, Hsi-An, Shensi Province, China. Ch'in Dynasty (221–207 B.C.). Terra-cotta, life size. Courtesy of the Cultural Relics Bureau, Peking, and the Metropolitan Museum of Art, New York.

THE ANCIENT ORIENT

31 Vase, China. Han Dynasty (1st–2nd century A.D.). Applied decorations and a runny green glaze, height 14.38″ (36.53 cm.). Victoria & Albert Museum, London (Crown Copyright).

Han to T'ang Dynasties Under the Han Dynasty (206 B.C.–A.D. 220) trade and prosperity increased, and China gradually achieved a size and power comparable to those of the Roman Empire. The political and social order reflected the strict hierarchical relationships advocated by the sixth-century B.C. philosopher Confucius. Pottery vessels replaced bronzes as preferred tomb offerings to the honored dead. Such vessels were often covered with a copper-green lead glaze (Fig. 31). Late in the period the ribbed decoration on large funeral jars was covered with a true, green, feldspathic glaze fired at 2282°F (1250°C), although slip-decorated earthenware jars continued to be made.

During the Han, Six Dynasties (265–589), Sui (581–618), and T'ang (618–907) eras, the use of ceramic tomb sculpture continued but included small genre figures of musicians, jugglers, dancers, and especially dynamically prancing horses (Fig. 32). Late in the T'ang Dynasty polychrome clay slip decoration gave way to a lead glaze (Plate 1, p. 39). This brilliant, but running, yellow, brown, and green glaze was also applied to the typical earthenware jars and covered vases in a pattern of dots, chevrons, and rosettes. The Yueh kilns in Chekiang Province in the southeast, however, were developing *Yueh* ware, the first gray-green *celadon* glazes on refined bodies that some consider stoneware and others consider porcelain—inspired, perhaps, by jade carvings, which the Chinese valued highly. In the north, a white porcelaneous ware called *Ting* ware was made in Ting-Chou, Hopei Province.

Sung Dynasty During the following Sung Dynasty (960–1279) these innovations were further expanded as potters achieved an unusual perfection of form and glaze. The white Ting ware continued, but further south at Ching-te-chen, in Kiangsi Province, a true porcelain was developed. This *Ch'ing-pai* ware was high fired, translucent in thin areas, and covered with a bluish white glaze.

Celadons were of several types: gray-green *Kuan* (Imperial) ware in the north (Plate 2, p. 39) and blue-green *Lung-Ch'uan* ware in the south, resembling jade. Other porcelaneous bodies such as *Chun* ware had a pale blue or lavender-gray glaze splashed with purple. *Chien* tea bowls, made in Fukien Province, had a dark iron-brown glaze with silvery "oil spot" or "hare's fur" markings. They were called *Temmoku* by the Japanese, who copied them. Strikingly handsome were tall *Tz'u-Chou* stoneware wine jars made in the north with incised or bold floral slip-painted patterns of brown-black over a cream slip (Fig. 33).

Korea

As China's neighbor to the northeast, Korea has always been affected by developments in China. Neolithic Korean pottery was a reddish earthenware for utilitarian purposes: bowls, flat-based vases with a straight neck, and large storage jars.

During the early historical period, Korea was divided into several warring kingdoms: Kokuryo (37 B.C.–A.D. 668) in the north, Paekche (18 B.C.–A.D. 663) in the southwest, and Old Silla (57 B.C.–A.D. 668) in the south. Eventually Silla, the most independent of the kingdoms, succeeded in uniting all of Korea (668–935). Kokuryo and Paekche produced earthenware showing Chinese influence. Silla made unglazed gray or red stoneware, particularly covered cups on a tall foot with cutout sections (Fig. 34). They were decorated with incised geometric patterns.

left: 32 Horse and rider, China. T'ang Dynasty (618–907). Terra-cotta covered with white slip and traces of red, green, and blue paint, height 9″ (22.86 cm). Museum of Far Eastern Antiquities, Stockholm.

bottom left: 33 Tz'u Chou vase, China. Sung Dynasty (11th century). Stoneware with vigorous sgraffito decoration, height 15.5″ (38.73 cm). Victoria & Albert Museum, London (Crown Copyright).

bottom right: 34 Covered stem cup with pierced base, Korea. Old Silla Dynasty (57 B.C.–A.D. 668). Gray stoneware, height 9.25″ (23.25 cm). Seattle Art Museum (Eugene Fuller Memorial Collection).

35 Graceful bottle, Korea. Koryo Period (918–1392). Light stoneware with carved and inlayed mishima decoration, height 13″ (33 cm). Metropolitan Museum of Art, New York.

36 "Sanggam" bowl, Korea. Koryo Period, 14th century. Porcelain with inlayed mishima decoration under a pale celadon glaze, diameter 1.75″ (20 cm). Seattle Museum of Art (Eugene Fuller Memorial Collection).

By the late seventh century Korea had adopted Buddhism from China, including the Buddhist custom of cremation of the dead. Thereafter, the most commonly found wares are cremation urns, consisting of a covered vase on a low foot with bands of stamped decoration. Later examples occasionally have a yellow-brown or olive glaze.

The golden age of Korean ceramics was the Koryo Period (918–1392). Although obviously influenced by Chinese Sung pottery, Korean potters were responsible for several unique innovations. The vase form in the shape of the stump of a flowering prunus tree and the tall, graceful bottle forms (Fig. 35) are refinements of the comparatively heavy Sung shapes. Experiments with glaze led to a delicate blue-green celadon color. This was especially remarkable since the ware was fired in immense, single-chamber, bank-climbing kilns (see Figs. 25 and 26), where controlling the reduction atmosphere required great skill.

The variously formed bottles, vases, bowls, and covered jars were typically decorated with delicate floral patterns in the *mishima* inlay technique unique to Korea (Fig. 36). The design was first incised or stamped on a leather-hard stoneware body. The incisions were then filled with a porcelain slip or a dark clay or both. When the excess was scraped away, the decoration was revealed through the semitransparent celadon glaze.

Japan

The 1300-mile (2,200-km) island chain of Japan has been isolated from mainland Asia during most of its history. Pressures from an expanding China encouraged migration from China and Korea via Korea over a long period. Mainland influence has been very important in Japan but, as a result of this isolation, changes in Japanese ceramics evolved very slowly. For instance, the black, cord-marked Jomon ware (Fig. 37) of the Jomon Period (10,000 to 200 B.C.) survived until about 250 B.C., long after the Chinese were developing new forms about 4000 B.C. The pottery of the Yayoi Period (c. 200 B.C.–A.D. 200), unlike Jomon ware, was wheel thrown, simple in form, thinner, higher-fired, and decorated with incised, geometric bands.

Haniwa Period   During the Haniwa Period (200–552), increased population, the introduction of bronze and iron, and the cultivation of rice led to prosperity, as evidenced by the huge burial mounds of feudal lords. Of special interest to the potter are the thousands of *haniwa* figures, which encircled the mounds (Fig. 38). The first haniwa were simple clay cylinders. Later ones were more elaborate representations of armored warriors, robed ladies, horses, and other attendant figures.

During the late Haniwa Period (after 400), many Korean potters, because of wars among the Silla and other Korean kingdoms, emigrated to Kyushu, the southernmost island of Japan. There they produced a new ware called *Sue,* a gray stoneware with a runny green ash glaze (Fig. 39).

Asuka, Nara, and Heian Periods   In the Asuka period (552–645), the Nara Period (645–794) and the early Heian Period (794–897), Japan adopted much of the civilization of T'ang China, including Buddhism and the use of Chinese characters to write the Japanese language. The Japanese made T'ang-influenced, lead-glazed pottery as well as the older Sue ware. Trade and other contact with China ceased during the turmoil of the closing years of the T'ang Dynasty (c. 906 A.D.). In the late Heian Period (897–1185), the isolated Japanese digested Chinese influences and revised them to suit Japanese taste.

***above left*: 37** Jar, Miyanomac, Nagano, Japan. Middle Jomom Period, c. 2500 B.C. Earthenware with incised and applied decoration, height 23.4″ (59.5 cm). Tokyo National Museum (gift of Sugihara Sosuke).

***above right*: 38** Haniwa warrior. Tochigi Prefecture, Japan. Haniwa Period (3rd–6th century). Terra-cotta, height 22.88″ (57.25 cm). Metropolitan Museum of Art, New York (gift of Mrs. John D. Rockefeller, III, 1958).

***below left*: 39** Sue jar, Obata, Kitaura-mura, Ibaraki, Japan. Heian Period, c. 1000. Stoneware with ash glaze, height 6.6″ (25.8 cm). Tokyo National Museum.

Kamakura Period The Kamakura Period (1185–1333) was an era of renewed contacts with China. The Sung pottery imported during this time had a lasting effect on the Japanese. Seto, on the island of Honshu, became a major ceramic center. It produced a variety of vases, bottles, pitchers, and tea bowls incised or impressed with bold floral motifs and covered with a glaze that imitated Sung celadon.

Pre-Columbian America

The Americas were first inhabited by bands of hunters and gatherers who migrated intermittently over the land bridge from Siberia to Alaska during the period 26,000 to 8000 B.C. Some of these bands settled down as farmers in fertile areas in what are now Mexico, Guatemala, Ecuador, and Peru. Their development may be roughly classified into the Preclassic (or Formative) Period (until 200 A.D.), the Classic Period (200–950), and the Postclassic Period (950 until the coming of the Spanish in the early sixteenth century).

Mesoamerica

Advanced cultures developed in the Valley of Mexico, the east and west coasts of Mexico, southern Mexico, and nothern Central America.

Olmec The first major Preclassic civilization in Mesoamerica was that of the Olmec (c. 800–400 B.C.), who inhabited the coast of the Gulf of Mexico and whose influence spread through a much wider area. At La Venta in Veracruz Province and at other sites they built stepped, temple-crowned pyramids of brick faced with stucco or stone. They carved stone reliefs and freestanding figures, including huge heads, and clay figurines. Their sculpture is noted for its rounded forms and often pouting, baby-faced expression, as seen in the so-called jaguar-babies (Fig. 40).

Tlatilco Contemporary with the Olmec were farm villages in the Valley of Mexico such as Tlatilco, which produced thousands of small, often charming figurines (Fig. 41). Tlatilco also made burnished black or red earthenware with simple, incised designs. In addition to conventional bowl and bottle forms there were pots modeled in the form of birds or fish. This interest in modeled form is characteristic of all Pre-Columbian pottery. The potter's wheel never developed in the New World.

Teotihuacán During the early Classic Period, Teotihuacán, which had previously absorbed Olmec civilization, was the most important center in the Valley of Mexico until A.D. 600. It was a large architectural complex planned for ceremonies of sacrifice to the gods conducted by priests. Structures included temple-pyramids decorated with stylized carving and painted stucco and residential quarters painted with murals of the gods or ceremonial scenes. The characteristic pottery of Teotihuacán, unique in Mexico, was a low, cylindrical ceremonial urn on three legs (Fig. 42). The brown body was often cut away and coated with red pigment to leave a stylized raised design. Reflecting temple decoration were a few unusual pieces whose fired clay bodies were covered with stucco painted in many colors.

40 Olmec seated figurine, Las Bocas, Mexico. 1000 B.C.–A.D. 300. Earthenware with white slip and iron-red decoration, height 13.36″ (33.93 cm). Metropolitan Museum of Art, New York (The Michael C. Rockefeller Collection, bequest of Nelson A. Rockefeller, 1979).

above: **41** Tlatilco figurines, Valley of Mexico. c. 1000–500 B.C. Terra-cotta; height of center figurine 3.75″ (9.5 cm). Metropolitan Museum of Art, New York.

left: **42** Teotihuacán tripod urn, Mexico. 200–600. Earthenware with incised and slip decoration, height 9.75″ (24.76 cm). Metropolitan Museum of Art, New York (bequest of Nelson A. Rockefeller, 1979).

Nayarit, Colima, and Jalisco In western Mexico the peoples of Nyarit, Colima, and Jalisco, unlike other Mesoamericans, had no temple-pyramids or powerful priesthood. They made pottery figurines, which, like their Chinese counterparts, were intended to be buried in tombs to provide the dead with companionship in the life hereafter. Although made in regional styles, the figurines depict a relaxed, fun-loving people playing games or at rest (Plate 3, p. 40). There were also pots modeled like vegetables, dogs, or humans.

Zapotec and Mixtec In southern Mexico in the valley of Oaxaca, the Zapotec developed a civilization centered in Monte Albán that reached its height during the Classic Period. The Zapotec built stone temple-pyramids and sculpted large, terra-cotta effigy urns, which depicted a stylized god or chieftain, seated, wearing a flamboyant feathered headdress (Fig. 43).

By 900, at the start of the Postclassic Period, the Mixtec had entered Oaxaca, possibly from the Gulf Coast, and taken over Monte Albán. They built their capital at Mitla, which also had previously belonged to the Zapotec. The Mixtec were excellent jewelers in gold and jade, as the finely detailed ornament on their potlike, seated figurines shows (Fig. 44). Their love of intricate design is also reflected in the repetitive geometric decorations in yellow, red, orange, and black slip on their tripod and flared-pedestal bowls.

above: **43** Zapotec funeral urn, Oaxaca, Mexico. c. 1000. Terra-cotta, in typical form of seated figure with elaborate headress, height 6.5″ (16.51 cm). Collection I.B.M. Corporation, Armonk, New York.

right: **44** Mixtec xantile figure, Pueblo, Mexico. 1250–1500. Earthenware with trailed slip decoration, height 25.63″ (57 cm). Metropolitan Museum of Art, New York (The Michael C. Rockefeller Collection, gift of Nelson A. Rockefeller, 1978).

Maya The most advanced civilization of Mesoamerica was that of the Maya, whose numerous temple complexes such as Palenque, Tikal, Copán, and Chichén Itzá are still being discovered in Tabasco, Guatemala, Honduras, and Yucatan. Little is known of the Maya during the Preclassic Period. Mayan art of the Classic Period is serene and confident. Realistic, painted bas-reliefs adorn temple-pyramids and palaces. Ceramic figurines display a fluid, plastic quality (Fig. 45). The straight-sided bowls and footed vessels of the Maya perhaps show the influence of Teotihuacán. They were decorated with incised hieroglyphs and patterns in polychromed slip resembling temple murals.

Neither the Toltec nor the Aztec, who dominated the Valley of Mexico and Yucatan in the Postclassic Period, attained the heights of the Maya.

Diffusion Northward Influences from the culturally advanced Indians of Mesoamerica slowly diffused northward, including the skills of raising corn, building permanent structures, and making pottery. The Casas Grandes Indians in northern Mexico made effigy jars in the shape of birds and other excellent pottery, both with bold slip decoration (Fig. 46). Pueblo Indians, who built multistoried apartment dwellings in what is now the southwestern United States, made fine ceremonial pottery decorated in slip-painted geometric designs. Indians of the Mimbres Valley (New Mexico) made a distinctive ware that combined stylized patterns and realistic depictions of birds and

above left: **45** Maya figure, Jaina Island, Mexico. 900–1200. Terra-cotta, height 14.5″ (36.83 cm). Museum of the American Indian, New York (exchange from R. L. Stolper).

above right: **46** Casas Grandes effigy jar, Chihuahua, Mexico. 1300–1450. Earthenware with slip decoration, height 8.75″ (22.22 cm). Metropolitan Museum of Art, New York (bequest of Nelson A. Rockefeller, 1979).

47 American Indian cooking pot in the shape of a tortoise, Arkansas, U.S.A. 1200–1600. Blackware. Museum of the American Indian, New York (Clarence B. Moore Collection).

animals in black on white slip. Farther north in the Mississippi Valley and in the southeastern United States, Indians erected large earthen temple-pyramids and burial mounds and made functional burnished black pottery with incised decoration (Fig. 47).

South America

In South America advanced cultures developed in the river valleys that crossed two main areas—the Pacific coast of what are now Ecuador and Peru and the Andean highlands of Peru and Bolivia. About 3000 B.C. Indians on the coast were beginning to raise corn and cotton. The first pottery, from the Colombian and Ecuadorean coast, was black or gray, round-bottomed, cord-impressed ware similar to Japanese Jomon ware and dated from 3000 to 2700 B.C.

Chavín By 1400 to 1000 B.C. during the Preclassic Period, the Chavín people of Chavín de Huantar and other centers in the north highlands and coast were building temple-pyramids, weaving textiles, working gold, and making pottery. Chavín pottery was burnished black ware in a bottle and jar form, usually decorated with a jaguar motif. The coastal Chavín at Cupisnique developed a unique form—the *stirrup-spout* bottle, which had a hollow, stirrup-shaped handle with a spout on top. Many were modeled in a great variety of human, animal, vegetable, and even house forms. Other, rounded vessels were decorated with incised patterns accentuated by rocker stamping.

Mochica, Nazca, and Tiahuanaco During the Classic Period, beginning about A.D. 200, the Mochica on the north coast excelled in stirrup-spout bottles mold-modeled in the form of figures and portrait heads (Figs. 48 and 49). They also made smooth-surfaced stirrup-spout bottles and other pottery with

delicately painted figures on white slip. About the same time, the people of
the Nazca Valley on the south coast produced rounded and modeled grave
pottery with double spouts and a strap handle and an emphasis on intricate
painted polychrome decoration on slip (Fig. 50). Bisque molds were commonly used to produce spouts and elaborate vessel sections that were later
joined. They were usually very light in weight with a uniform thickness, which
belies the opinion that some have concerning handbuilt ware.

In the early Postclassic Period, before 1000 the people of Tiahuanaco, who had developed a Classic civilization in the southern highlands, expanded west and north, overruning the declining Mochica and Nazca civilizations. Characteristic Tiahuanaco pottery included flaring goblets, wide-rimmed bowls, and oval and modeled vessels with two spouts and a strap handle. They were decorated usually in black-outlined white on a red body or in polychrome slip. Stylized motifs included a feline form.

Chimú and Inca   In the late Postclassic Period, in the thirteenth century the Chimú dominated the north coast from their great capital city of Chan Chan. By that time painted decoration on pottery had virtually disappeared. Old forms such as the Mochica stirrup-spout jars persisted, but the usual body was smoked black.

In the early fifteenth century the Inca began to expand from the central highlands. By the arrival of the Spanish they ruled much of western South America from their capital at Cuzco. The most distinctive form of Inca pottery was the aryballoid jar with a pointed base, long neck, flaring collar, and low side handles (Fig. 51, p. 41). Decoration was bands of triangular, crosshatched, and other geometrical motifs in polychrome slips. While Inca craftsmanship was an improvement over Chimú work, it hardly equaled the more imaginative pottery of the much earlier Mochica or Nazca ware.

The Ancient Middle East

Neolithic farmers of Mesopotamia (now Iraq), Palestine (Israel), Anatolia, (Turkey), Iran, and Egypt were making coiled pottery at an early date. Subsequently the rise and fall of a series of civilized peoples—notably Sumerians, Babylonians, Assyrians, and Persians—in western Asia and the exchange of influences between them and the various Egyptian dynasties in northeast Africa contributed to a rich complexity of art forms. Despite regional variations, certain characteristics remained constant. One is the use of repetitive patterns and symmetrical composition. Another is a preference for curved forms. A third is emphasis on bright color. These characteristics were basic to Middle Eastern art and continued much later in the Islamic era.

Mesopotamia, Anatolia, and Iran

The oldest pottery found in the Middle East was made in the Neolithic village of Çatal Hüyük in southeast Anatolia about 6800 to 5700 B.C. The earliest wares were crude and soft with a dark burnished body. Later wares were red, covered with cream-colored slip and decorated with bands of zig-zag and chevrons and circular motifs.

Slightly later in the sixth and fifth millennia B.C. Hassuna and Samarra in Mesopotamia were producing incised black ware and red-bodied painted ware. In the fifth millennium B.C. the peoples of Halaf, Arpachiyah, and Carchemesh, between Anatolia and Mesopotamia, were making large flat dishes covered with bands of intricate repeat motifs in lustrous brown, tan, red, white, and black slip. In the fourth millennium, Tepe Hissar and other centers in Iran were producing slip-painted ware thrown on the potter's wheel (Fig. 52, p. 41). Geometric motifs were combined with stylized flowers

left: **Plate 1** Camel. China. Sung Dynasty (A.D. 676–908). Lead glaze with polychrome decoration on terra-cotta, height 34.75″ (86.9 cm). Los Angeles County Museum (William Randolph Hearst Collection).

below: **Plate 2** Vase and incense burner. China. Sung Dynasty (A.D. 960–1279). Kuan porcelain with a heavy crackled celadon glaze; vase height 5.13″ (13 cm), diameter of incense burner 6.13″ (15.5 cm). Cleveland Museum of Art.

right: **Plate 3** Seated ball player. Nayarit, Mexico. About A.D. 500. Burnished earthenware with polychrome slip decoration, height 13″ (33 cm). Minneapolis Institute of Art.

below: **Plate 4** Hippopotamus from the tomb of Senbi of Meir. Egypt, XII Dynasty (2000–1788 B.C.). Faience body with painted decoration of water plants; height 4.6″ (11 cm). Metropolitan Museum of Art, New York (Gift of Edward S. Harkness, 1917).

51 Inca aryballoid jar, Peru. c. 1438–1832. Earthenware with a dark slip geometric pattern, height 8.5″ (20.95 cm). Metropolitan Museum of Art, New York (The Michael C. Rockefeller Memorial Collection, gift of Nelson A. Rockefeller, 1961).

52 Small cup, Tepe Hissar, Iran. c. 3500 B.C. Wheel-thrown buff earthenware with brown slip decoration, height 4.38″ (11 cm). Metropolitan Museum of Art, New York (gift of Tehran Museum, 1939).

53 Footed cup, Sialk, Iran. c. 3000 B.C. Earthenware with slip decoration, height 7″ (17.7 cm). Metropolitan Museum of Art, New York (Rogers Fund, 1955).

and animals, such as the graceful ibex on a footed cup from Sialk (Fig. 53). Middle Eastern love of color may be seen in the relief scenes of animals and court life, made of molded tiles covered with polychrome tin-lead glaze, that decorated the walls of cities and palaces of the Babylonians and Assyrians, who ruled Mesopotamia in the eighth, seventh, and sixth centuries B.C. (Fig. 54).

Egypt

The earliest pottery of Egypt was a crude, dark ware made in the Faiyum region of the lower Nile Valley during the Neolithic period, about 4500 B.C., later than that of the Sudan (7000 B.C.). More developed were the burnished red and black vases of the Badarian culture in northern Egypt (Fig. 55) made about 4000 to 3200 B.C. Because the pots were fired upside down in little more than a bonfire, the upper portions of the red clay were covered with ashes, which reduced the amount of oxygen and caused them to turn black, while the balance of the pot retained its original red color. The Amratian culture to the south (c. 3600 B.C.) also made a red polished ware with white incised decorations of geometric, plant, and animal motifs. The Gerzean people of the Nile delta made a ware that indicates use of a better kiln, as it had a light body with painted decorations in reddish brown slip depicting boats, birds, and hunting and religious scenes (Fig. 56).

At an early period the Egyptians developed a turquoise glaze called *faience*. It was made of silica (the chief ingredient of glass) and soda with some clay as a binder and copper or cobalt as a colorant. In drying, the water-soluble soda was drawn to the surface, and when fired it reacted with the silica to form a shiny alkaline glaze. It fused satisfactorily with sandy clay bodies common in Egypt but flaked off the more plastic clay bodies common elsewhere in the Middle East. The turquoise tiles in the tomb of the Old Kingdom Pharaoh Djoser at Saqqara (c. 2600 B.C.) are the first evidence of

54 Lion wall from Palace of King Nebuchadnezzar II, Babylon. 605–562 B.C. Glazed brick, length 7′ 5.5″ (227 cm). Metropolitan Museum of Art, New York (Fletcher Fund, 1931).

EARLY CERAMIC HISTORY

left: **55** Tall El Badari vase, Egypt. 4000–3200 B.C. Red and black earthenware, height 21″ (53.3 cm). Victoria & Albert Museum (Crown Copyright).

above right: **56** Gerzean vessel, Egypt. c. 3300 B.C. Buff earthenware with brown slip decorations of ibexes, ostriches, and boats; height 7.75″ (19.69 cm). Metropolitan Museum of Art, New York (Rogers Fund, 1920).

right: **57** Faience Ushabti of King Seti I, Thebes, Egypt. 1313–1292 B.C. Ushabti are small mummylike tomb objects thought to be useful to the dead in the after life. Height 11.75″ (29.4 cm). Metropolitan Museum of Art, New York (Carnavon Collection, gift of Edward S. Harkness, 1926).

faience. It was also used for beads, other jewelry, furniture inlay, and figurines (Fig. 57 and Plate 4, p. 40). It was not applied to pottery until the New Kingdom about 1500 B.C.

    In spite of the beauty of the early red and black vases, the decorated Gerzean ware, and the unusual turquoise faience, pottery as an art form did not prosper in Egypt. The agricultural wealth of the country flowed into the household of the Pharaoh, the priesthood, and the military caste. They preferred finely crafted vases of polished alabaster and other stone and vessels of silver and gold. Pottery in the dynastic era was primarily utilitarian.

Ceramics were a highly developed art form in the centers of civilization around the Mediterranean Sea, especially in Crete and Greece. Greek pottery was traded all over the ancient world.

Crete

Between 3000 and 2500 B.C. the Minoan civilization, named after the legendary King Minos, evolved on the island of Crete. Although it was influenced by the neighboring civilizations in Mesopotamia and Egypt, it was different from them. Without a dominant priesthood and protected from invaders by the sea and their navy, the Minoans developed a unique prosperity based on sea trade.

Neolithic Cretan pottery, like that elsewhere, was first a corded black ware, then a polished ware with simple crosshatched and dotted designs. Early Minoan pottery (2800–2000 B.C.) was wheel thrown and decorated with banded and geometric motifs in white over black slip. During the Middle Minoan period (2000–1550 B.C.), pottery forms became more graceful. Designs were curling plant and circular motifs in white, cream, and red on a dark body. These gradually gave way to dark designs on a light tan body.

In the closing years of this era and the early part of the Late Minoan era (1600–1500 B.C.), Minoan civilization reached its height and spread to islands in the Aegean Sea to the north and the Greek mainland. The flowing motifs of plant and sea life (particularly the octopus) were superbly suited to oval water bottles and rounded vase forms (Fig. 58). There were also huge palace storage jars for oil and wine. They stood nearly 6 feet (1.83 m) high and were decorated with bands of relief motifs (Fig. 59).

Remains of palaces at Knossos and other sites indicate a series of volcanic destructions and rebuildings. About 1450 B.C. as the result of a particularly violent eruption on the island of Thera (Santorini), huge tidal waves swept the populous north coast of Crete, palaces were destroyed, and a thick layer of volcanic ash covered the farmland. Also the island was invaded from the mainland. Crete never recovered its former glory.

58 Minoan flask with two pots, Palaikastro, Crete. 1600–1500 B.C. Flowing decorations of sea and plant life in red and black slips on buff-colored clay. Herakleion Museum, Crete.

left: 59 Pithos, Knossos, Crete. c. 1450–1400 B.C. Earthenware storage jar with applied rope decoration, height 4' (1.15 m). British Museum, London.

below: 60 Mycenaean stirrup jar, Crete. 1200–1125 B.C. Earthenware decorated with stylized octopi, height 10.25" (26 cm). Metropolitan Museum of Art, New York (Lousia Eldridge McBurney Gift Fund, 1953).

Greece

Neolithic peoples were farming and making pottery in Greece in the sixth millennium B.C. About 2000 B.C., Greek-speaking tribes, including the Achaeans of Homeric legend, were invading Greece from the north. They built fortress-palaces on hilltops that became the centers of such later Greek city-states as Mycenae, Tiryns, Thebes, and Athens.

Mycenaean Period By 1400 B.C. these Mycenaean princes had expanded their power throughout the eastern Mediterranean, including Crete. Many Cretan craftsmen migrated to the mainland; thus much of the goldwork and pottery found in Mycenaean Greece has Minoan characteristics. Vases had a higher foot and were more rounded at the shoulder. Cups were high stemmed and delicately formed. Mycenaean potters subdued and conventionalized the more dynamic floral decoration of the Minoans and often used simple banded decoration (Fig. 60). Later they depicted scenes of warriors and horses somewhat crudely drawn but a forecast of later Greek wares (Fig.

right: **61** Mycenaean krater, found in Enkomi Alasia, Cyprus. Early 14th century B.C. The sketchy riders and chariots represent a great change from the earlier stylized plant decorations. Height 15.16″ (38.5 cm). Cyprus Museum, Nicosia, Cyprus.

below: **62** Funerary vase, Cyprus. 8th century B.C. Earthenware with paneled and banded decoration of horses, deer, waterfowl, and double axes in the Geometric style; height 46.88″ (117.5 cm). Metropolitan Museum of Art, New York (Cesnola Collection).

61). During the thirteenth century B.C., new waves of Greek-speaking peoples from the north, the Dorians, overthrew Mycenaean rule and initiated a period of artistic decline.

Geometric Style   About 1050 B.C. the pottery in the area around Athens improved. The forms, although based on those of Mycenaean cups, vases, and jars, were better thrown and higher fired. Decoration, bands or concentric circles in dark slip on a red body, was executed with care and precision. About 900 B.C., the *Geometric style* developed. Decoration was enlivened with rows of triangles, zigzags, meanders (keys), and swastikas (Fig. 62). Eventually figurative elements were introduced. First came the horse, a prestige symbol, and later the chariot and driver, but all were drawn as stick-figures.

Oriental Style   As the Greek city-states grew and population pressures on limited farmland increased, the Greeks founded colonies in the eastern Mediterranean and expanded trade with older civilizations of the Middle East. As a result Greeks encountered the fantasy of so-called Oriental art: winged monsters such as gorgons and sphinxes, often in a floral setting. In the late eighth and seventh centuries B.C., Corinth became a center of this *Oriental style*. Rhodes, Cyprus, and other islands close to Syria at the eastern end of the Mediterranean were also centers. They produced fine pottery on which floral borders replaced the old zigzags, and stylized birds, animals, and finally figures from the Homeric legends filled the central panel. An effective *black-figure style,* in which humans were painted in black slip on red ware, was used on a series of miniature vases (Fig. 63). Athenian potters at this time continued to stress the human figure but in a sketchy outline style (Fig. 64).

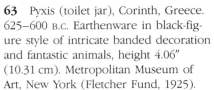

63 Pyxis (toilet jar), Corinth, Greece. 625–600 B.C. Earthenware in black-figure style of intricate banded decoration and fantastic animals, height 4.06″ (10.31 cm). Metropolitan Museum of Art, New York (Fletcher Fund, 1925).

64 Dipylon amphora, Athens, Greece. 8th century B.C. Terra-cotta, height 11.69″ (29.22 cm). Metropolitan Museum of Art, New York (Rogers Fund, 1921).

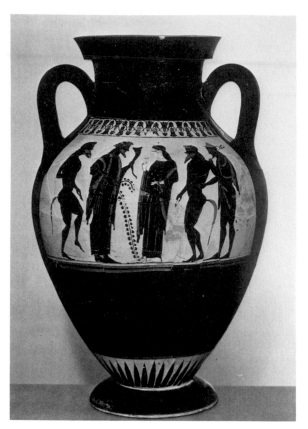

left: 65   Amphora, Greece. 6th century B.C. Earthenware, decorated with panels of Dionysiac and marriage processions in the black-figure style. Metropolitan Museum of Art, New York (Rogers Fund, 1912).

right: 66   Stammas, Greece. 470–460 B.C. Earthenware in red-figure style. Metropolitan Museum of Art, New York (Rogers Fund, 1918).

Black-Figure Style   Perhaps because pottery played an important part in burial rites, its forms had been codified. They included the tall wine jar, urn-shaped water jar, bowl, cup, pitcher, and bottle. The major area on each piece was devoted to a figure or group, at first representing heroes, gods, or episodes from Homer, later athletic and domestic scenes (Fig. 65). These were done in the black-figure style, which Athenian potters had adopted from Corinth in the late seventh century B.C. It was striking, but because details had to be made by incising the black slip, it provided little flexibility for the increasing skill of vase painters.

Red-Figure Style   After about 520 B.C. Athenian potters developed the *red-figure style,* in which the background was painted black and the figures reserved in the red of the unpainted clay body (Fig. 66). The so-called black glaze of the Greeks was not a true glaze but rather was made of a finely decanted red clay slip. When fired in a *reducing* fire (without oxygen) the entire pot became black. A later firing with oxidation turned the porous, red clay body back to its original color while the painted slip remained black. Details could then be added easily with fluid brush strokes. As the skill of the vase painters grew, they were tempted to create more and more extravagant effects. By the fourth century B.C., the decorative quality of Hellenistic pottery was destroyed by attempts at realism that resulted in confused overlapping of forms, excessive foreshortening of figures, and eventually multicolored landscape elements.

Etruria

After Crete and Greece, the third major area of early civilizations in the Mediterranean is Italy. The Etruscans are thought to have come from Asia Minor to western Italy during the ninth century B.C. at about the same time that the Greeks were founding colonies in Sicily and southern Italy. Eventually the Etruscans established twelve loosely allied city-states in an area between present-day Rome and Florence. They mined and exported iron and copper and had considerable trade with the Greeks. Greek potters likely emigrated to Etruria.

Etruscan pottery was uneven in quality, for it absorbed many influences without assimilating them into a coherent whole. These influences included the polished black ware of the older Villanovan people of northern Italy (Fig. 67), the Oriental style, later Greek styles (Fig. 68), and their own embossed metalwork. Early Etruscan pottery had a red polished body and was often incised with bands or cross-hatching. More characteristic was polished black *bucchero* ware with incised, pressed, or molded decoration.

The Etruscans were most noted for their terra-cotta sculpture. Their temples were roofed with tiles that terminated along the eaves in elaborate gorgan heads. Large polychrome terra-cotta figures of gods topped the ridgepole, and high-relief figures filled the triangular pediment over the entrance. Unfortunately, these temples and their sculpture were almost completely destroyed by the Romans. Large, ceramic sarcophagi have been found, however, in rockcut tombs that escaped looting (Fig. 69). They are surmounted by portrait figures of the dead, the most famous of which is a reclining couple who seem to be in easy, animated conversation with their friends.

67 Villanovan cinerary urn, Vulci, Italy. 9th–8th century B.C. Black polished earthenware. Villa Guilia Etruscan Museum, Rome.

***below*: 69** Etruscan urn in the form of a sarcophagus, Italy. 3rd century B.C. Terra-cotta decorated with battle scene and reclining woman. Metropolitan Museum of Art, New York (Subscription, 1896).

***below*: 68** Etruscan oenochoe (wine pitcher), Chiusi, Italy. 5th century B.C. Black polished bucchero earthenware in the Greek style. Art Institute of Chicago (gift of D. P. Armour and C. L. Hutchinson).

Rome

Shortly after 500 B.C. warlike Latin-speaking tribes around Rome began to expand north into Etruria and south into the Greek colonies. Neither the Greeks nor the Etruscans, often quarreling among themselves, put up a united front against the Latins. During the next two hundred years all Italy fell before the growing power of Rome, which eventually took over most of the empire of Alexander the Great in Greece and the Middle East as well as the lands bordering the western Mediterranean.

Roman art combined Greek and Etruscan elements. Ornate late Greek, or Hellenistic, pottery was popular among the Romans, as was Etruscan bucchero ware. Although the Romans hired subject Etruscans to make ceramic sculpture for early Roman temples, the Romans eventually followed the Greek preference for marble sculpture. They continued the Etruscan interest in realistic portraiture but expressed it in marble.

Roman conquests in Syria and Egypt eventually led to the use of the lead glazes that had developed in those regions (Fig. 70). The pottery style that is typically Roman is *terra sigillata* (Fig. 71). It is somewhat related to the Etruscan bucchero ware in that it has a raised sculptural decoration, but the body has a brick-red oxidized surface instead of a black, reduced one. Since the decoration was elaborate and detailed, the ware was often made in molds, one of which is shown in Figure 72. In general, however, the Romans neglected ceramics, giving greater attention and value to stone carving, metalwork, and architecture.

70 Footed bowl, Roman. 1st century A.D. Earthenware with sculptural relief and green lead glaze. Metropolitan Museum of Art, New York (Mr. and Mrs. Isaac D. Fletcher Collection, bequest of Isaac. D. Fletcher, 1917).

EARLY CERAMIC HISTORY

left: 71 Terra sigillata footed bowl, Roman. c. 10 B.C.–10 A.D. Molded red earthenware. Metropolitan Museum of Art, New York (Rogers Fund, 1910).

below: 72 Arretine mold with intricate relief, Roman. Late 1st century B.C. Earthenware. Metropolitan Museum of Art, New York (Rogers Fund, 1919).

3

Later Ceramic History

From the twelfth century, increased contact between the Orient, the Middle East, and the West led to many technical and stylistic changes in the ceramics of Europe and Asia but did not affect those of Africa. The Industrial Revolution, which began in eighteenth-century Europe, led to a greatly increased but mechanical production and to a decline in design. Hand-built, contemporary pottery developed in reaction to it.

The Orient

China continued to play a leading role in the history of ceramics, influencing not only Korea and Japan, as in previous centuries, but also the Islamic world and Europe.

China

left: **73** T'zu-Chou ware bottle, China. Yüan Dynasty (1115–1234). Stoneware with dark brown glaze, height 9.63″ (24.4 cm). Victoria & Albert Museum, London (Crown Copyright).

right: **74** Jar, China. Ming Dynasty (1368–1644), Hsüan-Tê Period (1426–1435). Porcelain with dragon decorations in underglaze Muhammadan blue. Metropolitan Museum of Art, New York (gift of Robert E. Tod, 1937).

Despite the immense distances over desert and mountain terrain between China and the Western world, Chinese military forces under the expansive Han Dynasty had gained control of the Silk Route between China and the eastern borders of the Roman Empire. During the T'ang Dynasty this overland trade to western Asia expanded, and maritime trade via the South China Sea was established with southeastern Asia and India. These contacts with the outside world were limited, however, and were interrupted during periods of domestic upheaval. This situation changed when Genghis Khan unified the nomadic Mongol tribes of central Asia in the late twelfth century. Fierce fighters and expert horsemen, the Mongols rapidly conquered an empire that stretched from Korea to Russia.

Yüan Dynasty The Mongol conquest of China was completed when Genghis Khan's grandson, Kublai Khan, conquered South China from the Sung and established the Yüan Dynasty (1280–1368). No longer a relatively isolated state but part of a great foreign empire, China was much more open to foreign influence and in turn inspired non-Chinese civilizations.

The Mongol love for elaborate, overall decoration consisting of intertwining forms influenced the art of both China and the Middle East. Celadon ware continued to be made but with ornate, more deeply carved designs. A good-quality cobalt was imported from the Middle East, which produced brilliant blue decoration on white porcelain instead of the brownish black previously obtained from inferior Chinese cobalt (Fig. 73).

Ming Dynasty Feuds among warlords and disastrous floods led to peasant uprisings and the founding of the Ming Dynasty (1368–1644), which gave imperial patronage to all the arts. In 1402 an official court factory was established at Ching-Te-Chên in Kiangsi Province. Its many potteries henceforth played the dominant role in Chinese ceramics.

White porcelain with blue underglaze decoration was in great favor during the Ming period. During the reign of Hsüan Tê (1426–1435) the blue-and-white style, with its delicate animal and floral patterns, was at its height (Fig. 74). Copper-red (*sang-de-boeuf*) glazes, attempted during the Sung period, were perfected by Ming potters (Fig. 75). Meeting the court taste for luxury were *famille verte* ("green family") porcelains, decorated in low-fired overglaze enamels of dark purple, green, yellow, and later a strong red, which gradually replaced blue-and-white ware (Fig. 76).

76 Teapot, China. Ch'ing Dynasty (1644–1912). Porcelain with famille verte decoration. National Palace Museum, Taipei.

75 Stemmed cup, China. Ming Dynasty (1368–1644), Hsüan-Tê Period (1426–1435). Porcelain; fish design copper-red glaze. Foot thrown separately, height 3.63″ (8.5 cm). Victoria & Albert Museum, London (Crown Copyright).

Ch'ing Dynasty   In the early seventeenth century, Ming China, weakened by rebellion, was taken over by Manchu tribes from the north, who established the Ch'ing Dynasty (1644–1912). The nomadic Manchus learned Chinese ways and continued the Chinese tradition of imperial patronage of the arts. In 1682 the imperial porcelain factories at Ching-Te-Chên, which had been largely destroyed during the Manchu conquest, were rebuilt and expanded. In addition to famille verte porcelains, a new *famille rose* ("rose family") porcelain was made, using colloidal gold in the glaze.

Unique to the Ch'ing period is an antiquarian mood in which many Sung and Ming pieces from the imperial collection were skillfully copied: celadons, ware glazed with copper-red, white Ting ware, and blue-and-white porcelain. Thus many pieces bearing a Sung or Ming mark are actually of Ch'ing origin. Wares made during the reign of Emperor K'ang Hsi (1672–1722) are particularly fine. Ch'ing potters produced work for a huge export trade with the Portuguese and later the Dutch and English. Chinese efforts to satisfy European tastes, such as that for chinoiserie, led to a deterioration of standards of design.

Korea

Korea, like China, was affected by the Mongol invasion of the thirteenth century. From 1231 to 1260 most of Korea was occupied by the Mongols. This disruption caused great changes in the Korean pottery traditions and decline in craftsmanship from the Koryo Period. Celadons and ware decorated with mishima practically disappeared, although a few porcelains were made during the latter years of the Koryo Period.

The Yi Dynasty (1392–1910) is divided into two periods, separated by the Japanese occupation of 1592–1598. Characteristic of the early Yi period were stoneware, including *Punch'ung* ware (Fig. 77), a white slipware with

77   Punch'ung ware bottle, Korea. Yi Dynasty, 16th century. Stoneware with black iron brush decoration over a coarse white slip. Seattle Art Museum (gift of Mr. Frank Bayley to the Thomas D. Stimson Memorial Collection).

left: **Plate 5** Tea bowl. Choniu, Japan. Handbuilt raku ware. About 1760. Height 3.5″ (8.75 cm). Metropolitan Museum of Art, New York (Howard Mansfield Collection, gift of Howard Mansfield, 1936).

right: **Plate 6** Hispano-Moresque platter. Manises, Spain. 15th century. Earthenware with a lead-tin glaze with overglaze decoration in luster and blue, diameter 17.63″ (44 cm). Metropolitan Museum of Art, New York (Cloisters Collection, 1956).

Plate 7 Peter Voulkos, U.S.A. Stoneware plate, altered form with thin colemanite glaze. Wood-fired, diameter 23″ (58.4 cm).

78 Bottle, Korea. Yi Dynasty, 19th century. Porcelain with underglaze blue decoration, height 7.5″ (19.05 cm). Victoria & Albert Museum, London (Crown Copyright).

vigorous sgraffito or iron-black brushwork; a coarse, brushed slipware called *hakeme;* and a stamped mishima ware. Later, white porcelain with underglaze blue decoration became important (Fig. 78). Vases and bottles were decorated with floral sprays in a free-brush manner. An iron-brown and an underglaze copper-red were employed as well as the popular blue. Ware made after the Japanese invasion lacked the strength of form and decoration characteristic of earlier periods.

Japan

The later ceramic history of Japan was affected principally by the growing influence of Zen Buddhism, which encouraged the uniquely Japanese cult of tea.

Muromachi and Momoyama Periods   Zen Buddhism, introduced to Japan from T'ang China, took hold in the twelfth century in the early Kamakura Period. As practiced by monks in Zen monasteries, it required long periods of meditation broken by a pause in which a cup of tea was served. During the Muromachi (1392–1573) and Momoyama (1573–1615) periods, the serving of tea became a codified ceremony and was adopted by the feudal nobility and then the rich merchant class. Most of the paraphernalia—tea bowls, water container, cake trays, and flower vase—were ceramic.

79 Oribe ware teapot, Japan. Momoyama Period (1573–1615). Stoneware with green and transparent glazes over a brown slip tortoise-shell decoration, height 7.63″ (19.25 cm). Seattle Art Museum (Eugene Fuller Memorial Collection).

80 Tea jar, Shigaraki, Japan. 19th century. Coarse stoneware, height 3.5″ (8.8 cm). Metropolitan Museum of Art, New York (Fletcher Fund, 1925).

In the Kamakura Period, as noted in Chapter 2, rare Sung bowls were imported from China for tea, but gradually they were thought not to be in keeping with the stress that Zen put on the natural, spontaneous, and simple. Eventually tea masters sought out the ordinary peasant earthenware made by the so-called six old kilns of Japan—Seto, Bizen, Shigaraki, Tamba, Tokoname, and Echizen. Later they also used the *Karatsu* ware made by Korean potters brought to Japan after the Japanese invasion of Korea. In the eyes of the tea masters the coarse imperfections of the clay, the careless touch of the potter's hand, and the accidental running of a glaze had a spontaneous quality associated with nature (Figs. 79 and 80). Typical of this influence is handmade *raku* ware, first made by Tanaka Chojiro for the great sixteenth-century tea master Sen-no-Rikyu (Plate 5, p. 57).

Edo Period The cult of tea continued into the Edo Period (1603–1867), when it was served by such outstanding artists as Ogata Kenzan. Kenzan, who was primarily a decorative painter like his brother Korin, made tea bowls and other tea ware decorated with a free brushwork and bold colors (Fig. 81) and in a style more Japanese than Chinese in feeling.

Porcelain was first made shortly after 1616 when kaolin was discovered by a Korean potter working for Lord Nabeshima near Arita on the island of Kyushu. At first, potteries produced a Korean-inspired underglaze blue-and-white ware. Later, more colorful ware in Chinese style with dark blue underglaze and strong red overglaze enamel became popular. Chinese motifs were soon replaced by motifs from Japanese painting, textiles, and lacquerware. Such porcelain, however, soon became ornate, quite unlike the rustic tea ware. Produced in large amounts and exported from the port of Imari, this *Imari* ware, as it was known in the West, was in great demand in Europe.

81 **Ogata Kenzan,** Japan. *Bellflowers,* fan-shaped cake tray. Edo period, 18th century. Stoneware with enameled decoration on a cream-colored glaze, length of sides 6.63″ (16.5 cm). Seattle Art Museum (Eugene Fuller Memorial Collection).

below left: **82** *Pine, Bamboo, and Flowering Tree,* Kakiemon ware plate, Japan. Edo Period, early 18th century. Porcelain with gold and enameled decoration, diameter 7.38″ (18.5 cm). Seattle Art Museum (Eugene Fuller Memorial Collection).

below right: **83** Nabeshima ware teapot, Japan. Edo Period, mid-18th century. Porcelain with pale celedon glaze in a "plum blossom and buds" design, height 6″ (15 cm). Seattle Art Museum (gift of Mrs. Charles E. Stuart).

In contrast to the vivid Imari ware were the small amounts of excellent porcelain produced by the potteries of the Kakiemon family and of Lord Nabeshima, also in Arita. *Kakiemon* enameled ware was in the Chinese tradition but was painted with greater restraint and delicacy of color and brush stroke and with more openness of design (Fig. 82). *Nabeshima* ware was delicately painted in motifs and style characteristic of Japanese painting (Fig. 83). *Kutani* porcelain, from the Kutani potteries on the island of Honshu, was also Japanese in feeling but had boldly brushed designs of birds, flowers, and landscapes in strong green, blue, yellow, and purple.

61

The Islamic World

In the sixth century the prophet Muhammed founded a religion in the remote southern Arabian desert that became the dominant political and cultural force for a large part of the Old World. In the century after his death in 632, his devout, war-minded followers burst out of Arabia, conquering the Middle East and expanding east into India and west across North Africa into Spain. The Islamic civilization that they developed synthesized ancient art traditions of the conquered lands. These included the flowing, interlaced curves of symmetrical floral motifs known as *arabesques,* intricate geometric patterns and other detail, and vivid color.

Mesopotamia

Pottery of the seventh and eighth centuries in Mesopotamia was simple utilitarian earthenware often covered with a transparent lead glaze in brown, green, or blue-green (Fig. 84). Improvements in pottery must be credited to the influence of Chinese ware, particularly porcelains, imported for the court of the Abbasid caliphs, who ruled from Baghdad and Samarra. It is to their credit that they encouraged local potters to imitate Chinese wares. In their efforts to do so, Mesopotamian potters, lacking kaolin, coated their earthenware with white slip. Such ware, incised with floral decorations and covered with a spotty, runny lead glaze in brown, green, and purple, showed the influence of T'ang pottery. Further improvements led to the replacement of the slip by a thick white glaze, made opaque by adding tin to lead glaze, which served as a background for painted decoration. Compared to Chinese porcelain, however, this Mesopotamian tin-lead-glazed ware was still heavy and coarse.

84 Amphora, Homs, Syria. Roman period, A.D. 1st–3rd century. Earthenware with rope handles and applied decoration under a blue glaze. Metropolitan Museum of Art, New York (gift of John D. Rockefeller, 1938).

85 Wall tile, Kashan, Iran. 13th century. Tin-lead glazed earthenware with luster decoration, diameter 5.75″ (14.5 cm). Metropolitan Museum of Art, New York (bequest of Edward C. Moore, 1891).

Often the decoration was in luster glaze, the most unusual achievement of the Islamic potters of Mesopotamia (Fig. 85). Luster is a thin coating of metallic salts, which is fused by low firing onto a glazed surface as a form of decoration. During the eighth century it was used in Egypt on glass to produce the effect of gold. In the early ninth century, Mesopotamian potters adapted luster to earthenware. At first they used lusters of ruby red, green, brown, and yellow. In time they applied pale golden brown luster as a background in conjunction with polychrome decoration in blue, turquoise, manganese purple, and pale green.

The Old Testament injunction against making graven images for fear of idolatry was continued in Islamic tradition, although it pertained only to religious art. Favorite motifs on pottery and tiles used to enrich the interior and occasionally the exterior of mosques were intricate arabesques. On pottery they often served as a background for stylized birds, animals, or human figures. Another common motif was koranic inscriptions in a bold, angular Kufic script, used alone or with other decoration.

Iran

Nomadic Turkish tribes from central Asia adopted Islam and established the Seljuk Empire in Iran and Mesopotamia in the eleventh century. Power shifted from the Abbasids in Mesopotamia to Cairo, Egypt, where Mesopotamian potters moved in search of patronage. Egypt then became a center of ceramic production.

above left: 86 Bowl, Rhages, Iran. 12th century. Earthenware with golden luster decoration. Metropolitan Museum of Art, New York (Rogers Fund 1920).

above right: 87 Jug, Iran. 13th century. Earthenware with Kufic decoration in dark slip under a clear glaze, height 5.75″ (14.6 cm). Victoria & Albert Museum, London (Crown Copyright).

right: 88 Ewer, Sultanabad, Iran. 13th–14th century. Earthenware body with decorations in a dark slip under a turquoise alkaline glaze. Art Institute of Chicago (Mr. and Mrs. Martin A. Ryerson Collection).

After the fall of the rulers of Egypt in the twelfth century, many Egyptian potters settled in Iran. Consequently, Iranian potters in Rhages, Kashan, and other cities, who had previously made slip-painted, lead-glazed earthenware, began to use luster (Fig. 86). By about the twelfth century they had developed a soft-paste porcelain. Firing at a low temperature, this new body was composed of powdered silica sand and alkaline *frit* (melted, reground glaze) held together with a white clay. It was not very plastic, which limited them to rather simple dish, ewer, bowl, and vase forms. Such wares were coated with an alkaline glaze originally invented in Egypt.

Some Iranian pottery was decorated with Kufic inscriptions (Fig. 87). In contrast, other pieces bore delicate *minai* decoration, inspired by manuscript illustration, which revealed great interest in human life. Minai painting in polychrome enamel over opaque white or turquoise glaze, represented in miniature scenes of horsemen, court life, and romantic legends. It became popular in the late twelfth century. A third, quite different ware had bold decorations in dark slip or sgraffito of animals and floral patterns under a transparent turquoise glaze.

The Mongols, who invaded China in the thirteenth century, as previously noted, also conquered the Seljuks in Iran. As a result of their invasion, production of luster ware and minai ware ceased, except in Kashan. Gradually they were replaced by ware decorated with black brushwork under a clear turquoise glaze (Fig. 88).

During the fourteenth century when both China and Iran were part of the Mongol Empire, contacts between the two countries were renewed. Designs from imported Chinese textiles and painting, such as clouds and dragons, were reflected in Iranian ceramics, although traditional Iranian bird and animal motifs with floral borders continued to be used. In the seventeenth century the luster technique was revived. Potters also produced a series of monochrome wares in Kerman and other cities, as well as fine earthenware and thin, soft-paste porcelain in blue and white (Fig. 89) or entirely in white with a pierced design in the body, which was filled and covered by a transparent glaze (Fig. 90).

left: **89** Jar, Iran. 16th–17th century. Copy in earthenware of a Chinese porcelain jar, height 7.5″ (19.05 cm). Victoria & Albert Museum, London (Crown Copyright).

right: **90** Footed bowl, Iran. 17th–18th century. White earthenware with elaborate pierced decoration, diameter 8.5″ (21.59 cm). Victoria & Albert Museum, London (Crown Copyright).

91 Dish, Iznik, Turkey. 1550–1560. Earthenware with tin-lead glazed polychrome decoration, diameter 14.5″ (36.83 cm). Victoria & Albert Museum, London (Crown Copyright).

Ottoman Empire

Many Seljuk Turkish tribes entered Anatolia (modern Turkey) from the eleventh through the thirteenth century. They built mosques enlivened by glazed tiles in the Iranian style. After the Mongol conquest of the Seljuks, one Turkish tribe, the Ottoman Turks, rose to prominence in Anatolia. In 1453 they conquered Constantinople, capital of the Byzantine Empire, which had succeeded Roman rule in the eastern Mediterranean and southeastern Europe. In the early sixteenth century, Syria and Egypt fell under Ottoman rule.

The Ottoman sultans imported Iranian potters to make tiles for new mosques in Bursa and Edirne. The tiles, in turquoise and blue on white, successfully combined Chinese and Iranian floral motifs. By the late fifteenth century, the potters of Iznik (formerly Nicaea) were making not only tiles but also large dishes, jars, ewers, tall-footed bowls, and mosque lamps in white with blue decoration. Gradually they added green and purple decoration and finally a brilliant iron-red. The most impressive examples of *Iznik* ware are large plates with a central floral spray—tulips, carnations, roses, or hyacinths—treated realistically (Fig. 91).

Spain

At the western end of the Islamic world, southern Spain prospered under Muslim (Moorish) rule from the eighth to the sixteenth century. Early *Hispano-Moresque* pottery of the tenth and eleventh centuries had stamped or slip-painted geometric motifs or koranic inscriptions.

The upheaval resulting from the thirteenth-century Mongol conquests in the Middle East benefited Spain as Iranian and other Middle Eastern potters, dispersed from their homelands, fled west. From them the Moorish and Christian potters of Málaga, Valencia, and nearby Manises learned the secrets of luster glazes. These lusters, composed of copper, silver, sulfur, red ocher, and vinegar, were applied to earthenware covered with white tin glaze with a

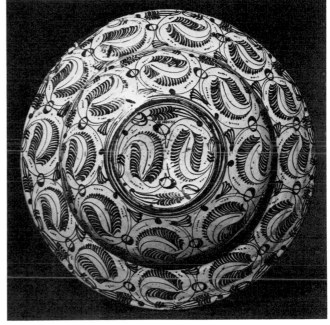

above: **92** Hispano-Moresque platter, Spain. c. 1450. Earthenware with tin-lead glaze decoration in blue with golden luster, diameter 17.75″ (45.08 cm). Victoria & Albert Museum, London (Crown Copyright).

right: **93** Bottom view of platter in Figure 92 showing double foot and decoration.

third low reduction firing only for the lusters. To save kiln space the large plates were placed on edge. The favorite colors were pale gold luster with details in blue. Decoration, on both front and back, reflected the arts of metal engraving and textiles in its overall patterns of stylized floral elements, chevrons, knotted ribbons, and koranic inscriptions (Figs. 92 and 93 and Plate 6, p. 57).

As Gothic influences from France crept into Spain, more naturalistic foliage and even animals, birds, horsemen, and other humans appeared. Of particular interest are large sets of lusterware plated with a heraldic coat of arms surrounded by an intertwined floral border. Owning such plates became a symbol of prestige for many small feudal states not only in northern Spain but also in southern France and Italy, where lusterware was in great demand.

94 Hispano-Moresque drug jar, Spain. c. 1440. Earthenware with tin-lead glaze decoration in blue and opal luster, height 15.13″ (38.4 cm). Victoria & Albert Museum, London (Crown Copyright).

above right: **95** Hispano-Moresque vase, Valencia, Spain. c. 1470. Graceful wing-handled vase derived from the earlier more austere Alhambra style. Earthenware with tin-lead glaze decoration in blue and golden luster, height 20.75″ (52.70 cm). Victoria & Albert Museum, London (Crown Copyright).

right: **96** Platter, Manises, Spain. 1468–1479. Earthenware with relief decoration and coat of arms of Castile, Leon, and Aragon in tin-lead glaze and golden luster, diameter 17.5″ (44.45 cm). Victoria & Albert Museum, London (Crown Copyright).

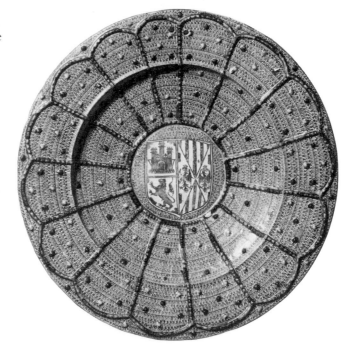

Interested primarily in painted decoration, the Hispano-Moresque potters of the fourteenth and fifteenth centuries never developed the more graceful shapes of Oriental ceramics. They preferred the flat painting surface of large platters or of the nearly cylindrical *albarelli,* or drug jars (Fig. 94). The graceful Alhambra vase with its winglike handles was the only innovation in form (Fig. 95).

68

Muslim influence waned as the Christians reconquered Spain. The last Moors and Jews, who were the chief farmers, craftsmen, and traders of Spain, were expelled when Granada fell to the Spanish monarchs Ferdinand and Isabella in 1492. The resulting damage to the Spanish economy was concealed for a while by the influx of gold and silver from Spanish conquests in the New World, but this treasure also made luster less appealing. Although attempts were made to shape plates with raised designs and bosses imitative of metalwork (Fig. 96), the association of lusterware with the Moors perhaps contributed to its decline.

Africa

Our knowledge of African pottery suffers from the lack of data that formerly characterized the study of all aspects of ancient African cultures. Rock paintings and stone engravings from the fifth millennium B.C. to the second, which were first discovered in the mountains of the Sahara and central and southern Africa early in this century, reveal a gradual change from a hunting to a pastoral culture. As the climate gradually became drier and population increased, peoples migrated, generally from north to south and from west to east. Trade between the ancient African kingdoms of Kush (now Sudan) and Punt (Ethiopia and Somaliland) and Egypt exposed Africans to the developments of Middle Eastern civilizations. Iron making spread west to northern Nigeria, where the Nok people (900 B.C–A.D. 200) worked in iron as early as the fifth century B.C. An extensive iron industry flourished at Meroë, capital of Kush, on the upper Nile in the first century A.D. Bronze casting, well-established along the Niger River between 600 and 950, spread south to Ife (Fig. 97) and Benin (now Nigeria), where it reached its height in royal portrait heads of the rulers of Benin between 1575 and 1625.

97 Ife figure, Tada, Nigeria. 10th–11th century. Bronze, height 20.5″ (50.93 cm). Department of Antiquities, Lagos, Nigeria.

98 Cast of Ife head called Lajuwa, Nigeria. c. 1200–1300. Terra-cotta, height 13.11″ (33 cm), width 7.48″ (19.6 cm). American Museum of Natural History, New York, Cat. No.: 90.2/249.

above right: 99 Benin head, Bini, Nigeria. 1560–1680. Terra-cotta, height 8.5″ (21.5 cm). Metropolitan Museum of Art, New York (The Michael C. Rockefeller Memorial Collection, bequest of Nelson A. Rockefeller, 1979).

African sculptors also worked in stone and especially in wood, creating ceremonial and religious figures according to tribal traditions. Some, however, worked in terra-cotta. Life-size terra-cotta heads and the fragments of figures made by the Nok about 500 B.C. have an impressive realism that is unique. Since clay is commonly used to make studies in preparation for sculpture in other materials, it is not surprising that many large terra-cotta portrait heads have been found that have the same feeling for plastic form and personal expression that characterize the bronzes of Ife and Benin (Figs. 98 and 99).

In addition to this large, rather formal ceramic sculpture, many tribes made small clay figures. The figurative earthenware bottles of the Mangbetu are best known (Fig. 100). These effigy heads, like those of the Mochica in pre-Columbian Peru, are stylized in a manner that is elusive but quite satisfying; they are an art form that, as exemplified in vacuous late Greek portrait vases and caricature English Toby jugs, often fails. Perhaps Westerners, who stress written and oral communication, have lost the plastic inventiveness that characterized so much of traditional African art.

The Africans also made pottery, which, as in most tribal cultures, was usually the work of women. In some instances, whole villages made pottery and traded their surplus to other areas. Except in a few Muslim-influenced regions in North Africa, all pottery was hand built in a combination coil and paddle technique. The gourd so commonly used as a container influenced many pottery forms. Large oval vases with collar rims served for food and water storage. Textural decorations were often applied in a basketlike weave or painted in iron oxides to produce a red or black design. Since most pottery was fired in an open pit with straw and twigs, it was not very hard; little early pottery has survived.

100 Mangbetu portrait bottle, Congo. 19th–20th century. Terra-cotta, height 11.38″ (28 cm). Metropolitan Museum of Art, New York (bequest of Nelson A. Rockefeller, 1979).

The West

The development of European ceramics, in general, depended on influences from the more advanced peoples in the Middle East and the Orient. Farmers from western Asia migrated to the Danube Valley in eastern Europe, where small agricultural villages were settled shortly after 7000 B.C. Excavations during the 1970s at Vinca in Yugoslavia, Varna in Bulgaria, and other sites reveal pottery decorated with black graphite and artifacts made of gold and copper dated shortly after 5000 B.C. Ceramic figurines date as early as 6500 to 6000 B.C.

The Celts, Indo-European people from the east, who spread over much much of Europe from about 1800 to 400 B.C., were primarily farmers and skilled metalworkers. They traded with the Greeks and Etruscans south of the Alps for fine pottery. From the Romans, who colonized Gaul, the Rhineland, and Britain from the first century B.C. to the fifth century A.D., European potters learned such advanced techniques as the use of the wheel and lead glaze. The decline of Rome, however, accompanied by new waves of barbarian invaders from the east, caused pottery skills to be forgotten not only in nothern Europe but even in Italy itself.

The Middle Ages

During the Middle Ages, contacts with the Byzantine Empire and the Islamic world encouraged Italian potters again to produce glazed ware. The simple earthenware bowls, jugs, amphoras, and pitchers of the seventh and

left: **101** Jug, Rouen, Normandy. Late 12th/13th century. Thrown earthenware with applied clay and slip decoration under a thin yellow glaze, height 9.5″ (24.13 cm). The Museum of London.

above right: **102** Jug, England. Late 13th/14th century. Earthenware, ram's head spout with pinched foot, green stripes under a yellow lead glaze; height 14″ (35.56 cm). The Museum of London.

eighth centuries had a runny yellowish or green lead glaze with *sgraffito* (scratched) decoration. France, farther from these advanced centers of civilization than Italy, was slower to recover lost skills. Green-glazed tiles may date from the ninth century, although glazes were not in widespread use until the thirteenth century (Fig. 101).

Britain was even more isolated by the departure of the Romans. By the tenth century Anglo-Saxon trade with the Continent had resulted in only a limited revival of the potter's wheel and lead glaze in England. In the late thirteenth and early fourteenth centuries, English potters became more innovative. The tall jug developed into a pitcher with a pinched-out lip and spiral patterns of clay applied under a green glaze. Finally faces appeared on the pitcher neck, the spout turned into an animal head (Fig. 102), and a few rare pieces had entire hunting scenes in relief.

Roman influences survived longer in the Rhineland, as seen in jugs with banded rouletted decoration. Increased trade with Italy reintroduced lead glaze as early as 900, but it never assumed great importance. Improved kilns and an abundance of stoneware clays encouraged potters to fire higher and produce a more durable ware. By the early twelfth century they were producing a proto-stoneware and by the late fourteenth century a true stoneware. Usually light gray in body, it was almost waterproof without a glaze.

The Renaissance

The Renaissance, a period of great economic growth, saw increased trade within Europe and between Europe and the Orient. It was a time of new ideas and important developments in all the arts, including ceramics.

Italy In Italy the older lead-glazed earthenware with sgraffito decoration continued to be made into the sixteenth century, but the early Hispano-Moresque ware was highly prized and then imitated. Since this Spanish tin-glazed lusterware was imported into Italy via the island of Majorca, the new Italian ware in the Spanish style was called *majolica*. Italian majolica of the late thirteenth and early fourteenth centuries was typically decorated with geometric and floral elements around a central human figure, animal, or coat of arms (Fig. 103). The usual green and brown on white tin glaze was occasionally relieved by cobalt blue. Popular shapes were the Spanish albarelli (Fig. 104); full, rounded vases; and graceful bottles and pitchers; as well as large, broad-rimmed plates.

Early in the fifteenth century, Florence and Faenza produced a blue and brown majolica of stylized floral and animal motifs reflecting Byzantine and Oriental influences. These colors soon gave way to a wider palette including

left: **103** Drug jar, Tuscany, Italy. Mid-15th century. Earthenware with majolica decoration of rabbit and flowers in blue, purple, and green tin-lead glaze; height 8.5″ (21.59 cm). Victoria & Albert Museum, London (Crown Copyright).

right: **104** Drug jar, Caffaggiolo, Italy. Early 16th century. Earthenware with majolica decoration in tin-lead glaze, height 8.88″ (22.55 cm). Victoria & Albert Museum, London (Crown Copyright).

105 Platter, Deruta, Italy. c. 1520. Earthenware with majolica decoration of young woman with floral border in blue tin-lead glaze and golden luster, diameter 15.75″ (40 cm). Victoria & Albert Museum, London (Crown Copyright).

106 Plate, Urbino, Italy. c. 1542. Earthenware with majolica decoration of *The Calydonian Boar* in polychrome tin-lead glaze, diameter 10.75″ (27.3 cm). Victoria & Albert Museum, London (Crown Copyright).

yellow, orange, and purple in the Iranian palmette and peacock feather motifs. Figures and portraits, which traditionally had been part of an overall decoration, became major design elements (Fig. 105). As the skill of pottery painters increased, they incorporated pictorial elements in their work; finally they copied complete panel paintings, including scenes from classical legends and the Bible, with perspective and atmospheric effects (Fig. 106). Although technically superior, this sixteenth- and seventeenth-century majolica lacked the union of form and decoration characteristic of earlier production.

Familiar with clay as a material for studies for sculpture, some of the many Renaissance sculptors were naturally intrigued with the marblelike effect of tin-glazed ceramics. The fifteenth-century Florentine sculptor Luca della Robbia produced subtly modeled terra-cotta madonnas glazed white against a pale blue background surrounded by an unobtrusive border of flowers and fruits; these relief plaques were remarkably popular decorations for churches and homes (Fig. 107).

107 **Luca della Robbia,** Florence, Italy. *Madonna and Child.* c. 1450. Relief in tin-lead glazed terra-cotta, white on pale blue background; height 31.25″ (79.38 cm). Metropolitan Museum of Art, New York.

France and The Netherlands In northern Europe tin-glazed earthenware became known as *faience* as a result of the popularity of the Italian majolica of Faenza. French faience potters imitated the blue-and-white porcelain of the Chinese, but none were as successful as the Dutch in Delft, who learned to throw thinner ware. Decoration became delicate until Delft potters were finally able to make reasonable copies in faience of the famous K'ang Hsi blue-and-white porcelain.

Chinese influence gradually gave way to European baroque influence in form and in landscapes, scenes, and decorative motifs copied from engravings and paintings. Eventually Dutch potters reproduced the colorful Japanese Imari ware and Chinese famille-verte ware. They also made glazed tiles. Tiles had long been made in Spain, Italy, and France to decorate churches and homes, but Dutch tiles were especially popular. Chiefly blue and white, they varied widely in motif, including flowers, ships, marine monsters, landscapes, and religious scenes.

England and Germany   The majolica tradition was never significant in England. More important was slipware made chiefly during the seventeenth century in Staffordshire, usually to commemorate weddings and christenings. Trailed in dots and dashes or applied by stamping, the white clay slip made a striking contrast with the red or dark brown body. Slip-trailed plates decorated with feather brushing were also popular. More elaborate slip-trailed dishes, such as those by the potter Thomas Toft, displayed mermaids, pelicans, and coats of arms with a lattice border of trailed red and brown slip on a white ground covered with a clear or pale yellow lead glaze (Fig. 108).

Although German potters made peasant earthenware decorated with sgraffito or slip, the most important German ware was the salt-glazed stoneware that had evolved by the close of the fourteenth century. Lingering Roman influence can be seen in the pressed foliage designs on tankards and jugs, especially the full-bodied *bellarmine* jug with its bearded face (Fig. 109). By the sixteenth century, stoneware was also being made in the Beauvais region of France and in the seventeenth century in Staffordshire, England.

The Eighteenth and Early Nineteenth Centuries

The Continent   The outstanding development in eighteenth-century ceramics was the discovery of the way to make porcelain. The impetus came from the importation of blue-and-white porcelain from China and, later, of Imari ware from Japan. Tremendously popular, these Oriental porcelains sold at fantastic prices. In an attempt to imitate them, the Medici family of Florence in the late sixteenth century had sponsored the production of soft-paste porcelain using kaolinic clay, a white earthenware, silica, and soda. In the seventeenth and eighteenth centuries, factories at Rouen, St. Cloud, Sèvres, and other French cities produced soft-paste porcelain made of clay and frit. These wares were attractive but fragile.

In 1707, J. F. Böttger, a young German alchemist employed by Augustus the Strong, ruler of Saxony, in the course of subjecting local minerals to heat, developed a hard, red stoneware (Fig. 110). About 1710 he produced a true, or hard-paste, porcelain. Augustus thereupon established a porcelain factory at Meissen, where there were large deposits of kaolin. Later, factories were built in Vienna, Strasbourg, Nymphenburg, Copenhagen, and other cities. In the 1770s porcelain was being produced at royal factories in Sèvres and Limoges in France.

The wares of the various soft-paste and hard-paste porcelain factories were technically superior to any ceramics previously made in Europe. In style, potters at first copied Oriental pieces (Fig. 111). Then baroque, rococo, and neoclassical elements borrowed from other European arts crept in, including landscape scenes. Elaborate rococo figurines displayed the great skill of the potters in modeling and glazing.

These eighteenth- and early-nineteenth-century porcelains are treasured by twentieth-century museums and private collectors. They are of less interest to present-day potters because their form and decoration did not grow out of regional ceramic traditions but was eclectic. Furthermore, through the use of plaster-of-Paris molds, they reproduced shapes and decoration originating in metal and other nonceramic materials (Fig. 112).

110 Flask, Meissen, Germany. c. 1710–1715. Early example of red stoneware by J. F. Böttger with impressed decoration. Metropolitan Museum of Art, New York (gift of Mrs. George B. McClellan, 1942).

left: **111** Covered vase, Meissen, Germany. c. 1725–1730. Hard-paste porcelain with polychrome overglaze decoration in a Japanese style, height 16.5″ (41.91 cm). Metropolitan Museum of Art, New York (bequest of Alfred Duane Pell, 1925).

right: **112** Vase, Sèvres, France. c. 1785. Porcelain with sprigged classical motifs and a blue and white glaze, height 16″. Victoria & Albert Museum, London (Crown Copyright).

England While Continental potters led the way in the manufacture of porcelain, other developments in ceramics took place in England. The chief center was Staffordshire, which was well supplied with clay and with coal for the kilns. Staffordshire potters produced both salt-glazed stoneware and a new *creamware,* a light, durable earthenware used for dishes for the table. Creamware eventually superseded the softer slipware in England and, to some extent, faience and majolica on the Continent.

Although the Wedgwood family potteries produced immense amounts of creamware, they are best known for their unglazed black *basalt* ware and *jasper* ware of various pale colors. Both types of stoneware were used chiefly for display. Their shapes and relief decorations, molded or applied, were derived from classical forms. Popular pale blue jasper ware vases with white figures in relief resembled glass cameos more than ceramics.

English potters also experimented with porcelain. By adding bone ash as a flux to soft-paste and hard-paste bodies, they produced a light, durable *bone china* fired at a somewhat lower temperature. Bone china was made at Chelsea, Worcester, and other potteries, notably that of Josiah Spode II, who developed the standard bone china formula. Spode (renamed Copeland), Minton, and other Staffordshire potteries also made *Parian* ware, a bisque porcelain that resembled marble.

English potteries were quick to adopt the mass-production techniques of the Industrial Revolution. Steam-powered machinery, plaster-of-paris molds, and *jiggering* (shaping clay on a turning plaster mold by means of a metal template on a moving arm) made production more efficient and therefore cheaper. Transfer printing of designs from engraved metal plates speeded up decoration but also led to the demise of most hand-painted ware.

America In colonial America the first pottery was a soft, lead-glazed red earthenware. That made by English colonists, if decorated at all, was in the English slipware tradition. Pottery made by German settlers in Pennsylvania was apt to imitate German slipware and sgraffito ware with figures and tulip and other floral designs (Fig. 113). Good stoneware clays were found in New

113 David Spinner, Bucks County, Pa., U.S.A. Pie plate. c. 1800. Red earthenware with sgraffito decoration, diameter 11.5" (29.3 cm). Brooklyn Museum, New York (gift of Mrs. Huldah Cart Lorimer in memory of George Burford Lorimer).

Jersey and New York and later in Ohio. The first surviving stoneware was made in New Jersey in 1775. Gradually stoneware displaced the more fragile red earthenware.

Imports from abroad, especially English creamware, made it difficult for American earthenware potters working on a small scale to compete either in tableware or in decorative pieces. Stoneware potters, producing functional salt-glazed jugs and crocks for a local market (Fig. 114), were more successful. Typical of such potteries was that in Bennington, Vermont. During the late eighteenth and nineteenth centuries, it first produced red earthenware, then stoneware, and finally a mottled-brown-glazed creamware called *Rockingham.* Bennington also used Parian ware copied from Minton and Copeland to make soft-paste porcelain figurines and elaborately modeled vases. Many had a blue background in imitation of Wedgwood jasper ware (Fig. 115). Although porcelain was made experimentally in New Jersey in 1826, it was not made commercially until after the Civil War.

The Late Nineteenth and Twentieth Centuries

Industrialization, beginning in eighteenth-century England, steadily increased thereafter in Europe, the United States, and later in Japan. In the process it nearly destroyed hand-thrown and hand-decorated ceramics. It forced individual potters into large factories where they performed a small, repetitive task in a huge mass-production enterprise controlled by an entrepreneur whose major interest was profit. Design decisions were no longer made by potters but by sales managers.

Preindustrial potters had worked basically within local traditions, reacting only slowly to new ideas and developments in other crafts such as metalwork. These local traditions succumbed to the immense popularity of imported ware. For example, Royal Copenhagen and Bing and Grøndahl in Denmark, Gustavsberg and Rostrand in Sweden, and Arabia in Finland were strongly influenced by the faience and porcelain of France and Germany. Commercial potteries in the United States, such as Bennington as previously noted, copied designs from abroad. The fact that until 1918 the china used in the White House was imported shows the pervasive influence of foreign wares.

Local traditions also suffered from the growing taste for extravagant display and the factory owners' desire for profit. In addition, the plastic quality of clay and the variety of glaze effects available made possible the manufacture of forms and decoration of poor quality and bad taste.

Early Attempts at Reform Gradually protest arose against this commercialized, industrialized ware. It began in mid-nineteenth-century England, when the writer John Ruskin, the writer and designer William Morris, and their followers, imbued with the Romantic ideal of return to the Middle Ages, tried to revive traditions of integrity in materials, design, and workmanship in the decorative arts. Although the Arts and Crafts movement they inspired faltered, Morris succeeded in drawing attention to the poor quality of nineteenth-century design. Later, the Art Nouveau movement of the 1890s and early 1900s in France, England, and the United States and the related *Jugendstil* in Germany were other forms of reaction against the prevailing state of the decorative arts (Fig. 116).

Meanwhile individual potters such as Theodore Deck, Ernest Chaplet, and Auguste Delaherche in France (Fig. 117) and the Martin brothers and William de Morgan in England carried out experiments to rediscover the lost

left: **116 Georges de Feure,** potted by E. Gerard, Limoges, France. Vase. c. 1898–1904. Porcelain with Art Nouveau design in green, lavender, and gray. Metropolitan Museum of Art, New York (Edward C. Moore, Jr. Gift Fund, 1926).

right: **117 Auguste Dalaherche,** Beauvais, France. Vase. c. 1900. Stoneware showing Oriental influence. Metropolitan Museum of Art, New York (gift of Edward C. Moore, 1922).

118 Adelaide Robineau, U.S.A. Vases. Late 19th/early 20th century. Porcelain with crystalline glazes. Everson Museum of Art, Syracuse, N.Y.

pottery secrets of earlier ages. They explored decorative techniques such as Islamic luster and Chinese copper-red glazes. The Victorian taste for ornate Ch'ing export porcelain was slow to die, but gradually an appreciation grew for the more subtle wares of the Sung period as well as those of Korea and Japan. In the United States the Art Nouveau movement and interest in Chinese ceramics played a part in giving new directions to potteries such as Rookwood, in Cincinnati, and to early pottery enthusiasts such as Adelaide Robineau (Fig. 118).

Interest in Avant-garde Design In the early twentieth century in both Europe and the United States, some potters became more concerned with good design. In Europe this tendency was in large part the result of government-sponsored craft schools founded in England, Germany, Italy, and Scandinavia and of the Bauhaus, a school of design that flourished in Germany in the 1920s and early 1930s. These schools encouraged the production of furniture, glassware, textiles, and metalware, as well as ceramics, which were designed to be beautiful, functional, efficient to manufacture, and reasonable in cost. In Scandinavia, industry, the schools, and government officials made a combined effort to reach these goals, perhaps as a result of the prevailing

119 Stig Lindberg for Aktielologet Gustavsberg Fabriker, Gustavsberg, Sweden. Functional ovenware. c. 1960. Brown and white.

socialist policies after World War II, which emphasized the well-being of the whole population (Fig. 119).

When the Bauhaus was closed by the Nazi government, many of its faculty went to the United States, where they spread Bauhaus principles. Frans and Margarite Wildenhain, former students at the Bauhaus, Maija Grotell from Finland, and Otto and Gertrude Natzler from Austria were among many emigrés who brought a fresh impetus to American ceramics. They built on a foundation already prepared by the English potter Charles Binns, who had become the first director of the New York College of Ceramics in Alfred, New York, in 1900. His work had been continued by his many students, such as Charles Harder and Arthur Baggs (Fig. 120), who laid the foundations for many ceramics programs later established in American colleges. *Keramic Studio* magazine, founded by Adelaide Robineau in 1899, played a helpful role.

120 Arthur E. Baggs, U.S.A. Jar. 1938. Salt-glazed stoneware. Everson Museum of Art, Syracuse, N.Y.

121 Shoji Hamada, Japan, shown decorating a vase, c. 1960.

Interest in Traditional Techniques The twentieth century also saw a reawakening of interest throughout the world in the fundamentals of ceramics. Many people took up pottery as an avocation or taught pottery making in schools. Quite naturally, potters focused renewed attention on native pottery traditions that had been by-passed by the Industrial Revolution—majolica and lusterware in Italy and Spain, salt-glazed stoneware in Germany and the United States, Pueblo pottery in the southwestern United States, and raku ware, used for the tea ceremony, in Japan and the United States.

The Japanese potters Shoji Hamada (Fig. 121) and Kanjiro Kawai together with Soetsu Yanagi, founder of the Mingei (folk art) Society, revived interest in traditional handmade pottery in the 1920s and 1930s. They influenced the architect Kenkichi Tomimoto, who made more personal pottery (Fig. 122) and founded the first Japanese college-level ceramics program.

122 Kenkichi Tomimoto, Japan. Jar. Mid-20th century. Porcelain with delicate pattern in gold and silver, height 7.5″ (19.05 cm). Japanese Embassy, Washington, D.C.

123 Bernard Leach, England. Plate. Made during his stay in Japan, prior to 1920. Raku-fired earthenware with slip-trailed decoration, diameter 13.5″ (34.19 cm). Victoria & Albert Museum, London (Crown Copyright).

In England, William Staite Murray and Bernard Leach, both of whom knew Shoji Hamada, led a revival in hand-thrown pottery. Murray made chiefly art pottery and taught at the Royal College of Art in London. Leach, who had studied ceramics in Japan before 1920, made functional ware. He encouraged understanding of Oriental folk pottery (Figs. 123 and 124) and rekindled interest in early English slipware. Through the many apprentices at his workshop in St. Ives, Cornwall, notably Michael Cardew (Fig. 125), and through his many books, he had great influence on ceramics in the English-speaking world.

In the United States on the West Coast in the 1930s Glen Lukens experimented with local minerals for glazes and encouraged his students in a wide range of projects. Since World War II Peter Voulkos (Plate 7, p. 58), Daniel Rhodes, Robert Turner (Fig. 197), Ted Randall (Plate 8, p. 91), Sheldon Carey, Karl Martz, and a host of other potters have continued to experiment with ceramic techniques.

Ceramics as an Art As a result of the revival of interest in pottery traditions and in new pottery design, ceramics has come to be accepted as an art

form. Many potters today have previously been artists in other fields. Exhibitions of ceramics, rare in the past, in the 1980s are commonplace. Exhibitors, less interested in functional, wheel-thrown ware than potters were earlier in the century, are more concerned with decorative or completely sculptural ceramics, often made by the coil and slab techniques. Various trends in the world of painting and sculpture such as Dadaism, Pop Art and funk art, Minimal Art, Environmental Art, soft sculpture, and the use of mixed media are all reflected in late twentieth-century ceramics. Thus the contemporary potters whose work is illustrated in the following chapters are a mixed group in background and goals.

The differences between these avant-garde ceramists and potters with a more traditional approach are likely to continue. Both groups, however, have brought experimentation and vitality to an ancient art that was nearly stifled by the demands of industrialization and a mass market.

left: **124 Bernard Leach,** England. Vase. 1931. Stoneware with form and brush decoration in an Oriental style, height 14″ (35.56 cm). Victoria & Albert Museum, London (Crown Copyright).

right: **125 Michael Cardew,** England. Mid-20th century. Covered jar. Stoneware with incised decoration.

4

Hand-building Techniques

Hand building with clay is one of the oldest craft activities known. The techniques are followed today in almost the same manner as they were ten or twelve thousand years ago. It is likely that small figurines and animals were modeled long before the first pots were made. Few of these unfired figures have survived, but some have been found in Middle Eastern burial mounds. They were probably used as fetishes in connection with hunting, planting, and harvesting ceremonies.

Throughout the history of ceramics, hand-building techniques have been used to make both functional and sculptural forms. In skilled hands pinching and coiling produce remarkably symmetrical pots. Even after the introduction of the potter's wheel, many cultures continued to prefer the flexibility of these hand methods.

Preparation of Clay

If a coil of moist clay cracks excessively when wound around the finger, it probably is not suitable for forming. Often, sand will cause this cracking; it can be removed by adding water to the body to make a slip and allowing the sand to settle out. But this procedure may require more effort than it is worth. If the base clay has possibilities but is only moderately plastic, an addition of 20 percent ball clay or 5 percent bentonite will improve the body. Some bodies contain up to 40 percent ball clay, but because ball clay absorbs a large quantity of water, the shrinkage rate increases.

126 In wedging, (a) the clay is compressed with the heel of the hand in a rocking motion. (b) A slight twist develops a corkscrew pattern, which forces out all the trapped air bubbles (page 89).

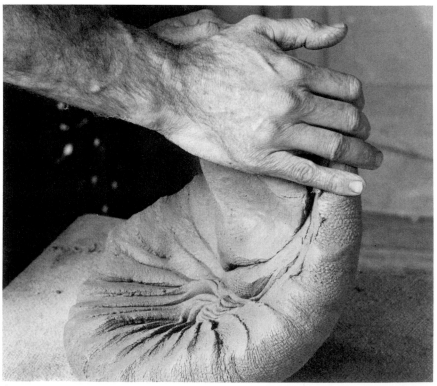

A

Aging

It is essential that even a satisfactory clay body be aged for at least three weeks in a plastic state. Aging allows the microscopic particles to become completely wet, causing them to cling together. If clay is aged for several months, a slight chemical breakdown occurs much like the original formation process. Even a nonplastic casting slip will become suitable for throwing if it is aged long enough. A small amount of clay can be aged in a plastic bag or plastic garbage can. For larger quantities an old refrigerator, a plastic-lined box, or a concrete vault can be used.

Wedging

Wedging (Fig. 126) is an important process in clay preparation. The clay is kneaded to force out air bubbles, to align coarse particles, and to develop a homogeneous consistency. The potter starts with a 5- to 10-pound (2.27–4.54-kg) ball of clay; the larger the clay mass, the greater the physical strength required. The clay should be softer than desired for forming, because some moisture is lost in the wedging process. A plaster wedging table provides an absorbent surface and should be at a convenient height. (The plaster surface should be scraped often to prevent the clay particles from clogging the plaster and making the clay stick.)

The clay mass is wedged with firm pressure from the heel of the hand to compress the clay. A rocking motion with a slight twist keeps the clay from flattening on the table. This pressing, rocking, and twisting will create a corkscrew effect, bringing all portions of the clay into contact with the surface and

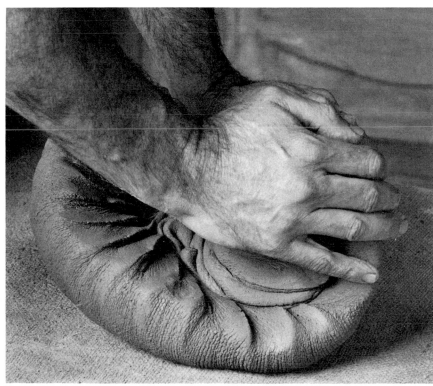

B

127 Wedging table with wire for cutting clay.

bursting trapped air bubbles. A comfortable and effective wedging rhythm will evolve only after practice. Beginning students tend to flatten and fold the clay, thus adding rather than removing air pockets.

A wire strung from a post at the rear of the table to a front corner will help to cut the mass of well-wedged clay into smaller pieces. The wire also aids in mixing a stiff mass of clay with a softer body. Both bodies are cut into thin slices and thrown onto the table, alternating soft and hard pieces. This cutting and throwing operation is repeated several times; then the clay is wedged in the usual manner to obtain a uniform consistency.

Depending upon the type of work, it may be necessary to wedge *grog* into the clay body. Grog (fired clay crushed to fine particles) helps plastic clay to stand up, prevents sagging, and lessens the chances of thick walls cracking. For throwing and for delicate sculptural work a minimum of fine grog is necessary; for large sculptural pieces as much as 20 to 30 percent of medium or coarse grog (mesh sizes 12 to 8) will be needed.

Grog should be wedged into the body in small quantities. Thin layers of the type needed are dusted onto the surface and wedged until they are evenly distributed through the body. Then more grog is added until the body seems right.

Unusual effects are achieved by adding colored grog to a contrasting clay body. Grog can be made by forcing plastic clay of the desired color through a coarse screen. The stringlike particles are allowed to dry and are bisque fired. The fired pieces are pounded with a mallet and put through a sieve to obtain the proper grog size.

Fiberglass is another material added to a clay body to lend greater strength. Since fiberglass is actually silica in another form, it fuses into the body during firing. Strands cut into 1-inch (2.54-cm) segments can be wedged into a plastic mass of clay in the same manner as grog (Fig. 11, p. 11). Fiberglass cloth in an open mesh size can be rolled between two slabs to create a slab with greater tensile strength.

HAND-BUILDING TECHNIQUES

Plate 8   Theodore Randall, U.S.A.
Planter. Coiled stoneware, stained with
iron, cobalt, and copper slips, diameter
20″ (50.8 cm), height 17″ (43.1 cm).

Plate 9   Hiroaki Morino, Japan.
Cube. Stoneware slab construction with
modeled additions, iron stain and low-
fire polychrome playing card design;
height 14″ (35 cm).

Plate 10 Marilyn Levine, U.S.A. *Two-Toned Golf Bag.* An amazing simulation in clay. Stoneware body with nylon reinforcement fired at cone 07–08; low-fired lusters on rivets and rings; length 35″ (89 cm).

128 Well-wedged mass of clay cut in half (left) and improperly wedged clay showing air pockets (right).

Pinching

Pinching requires only properly conditioned, plastic clay and the fingers. Small sculptural pieces can be pinched from one large mass of clay or built up from many units. Remarkably expressive forms can be made with this simple hand-building method, provided certain basic guidelines are kept in mind. Small cracks that appear during pinching can be smoothed over, but large cracks are likely to reappear during drying and firing. If the clay becomes too dry and cracks excessively, it is best to moisten it, wedge it, and begin again. Also important to pinching (and most hand-building methods) is gentle, even pressure to manipulate the clay.

A pinch pot is a good beginning project for students; making a simple bowl shape will help familiarize them with the qualities of clay. The basic steps are illustrated in Figure 129 on page 94. The potter starts with a small ball of wedged clay, the size of a tennis ball or slightly larger. A depression is made in the center with the thumbs. Then the ball of clay, held in one hand, is squeezed between the thumb and forefinger of the other hand. More pressure from the inside will make a wider bowl shape, while more pressure with the forefinger against the thumb will result in a taller form.

Steps in the Process of Pinching a Pot

129

A Make a depression with the thumbs in the ball of clay.

B Gradually thin the walls with gentle pressure between thumb and fingers.

C Smooth with thumb to eliminate small cracks.

D A coil may be added and joined to form a foot.

A

B

C

D

HAND-BUILDING TECHNIQUES

When the walls are of uniform thickness, the rim can be cut or smoothed with a piece of leather. Once this basic form is established, there are many decorative possibilities—pinched additions, incised lines, or the addition of a *foot*. The foot can be a simple coil or ridge of clay joined to the bottom to serve as a design accent, or it can be individually modeled pieces added to make tripod feet. Historically, cooking vessels had tripod feet to elevate them above hot coals.

Coiling

Coiling is done by rolling out coils or ropes of clay to a desired thickness (see page 96). Often these coils are joined to a flat or rounded base and gradually shaped to build up the desired form. The coils should be pressed together firmly and the join marks smoothed on the inside with a vertical wiping motion. Unless the piece is purely decorative, the coils should probably be joined on the outside as well. If a more refined form is desired, however, the surface can be finished with a wooden tool or metal scraper when the clay has begun to dry (Fig. 130). At this point clay can be added and incised in a decorative manner, as in Plate 8, page 91, and Figure 132, page 97. Coils can also be added to the rims of thrown forms, provided the clay has set up enough so that it will not sag. When coils are joined to a *leather-hard* surface—still moist but dry enough to hold its shape without distortion—the edge must first be scored and coated with slip. Coils may also be looped to create an openwork form (Fig. 133, page 97).

130 Winnie Owens-Hart, U.S.A.
Water jar. Variation of a traditional Nigerian water jar, coiled, burnished, and smoked earthenware, height 11.5″ (29.2 cm).

Steps in Coiling a Pot

131

A A flat slab of clay serves as a base for the coiled pot. Coils must be uniform and joined every three coils.

B The inside should be finished completely as the form rises. The exterior needs only a rough scraping.

C Large pots need a slight drying at the halfway point or the soft clay at the base will become deformed.

D Irregularities may be leveled out by patting with a block of wood.

E Coils may be smaller as one approaches the neck and flaring rim. When leather-hard, the surface may be finally scraped and slip or other decoration applied; height 24″ (60 cm).

A

B

C

D

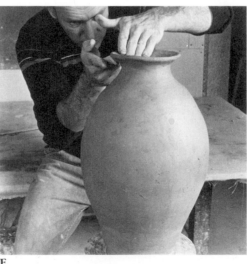

E

HAND-BUILDING TECHNIQUES

132 Sandra J. Blain, U.S.A. Planter. Coiled stoneware with coils partially exposed. Oxides wedged into clay and an Albany slip glaze over the impressed decoration. Thrown foot. Fired to cone 9, height 24″ (60 cm).

133 Susie Fowler, U.S.A. Fruit basket. Porcelain, made from rolled coils, formed inside a thrown bisqued mold, cobalt and copper colorant, clear glaze, fired at cone 10 reduced, height 7″ (17.78 cm).

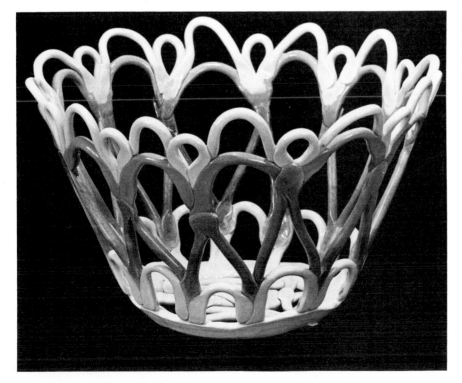

Thick Coil and Paddle

The size of many ancient pots amazes the modern potter. Intended for the storage of olive oil and wine, some Cretan jars are as tall as a person, with a nearly symmetrical swelling form (Fig. 59). These were doubtless made with the thick-coil method. Thick coils are joined, then thinned and shaped by beating a paddle against a rounded wooden anvil held inside. Wrapping the paddle with cord or covering it with fabric will reduce the tendency of clay to stick to its surface. When constructing a large, vertical piece, the potter should begin with a form that is taller and narrower than he or she wants it ultimately to be, because paddling will stretch the clay wider. The vibration of this forming method causes a tendency for the clay to settle. Burning a crumpled newspaper inside the pot will dry the clay sufficiently so that more coils can be added without making the structure collapse or sag unduly.

Coil construction is the basic technique for much sculpture, especially when used in combination with pinching and slabs. Bruno La Verdiere is a sculptor who works with coils to create works on a very large scale. The arch illustrated in Figure 135 is about 7 feet (2.13 m) tall and depends upon internal ribs of clay for support.

Problems in Coil Construction

Problems that arise in coil construction can often be attributed to one or more of the following:

○ coils that are too thick or thin for the size of the piece
○ clay that is either too soft and sticky or too stiff to join properly

134 Ruth Duckworth, U.S.A. Vase. Coiled porcelain with base coils 10 percent oxide, decreasing every three coils to a nearly white rim; height 20″ (50.9 cm).

135 Bruno La Verdiere, U.S.A. Huge arch. Earthenware, made in three sections with grog and sawdust added to the coiled clay, height 7′ 3″ (2.18 m).

136 John H. Stephenson, U.S.A. *Issue*. Stoneware and steel construction with bright polychrome surfaces, length 38″ (96.5 cm)

- ○ coils added so rapidly that the lower walls sag and thicken
- ○ a form that is too horizontal or has too flat a curve. (The wet clay cannot support too wide a shape and may also sag during firing.)

Slab Construction

Slabs are sheets or slices of clay that are rolled out, often with a rolling pin, to the desired thickness and wrapped, folded, or cut and joined together. The illustrations show the great variety of forms possible with slab techniques. Although beginning students tend to make slabs into square or rectangular boxlike shapes, there is just as much potential for round, oval, or flaring vertical shapes. When used in combination with modeled, coiled, or thrown sections, slab construction has many more possibilities. (See Plate 9, p. 91).

To make a number of slabs it is best to start with a large block of wedged clay and cut off thin square sections with a wire. These sections are rolled out on a piece of canvas or a sanded table top. Rolling the clay out diagonally will preserve the squared form, and turning the slab after two or three strokes of the rolling pin will keep the piece an even thickness. Fabric or such flat objects as leaves and dried flowers placed between the slab and rolling pin will produce interesting textures. Those working extensively with slabs might want to purchase a commercially manufactured slab roller (Fig. 138, p. 100). This machine consists of two rollers in an etching press arrangement that compress the clay between two pieces of canvas.

137 Square slab box with beveled edges scored and slipped. Seams are reinforced where possible.

138 Brent slab roller, bed size
60″ × 22″ (150 × 55 cm), slab thickness
0.13–1.5″ (0.3–3.1 cm).

139 Mary Frank, U.S.A. *Untitled (Lovers).* 1975. Stoneware, disjoin′ed figure
study made of thin slabs, fired to cone 6, length 5′ 2″ (1.55 m). Courtesy Zabriskie
Gallery, New York.

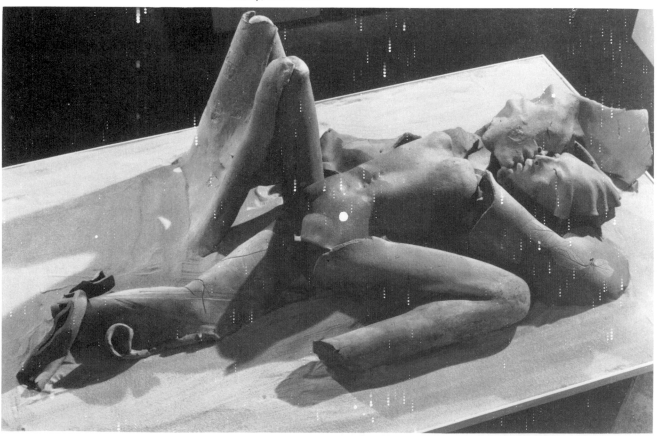

HAND-BUILDING TECHNIQUES

140 Marilyn Levine, U.S.A. *Brown Suitcase Without Handle.* Stoneware slabs reinforced with nylon fibers, engobe, iron stain and lusters, length 27.5″ (68.75 cm).

If the slabs are draped over a mold, they should be plastic; if formed into a vertical shape, the pieces should be allowed to dry sufficiently so that they can support themselves. They should not be allowed to dry too much, however, for they may crack as they are folded. As in other techniques, the edges that are joined should be scored and coated with slip to prevent them from coming apart during the drying process. Sharp angles and joints should be reinforced with a coil of moist clay on the interior seam. Horizontal spans may need to be reinforced with interior clay partitions to support the slab and prevent it from sagging.

Clay slabs can be smoothed and manipulated to create endless surface textures and sculptured effects. Some potters choose to fold and shape the plastic slabs just enough to suggest a form, but leave the method undisguised. Marilyn Levine, on the other hand, is a master of detail in the construction of objects in clay that resemble leather (Fig. 140 and Plate 10, p. 92). Figure 141 (pp. 102–103) shows her constructing *Brown Suitcase Without Handle.*

The stoneware body Levine uses includes 1.5 percent nylon fiber. The body is mixed in a dough mixer and then run through a slab roller until the fibers are properly aligned. The slabs are then covered with a layer of plastic to prevent drying and are cut with scissors to conform to a paper pattern. The clay is coated with colored *engobes*, and textures are imparted by pressing various materials into the slab. A roulette wheel is used to imitate the stitching common on leather articles. The sections, still covered with plastic, are joined and held together with masking tape while drying. Interior clay partitions are then constructed in an irregular grid pattern. These will support the lid and prevent it from collapsing. Details such as buckles and rivets are cut from the plastic-covered slab and joined to the clay while it is still damp. The suitcase cover is then placed over the base, and the entire piece is covered with more plastic and dried very slowly. The glaze firing is to cone 7, after which the "metallic" sections are coated with lusters before a second firing at a lower temperature.

SLAB CONSTRUCTION   **101**

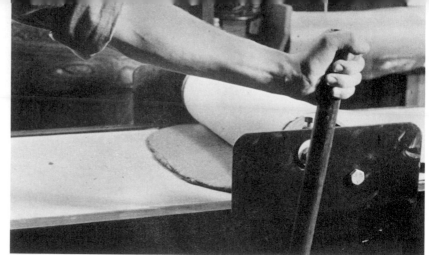

A

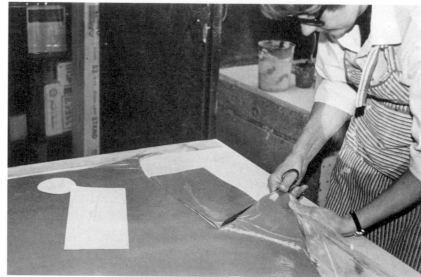

B

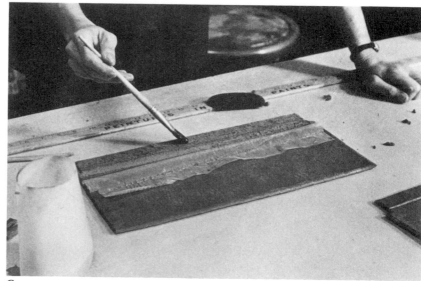

C

D

E

F

141

A A slab roller produces thin, uniform pieces of clay.

B A slab is cut to the pattern size.

C The plastic is peeled back and the slab is coated with an engobe (slip).

D Interior clay partitions are needed to support the lid.

E The lid is lowered carefully into place.

F Low-firing lusters are applied to simulate metal hardware.

142 Jane Peiser, U.S.A. Planter. Colored porcelain in millefiore technique, salt-glazed to cone 10, overglaze fired to cone 017.

Jan Peiser is a potter who uses slabs to create a totally different effect (Fig. 142). The technique, illustrated in Figure 143, is called *millefiore* and consists of joining pieces of colored clay inside a mold. Thus the slabs serve as a decorative as well as a structural element. Pieces and slabs of clay are arranged in a loaf form to create a design—in this instance, a fanciful figure of woman. The loaf is then cut into thin sections and rolled out, which joins the individual segments, at the same time stretching and elongating the design. The resultant slabs are taped together inside a plaster mold, in a shape that will allow the piece to shrink without damage. After the piece has been assembled, the inside surface is covered with coils to reinforce the structure and prevent the sections from shrinking apart. When the pot has shrunk from the sides of the mold, it is removed, covered with plastic, and uncovered for only about an hour every day. This final drying may take a week or longer, but it is essential for a work composed of so many different pieces. For more details about the decoration and glazing process, see Chapter 6.

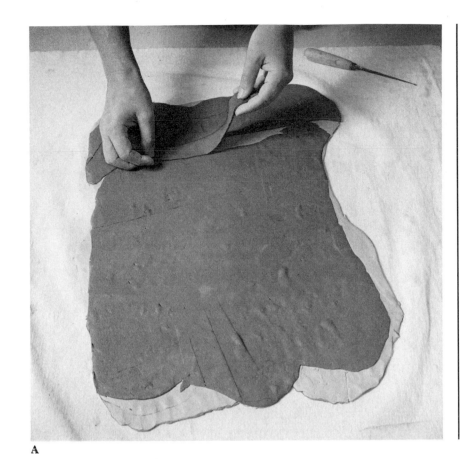

A

Steps in the Construction of Jane Peiser's Planter, Using the Millefiore Technique

143

A Two thin slabs of contrasting colors are joined together.

B The different segments of the design are placed together.

C The design is built up in a long loaf shape.

continued

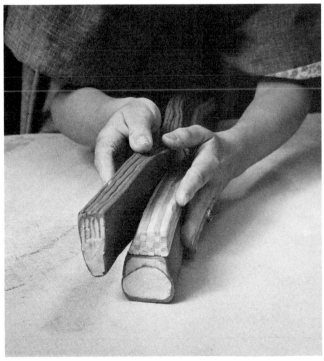

B

C

143, *continued*

D The completed clay loaf shows figure and background.

E The loaf is set on end, and thin slabs are cut with a wire.

F The sections are rolled out, elongating the design and thinning the slabs. They are now ready to be taped together inside a plaster mold in a shape that will allow the piece to shrink without damage.

D

E

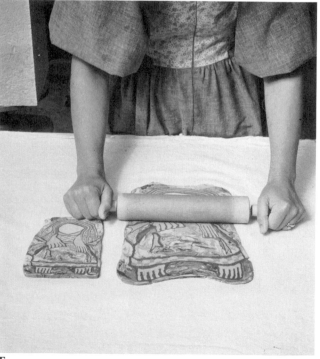

F

HAND-BUILDING TECHNIQUES

Molds

The use of molds to form clay is an ancient technique that is also adaptable to modern commercial production and new materials.

Hump and Press Molds

A mold can be almost any rounded shape, and the technique of molding will produce a finished pot in practically a single step.

For a *hump mold*, a slab of clay is draped over a convex form—a stone, gourd, kitchen bowl, beach ball, or plaster form made for the purpose. The slab is pressed to conform to the mold, and the excess clay is trimmed away. Strips of wet newspaper, paper toweling, or plastic will prevent the clay from sticking to the form (Fig. 144). After drying slightly—enough to maintain the shape without distorting—the mold is removed. If left on the form too long, the clay will crack as it contracts.

A convex form can also be covered with coils of plastic clay. The coils should be smoothed together with a tool or the fingers so they will not crack apart when drying. Coils and slabs can be joined over a preexisting shape, provided the seams are well sealed. This will create alternating smooth and rough textures. Join marks are smoothed on the exterior, so that any design will be seen on the inside surface.

Large abstract shapes can be made by placing slabs in a canvas sling extended between the backs of two weighted chairs. Another possibility is a completely round, closed form that results from joining plastic slabs around a heavy balloon. When the clay is leather hard, the balloon should be punctured to permit the clay to contract. The rubber will burn out during the firing. The firing should proceed slowly, however, to allow the moisture to escape through the puncture hole instead of turning to steam and causing the pot to explode.

144 Moist paper towels separate the clay from the mold, a stone.

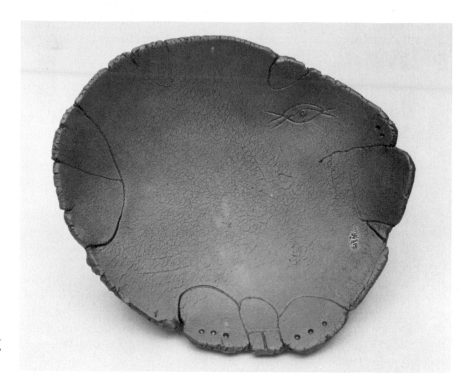

145 Jack Sures, Canada. *Nowhere to go Nothing to Do.* Platter. Rough stoneware formed on a mold, 18″ × 14″ × 6″ (45.7 × 35.5 × 15.2 cm).

146 William Daley, U.S.A. Stoneware planter, formed in styrofoam molds, 24″ × 20″ × 18″ (60.96 × 50.8 × 45.72 cm).

A

Commercial Press-molding

147

A A disc of plastic clay is placed on the plate mold.

B The disc is compressed between the two sections of the press mold to form the plate.

C As the upper section of the mold is raised, the plate form revolves and a trimming tool removes the excess clay.

B

C

A *press mold* is a concave form—the inside of a bowl or plate or a plaster mold—into which slabs and coils of plastic clay are shaped. The procedure is the same as for hump molds, except that the slabs or coils are pressed into a form rather than draped over it (see Plate 11, p. 125). In this method the smoothing and joining of coils and slabs is done on the inside surface, and the design will appear on the exterior.

Rounded forms can be constructed by joining two semicircular sections press-molded in a bowl shape. Both halves must have a similar moisture content. The edges should be scored and coated with slip. Once joined, the piece should dry very slowly to prevent cracking along the seam.

Commercially some very complicated forming machines are used to press-mold plates, bowls, cups, and similar vessels. As Figure 147 shows, production is very fast, several thousand pieces per day. Studio potters can hardly expect to compete by making prosaic types of functional ware. Their work must be unique in both form and decoration if it is to command the higher prices they must charge.

Slip Casting

Another possibility for hand building with molds is casting. Although casting is primarily a commercial production technique, some studio potters are interested in the clean lines and smooth surfaces that casting makes possible. The process is complicated, however, and is outlined only briefly here. Slip casting consists of pouring slip into a plaster mold. Depending upon the complexity of the piece, the plaster mold may consist of one to five or more parts. In order for the slip clay to dry and shrink away from the plaster mold, it is important that the form be of a smooth texture and the surface even, without crevices and undercuts.

148 Anne Currier, U.S.A. *Teapot with Two Cups.* 1975. Slip-cast earthenware with slab-built handles and spout, luster glaze; height 9″ (22.5 cm).

When the plaster mold sections have dried, they are scraped clean and clamped together for the casting. Slip is poured into the mold. Plaster draws the moisture from the slip and causes the clay surface in contact with the plaster to harden, or set up. The excess slip is poured or drained from the mold, and the piece is allowed to dry further. The mold is removed when the piece is leather hard, and then the surface is scraped or sanded to remove the join marks of the mold sections. (See Chap. 10 for more information about slip casting.)

Styrofoam as a Model Material

Nino Caruso, an Italian potter known for his architectural modular reliefs, has developed a casting method that uses styrofoam as a model material (Figs. 149–151). Styrofoam has a very dense consistency but is still lightweight and convenient to handle. A design is drawn on a block of styrofoam and then cut with a taut, hot wire. The wire is placed in an arrangement like a band saw, but the wire makes a sharper cut and leaves a smoother surface than a saw blade.

The various segments of the pattern are joined with cement to make the model, which is then coated with shellac to fill all the air pockets and repel the plaster. This model serves as the form for making the plaster mold.

149 Clay slip is poured into the plaster mold clamped together with a vise.

150 After drying, the plaster mold is removed from the clay.

151 The original model requires four plaster molds from which the final form is slip-cast.

When the plaster mold sections have been clamped together, slip is poured in, and after the clay has set up, a plug is pulled from the bottom of the mold to let the excess slip drain out. The mold is opened when the clay is leather hard. The resulting module is hollow and makes the drying and firing process less hazardous. Figure 152 shows an exhibit of Caruso's modular walls in the Piazza dei Consuli at Gubbio, Italy. The interchangeable modular units are easier to see in Figure 153, as is the smooth surface quality that slip casting imparts.

152 Nino Caruso, Italy. *Modular Sculpture*. Slip-cast fireclay with a white glaze fired to cone 10, each module 20″ × 16″ × 14″ (50 × 40 × 35 cm). Installed in the Piazza di Consuli, Gubbio, Italy.

153 Nino Caruso, Italy. *Modular Sculpture,* detail. Slip-cast fireclay with white glaze fired to cone 10; each module approximately 20″ × 16″ × 14″ (50 × 40 × 35 cm).

above: **154   Patti Warashina**, U.S.A.
Metamorphosis of an Angel. A delicate
series of small porcelain figures, height
19″ × 16″ × 1′ 61″ (48.2 × 40.6 ×
154.9 cm).

below: **155   Willis Bing David**,
U.S.A. *Ancestral Ritual Vessel.* Stoneware
slab form with a vigorous surface texture, variegated glazes, height 24″
(61 cm).

Modeling

Modeling directly in clay preserves the texture of the material and the feeling
of immediacy derived from manipulating hands and tools. The use of plaster
as a mold material results in a bland, more uniform surface. Since time imme-
morial, however, sculptors have modeled solid clay studies, made plaster
casts, and created a finished product in stone or metal. Usually, the final piece
does not resemble the original clay sketch, which would have been too difficult to fire. Solid masses of clay are apt to explode in the kiln.

Traditional Modeling Method

Over the years sculptors developed methods of modeling that permitted the original study to become the permanent record. If the study is on a
small scale and the clay walls are less than 1 inch (2.54 cm) thick, firing will
not present a problem. For larger pieces, it is necessary to hollow out the
excess clay inside. While the clay is still fairly plastic, the piece is cut in half
with a fine wire. With a wire looping tool the walls are trimmed to a thickness
of 0.5 to 1 inch (2.54 cm). When both halves have been trimmed, the cut
edges are scored and coated with slip. The two sections are pressed together,
and any surface defects are touched up with the fingers or a tool.

Sculpture should dry under plastic and be exposed to air slowly. This
will ensure an even drying of the thick areas. The kiln firing should also
proceed slowly. It is common practice to leave the kiln on low heat with the
door ajar for at least twelve hours before the actual firing begins.

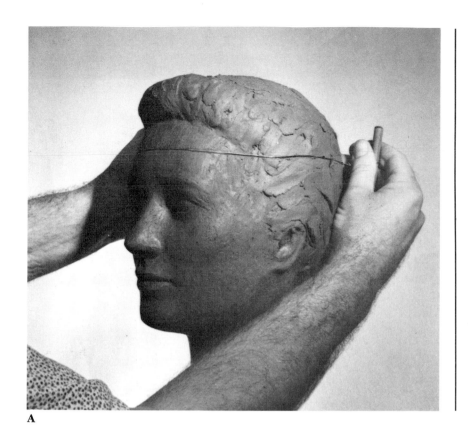

A

Hollowing a Solidly Modeled Head

156

A The top of the head is cut with a wire.

B Both the halves are trimmed to a thickness of about 0.75" (1.9 cm).

C The edges are scored, coated with slip, and then joined.

B

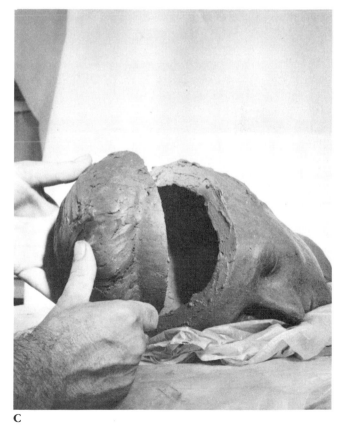

C

above: **157** **Ruth Duckworth**, U.S.A. Garden sculpture. Stoneware with copper-porcelain inlays, height 6′ (1.82 m), length 7′ 10″ (2.38 m).

below: **158** **Martha Jackson-Jarvis,** U.S.A. *Cambrian Explosion II.* Small delicate forms reminiscent of early plant and animal life, length 3′ (91 cm).

Plates 12 and 13 (pp. 125 and 126) and Figures 157 and 158 show the great range of effects possible with modeling techniques: from smooth, soft surfaces, hard-edged lines, and plastic additions to very rough surfaces and incised lines. Expressively modeled clay needs no further embellishment; brightly colored glaze, however, will lend more naturalistic effects.

Hollow-Tube Method

More complicated pieces can also be cut apart, hollowed out, and then joined, but problems are apt to arise from the joining of too many parts. It is simpler to construct the different parts from hollow sections and then join them together. The clay must be plastic enough during the joining process so that the joins can be smoothed over.

159 Jerry Rothman, U.S.A., *Opel in the Sky*. Stoneware, built and fired on a stainless steel armature, length of mule 6′ 8″ (2 m), width of hoop 10′ (3.04 m).

Sagging during firing is always a problem with sculptural projections that lack support. In figurative sculpture, heads especially are apt to tilt when the weight of the head puts pressure on the forward thrust of the neck. Clay tube supports should be made for the projections when both are leather hard, so that they will shrink at the same rate during both drying and firing. Small holes in several places will allow moisture and combustion gases to escape during firing.

Often, complicated sculptural forms will need some kind of interior support in addition to the exterior support to prevent sagging during drying and firing. Clay partitions that shrink with the form in drying and firing are the most practical solution, provided ample air passages are left. Metal rods and wires can be used temporarily, but these must be removed before major shrinkage occurs to avoid cracking the piece. Jerry Rothman, a sculptor who works in very large scale, has been experimenting with clay bodies that have the unusual potential of zero shrinkage, combined with a stainless-steel armature. The leaping mule in Figure 159 is 6 feet 8 inches (203.2 cm) long, the hoop is 10 feet (304.8 cm) wide. The form is supported by a welded armature of stainless steel bars and mesh. Its base is stabilized by concrete weights.

Combined Techniques

Once the basic hand-building methods have been mastered and the potter is familiar with the possibilities of each, it will become clear that many forms can be constructed only by combining the different techniques. Pinched and modeled shapes often require coiled accents. Slabs and coils reinforce each other structurally as well as aesthetically. Each method has structural advantages and limitations. If pinching a lump of clay does not produce the desired form, then perhaps a coil should be added to the rim, or a slab joined to the

above: **161   Pablo Picasso**, Spain. *Centaur.* 1950. Terracotta, combining thrown and hand-built forms, with painted design, height 17″ (42.5 cm). Courtesy the Arts Council of Great Britain, London.

above left: **160   Sally Michener**, Canada. Figure with coiled arch. Terracotta, figure life size, arch 7′ 4″ (2.13 m 10.16 cm).

below: **162   Winnie Owens-Hart**, U.S.A. *The last time I saw Egypt, it was in Africa.* Plaque. Stoneware with pressed, modeled, and hand-built elements, fired to cone 9 with second sawdust firing, height 16.5″ (41.9 cm).

coil. The potter discovers by experimentation how far plastic clay can be stretched and manipulated. Overly thin walls will sag, and walls that are too thick are likely to explode in the kiln. Plate 14 (p. 126) and Figures 160, 161, and 162 show the freedom of design that is possible when hand-building techniques are combined imaginatively to create both functional and sculptural forms.

Special Hand-Building Techniques

Potters have developed a number of special techniques to achieve special effects.

Extruded Forms

Extruded Coils   Many potters use clay extruders to save time in producing small coils in quantity for constructing or decorating pots and for creating fanciful strap handles (Fig. 163). To make small coils the barrel of the extruder should not be too large in diameter because the pressure required to extrude the clay through it would be too great.

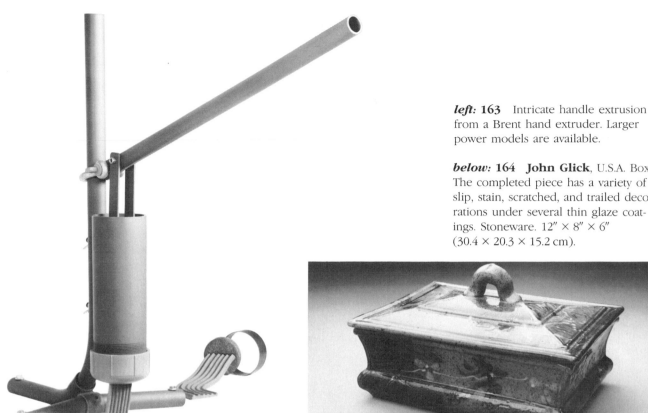

below: **164** **John Glick**, U.S.A. Box. The completed piece has a variety of slip, stain, scratched, and trailed decorations under several thin glaze coatings. Stoneware. 12″ × 8″ × 6″ (30.4 × 20.3 × 15.2 cm).

Extruded Slabs Depending on the shape of the die used, many forms other than the coil may also be extruded, such as the slab forms designed by John Glick to produce the rectangular covered box illustrated in Figure 164. The illustration sequence on pages 120–122 shows Glick forming this box with dies and an extruder that he made himself.

There are certain advantages to the extruded slab form. As a result of the process, the clay has a denser and better aligned composition, which is less apt to warp in drying and firing. Also, flanges and lips can be produced as part of the basic form.

To produce extruded slab forms, the potter makes a sketch of the projected work and a scale drawing of the forms to be extruded. The dies can be constructed of wood, metal, or even fired clay, but for ease of forming, a die of 0.5-inch (1.27-cm) acrylic mounted on a plywood base works very well. It must be beveled to produce a clean, even surface.

An extruder can be improvised out of a length of pipe and an old hydraulic jack. The handle should be of sufficient size to exert pressure. The extruder should be securely mounted on a study table or wall.

The clay must have been aged and wedged. Grog, if added, should be of a small size. Extrusions of up to 36 inches (91.4 cm) are possible. They should be laid out carefully on a table and allowed to dry before assembling.

For further information on extruding slab forms, see John Glick's article in Vol. 17, No. 1 of *Studio Potter*, pp. 55–61.

A

B

C

D

Construction of Extruded Forms

165

A Slabs are extruded from a hand-built bench model extruder.

B Clay extrusions with a 0.25″ (0.64 cm) acrylic die are mounted on a plywood base.

C Wooden templates allow the slabs to be cut at a uniform angle to the proper size.

D The edges are scored, coated with slip, and assembled.

E When joined, the side walls are placed on the base slab and further reinforced at the joints.

F Metal templates are used in cutting the more irregular forms making up the cover.

continued

E

F

G

H

165, *continued*

G Interior support is needed as the cover segments are scored, coated with slip, and joined.

H The completed cover is carefully lowered into place.

I A handle is attached and the box is coated with slip with a later scratched decoration.

I

166 Carol Jeanne Abraham, U.S.A.
Wall sculpture. Thixotropic clay and
cotton yarn, length 45″ (114 cm).

Thixotropic Clay

Thixotropy is the property exhibited by some gels of becoming fluid
when shaken or stirred and setting again to a gel when allowed to stand. In a
clay body this means that the clay becomes fluid when manipulated, then sets
up again when the motion is stopped. This action results from a reduced
attraction between the negatively charged silicate particles and the positively
charged chemical ions in the clay body. Normally, a clay body is stable because the charges on the ions are neutralized and cause *flocculation*, or
thickening. If large ions of sodium, lithium, or potassium are added, however,
they are not strongly attracted to the negatively charged particles, and this
causes *deflocculation*, or thinning.

While she was a graduate student in ceramics, Carol Jeanne Abraham
began a series of experiments in the particle suspensions of various clay
bodies. Eventually, she compounded a porcelain body with thixotropic properties (see Appendix for formula). The body is prepared in a slip form and
should be aged for a long time.

A thixotropic clay body cannot be formed by the usual hand-building
techniques or by throwing. The basic steps are shown in Figure 167. The clay

Steps in Thixotropic Forming

167

A Thixotropic clay is wedged by gently pulling the clay into ropelike strands.

B The strands are then folded.

C Vibration from the hands causes the clay to flow into a single mass.

continued

A

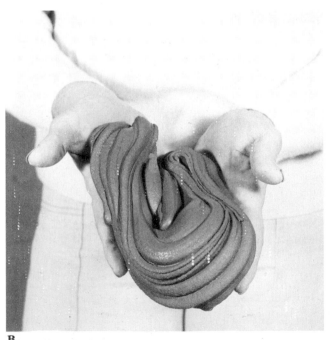

B

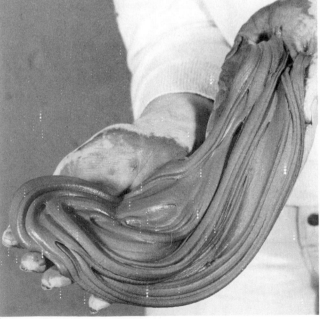

C

above: **Plate 11   John Mason**, U.S.A. Stoneware plaque made from a simple slab with impressed forms in relief, brilliant low-fire glazes, width 15.5″ (38.7 cm).

right: **Plate 12   Robert Arneson**, U.S.A. *Samuel Gompers,* an arresting portrait study. Modeled hollow with colored slips, low-firing glazes and luster accents, height 14″ (35.5 cm).

left: **Plate 13 Toby Buonagurio**, U.S.A. *Super Duesie,* an imaginative treatment of an antique hotrod. Earthenware with low-fire glaze and luster, acrylic paint, flocking, and glitter, length 90″ (228.6 cm).

right: **Plate 14 Victor Cicansky**, Canada. *Working: The Old Working Class.* Relief showing a couple in a short-order restaurant. Terra-cotta with low-fire glazes, height 5′ (1.52 m), width 6′ (1.82 m), depth 14″ (35.5 cm).

below: **Plate 15 Ruth Duckworth**, U.S.A. *Clouds over Chicago.* Stoneware mural constructed of slabs each 24″ (60 cm) and decorated with washes of iron, copper, nickel, and four glazes, 25′ × 9′7″ (7.2 × 3.2 m). Dresdner Bank, Board of Trade Building, Chicago.

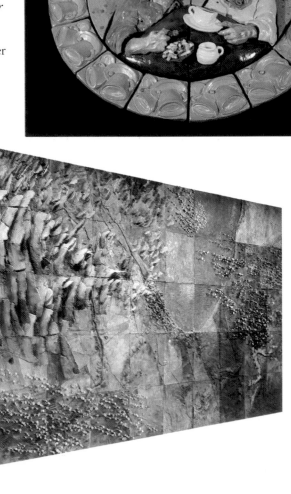

D

E

F

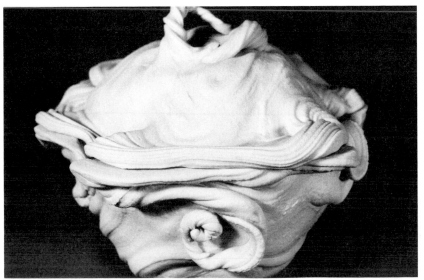

G

167, *continued*

D With further vibration the clay stretches into a single mass.

E The slab is then draped over a mold and pulled at the edges.

F After the form has set up, a cover is made by inverting the bowl shape, filling it with newspapers, and draping another slab over it. A dusting of alumina prevents the rims from sticking.

G Carol Jeanne Abraham, U.S.A. Covered jar. Thixotropic porcelain. The finished jar is characterized by a flowing form and twisted spirals.

appears to be firm but becomes increasingly fluid when manipulated. First the clay is stretched and folded until it becomes semifluid. Then it is gradually worked into a shape that can be draped over a mold. When it begins to set up again, plastic additions can be pulled and twisted from the draped clay. Because of shrinkage, the form should be removed from the mold as soon as possible to avoid cracking. The surface may appear deceptively dry, however, when the form is still quite plastic.

The technique will require some practice since the clay behaves very differently from other bodies. The effects of fluidity and apparent motion will appeal to many potters, especially those interested in decorative and sculptural forms.

Although Abraham has experimented with joining decorative forms made from a thixotropic body to a regular porcelain body, there are some problems. One is that the thixotropic clay sags. Moreover, the thixotropic body shrinks about 6 percent, while most other bodies shrink about 15 percent. One solution is to fire the porcelain piece to the bisque stage before adding the thixotropic clay, although this will require a great deal of planning during the forming stages, taking into account the different shrinkage rates. Another possibility would be to compound a porcelain body with a lower shrinkage rate, making only one bisque firing necessary.

With such unusual shrinkage rates, a typical porcelain glaze will not be satisfactory for thixotropic clay. A glaze formula suitable for cone 5 and lower is given in the Appendix. This glaze will craze slightly at cone 9.

Techniques for Architectural Use

Ceramic murals in relief differ from previously discussed forms because their large size requires that they be constructed of many units. They are discussed here because they are formed primarily by hand-building techniques.

The ceramic mural can be the focal point for an interior design or part of a continuous wall decoration. The mural shown in Figure 168 is of stoneware cemented into the wall. The irregularly shaped sections have been carved, cut, and added to, and then stained in a variety of colors. The mural in Figure 169 is composed of individual sections slip-cast in wet sand molds. This process allows the ceramist to develop intricate forms and textures.

left: **168 Frans Wildenhain**, U.S.A. *Allegory of a Landscape.* Mural. Stoneware in low relief with engobe and iron washes, 24′ × 9′ (7.2 × 2.7 m). Ingle Auditorium, Rochester Institute of Technology, Rochester, N.Y.

right: **169 Stig Lindberg**, Sweden. Section of a mural prior to glazing. Sand-cast stoneware.

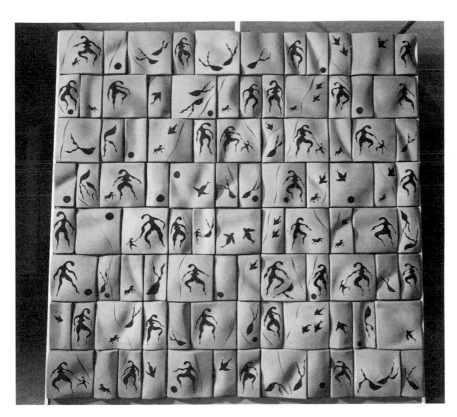

170 Thomas Kerrigan, U.S.A. *Brighton Shores*. Mural. Stoneware made with various figurative panels in a mishima and stain technique, 8′ × 8′ (2.4 × 2.4 m).

171 Jack Sures, Canada. Mural. A huge decorative design of 4200 varying red-hued stoneware tiles, height 56.5′ (17.1 m), width 64′ (19.4 m). Facade of the Sturdy-Stone Centre, Saskatoon, Canada.

William Daley Making a Mural Unit

172

A   Slabs 0.63″ (1.6 cm) thick are placed in the wooden mold and joined. Cloth lining prevents sticking.

B   A hinged mold allows the two segments to be formed and later joined.

C   A roller arrangement allows the heavy, nearly completed units to be easily rolled from side to side in order to join the end segments.

D   A dry completed unit is ready for loading and firing.

A

B

C

D

173 William Daley, U.S.A. Mural. Red-hued stoneware, length 20′ (6 m), height 10′ (3 m). The facade of the Ritz Theater, Philadelphia.

Ruth Duckworth's mural *Clouds over Chicago* (Plate. 15, p. 126) was conceived as a continuous, nonrepetitive composition, as was Frans Wildenhain's. It seems to have been inspired by an aerial photograph. We see a portion of the lake, as well as the winding paths of the Chicago and Des Plaines rivers. The main interest, however, is in the thin, platelike cloud forms that swirl through the mural and finally break up into small, textured areas. The individual stoneware panels making up this mural consist of base slabs 2 feet (0.61 m) square, on which modeling has been superimposed. Color washes of copper, iron, and nickel, with glazes of varying gloss or opacity, result in a panorama of muted tones.

Figure 173 shows a sectional mural by William Daley on a Philadelphia theater facade. The several basic segments were easily varied by slight changes in the mold. Daley's system is shown on page 130. An elaborate hinged mold allows the large vertical surfaces to be constructed and joined. Equally ingenious is the roller arrangement, which permits the heavy and nearly completed section to be rolled from side to side in order to join the end sections. Since the largest segments are 36 inches by 30 inches by 10 inches (91.44 cm by 76.2 cm by 25.4 cm) some such mechanical aids are necessary. Arm-size holes are cut in the end sections so that the slabs can be joined from the inside. Smaller openings are also made so that the mural units can be clamped together on the building site. After the section is completed and scraped to provide a textured surface, it is covered with wet cloths and plastic and allowed to equalize for a week. Then the cloth and plastic is removed for an hour and gradually longer periods each day to dry. When bone dry, the sections are fired very slowly in a 120-cubic foot (3.4 m³) kiln to a cone-6 reduction.

5

**Wheel
Techniques**

The introduction of the potter's wheel was a technical advance that gave a great impetus to ceramics. Before the development of the wheel, a simple turning device had aided potters in trimming and refining hand-built pots. This evolved into a weighted wheel head turning on a peg in the ground (Fig. 175). At first, the primitive wheel served only to shape plastic coils and to give a final finish to the lip. This method is still used by many Mexican and American Indian potters. In Figures 176 and 177 a remarkably symmetrical jar is made by rotating a coiled pot on *platos*—one shallow bowl resting on top of another inverted shallow bowl.

Although pots with wheel-turned feet dated as early as 3500 B.C. have been found in eastern Anatolia and northern Iran, it was not until about 3000 B.C. that small pots were thrown entirely on the wheel. By this time, improved agricultural methods and more prosperous villages led to the barter of goods. The crafts of the metalsmith, weaver, miller, and leather-worker, as well as the potter, developed for this market. Often an entire family engaged in pottery making and traded their wares for other goods. The potter's wheel was an essential tool, because it provided a more efficient method of making small and moderate-size pots. Larger pieces were still coiled or made by a combination of techniques.

left: **174 Robert Eckels**, U.S.A. Bottle. Stoneware with sgraffito and applied decoration, paddled leatherhard, with the glaze rubbed off in center panel for color and textural contrast; height 16″ (40 cm).

right: **175** Primitive potter's wheel, China. Probably 19th century. A type used by many early cultures. Base, wood; top, clay mixed with pig's hair. American Museum of Natural History, New York, Cat. No. 70/12797.

Throwing on the Wheel

The overriding advantage of the wheel is that one can make perfectly symmetrical rounded forms in a short time. Most student potters have greater initial success with coiling or slab techniques, but all are eager to try their luck on the potter's wheel. It is fascinating to watch an experienced potter take a ball of plastic clay and produce a form that evolves and changes shape in a seemingly miraculous fashion. Developing skill at throwing on the wheel, however, demands much practice and an understanding of the proper sequence of operations.

A student should choose a single form, preferably a cylinder, and throw it over and over again. When throwing a different shape each time, the student learns nothing from previous errors and misses the most natural method of developing form and design. It is important to learn how to center the ball of clay and bring it up into a cylinder quickly, before the clay begins to soften and sag from the water. Gradually, the potter gains a sense of how far to push the clay—how thin the walls can be and how wide a curve can open before the clay becomes distorted and collapses. With practice the potter learns to throw taller and thinner shapes from the same amount of clay. A greater ease and freedom in handling the clay ultimately brings a dynamic quality to throwing.

There is little point for the beginner to make drawings of an ideal pot. Until he or she gains a feeling for the clay and a knowledge of possible forms, there is likely to be no relationship between the drawing and the pot. The final details should grow out of the actual process of throwing. Plastic clay has a quality all its own and imposes certain restrictions upon the potter. Thus, there are certain forms and decorations that seem natural to clay, expressing a fluidity difficult to achieve with other media.

left: 176 Traditional forming techniques in the Mexican town of San Bartolo Coyatepic. A coil is attached to a pinched form by squeezing with an even pressure while the pot is rotated slowly on *platos*.

right: 177 Once the coil has been joined it is thinned and smoothed with a piece of leather.

178 Randall kick wheel with welded frame, splash pan, and adjustable seat.

Selecting a Wheel

A suitable wheel is even more important for the beginner than for the experienced potter. The potter who throws for many hours every day really needs an electric wheel, but for the beginner a kick wheel is preferable. During the critical moments in throwing one instinctively stops kicking, thus slowing the speed of the wheel. A beginner on a power wheel may actually increase the speed at a moment of crisis, causing centrifugal force to tear the pot apart.

The wheel should have a rigid frame that is free of vibration. Its seat must be comfortable and adjustable for both height and distance from the wheel head. On a foot-powered wheel, kicking should be an easy motion, not tiring or awkward, and the footrest must be in a convenient location. If the student is throwing on an electric wheel, the seat should be adjusted to a comfortable height and brought as close to the wheel head as possible. Most electric wheels manufactured today are very low. Depending upon the height of the potter it might be desirable to elevate the wheel slightly to avoid back strain from hours spent in a bent-over position.

On a power wheel the speed control activated by foot or knee must allow easy operation from either a standing or a sitting position. Excessive speed in the wheel is not necessary or even desirable; 80 to 100 r.p.m. is sufficient for centering, and even slower speeds may be desirable for throwing. The most critical factor is the torque transmitted through the reduction gears from the motor. A motor of at least ⅓ horsepower is essential for potters throwing large pieces, since the pressure needed to center a clay ball of 25 pounds (11.34 kg) or more may actually stop a ¼-horsepower unit.

179   Brent electric potter's wheel with splash pan, 1-horsepower motor, and foot control.

Preparing to Throw

A bowl of water and a few simple tools should be placed in easy reach. These tools are the following:

- a sponge to apply water and remove excess slip and water from inside the pot, plus a sponge attached to a long dowel
- a small piece of leather to compress and smooth rims
- a pin (or needle attached to a dowel) to remove uneven rims, pop air bubbles, or gauge the thickness of bottoms
- a rib, of metal or wood, to aid in refining the form
- a fine, double-twisted wire to cut the finished pot off the wheel head

Composition board, plywood, or plaster bats will prevent thin pots from sagging or becoming distorted when removed from the wheel. They are essential for large pieces and very wide bowl shapes. Some wheel heads are equipped with removable metal pins that can be inserted into corresponding holes in the bats. Otherwise, wooden bats can be attached with soft clay or plaster bats with slip.

From clay that has been thoroughly wedged (See Figs. 126–128, pp. 88–93), pieces are cut that can be held comfortably in one hand. If the clay ball is too small, it will be hard to manipulate; if too large, it will be difficult to center. The pieces are patted into balls, and all those that are not to be used immediately are covered with plastic. Even a slight drying of the surface will lessen the throwing qualities of the clay.

Centering

180

A A wedged ball of clay is slapped down on the wheel head.

B With the wheel turning, the clay is moistened and forced with the hands into a beehive form.

C The elbow must be braced as the heel of the hand forces the clay into the center.

D With the fingers encircling the clay, a hollow is formed with pressure from the thumbs.

A

B

C

D

The consistency of the clay is very important when the student is learning to throw. It should be soft enough to be wedged and centered easily, but not too soft to stand up or hold its shape as it is thrown. If a coil of moist clay cracks when wound around the finger, the clay is not suitable for throwing. Clay that is too hard can be very frustrating, for it is difficult to wedge and center. In this situation, softer clay should be wedged into it.

Centering

The first step in throwing is *centering* the clay, or forcing it onto the exact center of the wheel head, as illustrated in Figure 180.

- If a plaster bat is dry, moisten it slightly for better adhesion.
- Press the clay ball down in the center of the wheel head.
- Start the wheel turning.
- Dip your hands in water and wet the clay.
- With both hands apply pressure downward on the clay to seal it to the wheel and force it into a rounded beehive form.
- Depending upon your preference, brace either your left or right elbow on your thigh and force the clay towards the center with the heel of your hand, using the other hand to even out minor irregularities.
- When the beehive form is centered, flatten the form and make a depression in the center with your thumbs.
- Add a little water and enlarge the depression.

The student is now ready to begin throwing the desired form. No more water should be used than necessary. While throwing, the hands should not be washed off but rather stripped of the slurry, which is used as a lubricant.

Throwing Specific Forms

All forms evolve from a cylinder. Bowls and bottles, for instance, evolve from a low, thick cylinder. Unless the potter can throw a perfectly uniform cylinder, it is useless to try to develop the form further.

The Cylinder

The general procedure for throwing a cylinder is illustrated in Figure 182, pages 140–141.

- After you have centered the clay and formed a depression, open up the clay by pulling it toward you with one hand while the other hand remains steady.
- Develop a rounded bottom not more than 0.75 inch (1.91 cm) thick. Sponge out excess water so the base does not become too soft.
- Use only the fingertips to throw small forms, the knuckles for larger ones.
- With a firm pressure from the inside fingers, pull rather than thin the clay upward with the knuckles of the outside hand. The clay should not flare out at the base but rather be forced in and pulled up.

181 Roberta Griffith, U.S.A. Tall cylindrical bottle. Porcelain, fired to cone 9, with brown glaze and thin textural slab addition sand-blasted after firing, 24.5″ (61.2 cm).

A

B

C

D

Throwing a Cylinder

182

A   A small cup form can be opened up entirely with the thumb and fingers; a large form needs the pressure of the entire hand.

B   The hands are now reversed, the inside fingers held steady, and the clay is pulled up with the knuckle of the right hand.

C   A cut-away section shows the action of the clay as it is pulled upward.

D   Another cut-away section shows the increasing height of the form.

E   The form continues to grow as it is pulled upward.

F   The form is finally refined.

G   The throwing usually results in a slightly uneven top, which is cut off with a needle set in a dowel.

H   The rim is then moistened and smoothed with a soft leather.

E

F

G

H

- Should the cylinder flare outward, encircle the form with the thumbs and middle fingers of both hands and compress it into a smaller diameter. Eventually you should be able to throw a 12-inch (30.48-cm) cylinder with five or six pulls from bottom to top.
- If the clay begins to sag, ball it up, dry it, and rewedge it. It is a waste of time to fuss with a wobbly pot.
- A slight unevenness usually occurs at the rim. Cut off a segment with a needlelike tool. Moisten and finish the rim with a wet strip of glove leather.

Whenever possible while throwing, the elbow should be braced on one's side for greater control. If the potter is left-handed, he or she should hold the hands in a reverse form. The usual electric wheel turns in a counterclockwise direction. Therefore, a left-handed potter needs to reverse the direction. A few wheels can change direction.

The Bowl

Throwing a small bowl presents few problems. The essential fact to remember is that the potter does not develop the desired form and then merely make it thinner. Clay tends to sag as it is pulled outwards; therefore, the potter must begin with a form that is higher than the finished piece. Also, because the clay wall becomes thinner when it is expanded to form the bowl shape, he or she must start with a thick rim.

These problems are magnified when the potter wants to throw a really large bowl. Figure 183 (pp. 145–146) illustrates the steps involved in throwing a really large bowl from 50 pounds (22.68 kg) of clay.

- Wedge two 25-pound (11.34-kg) batches of clay separately and then join them together to form a 50-pound (20.68-kg) ball.
- After centering and opening the clay, form a low, thick cylinder.
- Pull this cylinder up quickly into a tall bowl shape.
- It is very difficult in a bowl of this size to end up with sufficient clay to form an adequate rim, which is necessary to provide a handhold for moving the pot and to reduce the tendency to warp in drying and firing. The best solution is to join a thick coil to the rim. This coil extends the size of the pot and enlarges the rim to form a focal point for the visual movement of the large, rounded bowl form.
- Finally, cut the bowl off the bat with a double-twisted wire. Do not remove it until it has dried to a leather-hard state. But unless you separate the base from the bat by the rough cut of the wire, the bowl will crack in drying.

The Bottle

The bottle is an intriguing project, not only for its technical problems but for its design considerations. Whereas the bowl is a relatively simple form evolving from a low, thick cylinder into a curved shape with accents possible only on the foot and rim, the bottle usually has a full, swelling body and a feeling of upward movement; infinite variations between foot, body, neck, and rim are possible. Plates 16 and 17 (p. 143) show only two of the many possibilities while steps in throwing the bottle form are illustrated in Figure 184 on pages 147–148.

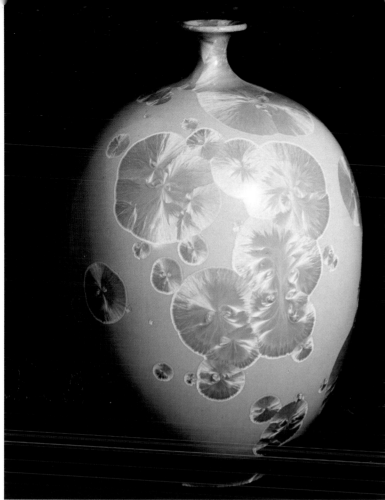

left: **Plate 16   Marc Hansen**, U.S.A. Porcelain bottle. The alkaline crystalline glaze was fired to cone 10, allowed to cool 100°F and held at that point for 4 hours, then cooled slowly, height 9.63″ (22.57 cm).

below left: **Plate 17   Harrison McIntosh**, U.S.A. Bottle. Stoneware with spiral engobe decoration in blue green and black. Gray mat overglaze, height 10.5″ (26.6 cm).

below right: **Plate 18   Peter Voulkos**, U.S.A. Monumental stoneware bottle, thrown and altered. Wood-fired, height 40″ (101.6 cm).

left: **Plate 19   Ken Ferguson**, U.S.A. Teapot. Porcelain with iron engobe under an opaque mat glaze with fluid green overglaze. Wood-fired, height 13″ (32.5 cm).

below: **Plate 20   Tom Turner**, U.S.A. Teapot. Fluted porcelain with slip trailed design under a celedon glaze. Cane handle, height 10″ (25.4 cm).

144

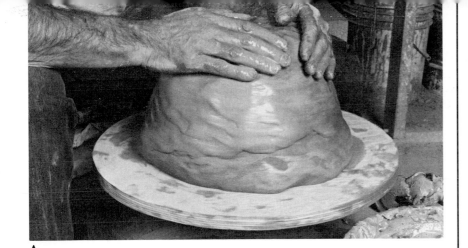

A

Throwing a Large Bowl

183

A Fifty pounds (22.68 kg) of wedged clay is pounded to form a rough bee-hive form on the wheel.

B After centering, a low thick cylinder is opened on the wheel head.

C A great deal of pressure is required to pull up the thick cylinder.

D Gradually the cylinder is pulled upward and expanded into a large bowl shape.

continued

B

C

D

E

F

E To increase the bowl size further an additional 25 pounds (11.34 kg) of clay is wedged and rolled out to form a thick coil.

F The coil is joined to the rim in the usual manner.

G The joined coil is compressed and pulled up to increase the bowl size further still.

H Finally a decorative rim is thrown. Height 18″ (45.7 cm), diameter 27″ (68.5 cm).

G

H

146

A

Throwing a Bottle Form

184

A After the basic cylinder is thrown, the base is flared outward by pressure from the inside finger tips.

B Use of a flexible scraper or rib produces less drag, and thus the wall is less likely to twist.

C Water or slip is applied and the neck portion is compressed by encircling with the fingers of both hands.

continued

B

C

D

E

D The compressed neck is pulled up and further constricted.

E After being trimmed with a needle tool the lip is finally finished with a wet soft leather.

F After excess clay has been trimmed from the base, the bottle is cut off the wheel head with a fine, twisted wire and lifted off.

F

- Begin the form with the basic cylinder as previously described, leaving it a little thick near the base since it will be flared out to form the round body of the bottle.
- Flare out the cylinder with the fingers or preferably with a flexible steel scraper or a wooden rib both inside and outside the form. In this manner the clay wall is not only expanded but compressed as well and thus is less likely to sag.
- Since the points of pressure are relatively small, you may work the clay in a drier state.
- After you have expanded the body, *neck in* (narrow) the top, using an upward movement of the encircled fingers, which thickens it.
- Carefully pull up the top with the fingertips. After repeating this process several times to bring the pot to the shape you desire, form the rim with a piece of leather.
- Remove excess clay from the base and cut the bottle from the bat with a fine, twisted wire.

The final bottle or vase should not be expected to be taller than the original cylinder. Although the necking in of the top section thickens the clay and allows it to be pulled up farther, the inevitable vibration of throwing causes the clay to settle. (See pp. 150–151 for steps in throwing a two-section vase.)

185 Bob Dixon, U.S.A. Bottle. An unusual form with brushed decoration in brown, tan, and blue-green. Barium-glazed at cone 10, height 31″ (78 cm).

A

B

C

D

E

F

Throwing a Two-section Vase

186

A A large bowl shape is thrown to form the base section of this large two-section vase.

B The upper section is slightly taller and smaller at the base but has the same diameter as the base section.

C After drying for a day the rims are scored and coated with slip prior to joining the two sections.

D The base of the upper section is cut away.

E A coil of clay is added to the junction of the two forms and compressed by using a rib on both the inside and outside of the form.

F After moistening, the top section is pulled up and flared outward to form a rim. An iron slip is applied prior to a sgraffito decoration. Height 28.5″ (72.3 cm), width 18.5″ (47 cm).

Problems in Throwing

The following situations and practices may cause difficulty in throwing:

- clay that is too stiff, too soft, or poorly wedged
- opening the clay before it is properly centered
- greater pressure with one thumb than the other when opening the ball, making the walls uneven
- applying too much water so that the clay becomes too soft
- unsteady pressure from inside the pot, making the pot wobble
- pressure from both the inside and the outside fingers, causing a thin spot in the walls
- throwing too slowly and overworking the clay, causing the pot to sag
- allowing throwing water to collect in the bottom of the pot, making the clay soft and the pot difficult to remove from the wheel, a practice that also creates a tendency for the pot to crack during drying

Multiple-Section Forms

There are limits to the potential size of forms thrown from one section of clay. Most students can comfortably center only about 20 pounds (9.07 kg) of clay at a time, and 50 pounds (22.68 kg) is certainly the maximum. It is foolish to try to stretch clay beyond its natural capacity. Trying to make the walls ever taller always leads to excessive thinness and may cause the form to flop.

Many potters find it more convenient to throw an extremely tall or large shape in sections (Plate 18, p. 143). The sections should be allowed to dry to a leather-hard state and then joined. The Greeks used this method for their funerary jars, which often stood more than 4 feet (1.22 m) tall (see Fig. 62).

If a smaller pot consists of different angular shapes, such as a teapot, it too can be thrown in multiple sections.

The Two-Section Vase

Figure 186 (pp. 150–151) shows the potter Jay Lindsay throwing a large, two-section vase. The clay used is approximately 30 to 40 pounds (13.6 to 18.4 kg) per unit. The base is a high bowl shape with the upper unit the same diameter but slightly smaller towards the top. When leather hard, the rims are scored and coated with slip and the upper section is carefully inverted over the base. Excess clay is trimmed from the old base, which is then moistened and pulled upward and necked in to form a flaring top. Clay is added if necessary, and the two sections are firmly joined, using a rib on the inside as well as the outside of the form. A dark red slip is applied, and then the vase is given carved and sgraffito decoration.

The Multiple-Section Pot

The pot by Don Reitz in Figure 187 is more than 42 inches (106.68 cm) tall and consists of five separately thrown sections. The following sequence of photographs illustrates twelve steps in the construction of the form (Fig. 188, pp. 154–157). Some general guidelines will help the beginner attempting a multiple-section pot.

- Make a sketch of the final form, deciding upon the number of pieces, how they will be thrown, and how they will be joined.
- Throw the sections from one clay body, wedge and prepare the pieces at the same time, and cover with plastic all but the one being thrown.
- Throw the pieces in a sequence so they will be of the same consistency as they dry.
- Cover the rims with plastic after they set up to promote an even drying.
- Join the top of one section to the top of another, and bottoms to bottoms, to ensure a similar moisture content.
- Score all joints, and thoroughly coat them with slip.
- Make curves round and uniform as in a bridge arch, for any flatness will cause the form to collapse.
- Cover the assembled form with plastic for three or four days. This will equalize the shrinkage of the different parts and prevent cracking.

187 Don Reitz, U.S.A. Five-section form. Stoneware, unfired; height 42″ (105 cm). The photographs that follow show its construction.

A

B

C

D

WHEEL TECHNIQUES

E

F

G

Throwing a Multisection Pot

188

A To open up a large mass of clay a wide plywood bat is attached to the wheel head with three concentric rings of clay to allow for the widest possible diameter of the base section.

B The base is thrown upside down in a flat cone shape; a cone will support the weight of the clay better than a rounded form.

C For the largest section of the form, two 25-pound (11.34-kg) balls of wedged clay are compressed together on a plywood bat.

D The clay is opened up to the edge of the bat (to conform to the width of the cone shape) and then thrown into a beehive shape.

E On a smaller plywood bat, a short cylinder (to sit on top of the beehive shape) is thrown and measured with calipers.

F The rim of a second, taller cylinder is measured with calipers to ensure a close fit with the rim of the shorter cylinder.

G When the base section is leather-hard, it is tooled and the rim is scored and coated with slip. A stiff slab of clay cut to fit the hole is then joined to it.

continued

H

I

J

WHEEL TECHNIQUES

K

L

M

188, *continued*

H After the base has become firm, it is inverted and recentered on the wheel head. A thick coil of plastic clay attaches the piece to the wheel and supports it while the other sections are added.

I The beehive shape is attached to the base section after both have been scored and coated with slip. The joint is reinforced by impressing with the thumb.

J The shorter cylinder is joined to the rim of the beehive shape. The thumb marks from the previous joint have been smoothed over.

K When the second cylinder is added, the rim is recentered and smoothed.

L To complete the form, a collar is joined to the rim of the cylinder.

M Finally, to counter the vertical movement of the vase, appendages of plastic clay are joined to the neck. These are attached like handles but instead of being pulled symmetrically are modeled into decorative shapes.

189 When throwing a series of mugs a movable pointer serves as a handy guide.

Throwing Aids

Most large pots and wide bowls must be thrown on a bat, but many pieces can be thrown conveniently right on the wheel head. These can be cut from the wheel with a wire or string, then lifted off with a slight twisting motion of the first two fingers of both hands. A thicker base and undercut with a wooden tool will provide an easier handle for the fingers and will lessen the tendency of the pot to become distorted.

A hinged, adjustable pointer is a handy guide for throwing pots of uniform height.

Small pieces such as cups, bowls, or bottles can be thrown "off the *hump*" (a larger mass of clay). This method is much faster when a great many pots of the same size are being thrown at the same time, for it is easier to center each ball of clay. To remove the thrown form from the larger mass of clay, a groove is cut at the bottom, and the string is pulled through with the wheel revolving slowly.

190 To remove the pot from the hump, a groove is cut under the pot and the end of a cord is placed in it and held steady. The slowly revolving wheel will cut the pot off cleanly.

Trimming

Trimming removes excess clay from the bottom of a pot, so that it is lighter and less likely to crack. If desired, trimming can give the pot a *foot*—a ridge of clay at the base to serve as a design accent. Some pots can be trimmed during the throwing stage and the mark of the cutting wire left as it is.

Most often, trimming or *tooling* is done when the pots have dried to the leather-hard stage. If the pot becomes too dry, there is a danger of cracking; if too soft, it will sag. A pot that becomes too dry after throwing can be restored to a leather-hard state by spraying it with a plant mister both inside and out. This should be done several times to ensure an even absorption of water. A plaster bat will absorb the excess moisture and prevent the bottom from becoming too soft. A pot that has become completely dry, however, should be discarded; it will take less time to throw a new one than to reclaim the old.

If thrown on bats, pots should be cut through at the bottom with a wire to allow the clay to contract evenly (see p. 148). Plates, platters, and wide

191 Large bowls must be reversed onto a large plywood bat, which is then centered on the potter's wheel.

192 Because the bowl was cut off the bat immediately after throwing, it is easily removed and trimming begins.

Plate 21 Charles Lakofsky, U.S.A. Covered jar. Slip-cast porcelain with lid modeled from a summer squash. Opaque glaze with yellow stain trailed decoration, height 8″ (20 cm).

Plate 22 Paul Dresang, U.S.A. Fanciful raku teapot with double spout, wire handle. Airbrushed colorants and cone 05 glaze. Luster accents fired with propane torch, height 16″ (40.6 cm).

Plate 23 Dick Evans, U.S.A. *Landscape bowl.* Formed from thin porcelain slabs draped over a plaster mold with a later-thrown foot. Spodumene glaze with yellow stain. Cone 10 oxidation, diameter 6″ (15.24 cm).

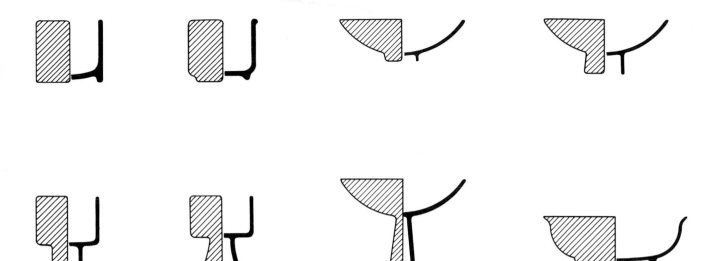

bowls should be inverted on a wooden bat after they have stiffened slightly to allow the thicker bottom to dry (p. 160). This will also prevent the rims from drying too quickly and thus reduce the chances of warping and cracking.

When the pot is leather-hard, the potter should observe its inside shape and judge its thickness to determine how much clay needs to be removed. If unsure, he or she inserts a pin.

193 Various types of feet are shown in cross section. Some may be trimmed on the pot while others are thrown separately.

o Place the pot upside down on the wheel and center it. A tall vase or bottle can be placed inside a wide-mouthed glass or ceramic jar or a plaster chuck that has been centered and secured to the wheel.

o Press a roll of clay around the circumference, and attach the pot (or the supporting jar) securely to the wheel. Avoid using random lumps of clay, for these place a strain on the rim and cause cracks.

o With the wheel turning at a moderate speed, apply the trimming tool to the pot and shape the bottom.

o Begin by reducing the diameter of the base, where most of the clay tends to be. Trimming will help to control a foot that is too wide.

In trimming, the potter tries to maintain the same fluid motion as in throwing, so that the foot seems like a natural extension of the pot. The inside curve of the foot should repeat the curve of the exterior. It is interesting to note that while Japanese potters throw with the wheel turning in a clockwise direction, they trim pots turning in a counterclockwise motion. This makes the trimming marks blend into the throwing rings without changing the surface texture.

Although the height and contour of a foot depend on the overall design, the base edge should have a slight bevel to make it less susceptible to chipping. An outward taper of the foot will give the pot both an actual and a visual stability. Especially wide shapes such as platters may need a second foot to support the large expanse of clay and prevent sagging. Tall pedestal-type feet can be thrown separately, tooled, and then joined to bowl or cup shapes when the clay is leather hard. Hand-built feet can also be applied to the tooled bottom at the leather-hard stage. After firing, the bottoms of tooled pots are sanded to remove any roughness and prevent scratching of furniture. In some cases it may be desirable to glue a felt pad to the bottom of the pot.

194 David Nelson, U.S.A. Large basket. Porcelain, with the handle flowing into the body, wax-resist design with an ash and copper-green glaze; height 12″ (30.4 cm), width 16″ (40.6 cm).

Appendages

A basic form can be given various appendages to make it more functional. These include handles, spouts, and lids. Any appendage attached to a thrown pot should be the same moisture content so that in drying the two parts will shrink at the same rate. This makes the join stronger, less apt to separate and crack.

Handles

Handles are joined to a form after it has been trimmed and while it is still leather hard. A pulled handle such as that in Plate 19 (p. 144) is made in the following way:

○ Wedge clay that is slightly stiffer than throwing consistency, and roll it into a thick taper.
○ Hold the butt end in the left hand, wet the right hand, and pull the clay in a swift, downward motion.
○ Pull the clay three or four times, wetting the hand each time and turning the mass of clay.
○ Apply even pressure that is lighter toward the end of the elongated strip.
○ If the thickness varies, cut off the uneven part, because it will weaken the handle.
○ Pressure with the thumb against the fingers during the pulling motion will result in a more comfortable handle (see Fig. 206F, p. 173).
○ Score and apply slip to the two points of attachment on the pot.
○ Pinch or cut the butt end of the handle, and press it firmly against the upper section of the pot, smoothing the clay to strengthen the join.
○ Correct the curve, and fasten the bottom of the handle to the score marks.

Handles for cups and other small objects can be made by attaching the thicker end of the handle to the upper score mark and pulling the handle directly on the pot. The handles in Figure 195 were joined in this manner

with small knobs of clay placed on the upper ridge for a thumb rest. Decorative handles made of coils or slabs of clay are also possible.

Whichever method is used, after the joining is completed the ware should be placed in a damp room or covered with plastic to allow a slow and even drying. This will prevent the small diameter of the handle from drying and contracting faster than the body of the pot, causing cracks to develop.

The beginner may have to pull many handles in order to achieve one that looks and fits well on a pot. At first it may help to let the handle dry slightly after pulling. The joining process is easier if the surface of the handle is not wet with slip.

198 Warren MacKenzie, U.S.A. Teapot. Stoneware with a wax-resist decoration under a red kaki glaze, cane handle; height 6.5″ (16.2 cm).

When a high, rising handle, as for a teapot, is needed, the potter may prefer to purchase a readymade one of cane, as in Plate 20 (p. 144) and Fig. 198. In this event, a ring of clay is attached later to two sides to accept the handle. The rings should be joined, with scoring and slip, in the usual manner. A conventional pulled handle can also be used on a teapot.

Spouts

Pitcher spouts are made just after the pot has been thrown, while the clay is still soft.

○ Place the thumb and index finger against the rim to act as a support.
○ Form the spout with a wiping motion of the other hand.
○ Keep the width of the spout in proportion to the size of the pitcher.
○ If the wiping motion is continuous and the edge sharp, the pitcher will not drip.

A spout need not be an extension of the rim. It may also be formed from a slab of clay that is folded into a V-shape and attached to the rim.

A teapot spout is thrown at the same time as the pot and the cover, so that all will shrink at the same rate. This kind of spout is more complicated because there are many functional and aesthetic considerations. The spout must be long enough to reach above the rim of the teapot, or else the pot cannot be filled to the top. The base must be broad and low on the pot so as not to become clogged with tea leaves.

199 Making a pitcher spout with a wiping motion of one finger with the soft rim supported by the fingers of the other hand.

- Once the placement has been established, trace the outline of the spout on the pot. Score the outline and coat it with slip.
- With the fettling knife, make as many strainer holes as the space will permit in the portion of the pot wall to be covered by the spout.
- Wait until the clay has dried to brush away any rough burrs, for otherwise they will stick in the holes.
- Join the spout to the pot while it is still somewhat soft. At this point the base can be pinched into a graceful curve.
- Make the pouring lip sharp in profile to prevent dripping. If the clay is too hard to manipulate, cut a groove in the lip.

Lids

There are many different ways of making covers for pots. All, however, are thrown at the same time as the pot and are measured accurately with calipers to ensure a tight fit. A lid should always conform to the shape of the pot and complement its lines. Care must be taken when removing a lid from the wheel or bat and during trimming. If the lid is distorted while it is still soft, it will most likely warp as it dries and not fit correctly. It is almost impossible to make a lid for a pot that is too dry. Because of the different shrinkage rates, the lid will not fit the pot.

One of the simplest types of lid is a flat disk with a knob thrown on top. If small, it can be thrown off the hump, but a wide lid should be thrown on a bat. The vessel must have a depressed inner flange to support the flat lid.

200 Jack Sures, Canada. Covered jar. Porcelain with carved decoration. Amusing knob is entitled "Coming and Going." Height 12″ (30.4 cm).

201 Gary Gogerty, U.S.A. Cheese cover. Stoneware with a cherrywood base, iron-blue glaze with brush decoration over white slip; height 5.5″ (14 cm).

168

202 Don Pilcher, U.S.A. Covered bowl. Porcelain, transparent glaze with iron spots; diameter 14″ (35.56 cm).

Casseroles or teapots must have an inner flange below the pot rim to hold the lid. This prevents moisture and escaping steam from running down the sides of the pot. In throwing the pot, the rim is kept a little thicker than usual. Then, with the finger, a portion of the rim is depressed to form the inner retaining ring. The rim is finished with a soft leather.

A domed or slightly rounded lid is thrown like a simple bowl. The rim is thick enough to allow an inner retaining ring to fit inside the top of the pot. When leather hard, the lid is inverted and the top tooled. A knob can be thrown on the lid or thrown separately and attached with slip. Knobs can also be made of pulled strips or coils attached to the lid.

203 David Shaner, U.S.A. Hand-built stoneware sphere with black crystalline glaze, stopper not glazed. Diameter 14″ (35.56 cm).

Another kind of lid is actually a shallow bowl that conforms to the slightly flared rim of the pot it covers. The knob is thrown on the lid at the same time. Later, the bottom is trimmed of excess clay. This method works especially well when a great number of lids are being thrown, because they can be thrown off the hump, the tooling process is faster, and there is a wider margin of error in the fit.

Once students understand the basics of making a lid, they can explore a great variety of shapes (Fig. 204). There are also many possibilities besides thrown clay. For example, corks make very tight-fitting lids and provide an interesting contrast to clay. The unusual lid of Charles Lakofsky's pot in Plate 21 (p. 161) was slip-cast from a mold made from a summer squash.

204 Different types of lids shown in cross section.

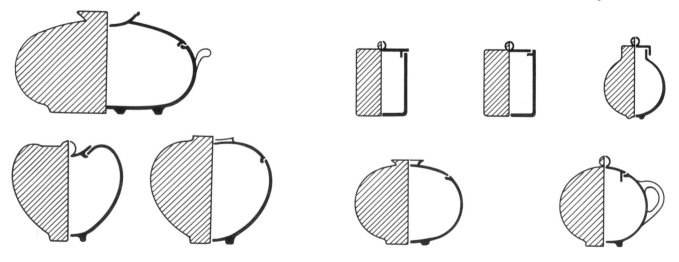

The Teapot

The teapot offers an unusual challenge to the potter, since it generally consists of four separate parts that must be combined to form a unified whole that is both functional and pleasing in design. However fanciful the conception, the teapot should have a well-balanced handle, an efficient pouring spout, a lid that will not fall off when pouring, and a body appropriate for holding the tea and retaining heat (See Plate 22, p. 162).

The four components must be thrown at the same time so that they will all shrink at the same rate, as mentioned earlier. Detailed instructions for making lids and for making and joining handles and spouts were given earlier, but the procedures as they relate to the teapot are illustrated on pages 172–173 by Jay Lindsay, who is shown throwing a spout and lid off the hump and later throwing the vessel itself. The flange on the teapot cover is deep to prevent its being dislodged when the tea is poured. A small hole should be made in the cover to prevent a vacuum. An inner rim is thrown on the vessel. After a slight drying the vessel and cover are trimmed. The spout is kept a bit softer, since after trimming it will be pinched out to flare into the vessel form. As previously noted, the spout level must reach the vessel rim and the strainer holes be cut as low as possible. To prevent dripping, the rounded rim of the spout is cut at an angle. Due to the torque of the spout during throwing, the clay will unwind in drying and firing; the spout is therefore cut at a slight angle. Finally the handle is pulled and joined. The curve of the cover, spout, and handle should flow into each other, forming a pleasing whole. (See Plates 19, 20, and 22, pp. 144 and 162.)

205 Donald Frith, U.S.A. Miniature tea set. Porcelain with pale celedon glaze fired to cone 10, cherry handle; teapot 2.5″ (8.9 cm).

A

B

C

D

172   WHEEL TECHNIQUES

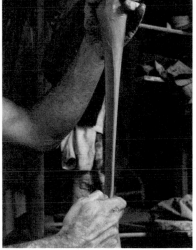

E

F

G

H

Throwing a Teapot

206

A A wide-based spout is thrown off the hump. A groove is cut to guide a string to cut the spout off the slowly turning wheel head.

B A deep flange cover is thrown and cut off the wheel. When leather-hard it is trimmed and a knob is thrown.

C The inner rim of the teapot is carefully measured to ensure a perfect fit with the cover.

D After the leather-hard stage, the vessel is trimmed, large numbers of strainer holes are cut in the teapot, and the point of juncture is scored and coated with slip.

E After being trimmed and pinched, the spout is flared into the body of the teapot.

F Finally the handle is pulled and joined to the teapot.

G After the edges are scored and coated with slip, the handle is joined to the pot. If very soft, the handle may be suspended from a table edge to stiffen prior to the joining process.

H The completed teapot before the bisque fire.

A Bowl Being Formed From Thin Porcelain slabs

207

See fired bowl, Plate 23 (p. 162).

A Thin porcelain slabs are sliced from a block of clay.

B The slices are placed on a plaster bowl form.

C A foot is then thrown.

D When leather-hard the complete bowl is lifted off the form.

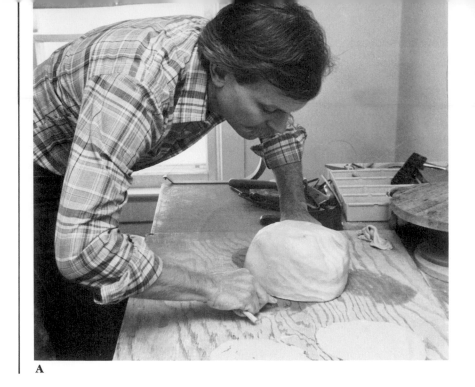

A

B

C

D

Combined Techniques

As mentioned in Chapter 4, many forms can be created only by combining techniques. Figure 207 shows Dick Evans combining hand-built and wheel-thrown forms to create a bowl that reflects the recent interest of potters in porcelain objects that have the delicate, translucent quality of thin, frosted glass. Evans slices thin porcelain slabs and places them upon a bisqued porcelain bowl form that serves as a mold. Later he throws a foot upon the thin, layered slabs. The final fired bowl is shown in Plate 23, p. 162.

6

Decorating and Glazing

Decoration should complement and not overwhelm a ceramic form. The character and shape of a piece will suggest an appropriate type of decoration. There are many methods of decoration, including manipulation of the clay itself and the use of colored clay bodies, slips, and glazes. However, there is never only one method suitable for a particular shape.

Decorating

The potter should decide how he or she wants to decorate a piece during the forming stages, because some types of decoration are undertaken while the clay is still plastic. Often, freely thrown or elaborately hand-built forms are complete in themselves, and some may need only a coating of a single glaze. Other, simpler shapes may benefit from plastic additions or a painted design in slip or underglaze. Planning the decoration and glazes for a form while it is being made will help to create a more unified result.

208 Harlan House, Canada. *Iris with Picket Fence.* Oval vase. 1980. Porcelain with cut-out, incised, and modeled decoration, Thomas glaze with brush-work in cobalt and chrome; height 18″ (45.7 cm).

above: **Plate 24 James F. McKinnell**, U.S.A. Baroque fruit bowl. Coiled stoneware with elaborate slab additions and incisions. Opaque glaze with stain and luster accents, diameter 16″ (40 cm).

left: **Plate 25 Kenneth Green**, U.S.A. A rocklike form of iron-stained stoneware with glazed porcelain disk, height 8.5″ (21.5 cm).

right: **Plate 26** **Donald Frith**, U.S.A. Bottle. Porcelain with delicately carved floral pattern.

below: **Plate 27** **Harrison McIntosh**, U.S.A. Plate. Stoneware with sgraffito design through a beige glaze to reveal the dark engobe beneath.

When faced with the many potential glaze colors, textures, and methods of application, the novice potter often tends to try a little of everything on one pot. The result usually resembles a discarded paint can, devoid of accidental charm. With experience it is possible to use a single stroke of color or a single glaze and produce a free and fluid effect or to allow a heavy application of glaze to make its own design.

Clay in the Plastic State

Decoration can be incorporated into a form while the clay is still soft (Fig. 209). In a wheel-thrown piece, deep throwing rings, pinched depressions, or modeled designs will provide decorative accents. After removal from the wheel, the form can be modeled even more, although care must be taken not to stretch the clay too much, or it might collapse.

In the hand-building process there are many possibilities for decoration. Coils or slabs can be pinched together or modeled into an endless variety of shapes for both functional and decorative purposes. See Plates 24 and 25, page 179.

Colored clay bodies offer one of the most basic means of decoration in both throwing and hand building. Oxides are added to dry clay ingredients, and then the batch is mixed with water and dried until it reaches wedging consistency. (See the Appendix for amounts of colorants added to bodies.) Some of the possibilities for colored clays include neriage, millefiore, Egyptian paste, and marbling.

left: **209** Plastic clay can take on any form or texture.

right: **210 Susanne Stephenson**, U.S.A. Vase. 1982. Porcelain, with elaborate slab-foot sections; pink, blue, and brown slips under a clear glaze; height 19.5″ (49.5 cm).

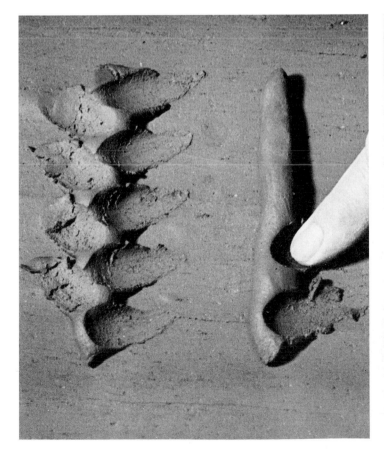

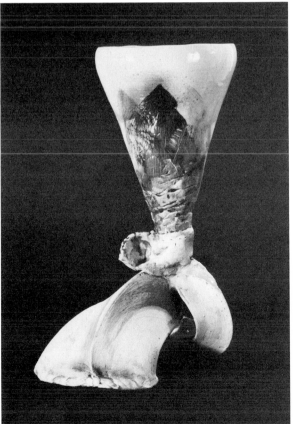

211 Don M. Olstad, U.S.A. Small covered jar. Blue and white porcelain sections with black slip in the laminated neriage technique, formed solid and then trimmed; width 3.5″ (8.9 cm).

Neriage The neriage technique uses colored clays pieced together in molds. Shaped segments of plastic clay are joined in a concave mold to make a pattern identical on both the interior and exterior surfaces of the pot. The contrasting clay pieces can be strips, coils, or small slabs. They must be joined well and allowed to dry slowly.

Millefiore The millefiore technique, which also uses colored clays in molds, is a more complicated procedure evolved from glass making. The different-colored clays are rolled into slabs, then layered in "loaves" or long rectangles that show the colored design in cross section. The loaf is sliced through to make a slab, then this slab is joined with other slabs and small pieces of clay in a plaster mold. (See Chap. 4 and Fig. 143 for forming techniques.) Needless to say, the decorative possibilities with this technique are great, for the colored clays combined with glazes, lusters, or decals can create an ornate design (Fig. 142).

Egyptian Paste Another technique in which both decoration and glazes are combined in a plastic clay is Egyptian paste. The paste has colorants and glaze-forming materials incorporated into the body in a soluble form. The actual clay content is very low—no more than about 20 percent of the body—with the major portion being nonplastic materials such as flint. As the clay dries, sodium is deposited on the surface and combines with the flint and colorants to create a glaze. Developed by the Egyptians before 3000 B.C., this paste was the earliest form of glaze known. It is most often seen in turquoise-colored beads and small, modeled figurines (see Plate. 4, p. 40).

Egyptian paste is highly nonplastic and suitable mainly for simple hand-built forms and beads. Another limitation is that excessive handling will remove the surface coating of sodium. Because fingerprints on the paste will leave unglazed patches, pieces should be dried and fired on stilts, or, for

212 Different-colored clays are wedged separately, then the clay slabs are pounded together with little further wedging, thus creating color striations when thrown.

213 Incising design and cutting away background slip applied on the pot shown in Fig. 186F. Potter, Jay Lindsay.

small objects such as beads, strung on Nichrome wire. When completely dry, the finished piece can be once fired to cone 08 to 07, depending upon the formula. (See Appendix for an Egyptian paste body.)

Marbling The ancient technique of marbling to make clay look like stone became popular in Europe during the eighteenth century and was termed *agateware* by the English. Slabs of different-colored clays are placed on top of each other and wedged just enough to remove air pockets. The mass is then thrown in the normal manner, with the layers creating color striations.

Leather-Hard Clay

The term *leather hard* refers to clay that has dried enough to be handled without becoming distorted but contains sufficient moisture to permit joins to be made and slips applied without cracking. Incising, carving, and stamping are most conveniently done at this stage, because the clay cuts cleanly and does not stick to the tool.

Thrown forms that have set up can be paddled to flatten the sides. If the walls are very thick, they can be cut with a fettling knife and then carved. Elaborate handles joined to thrown or hand-built forms can serve as decoration and a design accent.

Incising The technique of incising consists of carving lines with a tool into a clay surface (Fig. 213). These lines can be deep cuts providing a strong accent or shallow ones following the contour of the pot. Incised lines can also carve out a design that may be glazed later in a contrasting color as in Plate 26 (p. 180), where the contrast of the light blue glaze is accentuated as it collects in the carved floral pattern of Donald Frith's porcelain bottle.

214 Richard Peeler, U.S.A. Intricate castle form with birds. Incised stoneware slab construction with white mat glaze, height 43″ (109.3 cm).

DECORATING

right: 215 **Marj Peeler**, U.S.A. Stoneware vase thrown in sections, with incised decoration filled with an opaque glaze, height 13″ (33 cm).

below: 216 **Hans de Jong**, Netherlands. Stoneware vase with intricate stamped and incised patterns, beige glaze with gray-blue and green colorants in the recesses, height 8″ (20 cm).

Stamping One of the oldest decorative techniques for ceramic objects is stamping. Many Neolithic pots have impressed designs of weaves, cords, or basket patterns. These devices are still used today to provide interesting textural decoration. Other possibilities for stamps include shells, leaves, pebbles, and an infinite variety of found objects.

Potters also carve stamps out of clay and bisque-fire them for increased durability and to prevent their sticking to wet clay. Stamps should be applied with a fair amount of pressure to make a clear impression. If a vertical wall is being stamped, the wall must be supported with the hand to determine the proper pressure needed. The moisture content of the clay is important. If it is too dry, the clay may crack; if too wet, the stamp may stick.

Rolled stamp decoration has the advantage of greater speed in application but generally produces a less complex design. Applied clay pressed with a finger or a stamp will create a raised pattern and a more ornate, textured effect.

Slip Decoration Slip can be applied to leather-hard clay in many ways. For decorative purposes, oxides are added to the liquid slip to produce colors. Slip can be brushed over the entire surface of a pot, painted on in designs, or applied in bands. Once the coating has dried, lines can be scratched through to the clay beneath, as in Figure 213. This technique is called sgraffito. The incising should not be done when the slip is completely dry because it might flake off. On the other hand, if the slip is too wet, the design will smudge. The rough edges should not be brushed away until the slip has dried completely because this, too, will smudge the design (see Plate 27, p. 180).

Sprigging Applying relief designs with slip onto a leather-hard surface is called sprigging. Perhaps the best-known examples of sprig designs are the Wedgwood cameos and vases. Sprigs can be formed individually of leather-hard clay, but generally they are made in plaster or bisqued clay molds. First, plastic clay is pressed into the mold. When it begins to dry and shrink away from the form, it is removed, scored and slipped, and then pressed onto the pot's surface. If a sprig is too large, it is apt to shrink away from the pot. It is better to build up designs from smaller units.

Slip Trailing Applying slip with a syringe is called slip trailing. The line created by this method is very flexible and shows a slight relief effect, as in Figure 219 on page 186 (see also Figs. 108 and 174).

A variation of slip trailing is *combed* or *feathered* slipware, a technique popular in Europe, especially England, from the fifteenth through the eighteenth centuries. The procedure is unusual and can be applied only to wide, shallow shapes. In this method, slip is trailed in parallel lines across the entire surface. Then the piece is lifted a few inches off the table and dropped. The impact flattens the lines, causing them almost to touch each other. A feather or comb brushed gently across the surface at right angles to the lines creates a delicate pattern. If desired, the slip trailing technique can be used on a clay slab, and the slab can later be draped over a mold for shaping.

217 Bisque stamping is an easy technique to provide a variety of textural patterns.

218 Bernard Palissy, France. This oval lead-glazed earthenware platter in the manner of the eccentric late-16th-century potter runs the gamut of all decorative techniques. After this, contemporary pottery does not seem so strange. Length 20.5″ (51.2 cm). The Metropolitan Museum of Art, New York (gift of Julia A. Berwind, 1953).

above: 219 **Robin Hopper**, Canada. *Corinthian Bowl*. Raised trailed slip decoration under a porcelain alkaline green slip. Single fire; width 16″ (40 cm).

right: 220 Combed slip decoration on a red earthenware platter, from Staffordshire, England. 18th century. Length 20.5″ (51.2 cm). Victoria & Albert Museum, London (Crown Copyright).

below: 221 **Harrison McIntosh**, U.S.A. Stoneware bowl with incised lines, later filled with light and dark engobe, scraped and then glazed. Cone 5; diameter 4.5″ (12.2 cm).

Inlay Decoration The early and widespread use of incised lines and slip decoration eventually led to a combination of these techniques. One of the simplest methods is to apply a light-colored slip to incised lines in a darker clay body. After the slip has dried slightly, the surface is wiped clean with a scraper, further defining the color contrast. The bowl in Figure 221 has horizontal lines that were incised while it was on the wheel. These were filled with a light and a dark engobe (a kind of slip), and the piece was covered with a thin gray mat glaze.

DECORATING AND GLAZING

Mishima   In mishima, an inlay technique of Korean origin, incised lines are filled with clay of a contrasting color. When partially dry the surface is scraped flush. (See Fig. 36).

Clay in the Dry State

When a clay body has dried completely it is known as *greenware*. Decorative possibilities become more limited because of the fragility of clay in this state. Greenware is likely to crack and break when knocked or held by the rim. Provided the ware is handled gently, however, there are some decorating techniques possible on dry clay bodies.

Engobes and Oxides   Dry clay may be brushed with engobes and oxides to create colored designs and patterns. An engobe is a slip that has a reduced clay content to lessen contraction problems. Usually, half the clay is replaced by feldspar, silica, and a flux, and a small percentage of such plasticizers as bentonite or macaloid can also be added. Coloring oxides and stains are also painted on raw clay, but too thick an application will flake off or cause faulty adhesion of the glaze. A small amount of flux or feldspar added to the colorant and water mixture will help seal the color to the body and make it less susceptible to flaking during the glaze firing.

Wax-Resist Method   Decoration by the wax-resist method is generally used in conjunction with coloring oxides. The wax may be hot paraffin or beeswax thinned with turpentine; a more convenient water-soluble wax emulsion can be applied cold. The hot preparation makes a cleaner definition and is less apt to pick up specks of color. A brushed-wax design repels the applied stain, making the stain the background color. Lines incised through a band or panel of wax will absorb the stain or glaze application and produce a decoration of contrasting color.

Safety Caution

Be careful not to overheat the wax, because the mixture can ignite.

222   Floral pattern is brushed on a dry porcelain bowl with a cobalt oxide solution.

above: **223** Applying coloring oxides over a wax-resist design.

right: **224 Thomas Kerrigan**, U.S.A. *Rock Drawing*. Double-walled bowl with wax-resist and engobe decoration, raku firing. Diameter 17.5″ (44.4 cm); height 7.5″ (19 cm).

below: **225 Hans Coper**, England. Pilgrim bottle shape. 1958. Stoneware assembled from flat bowl shapes, joined to foot and rim, dry textured surface. Victoria & Albert Museum, London (Crown Copyright).

Glazes Glazes with a high clay content, such as the Bristol type or a slip glaze, can be applied to dry ware and fired only once. The ware must be of a uniform thickness and the glaze applied quickly to prevent excessive absorption, which will result in cracks. This procedure is most successful on tiles.

Clay in the Bisque State

After a clay body has been bisque fired, the major decorative techniques are associated with glazes and their methods of application. A few techniques, however, can be used for underglazing or even to replace a glaze.

Engobes Bisqued ware can be given applications of engobes to create a rough texture or to alter the color of the body. The engobes must contain sufficient fluxes to fuse with the body, but they should not be so fluid that they create a glossy surface. The dark engobe on the vase in Figure 225 has been wiped off in most areas, leaving a dry, textured surface.

DECORATING AND GLAZING

Coloring Oxides and Underglazes   Sometimes coloring oxides or underglazes (oxides mixed with flux or feldspar) can be used as brush decoration, bands of color, or an overall colorant on a bisqued body or a glazed surface (Plate 28, p. 197). Groggy, textured clays or incised designs can be coated with an oxide-and-water solution and then the excess wiped off. This technique works well on large sculptural pieces where a glaze application is not necessary. Underglazes produce more uniform colors and are less likely to cause running than oxides mixed just with water.

Decorating Pencils   Another technique requires the use of decorating pencils, which are manufactured commercially in a variety of colors. These are actually oxides or stains in a pencil form. On a bisque surface the potter can draw fine lines not possible with brushes. The pencils are most successful on smooth, white clay bodies later to be glazed in a clear or translucent white. The decoration can be very intricate, especially when used under a crackle glaze with portions inked for further contrast, as in Figure 226.

Wax-Resist Decoration   Wax can be brushed on bisqued ware before glazing. The result is a strong contrasting pattern of surface texture with the smooth glaze color. Often, the wax coating does not resist all the glaze, but this accident can be incorporated into an abstract design.

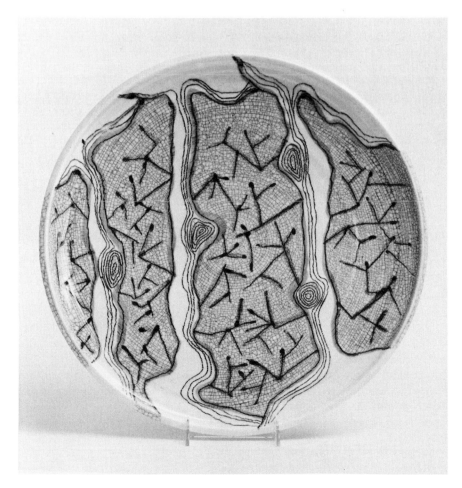

226   Carl E. Paak, U.S.A. *Tree Scape #2*. Porcelain plate with black decorating-pen design under a clear crackle glaze fired to cone 07, portions inked after firing; diameter 16″ (40 cm).

Glazing

Glazing in the raw clay state has definite advantages. By eliminating the bisque fire, there are savings not only in the labor needed for the extra stacking, unloading, and operation of the kiln but also in the fuel or power needed for the extra firing. A single firing also promotes a better union between the body and the glaze, because the two shrink simultaneously. There are, however, several disadvantages to the combined firing. Because of its fragility, the dry raw-clay vessel may be broken in handling. Expansions caused by the moisture absorbed into the dry clay may cause the vessel to crack. In general, only when the body of a piece is rather thick and uniform can glaze be poured safely. Other pieces should be sprayed, since the glaze, with its troublesome moisture content, can then be applied at a slower rate. One additional precaution must be taken in glazing raw ware: alkaline fluxes must first be fritted. These compounds have a high coefficient of thermal expansion. When they are absorbed into the outer portion of the clay, their expansion and contraction rate during firing and cooling is so great in contrast to the rest of the body that they will cause it to crack.

Glazing in the bisque state is the most common procedure. Normally, bisque ware is fired between cones 010 and 06 (1641°–1830°F, 894°–999°C). At this stage the bisque is hard enough to be handled without mishap yet sufficiently porous to absorb glaze readily. Bisque ware fired at lower temperatures will absorb too much glaze, and the clay structure may break down; if fired too high, it is especially difficult to glaze, for the glaze tends to run off. An exception to the normal bisque firing is high-fire chinaware. Such pieces as thin teacups, which are fragile and likely to warp, are often placed in the kiln with supporting fireclay rings inside their lips, or they are stacked upside down and then fired to their maximum temperature. Later, these chinaware pieces are glazed and fired on their own foot rims at a lower temperature where warpage losses are much less.

How to Glaze

Before the actual glazing operation takes place, a few precautions must be taken. If bisque ware is not to be glazed immediately upon its removal from the kiln, it should be stored where dust and soot will not settle on it, or it should be covered with plastic. The bisque ware should not be handled excessively, especially if the hands are oily with perspiration, for this will deter the glaze from adhering properly. All surfaces of the bisque ware should be wiped with a damp sponge or momentarily placed under a water tap to remove dust and loose particles of clay. The moisture added to the bisque ware by this procedure will prevent an excessive amount of glaze from soaking in and thus allow a little more time for glazing. Extra moisture also helps to reduce the number of air pockets and pinholes that form when the glaze dries too quickly on a very porous bisque. The amount of moisture required depends upon the absorbency of the bisque, the thickness of the piece, and the consistency of the glaze. Should the bisque-fire temperature accidentally rise much higher than cone 06, the ware should not be dampened at all.

The glaze must be cleaned completely off the bottom of the pot and 0.25 inches (0.64 cm) up the side as soon as it is dry enough to handle. Excess glaze will always run, so it is never advisable to allow a heavy layer of glaze to remain near the foot rim. The cleaning operation can be simplified by dipping the bottoms of bisque pots in a shallow pan of hot paraffin before glazing.

Brushed Glazing   A brushed glaze is easiest for the beginner, although experience is needed to produce an even glaze coating. The technique is best suited for the glossy surface of low-fire glazes. It requires a flat brush, at least 1 inch (2.54 cm) in width and possibly larger. An ox hair bristle is preferred, for camel hair is much too soft and floppy. Unless a considerable amount of clay is in the glaze, the addition of bentonite or a gum binder is necessary for proper adhesion. The glaze must be applied rapidly, with a full brush, and the piece must be covered with a second and third coat before the bottom layer is completely dry, for otherwise blisters will develop. The glaze must be neither too watery nor so thick that it will dry quickly and cause uneven laps and ridges.

Dip Glazing   The simplest glazing method is probably dip glazing. After the vessel has been cleaned and moistened with a damp sponge, it is plunged into a large pan of glaze. It should be withdrawn almost immediately and shaken to remove the excess glaze. The object is then placed on a rack to dry, and any finger marks are touched up with a brush. Small-size pots can be dip glazed with metal tongs (Fig. 228), which come in several shapes. The slight blemishes in the glaze caused by the pointed tips usually heal in firing. A more uniform surface is produced if the glaze is thin enough to allow dipping two or three times within a few seconds. Interesting patterns and colors evolve when a piece is dipped in two different glazes that overlap.

left: **227**   Brushed glazes must be applied quickly and evenly with a wide brush.

right: **228**   Glaze tongs are convenient for dip-glazing small objects.

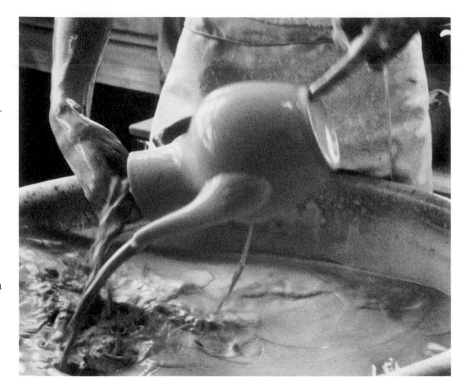

right: **229** A coffee pot being glazed by the traditional dip method.

below left: **230** Pouring glaze from a pitcher over a large platter, with a tub underneath to catch the excess.

below right: **231** The large bowl is filled with glaze and quickly rotated and the excess is poured out.

DECORATING AND GLAZING

Poured Glazes Pouring requires less glaze than dipping, and the technique can be applied to a greater variety of shapes. For example, the insides of bottles and deep, vaselike forms can be glazed only in this manner.

If the object is a bottle, the glaze is poured through a funnel, and then the vessel is rotated until all its surfaces are covered. The remainder is poured out and the bottle is given a final shake to distribute the glaze evenly and to remove the excess. Glazes that are poured or dipped must be a little thinner in consistency than those that are brushed on. The insides of bowls are glazed by pouring in a portion of the glaze, spreading it by rotating the bowl, and then pouring out the excess. This must be done rather quickly, or an overabundance or uneven amount of glaze will accumulate.

The exterior of a bottle is glazed by grasping the bottle by either the neck or the foot rim and pouring the glaze from a pitcher, allowing the extra to run off into a pan beneath. Finger marks are then touched up with a brush, and the foot rim is cleaned when dry. The outside of a bowl is glazed in the same manner, provided the foot is large enough to grasp. Otherwise the bowl can be placed upside down on wooden dowels extending across a pan. It is better to glaze the interior of a vessel first and the exterior later.

Sprayed Glazes Spraying permits subtle variations of color and control over glaze thickness and coverage. A thin overall glaze coating over delicate designs is most easily applied with the spray method. However, sprayed glazes are more common in commercial ceramics than among studio potters. Dipped and poured glazes are quicker to apply, less wasteful of glaze, and less liable to damage in loading. Another drawback is that brush and wax-resist decoration cannot be applied over a sprayed glaze.

The glaze for spraying should be more fluid than usual and should be

left: **232** Glazes that are too thick will produce an uneven glaze coating, as shown here. Note the dowels for supporting the bowl upside down in order to glaze the exterior.

right: **233** The glaze must be sprayed in several thin uniform coatings.

![Safety Caution icon] **Safety Caution**

Because many glaze materials are toxic, you should spray in a properly ventilated booth. You should always wear a mask when spray glazing.

left: **234**   A properly sprayed glaze develops a soft woolly surface with an even thickness.

right: **235**   Too fast or too heavy a glaze application will run.

run through a fine mesh sieve. Alkaline compounds that tend to settle or become lumpy must be replaced by fritted substitutes. The small electrically powered spray units for paint work well for glazes. Airbrushes, commonly used by graphic artists and for photo touch-ups, can produce overlapping color fields on a much smaller scale.

The insides of deep bowls or closed forms should be glazed before spraying the outsides. To obtain an even layer, the glaze is sprayed slowly at a moderate distance from the pot. The pot is turned as the spraying progresses, building up a soft, "woolly" surface. If the application is too heavy, the glaze will run. When that happens, the glaze must be scraped off and the pot dried and then reglazed. When the spraying is completed, handle the pot as gently and as little as possible. Dipping the foot in paraffin before spraying will eliminate the need to handle the pot while cleaning off the bottom.

Decorating with Glazes

The manner in which a glaze is applied can become a decorative technique. A single glaze will vary in color if applied in layers of different thicknesses. Several glazes dipped or poured over each other will create contrasting color fields. An interesting design often results from brushing an oxide or second glaze over a dipped or poured surface. If the base glaze is completely dry, however, another glaze applied on top may crack or peel off.

A simple decorating technique consists of wiping away a portion of the glaze. On a textured surface, this will leave glaze in the rougher sections. If the glaze is wiped away from a smooth surface, the slight residue of flux from the glaze may alter the color of the clay body. A variety of textures will also result from the glazes themselves—from a very dry through a smooth mat to a glossy finish.

When a glaze has dried to a firm coating, lines scratched through the glaze to the body will create a subtle relief pattern. Wax designs can also be applied to a firm coating of glaze, and lines can be incised through the wax. These lines can then be filled in with an oxide stain or a glaze of a different color to contrast with the body or base glaze. The bowl in Figure 237 has a wax design painted over the glaze. A cobalt wash is being brushed over the wax. In the finished bowl (Plate 29, p. 197) the waxed areas are the color of the original glaze, while those covered with cobalt are darker.

left: **236** **Warren MacKenzie**, U.S.A. Stoneware bowl with a thick glaze and finger-combed decoration; diameter 17″ (43.1 cm).

right: **237** Applying a cobalt colorant with a wide brush over a wax design on a glazed surface.

238 **David Nelson**, U.S.A. Platter. Porcelain with geometric wax-resist design and ash glaze with iron- and copper-red colorants; diameter 18″ (45.7 cm).

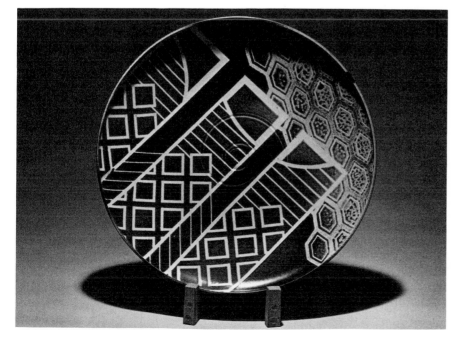

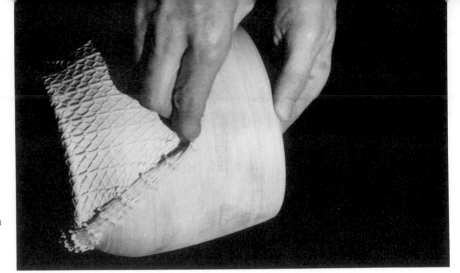

239 After bisque ware is covered with elasticized netting, the ware is sprayed with a temmoku glaze and the netting is carefully removed.

Moist paper stencils may also be placed on the bisque ware; after the ware is sprayed with glaze, the stencil is peeled off. The resulting decoration presents a contrast between the dry body surface under the stencil and the glaze.

More intricate effects result from using a flexible mesh as shown in Figure 239. In this instance the mesh-covered ware is sprayed with a temmoku glaze. After the mesh is carefully removed, the ware is sprayed with a light coating of a white mat glaze, which provides a greater contrast, as seen in the vase in Figure 240.

240 Barbara Pinsky, U.S.A. Vase. Porcelain with design created by elastic netting, Temmoku and white mat glaze, fired to cone 010 reduction; height 10″ (25.4 cm).

Plate 28 Judith Salomon, U.S.A. Slab bowl with tripod feet of low-fired whiteware. Brush decoration with yellow, blue, black, and red stains, 19″ × 11″ × 16″ (48.2 × 28 × 40.6 cm).

Plate 29 Jay Lindsay, U.S.A. Stoneware platter with wax-resist and cobalt stain decoration over a white semi-mat glaze, diameter 16″ (40 cm).

197

right: **Plate 30   Patti Warashina**,
U.S.A. Wall plaque, *You Captured My
Heart.* Intricate polychrome composition with under- and overglaze brush
and airbrush colorants. White ware
body, height 30″ (76.2 cm).

below: **Plate 31   Dick Evans**, U.S.A.
Untitled Form #23A. White stoneware
body with porcelain slip fired to cone
01. White glaze fired to cone 05, and
gold and mother-of-pearl lusters fired
to cone 020, length 18″ (45 cm).

Glaze-Fired Ware

Until recently, most hand potters were concerned with functional ware decorated with glazes formulated in the studio. Decorating techniques associated with commercially manufactured ceramics (or those that made the ware unsuitable for practical use) were largely neglected. Contemporary potters are now experimenting with low-fire techniques that result in less durable finishes characterized by bright colors and metallic lusters.

One possibility for decoration on glaze-fired ware is the application of acrylic or oil-base paints onto the glazed surface. Although acrylic paints adhere best to bisqued ware, oil and enamel paints work well on both bisqued and glazed surfaces.

Overglazes, lusters, and decals are fired between cones 020 and 015 (1175°–1479°F, 635°–804°C) in an electric kiln. This extremely low temperature fuses the colors to the previously glazed surface; the finishes would probably burn out above cone 010. Hard, glossy glazes are more reliable bases for these effects than rough or mat surfaces. The application and firing processes are exacting. The work area must be clean and free of any dust, and the ware should be wiped with alcohol to remove dirt and oily fingerprints. Although it is possible to compound overglazes and lusters, the ingredients are expensive and the process time-consuming. It is more profitable to choose from the commercially manufactured products.

Overglaze Colors Overglaze colors contain coloring oxides or stains, a flux, and a binder, such as oil of lavender. They can be purchased in small containers and applied directly from the bottle. The vials must be fresh, for if the colors are too old, they will become gummy and form a jellylike mass. The manufacturer's instructions should be carefully followed, and note should be taken of which type of medium is recommended for thinning and cleaning purposes.

Thin coats of color are applied with soft camel-hair or sable brushes. The brushes should be kept very clean and used only for overglazes. Mistakes can be wiped off with a cloth dipped in the proper thinner. A spray gun or airbrush will create subtle modeling details. The colors should be thinned to a more fluid consistency, however, to prevent the spraying mechanism from clogging. See Plate 30, p. 198.

If the design is complicated, the piece cannot be painted and fired in one operation. First, the broad color washes are applied; they can be intensified later if necessary. Then the finer details are painted. Many unusual color effects can be achieved by applying different colors over each other.

Most overglaze colors are fired between cones 020 and 015. The temperature is critical and should be controlled to the exact degree stated in the manufacturer's instructions. Overfiring will cause the colors to burn out; underfiring will prevent them from developing. The ware should always be handled with caution to avoid damaging the fragile surface.

Luster Glazes Metallic, iridescent, and pearlescent colors can be produced on glazed surfaces by means of luster glazes. They are available in a large selection of hues and in such liquid metal colors as gold, silver, and bronze.

Like overglazes, lusters can be brushed or sprayed onto a glazed surface in thin, even coats. Lusters will become increasingly brilliant with repeated firings; unusual effects result from applying colors over each other.

 Safety Caution

Make sure your kiln room is well ventilated when firing overglazes and lusters in order to rid the atmosphere of toxic fumes from the glazes.

Firing should proceed slowly, with the kiln door left open in the beginning to allow toxic fumes to escape. Most lusters mature between cones 020 and 018, although these temperatures may vary with the product. See Plate 31, p. 198.

Decals Several commercial firms produce decals, which are available from many ceramic supply houses. Watermount decals are printed by either a lithographic or a silk-screen process onto a thin paper sheet coated with water-soluble film. Lacquer is then applied over the decal material.

To apply the decal, the desired design is cut from the sheet and soaked in room-temperature until the paper has become saturated. (If it is left in the water for too long, the adhesive quality will be diminished.) When the backing paper has released the design, the decal is lifted from the water, drained, and slid from the backing onto the clean, glazed surface. The position is adjusted, and the excess water is patted away with a cotton pad. If the decal is large, a squeegee may be used to seal the decal to the surface. It is important to remove all water and air bubbles, or the decal will not adhere properly during the firing. Application on curved surfaces is facilitated by first heating the ware to about 85°F (29°C). This will cause the lacquer backing to stretch and conform to the surface when the decal is pressed onto the form.

The decal must dry completely before firing. Most decals mature between cones 020 and 018 and should be fired in an electric kiln.

241 Jug. Earthenware, printed in black; height 7.5″ (19.05 cm). Victoria & Albert Museum, London (Crown Copyright).

Photographic Silk-Screening The photographic silk-screen process may be used to make a decal, although the design may also be screened directly upon a vessel or a clay slab. The student in a school with a photographic and a print department should have no difficulty obtaining instruction in preparing a silk screen. The process is widely used commercially to produce advertising posters and, more recently, T-shirts with photographic images. Therefore, the potter in any urban area should be able to find a firm to furnish a photographic silk screen.

To make a silk-screen design, an image on a film negative is projected through a halftone (grid) screen to form a film positive. This positive image is in turn projected upon a silk screen coated with a light-sensitive emulsion. The coating on those portions of the screen receiving the greatest amounts of light is washed away when the image on the screen is developed. Ink, consisting of equal parts of turpentine, varnish, and linseed oil mixed with a colorant, is then brushed on the screen, penetrating the uncovered section directly onto the pot or on to transfer paper to make a decal. The pot, bearing the design, must then be fired to fuse the color to the surface and also to burn off the linseed oil if the pot is then to be overglazed.

Glaze Defects

Opening the kiln and finding a runny, crawling, or rough glaze is one of the greatest disappointments faced by the potter. Because glaze chemicals vary slightly in their composition and because potters are always tempted to experiment with new combinations of glazes, the problem of glaze defects is a continuing one.

There are usually several reasons, all logical, why a particular glaze fault occurs, but trying to deduce the cause from one piece may prove quite difficult. When there are a number of pots having the same glaze from a single kiln load or when there are several glazes on a single body, the problem of deduction is much easier. The following section outlines some of the factors that can cause glaze defects. Glaze faults may result not only from the composition of the glaze but from the improper selection or preparation of the clay body, faulty kiln operation, or, as happens most frequently, lack of skill and care in application.

Defects Caused by the Body

○ A body that is too porous because of improper wedging, kneading, *blunging* (mixing with paddles), or *pugging* (mixing in a pug mill) may cause small bubbles, beads, and pinholes to form in the glaze as the body contracts and the gases attempt to escape.
○ Excessive water in the body can result in similar conditions.
○ A large amount of manganese dioxide used as a colorant in a body or slip may cause blisters to form in both the body and the glaze.
○ Soluble sulfates are contained in some clays and come to the surface in drying, forming a whitish scum. Pinholes and bubbles develop as these sulfates react with the glaze to form gases. This condition can be eliminated by adding up to 2 percent barium carbonate to the body. A slight reduction fire at the point when the glaze begins to melt will reduce the sulfates and allow the gas to pass off before the glaze develops a glassy retaining film.

- If the body is underfired in the bisque and therefore very porous, it may absorb too much glaze. Soluble fluxes in the glaze, because of their higher thermal expansion and contraction rates, can cause the body to crack. In any event, a glaze applied to a very absorptive body could have a coarse, or even a sandpaperlike surface.

Defects of Application

- Blisters or pinholes may result if the bisque ware has not been moistened slightly before glazing. The glaze traps air in the body's surface pores.
- Dust or oil on the surface of the bisque ware may cause pinholes, crawling, or a scaly surface in the glaze.
- If the glaze is applied too heavily, it will run and obscure the decoration, perhaps causing the pot to stick to the kiln shelves.
- In addition to flowing excessively, glazes that have been applied too thickly will usually crack in drying. When the piece is fired, these cracks will not heal but will pull farther apart and bead at the edges. If the drying contraction is great enough, the adhesion of the glaze to the body will be weak, causing portions to flake off during the initial water-smoking period of the cycle.
- On the other hand, a glaze application that is too thin will result in a poor, dry surface. This is especially true of mat glazes.
- If a second glaze coating is applied over a completely dry first coat, blisters will form. The wetting of the lower glaze layer causes it to expand and pull away from the body.
- If the bisque ware is considerably cooler than the glaze at the time of application, bubbles and blisters may develop later.
- Glazes high in colemanite should be applied immediately after mixing. If they are allowed to set, they thicken from the deflocculating effect of the colemanite. The extra water necessary to restore their consistency causes the glaze to separate and crawl in drying. A type of colemanite called gerstley borate should be used if possible, because it is less apt to settle. The addition of 0.5 to 1 percent soda ash or 3 percent Veegum T will retard the tendency of colemanite to thicken.
- Bristol glazes require perfect surface application. Because of their viscosity, thin areas will pull apart and crawl when fired.

Defects Originating in Firing

- If freshly glazed ware is placed in the kiln and fired immediately, the hot moisture will loosen the glaze, causing blisters and crawling.
- Too-rapid firing will prevent gases from escaping normally. They will form tiny seeds and bubbles in the glaze. For some especially viscous glazes, a prolonged soaking period is needed to remove these bubbles.
- Excessive reduction will result in black and gray spots on the body and glaze and will produce a dull surface.
- Gas-fired kilns with poor muffles using manufactured gas are troublesome to use with lead glazes. The sulfur content in the combustion gases will dull the glaze surfaces and possibly form blisters and wrinkles.
- Overfiring generally causes glazes to run excessively and clay bodies to distort and crack.

Defects in Glaze Composition

- Glazes that are not adjusted properly to the body are susceptible to stresses that may cause the glaze, and at times even the body, to crack. If the glaze contracts at a slower rate than the body does in cooling, it undergoes compression. This causes the glaze to crack and, in places, to buckle and separate from the body. This defect is commonly known as *shivering*.
- Slightly similar to shivering, and also caused by unequal contraction rates in cooling, is *crazing* of the glaze. When this happens, the glaze contracts at a greater rate than the body, causing numerous cracks to form.
- Glazes that run excessively at normal firing temperatures should be adjusted by the addition of kaolin to increase the refractory quality of the glaze or, if possible, by changing the bases.
- A dull surface will result if the proportion of silica to alumina or barium is too low.
- An excessive amount of tin, rutile, or colored spinels, which are relatively insoluble, will also cause a dull or rough-surfaced glaze.
- Bristol and colemanite glazes not fitted properly to the body will tend to crawl or to crack. This may be due in part to an excess of zinc, usually contained in these glazes. Zinc has a very high contraction rate at greater temperatures.
- Glazes ground too finely—thus releasing soluble salts from the frits, feldspar, and so forth—will develop pinholes and bubbles.
- Glazes that are allowed to stand too long may be affected by the decomposition of carbonates, organic matter in ball clay, or gum binders. Gases thus formed can result in pinholes and bubbles in the final glaze. In some instances, preservatives like formaldehyde will help. If washed, dried, and reground, the same glaze can be used again without difficulty.

7

Glazes: Formulation and Types

A ceramic glaze and its formulation are not as mysterious as they seem to most beginning pottery students. Basically, a glaze is nothing more than a thin, glasslike coating that is fused to a clay surface by the heat of a kiln. While some glaze compositions are quite elaborate and use a variety of chemical compounds, a glaze can be made from only three necessary elements: silica, the glass former; a flux, or glass melter; and alumina, the refractory element.

Silica The essential glaze ingredient is *silica*, also called flint. In its pure, crystalline state it is known as quartz. Were it not that the melting point of silica is so high—about 3100°F (1700°C)—this single material would suffice to form a glaze. Most earthenware clays, however, mature at about 2000°F (1093°C) and will seriously deform if fired higher, while most stoneware and porcelain bodies mature between 2250°F and 2400°F (1238–1315°C). Thus, pure silica cannot be used alone on these bodies.

242 Pat Probst Gilman, U.S.A. *Dragon and Hibiscus.* Vase. Porcelain, with carved decoration and elaborate handles, fired to cone 10, clear glaze; height 24.5″ (62.2 cm).

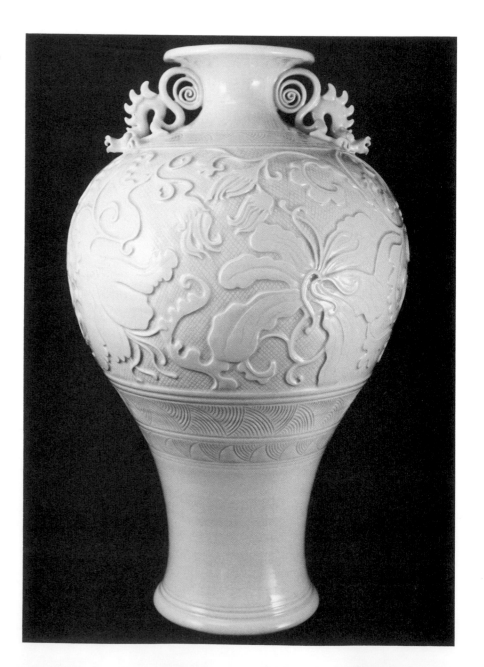

Flux A compound that lowers the melting point of a glaze is called a *flux*. Fortunately, many chemicals with a low melting point will readily combine with silica to form a glassy crystal. Two types of materials are commonly used as fluxes in low-fire glazes: *lead oxides* (lead carbonate, red lead, galena, and litharge) and *alkaline compounds* (borax, colemanite, soda ash, boric acid, and bicarbonate of soda). Although these two categories of low-fire fluxes have comparable fluxing power, their effects on glaze colorants and many of their other qualities are different (see Chap. 8). The chief high-fire fluxes are the alkaline earth compounds that melt at higher temperatures: calcium carbonate (also called whiting), dolomite (containing both calcium and magnesium), and barium carbonate.

Refractory elements A *refractory element* helps to form a stronger glaze that will better withstand the wear of normal use. The glaze produced solely by a mixture of silica and a flux would be soft and rather runny. A third ingredient, alumina, is therefore added to the glaze to make it harder and to prevent excessive running. Silica and alumina unite to form tough, needlelike mullite crystals, creating a bond more resistant to abrasion and shock.

Simple Formulation

In its final composition, then, a glaze includes its three necessary elements: silica, the glass former; a flux, which lowers the fusion point of silica; and alumina to give increased hardness to the glaze and increased viscosity.

It is not economically practical to use refined and pure ingredients to make up glazes. The compounds employed by the potter are usually those minerals that are abundant in nature in a relatively pure state. Therefore, a simple, low-fire glaze will consist of the following:

kaolin ($Al_2O_3 \cdot 2SiO_2 \cdot 2H_2O$)
potash feldspar ($K_2O \cdot Al_2O_3 \cdot 6SiO_2$)
gerstley borate ($2CaO \cdot 3B_2O_3 \cdot 5H_2O$)

The silica content will be provided by both the clay (kaolin) and the feldspar. Alumina is also a constituent of both kaolin and feldspar. *Feldspars* are minerals that contain alumina, silica, and varying amounts of potash, sodium, and calcium. The predominant flux gives its name to the compound, such as soda feldspar. Potash feldspar, the more common type, is slightly cheaper and fires harder and higher than soda feldspar. Feldspar should be considered only incidentally as a flux in the low-fire range, since it is an important source of silica and alumina. In addition to aiding the fusion of the glaze ingredients, a flux also combines with the silica contained in the clay body of the pot to form a bond uniting the body and the glaze. This union becomes stronger as the temperature increases. Occasionallly, a porous clay will absorb so much flux that the glaze will become thin and rough and require adjustments to either the glaze or the body.

Low-Fire Glaze Tests

In order to gain an understanding of the qualities imparted to the glaze by silica, alumina, and the flux, the beginner should make several tests with varying proportions of feldspar, kaolin, and gerstley borate fired to cone 04.

Earthenware tiles 2 by 3 inches (2.54 to 7.62 cm) and 0.25 inches (0.64 cm) thick make satisfactory tests. These should be bisque fired to about cone 010. The glaze samples should always be fired upright to detect a tendency in the glaze to run. The bottom quarter inch of each tile is left unglazed to catch the drips and evaluate the fluidity of the glaze.

A suggested beginning formula for a cone 04 glaze test is the following:

3 parts gerstley borate
3 parts feldspar
4 parts kaolin

Unless the scales are extremely accurate, a total sample of 100 grams is advisable. After weighing, the ingredients are ground in a mortar, and water is added until a creamy consistency is obtained. Modern ceramic materials are finely ground, so only a brief mixing is needed for a small sample. The glaze is brushed on a clean, dust-free tile in several thin coats. Experience is the only guide to the proper thickness of application. Cracks will develop if a layer is too heavy. In succeeding tests the feldspar is left constant, the kaolin decreased, and the gerstley borate increased by the amount necessary to replace the kaolin. The total number of parts should be kept at 10, so that valid comparisons can be made. This process is repeated until the clay content is reduced to one part. The clay also functions as a binder to hold the nonplastic ingredients together; thus, if no clay is present, methocel or another binder must be added.

The fired samples will show a gradual change from a claylike white coating to one that becomes more fluid and glassy as the increased flux combines with the silica. Finally, a point is reached at which the glaze runs excessively. This tendency can be retarded by substituting additional feldspar for some gerstley borate. At different firing temperatures the necessary proportions of flux, alumina, and silica will vary. When the temperature exceeds 2050°F (1130°C), the low-fire fluxes in the glaze must be replaced gradually by calcium carbonate (whiting), the principal high-fire flux. At temperatures above 2100°F (1150°C) the lead and alkaline fluxes will tend to run immoderately and are used only in minute quantities. A glaze can have a different crystalline surface structure because of variations in the proportion of alumina to silica. A slight excess of alumina produces a mat instead of a glassy finish; either too much or too little silica will result in a rough surface. Silica in its pure form can easily be added to a glaze if this should prove necessary.

After completing successful glaze test with these three basic ingredients, the potter can substitute for all or part of the feldspar other materials such as nepheline syenite, spodumene, lepidolite, or Cornwall stone. Further possibilities are cryolite, talc, and dolomite, which fire at slightly lower temperatures. Although some of these compounds contain silica and alumina, their main purpose is in varying and increasing the proportion of flux. These additions can affect the color and surface quality of the glaze. The principal advantages of having several fluxes in a glaze are the extension of the firing range and the more complete fusion of the chemicals with fewer glaze defects. (See Chap. 8 for more specific details about these materials.)

Barium carbonate additions will produce a mat glaze in situations where increasing the alumina content is not convenient. Zinc oxide can be added to the glaze in small quantities to obtain more fluxing action and reduce surface defects. It is essential that the glaze and the body cool and contract at the same rate after firing. If the body is weak and underfired, a contracting glaze may cause it to crack. Uneven contractions are also responsible for crazing. If sufficient tensions exist, the glaze will eventually craze, although this may not occur for days or even years. Expansions resulting from moisture collecting in a porous body may have a similar effect. On a decorative piece, tiny hairline cracks can add to the interest of the total design. If they are intentional, such effects are called *crackle glazes* to distinguish them from the unexpected and undesirable crazing.

Elimination of crazing is necessary in all functional ware to prevent seepage of moisture and to avoid odors resulting from trapped food particles. Changes can be made in the clay body to increase or reduce contraction and thereby adjust it to the glaze. The addition of silica to either the body or the glaze is one method used to prevent crazing. In the body the crystal formation developed by excess silica usually increases contraction, but in the glaze's glassy state silica is more likely to produce an expansion. Generally a potter has developed a satisfactory body with desired plasticity, vitrification, and so forth, and for this reason experimental glazes are adjusted to fit the body, rather than the other way around.

Although gerstley borate and colemanite are roughly similar in composition, colemanite has a greater tendency to settle in the glaze, making gerstley borate the preferred flux.

High-Fire Glaze Tests

High-fire glazes tests differ from those in the low-fire range only in the substitution of calcium carbonate ($CaCO_3$), commonly called whiting, for the low-melting lead and alkaline compounds. In this experiment tiles must be made from a stoneware or porcelain body. A good starting formula for a cone 6 to 8 glaze would be the following:

4 parts kaolin
4 parts potash feldspar
2 parts whiting

This will produce a sample that is white and claylike in character. In succeeding tests the whiting is held constant, the amount of feldspar gradually increased, and the proportion of the more refractory kaolin decreased. As the kaolin is lessened, the test glazes will become smoother and glassier. Depending upon the temperature, a satisfactory glaze should be achieved at the point when the kaolin content is between 10 and 20 percent. Throughout this series of tests the fusion point of the glaze has been lowered by the addition of the active flux, potash, which is contained in the feldspar. Only at higher temperatures can feldspar be considered a flux, since it is also a major source of alumina and silica.

A successful stoneware glaze can be made using only feldspar, kaolin, and whiting. As mentioned earlier, however, it may be desirable to add small amounts of other chemicals to obtain a greater firing range, achieve a better adjustment to the body, provide a more varied color spectrum, and develop a surface free from minor defects. Flint can easily be added to supply silica, if it should be needed.

The potter should attempt to vary the basic glaze to produce a glossy surface, a mat surface, and one that is fairly opaque (without the use of an opacifier such as tin oxide). Substitutions of some of the feldsparlike materials with different fluxes, such as lepidolite or nepheline syenite, can be tried.

Safety Caution

You must observe certain precautions in using glaze chemicals and certain glazes and in firing procedures. The various glaze chemicals, while often not toxic in themselves, are, like clay dust, injurious when inhaled. These effects are multiplied if you are a cigarette smoker. Therefore, you should wear a mask when emptying large vats of chemicals, which is a dusty operation. A well-ventilated spray booth is a must when spraying glazes.

Certain chemicals are very toxic when inhaled in dust form, allowed to enter the body through a cut in the skin, used in an unstable glaze, or given off as a gas during firing. Lead is well known today as a poison, but other fluxes such as barium, boric acid, borax, sodium, lithium carbonate, arsenic, and antimony are also toxic, often in minute amounts. Many colorants such as cadmium, chromium, copper sulfate, ferrous sulfate, iron chromate, manganese dioxide, vanadium pentoxide, and praseodymium are all toxic when used improperly. Of course, there are many other toxic chemicals, but they are rarely used in ceramics.

You must not only avoid breathing in the chemical dust and beware of skin cuts and food contamination, but you must also make certain that the glaze used is stable. A formula for a safe lead cone 06 glaze is given on p. 327. Glazes that are improperly compounded or underfired and therefore rough and scaly should not be used for food containers.

While most injurious gases pass out of the chimney during the firing of a fuel kiln, there is some leakage. During a reduction the kiln room must be especially well ventilated for the release of CO, which can cause asphyxiation. If the kiln is in the studio, drop panels from the ceiling should enclose the kiln area to localize the fumes and allow for an efficient use of the exhaust fan. Salt kilns need special precautions since the chlorine released is very toxic. Usually, however, such kilns are placed in an outside shed. Contrary to popular belief, an electric kiln should also have a hood and an exhaust fan, as toxic fumes seep out of the kiln during firing. A very small port, both below and above, is also desirable to clear the kiln atmosphere (see p. 278).

Often small amounts of another flux will result in a great improvement in a glaze. Other suggested additions are zinc oxide, talc, and barium carbonate. (See Chap. 8 for more detailed information on these and other chemicals, including colorants that will be used in further tests.)

Glaze Types

At the beginning of this chapter we stressed the simplicity of formulating a glaze. Indeed, a functional and attractive glaze can be made from only a few materials. Several glazes, however, use rather uncommon ingredients or require special firing techniques. The glaze recipes in the Appendix will clarify the general descriptions of the glazes that follow.

The glaze types have been grouped into two general categories—low fire and high fire. Low-fire glazes are those that fire generally between cone 020 and cone 04. High-fire glazes mature between cones 6 and 10. Some identify a third classification—medium-fire glazes, which mature between cones 02 and 4. Medium-fire glazes frequently exhibit some qualities of each of the two extremes.

In addition to these temperature categories, there are a number of special glazes formulated to give particular effects. Some of these fire predominantly in either the high or the low range, but others span the entire firing spectrum.

High-Fire Glazes

High-fire glazes generally are compounded to fire in a range from cone 6 to cone 14, or 2250°F to 2500°F (1230–1370°C). At these extreme temperatures, common low-fire fluxes, such as lead and borax, must be replaced with calcium carbonate, which has a higher melting point—about 1500°F (816°C).

Porcelain and stoneware glazes are identical, except in situations where adjustments must be made to accommodate a difference in firing shrinkage. Because feldspar is a major ingredient in such glazes, the term *feldspathic glaze* is often applied to stoneware glazes. Because of the high temperature, the union of glaze and body is quite complete. The interlocking mullite crystals prevent detection of the line of junction that is easily visible between a glassy glaze and a porous earthenware body. Feldspathic glazes are very hard (they cannot be scratched by steel), and they resist most acids, the exceptions being hydrofluoric, phosphoric, and hot sulfuric acids. The surfaces may be either mat or smooth, but they never reveal the high gloss of low-fire glazes.

Medium-Fire Glazes

Glazes firing between cones 02 and 4 contain both high- and low-fire fluxes in order to adjust to these temperature limits. (See Appendix for glaze recipes.) Generally, they combine the smooth, glossy surface and potential for bright colors of lead and alkaline glazes with the more durable heat and shock resistance of higher-firing glazes. There are also many commercially prepared glazes available in the medium-fire range providing a wide spectrum of colors—purples, yellows, reds, and oranges—difficult to achieve in the high-fire glazes and more likely to chip and crack in the lower-fire range. Many hand potters and sculptors are working with the very stable glazes in this medium-fire range for the bright designs and details they make possible. Another desirable feature is the energy saving in firing to lower temperatures.

Low-fire Glazes

Most low-fire glazes can be further subdivided into two distinct groups—alkaline or lead—according to the major flux included in the glaze. Both fire in the range of cone 016 to cone 02, and both result in smooth, glossy surfaces. They often are characterized by bright, shiny colors.

Alkaline Glazes   Alkaline glazes use such fluxes as borax, colemanite, or soda ash, which encourage bright color effects, particularly turquoise-blues. Because of their extreme solubility, alkaline glazes should never be applied to raw ware. When absorbed into the clay, the expansions and contractions that alkaline compounds undergo during firing and cooling will cause the body to crack.

A very soft bisque ware also reacts poorly to an alkaline glaze, for it will absorb a portion of the flux, leaving an incomplete and usually rough-textured glaze after firing. Becuase of their solubility and tendency to become lumpy in the glaze solution, the alkaline compounds (such as borax) are often fritted into a nonsoluble silicate form. Colemanite gives a milky blue tinge to the glaze, while the lead compounds are completely transparent. Alkaline glazes are generally more successful when used on a body fairly high in silica.

Lead Glazes The most common fluxes for lead glazes are oxides of lead compounds—lead carbonate and red lead. A very active flux that melts at about 950°F (510°C), lead gives glazes a bright and glossy surface.

In general, the lead glaze should be high in alumina and calcium. Additions of zinc, barium, and zirconium will also make the glaze more successful. Lead has the disadvantage of being very poisonous. Because lead dust or particles are dangerous, lead is often converted into a nontoxic silicate form by *fritting*. Fritting is a procedure by which a flux and silica are melted and later ground. The resulting frit, which is added to the glaze, makes the glaze both nontoxic and insoluble in water and should pose no problems during application. However, if the final composition is unstable, the ware should not be used to store food.

In spite of their being a potential health hazard, lead glazes should not be overlooked. They produce uniquely soft and shiny surfaces. In the past, lead glazes made opaque and whitish by the addition of tin to the glaze were commonly used on Spanish and Italian earthenware (see Chap. 3 and Plate 6, p. 57. Today lead glazes are ideal for low-fired earthenware sculpture.

243 Leoni Alfonso, Italy. Sculptural construction. Earthenware, with a tin-lead-based white majolica glaze; height 12″ (30 cm).

Special Glazes and Effects

Ash Glazes Ash glazes were probably the first glazes used. At present they have no commercial application, but they are of interest to the studio potter. The ash can derive from any wood, grass, or straw. Depending upon the specific source, the chemical composition can vary considerably: it is generally very high in silica and contains some alumina and calcium; moderate amounts of fluxes, such as potash, soda, and magnesia; plus iron and small quantities of numerous other compounds. Because of the high silica content, ash can seldom be used in low-fire glazes in amounts over 15 to 20 percent. This is not sufficient to make much change in the basic glaze.

A suggested starting point for a stoneware ash-glaze test would be the following:

40 parts ash
40 parts feldspar
20 parts whiting

244 Bernard Leach, England. Vase. Stoneware with a combed decoration and a runny ash glaze.

245 John Gill, U.S.A. *Housepot.* Stoneware with slip and sgrafitto decoration under a wood-ash glaze.

Fireplace ashes should be collected in a fairly large quantity and then mixed thoroughly to ensure uniformity. The ash is first run through a coarse sieve to remove unburned particles. It can then be soaked in water that is decanted several times to remove soluble portions. Many potters, however, prefer to run the dry ash through a fine sieve without washing (taking care not to inhale the fine ash particles), and thus retain the soluble fluxes. The latter procedure will allow a larger percentage of ash to be used in the final glaze.

While wood ash can be incorporated into a glaze and fired in an electric, oil, or gas kiln, an ash glaze can also be the accidental result of a long firing in a wood-burning kiln. Results are not predictable, because much depends upon the placement in the kiln, the path of the flame, and the length of firing. These factors cause the ash to be deposited on the ware in an uneven fashion, much like the effects of salt glazes. See Plates 32 and 33, p. 215.

Salt Glazes Salt glazes have enjoyed a revival in recent years after a long period of neglect by the studio potter. From the twelfth to the mid-nineteenth century, such glazes were common in Germany and England and, in the later two centuries, in Colonial America. Commercial applications today are limited to stoneware crocks, glazed sewer pipe, hollow building brick, and similar products.

Salt-glazing is a simple procedure. The ware is fired to its body-maturing temperature, at which time common salt (sodium chloride) is thrown into the firebox or through ports entering the kiln chamber. This sodium combines with the silica in the clay to form a glassy silicate. Adding a small amount of borax will reduce the firing temperature but often results in a shiny glaze.

246 Tim Storey, Canada. *Definitive Dragon.* Porcelain body with sprigged and stamped decoration, slip and stain under a salt glaze, low-fire metallic lusters added later; length 14″ (35 cm).

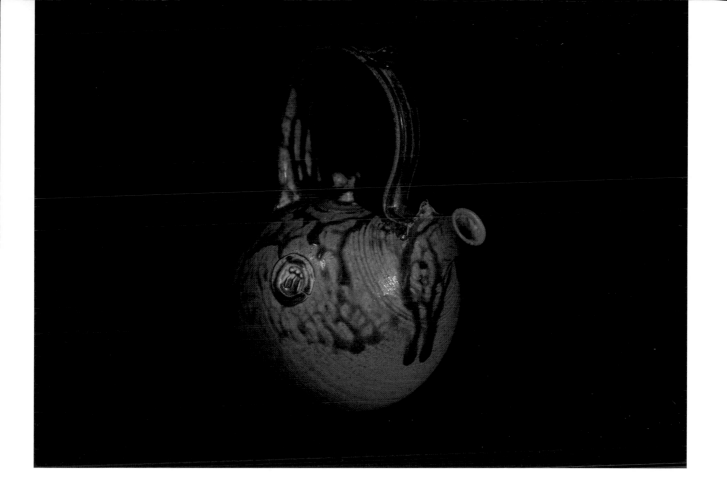

above: **Plate 32   Angelo Garzio**, U.S.A. Stoneware teapot. Thrown as a bottle form, then flattened on the side to form a base. Opening cut to form cover, with a pulled handle added. Runny wood ash glaze, height 10″ (25.4 cm).

left: **Plate 33   Paul Dresang**, U.S.A. Footed jar with applied and carved clay decoration. Stoneware with wood ash and salt glaze at cone 10, height 5.5″ (14 cm).

above: Plate 34 Don Reitz, U.S.A.
Platter. Sprayed color accents of rutile,
cobalt, and iron under a salt glaze.
Form altered with clay additions,
diameter 22″ (55 cm).

right: Plate 35 David Keator, U.S.A.
Covered jar. Raku black smoked body
with varied decorations in a crackled
white slip and low-fired glazes, height
14″ (35.5 cm).

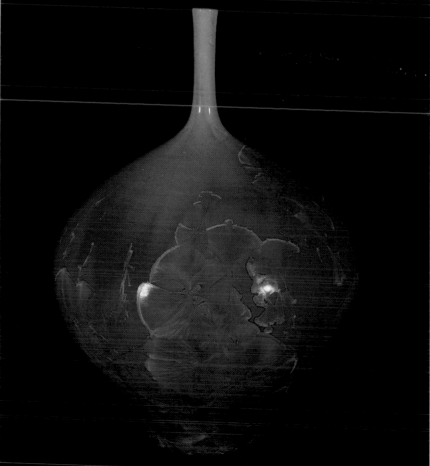

Plate 36   Tom Turner, U.S.A.
Covered bowl. Porcelain with copper-red reduction glaze and a trailed decoration, diameter 8.5″ (21.6 cm).

Plate 37   Tony Menzer, U.S.A.
Porcelain bottle. Zinc crystalline glaze with yellow, cobalt, and copper colorants, height 18″ (45.7 cm).

217

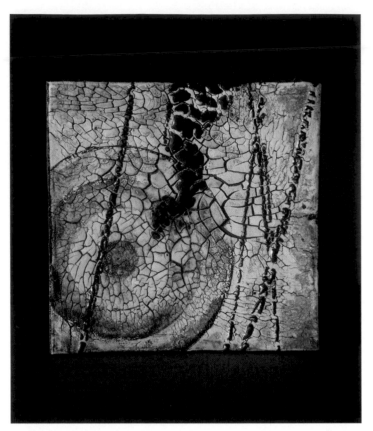

Plate 38 Robert Sperry, U.S.A. Wall tile. Stoneware with thick crackled engobe. Low-fire glaze accents, 16″ (40 cm) square.

Plate 39 Walter Hyleck, U.S.A. Porcelain dish. Cobalt stain and clear glaze fired to cone 10. Low-fired overglaze colors and luster fired to cone 016 to 020, diameter 16″ (40.6 cm).

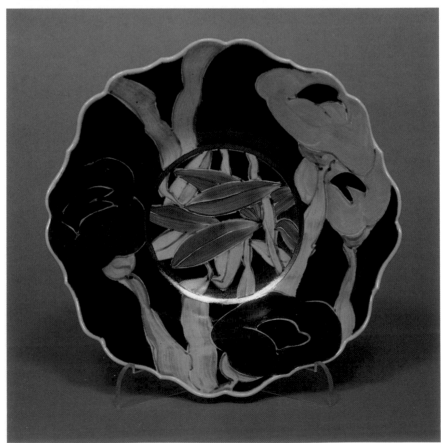

For salt-glazing, the usual stoneware or porcelain body is often satisfactory. Additionals of silica and feldspar may be necessary, however, to obtain a good glaze coating. Under reducing conditions (incomplete combustion to introduce carbon into the kiln atmosphere), buff or red clays will develop a pebbly brown or black glaze. Other colors can be obtained only by using colored slips or body stains. In addition, iridescent effects much like lusters can be produced by fuming. The kiln is cooled to a low red heat (about cone 020). With the draft and burner ports open, combinations of stannous chloride, ferric chloride, and bismuth, sodium, or silver nitrates are introduced into the kiln through the burner ports. Unique copper-reds are achieved by reducing the ware after copper oxide has been introduced by fuming. Other color oxides can be thrown into the kiln during the salting procedure. See Plate 34, p. 216.

Whatever coloring devices are employed, the glaze will have a mottled and pebbly surface. The salt does not collect on the sharper edges of plastic additions or in incised decoration, so that a natural contrast develops between fully and thinly glazed areas. Because the salt does not reach the insides of closed forms or tall bottles, the insides should be glazed in the normal manner.

The major disadvantage of the salt glaze is that it coats the whole interior of the kiln. This makes the kiln unsuitable for bisque and other types of glaze firing. The firing range of salt glazes is wide, from cones 02 to 12, but the most common firings are between cones 5 and 8. (See Chap. 9, p. 287, for more specifics on the salting technique.)

Raku Glazes Raku glazes are applied to stoneware bodies containing a high proportion of grog, usually 30 percent of the body, in order to withstand the rapid heating and cooling involved in the firing process. (See Chap. 9 for raku firing techniques.) Because the firing temperature may be as low as 1750°F (955°C) or cone 09, the glaze can consist of 80 percent gerstley borate and 20 percent potash feldspar. Low-firing borosilicate frits can also be used and will eliminate the lumpiness resulting from the borax.

The glaze is applied to bisque ware. Because of the low firing temperature, the stoneware body remains underfired, and the glaze is not waterproof. The speed of the firing, the exposure to open flame, and the reducing atmosphere and smoking result in a great variety of unusual and unpredictable glaze effects. Copper oxides tend to develop reds and lusters, red iron oxide becomes black, and deep crackle patterns occur.

Raku ware is associated with the Japanese tea ceremony as described in Chapter 3. Raku tea bowls are usually handbuilt and irregular, allowing the effects of the firing to complete the decorative design. The high grog content and the firing process tend to limit the size and shapes of raku forms, although many contemporary potters have greatly expanded the scope of raku ware. See Plate 35, p. 216.

Reduction Glazes Reduction glazes are those especially compounded to develop their unique color characteristics only if fired in a kiln capable of maintaining a reducing atmosphere during certain portions of the firing cycle. The normal kiln firing is an oxidizing fire. An electric kiln always has an oxidizing fire, since there is nothing in the kiln atmosphere to consume the oxygen that is always present. To reduce the atmosphere in a gas or oil kiln, the draft is cut back to lessen the air intake, resulting in an incomplete com-

 Safety Caution

Since deadly chlorine gas is released at the moment of salting, you should have a well-ventilated studio. The toxic chlorine and hydrochloric fumes have caused potters to search for alternatives to sodium chloride. Of these, sodium bicarbonate seems the most successful. Because of its higher melting point and lower vapor pressure, you should introduce the sodium bicarbonate through a burner or porthole with a blower attachment to ensure its distribution throughout the kiln.

bustion that releases carbon into the kiln interior. In a closed blower-type kiln with a forced-air system, the air intake is reduced. In a muffle kiln, some of the muffles will have to be removed to allow the combustion gases to enter the kiln chamber.

Carbon has a great affinity for oxygen when heated and will steal it from the iron and copper-coloring oxides in the glaze. It was in this manner that the Chinese produced their famous copper-reds (sang-de-boeuf) and gray-greens (celadons). See Plate 2, p. 39. When either copper or iron oxide is deprived of its oxygen, it remains suspended in the glaze as the pure colloidal metal. Thus a normal green copper glaze becomes a beautiful ruby red (Plate 36, p. 217) with occasional blue or purple tints. The iron oxide loses its customary brownish-red tone and takes on a variety of soft gray-green hues. In small muffle kiln, a reduction can occur if pine splinters or moth balls are inserted into the peephole. The usual reduction fire starts with an oxidizing fire, and reduction does not begin until just before the melting of the first elements of the glaze. After the reduction cycle, the firing must return to oxidation in order to develop a surface free from pinholes and other defects (see Chap. 9).

Reduction can also affect the color of a stoneware body. Stoneware that is light gray or tan in oxidation becomes darker gray or even brown under reducing conditions. The iron particles contained in most stoneware become darker and melt into the glaze, making it speckled.

A local copper reduction can be achieved by using a small amount (about 0.5 percent) of silicon carbide (carborundum) in the glaze. The effects are slightly different from the standard reduction, for the color is concentrated in little spots around the silicon carbide particles. But this technique has an advantage in that it can be used in an electric kiln, since the heating elements are in no way affected. The firing range of copper-red and celadon reduction glazes is quite wide, ranging from about cone 08 all the way up through the porcelain temperatures.

247 Mayer Shacter, U.S.A. *Comet Catcher #11.* Covered jar. 1982. Porcelain, thrown with pinched-slab handle, celedon glaze with copper-red accents, 13″ × 11″ (33 × 28 cm).

Mat Glazes Mat glazes generally are formed either by adding an excess of alumina or by substituting barium carbonate for some of the flux in the glaze. Therefore, they are often called alumina mats or barium mats. A mat glaze should not be confused with a thin, rough, or underfired glaze. It should be smooth to the touch, with neither gloss nor transparency. The mat effects sometimes observed on an underfired glaze are caused by incompletely dissolved particles, whereas a true mat develops a different surface crystalline structure. An unusually long cooling time will encourage the formation of mat textures. One test for a true mat is to cool the glaze quickly to see if it will develop a shine. A mat surface caused by the incomplete fusion of particles will continue to have a mat surface, regardless of the cooling time. It is generally a bit rough to the touch and lacks the smoothness of a true mat. Mats can be calculated for all temperatures, but they are particularly attractive in the low-fire ranges, since typical lead and borax glazes are so shiny that their glare tends to obscure all decoration and form. Mat glazes are related to the crystalline group, because both depend upon the surface structure of the glaze for their effects. Therefore, mats can also be made with iron, zinc, and titanium (rutile) when properly compounded and cooled slowly.

Crackle Glazes Crackle glazes cannot be characterized by their composition, for they are merely the result of tensions that arise when a glaze and a body expand and contract at different rates. In most glazes, except perhaps the mats, a crackle can be produced. The simplest way is to substitute similar-acting fluxes for others having difficult contration rate. The reverse is true if a noncrackling glaze is desired. Sodium has the highest expansion rate, followed by potassium. Calcium has about half the rate of expansion of these, lead and barium follow, with boron and magnesium having the lowest expansion rates of commonly used fluxes.

A crackle is a network of fine cracks in the glaze. It must be used on a light body to be seen properly. To strengthen the effect, a coloring oxide or

above: **248 Luke Lindoe**, Canada. Footed bowl. Stoneware with incised decoration and heavy crackle glaze; height 9″ (22 cm).

left: **249 Harlan House**, Canada. Bowl and vases. Porcelain with crackle glazes; vase height 9.5″ (24.1 cm), bowl width 10″ (25.4 cm).

strong black tea is often applied to the crackled area. The Chinese were able to achieve, by successive firings, a network of both large and fine crackles, each stained with a different coloring oxide. A crackle glaze is more practical on a vitreous stoneware or porcelain body because a crackle on a porous earthenware pot will allow liquids to seep through. See Plate 38, p. 218.

Crystalline Glazes There are two types of crystalline glazes. The more common, macrocrystalline, has large crystal clusters embedded in or on the surface of the glaze; the second type, called aventurine, has single crystals, often small, suspended in the glaze, which catch and reflect the light. These are interesting glazes technically, but they must be very careful related to the pot shape. The jewellike effects seem to float off the surface of all but the most simple and reserved forms. See Plate 37, p. 217.

The crystalline formation is encouraged by additions of zinc and iron or by titanium (rutile). Borax and soda can also be used, preferably in a fritted form, but lead is not advisable. The alumina content must be very low and is in fact absent from some crystalline formulas. The silica content is also lower than in most glazes.

A mat glaze is actually an example of a microscopic aventurine-type glaze. Possible firing ranges are wide, and, as with mat formations, the rate of cooling is most important. In order to allow the crystals to develop properly, the temperature of the kiln should be permitted to drop only about 100°F (38°C) after maturity, and it must be held at this level for several hours before slow cooling. Crystalline glazes are quite runny, so a pedestal of insulating

250 Tony Menzer, U.S.A. Jar. Porcelain with zinc crystalline green and blue-green glaze; height 12″ (30.48 cm).

GLAZES: FORMULATION AND TYPES

brick should be cut to the foot size and placed under the ware. The potter can also throw a separate foot ring, coat it with kiln wash, and place it under the ware. If fired high or given an especially heavy glaze application, the piece can be set in a shallow bisque bowl that will collect any excess glaze that might run off the sides.

Luster Glazes Historically, luster glazes consisted of a thin, decorative metallic coating fired over a tin-lead glaze. This coating was a solution of pine resin, bismuth nitrate, and a metallic salt dissolved in oil of lavender. The luster was then fired to a low red heat in a reducing atmosphere sufficient to fuse the metal and burn off the resin, but not to melt the original glaze. This procedure made possible a variety of colors as well as iridescent sheens. The metals employed were lead and zinc acetates; copper, manganese, and cobalt sulfates; uranium nitrate; and even silver and gold compounds. Bismuth generally served as the flux. The luster was rarely an overall coating; rather it was applied in the form of a decorative design. This is especially true in Islamic ceramics, which featured intricate, interlocking decorative motifs, as described in Chapter 3.

Whereas the lusters of the Islamic potter contained imputities to soften their brilliance, commercial lusters used today are bright and strident. Their popularity reflects the chrome, stainless steel, and fluorescent lights of much contemporary sculpture. The lusters usually are fired in an electric kiln between cone 020 and cone 014 and are available in pearl-like iridescent hues and various colors—turquoise, blue, pink, red, gold, and silver. They can be brushed, sprayed, or drawn with special pens onto nearly any low-fire or stoneware glaze. See Plate 39, p. 218.

Frit Glazes Frit glazes may be little different chemically from the two low-fire types described earlier. Fritting is a process that renders raw-glaze materials either nontoxic to handle or nonsoluble. Lead or alkaline fluxes (borax or soda ash) are melted in a frit kiln with silica or with silica and a small amount of alumina. When the glaze becomes liquid, a plug is pulled in the bottom of the frit furnace, and the contents are discharged into a container filled with water. The fractured particles are then ground to the necessary fineness. Small amounts can be made in the studio using a crucible. One disadvantage of studio manufacture is the extremely long grinding time necessary to pulverize the frit to adequate fineness.

Many different types of frit glazes are commercially available. Frit composition is complicated, for nontoxic or nonsoluble elements must be completely absorbed within a satisfactory firing range and without creating later adjustment problems.

A frit glaze is seldom a complete glaze for several reasons. Since it is usually colorless, opacifiers or colorants must be added. The frit has little ability to adhere, so it is usually necessary to add a small amount of plastic clay or bentonite. Adjustments for the final firing ranges must also be made. Frits have extensive commercial use where large amounts of standard glaze are employed. For the studio potter, frits are of most value in eliminating the lumpy quality of borax needed in crystalline, copper reds, and similar glazes. Purchased in 100-pound (45.36-kg) lots, low-fire frits might well be used in schools to replace the small and expensive colored glaze packets often purchased. The addition of a few color oxides and kaolin would not raise the cost substantially.

 Safety Caution

A lead frit may be nontoxic to handle, but still you should not use it on pots that will hold acid foods.

Bristol Glazes   Bristol glazes are very similar, in most respects, to the typical porcelain glaze, except that a relatively large amount of zinc oxide is added. In most instances, this tends to lower the melting point and to add a certain opacity to the glaze. Calcium and barium should be included in the fluxes. Most Bristols fall into the cone 5 to 9 range, although formulas have been successfully developed for cones 3 to 14. The most common use of the Bristol glaze is for architectural tile and bricks.

Since a large amount of clay is normally used, the ware is generally given a single firing, and there is no problem of shrinkage. However, by calcining part of the clay, the glaze can be fitted to double firings. The commercial single fire usually takes 50 to 60 hours, not only because of the thickness of the ware being fired but also because of the extremely viscous nature of the Bristol glaze. It is this quality of the glaze that makes it valuable to the studio potter. Interesting effects can be achieved by using a Bristol glaze over a more fluid glaze that breaks through in spots. The application of the glaze must be perfect because its viscosity prevents any cracks that may occur from healing. Moreover, in firing, the edges of the cracks will pull farther apart and bead. In general, Bristol glazes are shiny, but they can be given a mat surface by increasing the amount of calcium while reducing the silica content.

Slip Glazes   Slip glazes are made from raw natural clays that contain sufficient fluxes to function as glazes without further preparation beyond washing and sieving. In practice, additions are often made to enable the slip glaze to fit the body or to modify the maturing temperature, but these changes are minor.

Slip glazes were commonly used by early American stoneware potteries that produced such utilitarian objects as storage crocks, bowls, mugs, and pitchers. Albany slip clay is the only commercial variety that is used widely. It fires brown-black at cones 6 to 10. The addition of 2 percent cobalt to Albany slip will result in a beautiful, semigloss jet black. Many slip clay deposits are not recognized as such. They are particularly common in the Great Lakes region—Indiana, Michigan, Minnesota, Wisconsin—and, like those in New York, are probably of glacial origin.

Barnard slip clay is somewhat similar to Albany slip clay, but it is lower in alumina and silica and has a much higher iron content. Red Dalton is higher in alumina and silica, but lower in fluxes. All fire to a brownish black and can be used in a combination or, depending upon the firing temperature, with added fluxes. Because of the natural contraction of slip clay during drying, the ware is best glazed and decorated in the leather-hard stage.

Frequently, earthenware clays can be used as slip clays when fired high enough and with the addition of small amounts of flux. Most slip clays fire from cone 4 to cone 12. Slip-clay fluxes are generally the alkaline earth compounds, plus iron oxide in varying amounts. A high iron content serves also to produce a color ranging from tan to dark brown.

The potter must be careful in using slip clays, for they are generally mined in small pits, and their composition will vary slightly. Each new shipment of material should be tested before being used in quantity. Some Albany slip is so lacking in the usual brown colorant that the resulting glaze is a pale, semitransparent tan. Studio potters should pay more attention to this group of glazes. Slip clays are easy to apply, adhere well, and fire with few, if any, defects. The composition, chemically, is most durable, and, since addi-

tions are few, much time can be saved in glaze preparation. Slip clays are particularly well suited for single-fire glazes.

Terra Sigillata Roman terra sigillata relief ware, black Etruscan bucchero pottery, and the so-called black varnish of the Greek red-and-black ware and some Pueblo pottery all had essentially the same semiglaze finish. These glazes were actually slips fired to low temperatures so that the surface was easily scratched and not completely waterproof. However, the unusual decorative qualities of the soft black and red colors have made terra sigillata ware popular with modern hand potters.

To prepare the slip, a low-firing, high-iron-content clay body in a dry state is mixed with a large quantity of water. To make a thinner slip, 3 or 4 percent soda ash will help to flocculate the clay. A large, plastic garbage can makes a good container. The slip should be allowed to settle for a day or two, and then the clear water on the surface should be siphoned off. The upper portion of slip should be poured off and the coarser clay that has settled to the bottom discarded. Adding more water to the slip and repeating the process will ensure that only the finest colloidal clay particles remain.

Like the higher-fire slip glazes just described, the terra sigillata slip should be applied when the body is leather hard. This reduces the flaking that can result from the different shrinkage rates of the body and the glaze. For a smoother surface, the glaze can be burnished with a hardwood or bone tool. The glaze can be sprayed on to form an overall coating or brushed on to create a pattern.

The firing technique is an important factor in revealing the decoration. If the atmosphere is oxidizing, the color will be a soft, semigloss red; in a reducing fire, the color will be black.

8

Glazes:
Calculations
and Chemicals

253 Masayuki Imai, Japan. Vase. Porcelain, with calligraphic wax-resist design under a brown-black mat glaze.

Years ago as a ceramics student the author was subjected to several lectures on glaze calculations. Neither he nor the other students had the slightest idea of what the instructor was talking about. Although there were one or two ceramic texts on the market, it was several years later before the author came across them and was able to gain an idea of what ceramic calculations were all about.

His first reaction was jubilation that he had discovered the perfect, scientific way to prepare glazes. Later he made his students do all these calculations in hopes that they too would come to this wonderful understanding. But as time went on he discovered that there were several flaws in the standard methods of glaze calculations, which meant that the final results were not completely accurate.

For example, feldspar is usually classified as only soda or potash feldspar. Yet, a look at the table in the Appendix reveals a great variety among the feldspars, including many elements not included in the basic formula used. The same is true of other complex compounds such as cornwall stone, nepheline syenite, plastic vitrox, and spodumene. Ceramic chemicals are not like pure drugs but rather are minerals dug from the earth and pulverized. The composition varies from mine to mine and even from year to year.

Yet there are certain ideas to be gained from a study of ceramic calculations, despite their inaccuracies. For example, the previous chapter mentioned the three parts of a glaze: silica, the glass former, flux, such as lead or potash; and alumina, the refractory agent. It is only through the process of glaze calculations that potters can separate the complex chemicals used in a glaze and finally end up with the total amounts of silica, flux, and alumina. In this manner one glaze can be compared with another. There are rough limits to the proportion of silica, flux, and alumina needed to produce a satisfactory glaze at a specific temperature. By reducing a problem glaze to an empirical glaze formula potters can better see and correct any deficiencies.

Calculations

A glaze may be written either as a batch glaze, consisting of the weights of the raw chemicals making up the glaze. Or it may be shown in the form of an empirical glaze formula in which the active ingredients are expressed in molecular proportions.

Molecular Formula

All matter is made up of approximately one hundred chemical elements in the form of atoms. These elements do not occur in nature in a pure form but in compounds, which are groups of atoms held together by an electrical attraction, or bond. The atom is much too small to be weighed, but it is possible to determine the relative weights of atoms to each other. They are assigned weights corresponding to their weights in relation to that of hydrogen, the lightest atom. For example, oxygen, symbolized by the letter O, has been given the atomic weight of 16 becuase it is sixteen times heavier than hydrogen.

GLAZES: CALCULATIONS AND CHEMICALS

Raw Material	Equivalents		Molecular Weights		Batch Weights
soda feldspar	.16	×	524	=	83.84
gerstley borate	.105	×	412	=	43.26
white lead	.21	×	775	=	162.75
boric acid	.175	×	124	=	21.70
kaolin	.12	×	258	=	30.96
silica	1.60	×	60	=	96.00
zirconium oxide	.03	×	123	=	3.69
					442.20

Dividing the individual batch weights by 442.20 produces a batch recipe expressed in percentages. This is the original glaze recipe.

Original Batch Recipe

Raw Material	Parts by Weight
soda feldspar	18.95
gerstley borate	9.78
white lead	36.78
boric acid	4.90
kaolin	6.80
silica	21.70
zirconium oxide	.83
	99.74

Limit Formulas

In the glaze experiments described in Chapter 7, no definite limits were mentioned regarding the ratio between the RO, R_2O_3, and RO_2 parts in a glaze. This is because the major purpose of these glaze tests was to gain familiarity with the qualities of the various glaze chemicals. The previous analyses have shown that there are general limits to the amounts of alumina and silica that can be used successfully in relation to a single unit of flux. The firing temperature and the type of flux are also important factors in establishing limits.

256 Dieter Crumbiegel, West Germany. Bottle. Stoneware construction of textured slabs with overlapping glazes; width 12″ (30 cm).

In the several limit formulas a number of possible fluxes are indicated; however, the total amount used must add up to a unit of one. In general, a higher proportion of alumina will result in a mat surface, provided the kiln is cooled slowly. Barium will also tend to create a mat surface. A study of these formulas indicates how the ratio of alumina and silica rises as the temperature increases. While not intended to take the place of glaze formulas, the listing should be a helpful guide to those seeking to change the temperature range of a favorite glaze. Some glaze chemicals are quite complex, and under certain conditions an addition to a glaze will not have the desired effect. By converting the batch recipes to empirical formulas and comparing them with the suggested limits, it ought to be possible to detect the direction of the error.

Limit Formulas

Cone 08–04 Lead glazes				Cone 08–04 Alkaline glazes			
PbO	0.2–0.60	Al_2O_3	0.15–0.20	PbO	0 –0.5	Al_2O_3	0.05–0.25
KNaO	0.1–0.25	B_2O_3	0.15–0.60	KNaO	0.4–0.8		
ZnO	0.1–0.25			CaO	0 –0.3	SiO_2	1.5 –2.5
CaO	0.3–0.60	SiO_2	1.5 –2.50	ZnO	0 –0.2		
BaO	0 –0.15						

Cone 2–5 Lead calcium glaze				Cone 2–5 Lead-borax glaze			
PbO	0.4–0.60	Al_2O_3	0.2–0.28	PbO	0.2 –0.3	Al_2O_3	0.25–0.35
CaO	0.1–0.40			KNaO	0.2 –0.3	B_2O_3	0.20–0.60
ZnO	0 –0.25	SiO_2	2.0–3.0	CaO	0.35–0.5		
KNaO	0.1–0.25			ZnO	0 –0.1	SiO_2	2.5 –3.5

Cone 2–5 Colemanite glaze				Cone 8–12 Stoneware glaze			
CaO	0.2–0.50	Al_2O_3	0.2–0.28	KNaO	0.2–0.40	Al_2O_3	0.3–0.5
ZnO	0.1–0.25	B_2O_3	0.3–0.6	CaO	0.4–0.70	B_2O_3	0.1–0.3
BaO	0.1–0.25			MgO	0 –0.35		
KNaO	0.1–0.25	SiO_2	2.0–3.0	ZnO	0 –0.30		
				BaO	0 –0.30	SiO_2	3.0–5.0

Variables in Glaze Formulation

Potters are frequently disappointed when a glaze obtained from a friend or from a textbook produces quite unexpected results. Several factors may be involved in this problem. Ingredients that are more finely ground than usual will melt at a slightly lower temperature. In the same way, fritted glaze additions melt more quickly than do raw compounds of a similar composition. Occasionally the thickness of application or reaction with the clay body will produce slightly different results. More distressing and troublesome is the variable nature of such major glaze ingredients as Cornwall stone and the feldspars.

In attempting to alter a glaze that has proved unsatisfactory, the potter has several simple remedies. If the glaze is too runny, the addition of flint or kaolin usually will raise the melting point; if it is too dry, an increase of flux will develop a more fluid glaze. Sometimes, however, the effect is quite the opposite, and in such situations the student, quite justifiably, may feel that the instructor who suggested the change does not know a great deal about glaze chemistry.

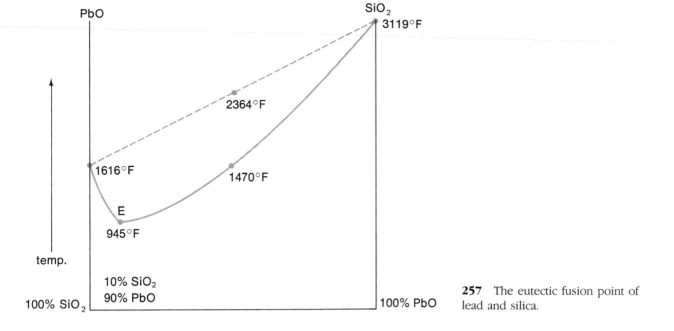

PbO

SiO$_2$
3119°F

2364°F

1616°F

1470°F

E

945°F

temp.

10% SiO$_2$
90% PbO

100% SiO$_2$

100% PbO

257 The eutectic fusion point of lead and silica.

The real culprit in many glaze failures is the chemical phenomenon known as a *eutectic*. A eutectic is the lowest point at which two or more chemicals will combine and melt. It is much lower than the melting point of any of the individual chemicals. For example, lead oxide has a melting point of 1616°F (880°C), and silica melts at 3119°F (1715°C). One might expect that a half-and-half mixture of lead and silica would melt at the halfway point, 2364°F (1300°C), yet the actual melting point is much lower, about 1470°F (800°C). The lowest melting point of lead and silica (the eutectic point) occurs at about 945°F (510°C), with a mixture of approximately 90 percent lead oxide and 10 percent silica. The line diagram in Figure 257 illustrates the relatively simple reaction between lead oxide and silica and the eutectic point at E.

In an actual glaze—compounded of complex minerals and containing several fluxes, alumina, and even different types of silica—the firing reaction is much more complicated. It is quite possible for there to be two and even more eutectic points.

Figure 258 (p. 238) shows a hypothetical reaction, with two eutectic points, between several fluxes and silica. The vertical movement represents the changing temperature of fusion as a portion of flux is replaced with a like amount of silica. Glazes that fall in areas B and C are more troublesome to potters, since a slight change in composition or temperature is critical. These are generally high-gloss glazes. In area B a small increase in silica will increase the gloss and raise the melting temperature, but in area C an increase in silica will lower the melting temperature and create a very runny glaze. The points E1, H, and E2 are especially troublesome, for a very slight temperature rise will change the character of the glaze. The most satisfactory glazes fall in the lower ranges of A and D. Because of the flattened curve in these areas, a slight change in temperature or silica is not likely to cause a great variation in the fired glaze. The alumina, calcium, zinc, and dolomite mat glazes fall in the lower area of A. As the silica is decreased in area A, the glazes

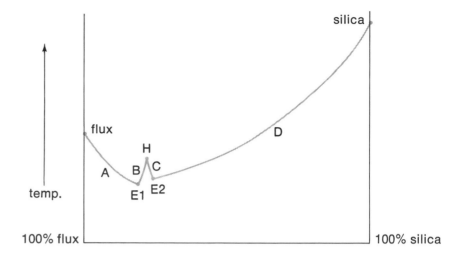

258 Although exaggerated, this line drawing demonstrates the unpredictable results caused by eutectic points in a glaze.

become more mat and finally become rough and incomplete with a very low proportion of silica. Transparent and majolica glazes fall in the lower area of D; these become less glossy as the ratio of silica and the temperature are raised. Although the area D glazes can be glossy like the unpredictable glazes in B and C, they are quite stable and little affected by slight changes in silica or temperature. Ash glazes fall in all areas; those in areas B and C are runny and unpredictable.

Figure 258 is a purely theoretical attempt to visualize the reactions betweeen the fluxes and silica. It does not represent an actual glaze, since the function of alumina is ignored. The more usual method of diagramming a glaze is shown in Figure 259. Here are the three major components of a glaze: fluxes, silica, and clay (alumina-silica). The small triangle at each apex contains 100 percent of the compound used. Moving along the base line of the

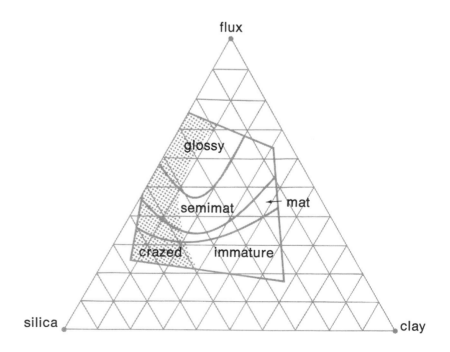

259 This chart shows the glaze types possible at cone 10 with various amounts of clay, silica, and fluxes.

238   GLAZES: CALCULATIONS AND CHEMICALS

silica-clay axis, the ratio becomes 90 percent silica to 10 percent clay (kaolin), then 80 percent silica to 20 percent clay, and so forth. Progressing vertically, the triangles contain an increasing amount of the first glaze components, the fluxes. The roughly square section in the center covers those glaze tests that at cone 10 (2426°F, 1330°C) fuse to form a glaze. As the gradient indicates, there is a change from mat to glossy as the fluxes are increased, and an area of crazed glazes where the alumina content is low. The clay content also has a decisive effect upon whether a glaze is to be glossy or mat. As indicated in both Figures 258 and 259, the mat and semimat glazes cover a much wider range of possible combinations at a given temperature. The sharp gradient of the glossy area in Figure 259 would suggest that the eutectic points for this particular glaze would fall in this range.

The use of a triaxial diagram for planning experiments has many applications in ceramics. It takes a lot of time to complete the entire sequence, and considerable effort can be saved by concentrating on those areas in which meaningful results can be expected. This system is especially helpful in gaining knowledge about the relative fluxing power of various compounds, their effects on colorants, and blending of colorants and opacifiers.

Chemicals

The chemicals used by the potter are generally not pure single oxides but more complex compounds that are available for industrial uses in a moderately refined form at low cost. Because of differences either in the original mineral or in refining methods, the ceramic chemicals available from different dealers can vary slightly. Even items from the same supplier can change minutely from year to year. Commercial potteries constantly check new shipments of chemicals, but this is seldom done in the small studio. If a favorite glaze reacts strangely, the potter should consider this factor, provided, of course, there was no deviation from the normal glazing and firing procedure. The feldspars, in particular, vary in their fluxing power. It is for this reason that the author has not stressed the importance of a glaze formula but rather the experimental knowledge of the properties in glaze ingredients. The batch glazes listed in the Appendix are mainly for purposes of illustration, and they may have to be adjusted slightly to fit the materials available.

For the convenience of students converting an empirical glaze formula into a batch recipe, a listing follows that gives the major sources of the various oxides in the RO, R_2O_3, and RO_2 groups. A more complete chemical description will be found in the alphabetized list at the end of this chapter.

Sources of Base (RO) Oxides

Barium Oxide Barium oxide (BaO) is a very active flux under some conditions. Its glass formation has a brilliancy second only to that of the lead silicates. Barium's effect on the thermal expansion of the glaze is less than that of the alkalies and calcia. Like lead, its fumes are toxic. It is one of the alkaline earth minerals, a category that also includes calcium, strontium, and radium. The best source for barium is

barium caronate ($BaCO_3$)

Calcium Oxide   Calcium oxide (CaO), in comparison with the other alkaline oxides, produces a glaze more resistant to abrasion, mild acids, and weathering. It also lowers the coefficient of thermal expansion, thereby increasing tensile strength. Although it is often used in small amounts with other fluxes in low-fire glazes, calcium should not be used as the sole flux at temperatures below cone 3. As with alumina, an excess of calcium tends to produce mat textures. Sources of calcium are

calcium carbonate ($CaCO_3$), also called whiting
calcium borate ($2CaO \cdot 3B_2O_3 \cdot 5H_2O$), more commonly known as colemanite
    or gerstley borate
dolomite [$CaMg(CO_3)_2$]
calcium fluoride (CaF_2), better known as the mineral fluorspar
bone ash, refined [$Ca_3(PO_4)_2$]
wollastonite ($CaSiO_3$)

Lead Oxide   Lead oxide (PbO) has been mentioned frequently as one of the major low-fire fluxes. There are several reasons for its popularity. It combines readily with all other fluxes and has a lower coefficient of expansion than do the alkaline fluxes. Lead gives greater brilliancy to the glaze, although at times this can be a disadvantage. Lead glazes melt and flow well and thus tend to reduce pinholes and other defects of the more viscous type of glaze. The chief drawbacks are the poisonous nature of lead compounds (unless they are carefully compounded) and their susceptibility to attack by strong fruit acids. Lead tends to blacken or develop a film if slightly reduced. The surface of a lead glaze will scratch easily unless an alkaline flux is added. There are many forms of lead, such as

litharge (PbO), a lead oxide
red lead (Pb_3O_4), a lead oxide
white lead [$2PbCO_3 \cdot Pb(OH_2)$], also called lead carbonate
lead monosilicate, the fritted lead silicate composed of approximately 16
    percent SiO_2 and 84 percent PbO
lead bisilicate, another commercial lead silicate, with the approximate composition of 65 percent PbO, 33 percent SiO_2, and 2 percent Al_2O_3
lead sulfide (PbS), also called galena

Lithium Oxide   Lithium oxide (Li_2O) is more commonly used by glass manufacturers, but it has several important qualities that make its occasional use in glazes valuable. Lithium (the oxide or carbonate) is expensive, because it is present in very small quantities (3 to 8 percent) in the producing ores. It has a much lower atomic weight than does either sodium or potassium (ratio of 1:3 and 1:5); therefore, a smaller amount of material can be used without lessening the fluxing action. This has the effect of decreasing tensions caused by thermal expansions and contractions and thus promoting a more durable glaze. Lithium is one of the alkaline metals, a category that also includes sodium, potassium, rubidium, and cesium. Sources of lithium are

lepidolite ($LiF \cdot KF \cdot Al_2O_3 \cdot 3SiO_2$)
spodumene ($Li_2O \cdot Al_2O_3 \cdot 4SiO_2$)
lithium carbonate (Li_2CO_3)
petalite ($Li_2O \cdot Al_2O_3 \cdot 8SiO_2$)
amblygonite ($2LiF \cdot Al_2O_3 \cdot P_2O_5$)

Magnesium Oxide Magnesium oxide (MgO) is frequently found combined with the feldspars and limestones. It lowers the thermal expansion more than do other bases, and it is as satisfactory as the alkaline fluxes in developing a durable glaze. In some combinations it will produce a slight opacity. Used with low-fire glazes, magnesium has a refractory effect and lends opacity and a mat quality; it fluxes easily at higher temperatures and becomes quite fluid. Sources of magnesium are

magnesium carbonate ($MgCO_3$)
dolomite [$CaMg(CO_3)_2$]
talc (varies from $3MgO \cdot 4SiO_2 \cdot H_2O$ to $4MgO \cdot 5SiO_2 \cdot H_2O$).
     In the solid and more impure form it is also known as steatite or soapstone.
diopside ($CaO \cdot MgO \cdot 2SiO_2$)

Potassium Oxide Potassium oxide (K_2O) is similar in fluxing action to sodium. It has a lower coefficient of thermal expansion, thus increasing the hardness and brilliance of a piece and lowering the fluidity of the glaze. Sources of potassium are

potassium carbonate (K_2CO_3), more commonly known as pearl ash
potash feldspar ($K_2O \cdot Al_2O_3 \cdot 6SiO_2$)
Cornwall stone, a complex compound of variable composition, roughly similar to a feldspar and having fluxes of calcium, sodium, and potassium
    ($1RO \cdot 1.16Al_2O_3 \cdot 8.95SiO_2$)
Carolina stone, a domestic product similar to Cornwall stone
volcanic ash (see analysis in Appendix)
plastic vitrox ($1RO \cdot 1.69Al_2O_3 \cdot 14.64SiO_2$)

Sodium Oxide Sodium oxide (Na_2O) is one of the more common low-fire fluxes. It has the highest coefficient of expansion of all the bases and generally gives a lower tensile strength and elasticity to the silicates formed than do most other fluxes. The usual ceramic sources of sodium are

sodium chloride ($NaCl$)
sodium carbonate (Na_2CO_3),
    more frequently called soda ash
sodium bicarbonate ($NaHCO_3$)
borax ($Na_2O \cdot 2B_2O_3 \cdot 10H_2O$)
soda feldspar ($Na_2O \cdot Al_2O_3 \cdot 6SiO_2$)
cryolite (Na_3AlF_6)
nepheline syenite ($K_2O \cdot 3Na_2O \cdot 4Al_2O_3 \cdot 9SiO_2$)

Zinc Oxide Zinc oxide (ZnO) can contribute several different qualities to a glaze. It can be used to replace some of the more soluble alkaline fluxes. Zinc is second only to magnesium in reducing thermal expansion and to calcium in increasing the strength and resistance of a glaze. It contributes some opacity to the glaze and is helpful in reducing crazing defects. The major zinc compound used in ceramics is

zinc oxide (ZnO)

Sources of Neutral (R$_2$O$_3$) Oxides

Unlike the RO group, which has numerous similar compounds, the R$_2$O$_3$ group is almost limited to alumina (Al$_2$O$_3$) and a few oxides that have the same oxygen ratio. The greatest difference between a glass and a glaze is the presence of alumina in the glaze. The alumina content is a most important factor in a successful glaze. It controls the fluidity of the melting glaze and enables it to withstand the temperatures needed to mature the body. Greater amounts of alumina increase the hardness of the glaze and its resistance to abrasions and acids. Crystalline glazes must necessarily be low in alumina, since alumina prevents the devitrification that accompanies the crystal formation.

Alumina Alumina (Al$_2$O$_3$) in a glaze can vary from 0.1 to 0.9 molecular equivalents, depending upon the firing temperatures. The equivalent ratios between the alumina and the silica groups can be from 1:4 to 1:20. For glossy glazes the ratio is about 1:10. As mentioned before, an increase of alumina will tend to produce mat textures. A glossy porcelain glaze firing from cones 10 to 12 will have an alumina-silica ratio of between 1:7 and 1:8, whereas mat glazes will have a ratio of between 1:3.2 to 1:3.8. The refractory properties of alumina are more like those of the acid silica than any of the bases. Alumina also has an effect on the colors developed. The normal blue of cobalt oxide will become a rose pink in the absence of alumina. Chromium oxide, which usually gives various green tones, will tend to become reddish in the presence of excess alumina. Sources of alumina are

alumina hydrate [Al(OH)$_3$]
feldspar and Cornwall stone, see sections under RO oxides
kaolin or china clay (Al$_2$O$_3$·2SiO$_2$·2H$_2$O), see sections under clay
nepheline syenite (K$_2$O·3Na$_2$O·4Al$_2$O$_3$·9SiO$_2$)
plastic vitrox (1RO·1.69Al$_2$O$_3$·14.64SiO$_2$)
pyrophyllite (Al$_2$O$_3$·4SiO$_2$·H$_2$O)

Antimony Oxide Antimony oxide (Sb$_2$O$_3$) is primarily used as an opacifier and a coloring agent. It is found in

antimonious oxide (Sb$_2$O$_3$)
basic antimonate of lead [Pb$_3$(SbO$_4$)$_2$], also known as Naples yellow

Boric Oxide Boric oxide (B$_2$O$_3$) is one of the neutral oxides (R$_2$O$_3$). As previously noted, it can react either as a base or an acid. Boric oxide has a number of characteristics similar to alumina: the alumina of mat glazes can be satisfactorily replaced by boric oxide; color effects do not change by this substitution; both alumina and boric oxide harm underglaze red and green colors; and both can form mixed crystals. On the whole, however, boric oxide functions as a flux, since in comparison with silica it increases elasticity, lowers tensile strength, and, in limited quantities, lowers the thermal coefficient of expansion. Like lead, it increases the gloss and refractive index. Major compounds containing boric oxide are

boric acid (B$_2$O$_3$·2H$_2$O)
borax (Na$_2$O·2B$_2$O$_3$·10H$_2$O)
colemanite (2CaO·3B$_2$O$_3$·5H$_2$O), also called calcium borate
gerstley borate (2CaO·3B$_2$O$_3$·5H$_2$O)

Chromic Oxide   Chromic oxide (Cr_2O_3) is derived from the mineral chromite ($FeCr_2O_4$). It is used as a colorant in glazes. The fact that the mineral form is a natural spinel would indicate its use as a stain.

Red Iron Oxide   Red, or ferric, iron oxide (Fe_2O_3) is commonly used as a coloring agent to form brownish-red hues and also to modify copper and cobalt. It would serve well as a flux except for its strong coloring action. Its presence in many compounds is regarded as an impurity, and considerable effort goes into removing iron flecks from whiteware bodies. Red iron oxide conforms to the R_2O_3 oxide ratio but has none of the refractory qualities that alumina has.

Sources of Acid (RO$_2$) Oxides

The important oxide in this group, silica, has a refractory effect on glaze, while the others function largely as opacifiers or coloring agents.

Silica   Silica (SiO_2), also called flint, combines readily with the bases to form glassy silicates. It is the most common element in glazes, comprising about 50 percent by weight. In a glaze it has the effect of raising the melting point, decreasing fluidity, increasing resistance of the glaze to water and chemicals, increasing hardness and tensile strength, and reducing the coefficients of thermal expansion. The amounts of silica used depend upon the flux and the maturing point of the glaze, but it is generally between 1 and 6 molecular equivalents.

Silica is commonly obtained from sandstone, quartz sands, or flint pebbles. Silica is found combined with many ceramic materials. Below are listed a few of the more frequently used silica compounds.

ball clay ($Al_2O_3 \cdot 2SiO_2 \cdot 2H_2O$)
kaolin ($Al_2O_3 \cdot 2SiO_2 \cdot 2H_2O$)
soda feldspar ($Na_2O \cdot Al_2O_3 \cdot 6SiO_2$)
potash feldspar ($K_2O \cdot Al_2O_3 \cdot 6SiO_2$)
Cornwall stone ($1RO \cdot 1.16Al_2O_3 \cdot 8.95SiO_2$)
wollastonite ($CaSiO_3$)
petalite ($Li_2O \cdot Al_2O_3 \cdot 8SiO_2$)

Tin Oxide   Tin oxide (SnO_2) is used primarily as an opacifier in glazes. Although rather expensive, it remains popular because it has greater covering power than any other opacifier. The chief form of tin is

tin oxide (SnO_2), also called stannic oxide

Titanium Oxide   (TiO_2) is probably the only other oxide in the RO_2 group that has some of the refractory qualities of silica. Its use in glazes, however, is entirely for its effect upon other colors and its action as an opacifier.

titanium dioxide (TiO_2)
rutile (TiO_2), an impure form containing iron and vanadium oxides

Characteristics of Chemicals

Albany Slip   Albany slip is a slip clay, which is a natural clay containing silica, alumina, and fluxes in the correct proportions to function as a glaze. It

260   Warren MacKenzie, U.S.A. Covered jar. Stoneware, with iron-saturated glaze over an opaque glaze with wax-resist decoration, reduction-fired to cone 10; height 11" (27.5 cm).

is mined in the vicinity of Albany, New York. Since it occurs in small pits, its composition and color will vary. Usually, it fires to a glossy brown-black at temperatures between cones 4 and 12. Occasionally, it may fire to a pale, nearly transparent tan. Slip clays are very easy to apply, and they fire with few, if any, defects.

Alumina Hydrate Alumina hydrate [$Al(OH)_3$] is preferred to the calcined form (Al_2O_3) for some uses, since it has better adhesive qualities and remains suspended in the glaze longer. Introduction of alumina for mat effects is considered to be more effective in the hydrate form than in such compounds as clay or feldspar.

Antimonate of Lead Antimonate of lead [$Pb_3(SbO_4)_2$], also known as Naples yellow, is primarily used as a paint pigment. It is a source of low-fire yellows. The presence of lead in Naples yellow is an advantage, since antimony will not produce a yellow unless combined with lead or iron.

Antimonious Oxide Antimonious oxide (Sb_2O_3) is poisonous and slightly soluble in water. For a satisfactory effect as an opacifier, it must be used in glazes fired below cone 1. Antimony will also produce yellow and orange colors for glazes. The most common mixture, known as yellow base, has the following composition:

red lead	15 parts
antimony oxide	10 parts
tin oxide	4 parts

The mixture is calcined to cone 09, then ground and washed.

Barium Carbonate Barium carbonate ($BaCO_3$) is usually used in combination with other fluxes, since at low temperatures it combines very slowly and acts as a refractory element to form mat textures. At higher temperatures it reacts strongly as a flux.

Barium Chromate Barium chromate ($BaCrO_4$) will produce colors in the pale yellow to light green range. It is generally used in overglaze decoration, since it is fugitive at temperatures above cone 04.

Bentonite Bentonite ($Al_2O_3 \cdot 4SiO_2 \cdot 9H_2O$) is of volcanic origin. The formula is not quite correct, since bentonite contains other impurities (see the analysis of South Dakota bentonite in the Appendix). Bentonite generally fires to a light cream color and fuses at about 2400°F (1300°C). Its chief value is as a plasticizer for short (lacking plasticity) clays. As such it is about five times as effective as ball clay. Purified bentonite will also make a stronger glaze covering and will help prevent settling in the glaze. An addition of about 3 percent is sufficient.

Bicarbonate of Soda   (see sodium bicarbonate)

Bismuth Subnitrate Bismuth subnitrate ($BiONO_2 \cdot H_2O$) generally contains impurities such as arsenic, lead, and silver carbonates. It melts at a low temperature and will produce pearly metallic lusters under reducing conditions.

Bone Ash   Bone ash in the unrefined state has a formula of $4Ca_3(PO_4)_2 \cdot CaCO_3$ with a molecular weight of 1340. The material generally available today is the refined calcium phosphate $Ca_3(PO_4)_2$ with a molecular weight of 310. It sometimes serves as a glaze flux but more commonly as a body ingredient in bone china, chiefly in the kind produced in England. It lowers the firing temperatures required and increases translucency.

Borax   Borax $(Na_2O \cdot 2B_2O_3 \cdot 10H_2O)$ is, next to lead, the major low-fire flux. It has a strong action on all ceramic compounds and may even be used in small amounts in the high-fire glazes that tend to be overly viscous in nature. Borax has an effect on coloring oxides different from that of lead; for this reason it is often combined with lead. Borax absorbs moisture and should therefore be kept dry, or weight calculations will be inaccurate. As mentioned earlier, borax is very soluble in water and should not be applied to raw ware.

Boric Acid   Boric acid $(B_2O_3 \cdot 2H_2O)$ is a flaky material soluble in water. It is available in a fairly pure state at low cost. Although boric acid is one of the neutral oxides (R_2O_3), it functions more as a flux, since it increases the gloss in glazes. Unlike silica, an acid, boric acid lowers the expansion coefficient and helps to increase elasticity.

Cadmium Sulfide   Cadmium sulfide (CdS) is a low-fire yellow colorant. It is usually combined in a stain made of cadmium, selenium, and sulfur frits. Unfortunately, it is fugitive above cone 010 and can be used only for overglaze decorations.

Calcium Borate   (see colemanite and gerstley borate)

Calcium Carbonate   (see whiting)

Calcium Fluoride   (see fluorspar)

Calcium Phosphate   (see bone ash)

Calcium Zirconium Silicate   Calcium zirconium silicate is a commercially produced opacifier with the composition of ZrO_2, 41.12 percent; SiO_2, 25.41 percent; CaO, 22.23 percent. It does not have the strength of tin but is considerably cheaper. It will reduce slightly the maturing temperatures of the lower-fire glazes.

Carolina Stone   Carolina stone is similar in composition to imported Cornwall stone, but is mined domestically. However, it is not commonly available.

China Clay   (see kaolin)

Chromic Oxide   Chromic oxide (Cr_2O_3) and other chromium compounds are often used in glazes to produce green colors. Dichromates are preferred because of the greater amounts of chromium per weight. Care must be taken in the glaze composition, for, when chromic oxide is combined with tin, a pink color results. Zinc and chrome will form a brown, and high-lead glazes may develop a yellow-lead chromate. Reducing conditions in the kiln will blacken the color. In fact, even adjacent tin-glazed and chrome-glazed pieces

261 Roberta Griffith, U.S.A. *Isadora with Gray Beige Lace.* Plate. Stoneware with speckled glaze, reduction-fired at cone 10. Thin clay ribbons with nylon fiber are impressed with lace and coated with colored slips; width 16.75″ (42.54 cm).

may affect each other in the kiln. Bright, low-temperature reds (below cone 010) can be produced by chrome oxide in a high-lead and low-alumina glaze.

Clay   Clay is a decomposed feldspathic-type rock consisting chiefly of silicates of aluminum but often containing numerous other ingredients, such as quartz, micas, feldspar, iron oxides, carbonates of calcium and magnesium, and organic matter (see Chap. 1).

Cobalt Carbonate   Cobalt carbonate ($CoCO_3$) is used to introduce a blue color in glazes. When combined with manganese, iron chromate, or ochre, it will produce colors ranging from gray to black.

Cobalt Oxide   Cobalt oxide (Co_2O_3) is the major blue colorant. It is extremely strong and therefore is often fritted with alumina and lime or with lead for lower-fire underglaze colors. The frit allows a lighter and more even color dispersion. Color stains made of cobalt, alumina, and zinc are uniform at all temperature ranges. Small amounts of cobalt in combination with magnesium carbonate, silica, and boric acid will produce a variety of hues in the pink and lavender range.

Cobalt Sulfate   Cobalt sulfate ($CoSO_4 \cdot 7H_2O$), unlike the other cobalt compounds mentioned, is very soluble in water. It melts at a low temperature and is primarily used in decorative work or lusterware.

Colemanite   Colemanite ($2CaO \cdot 3B_2O_3 \cdot 5H_2O$) is a natural hydrated calcium borate, which has the advantage of being only slightly soluble in water. Therefore, it does not develop the granular lumps in the glaze so characteristic of borax. Colemanite serves as low-fire flux, since the boron present melts at a fairly low temperature. It tends to prevent crazing and also functions partially as an opacifier. Colemanite can be substituted for calcium in some glazes where calcium would harm the pink or red colors desired. In both high- and low-fire glazes, colemanite tends to develop a milky-blue opalescent color. Gerstley borate, a type of colemanite, is preferred by many potters because it has less tendency to settle in the glaze and is less variable in quality.

Copper Carbonate Copper carbonate ($CuCO_3$) is a major green colorant in glazes. The carbonate form is preferred to the oxide form in the production of blue-greens or copper reds under reducing conditions.

Copper Oxides Copper oxide is available in two forms: cupric, or black, copper oxide (CuO), or cuprous, or red, copper oxide (Cu_2O). Copper is one of the few colorants that does not change greatly under normal oxidizing conditions. Additions of 2 percent or more of copper will decrease markedly the acid resistance of lead glazes. Lead fluxes tend to produce a blackish green. When copper and tin are combined with an alkaline flux, a turquoise will result. Potash will induce a yellowish green, while zinc and copper with fluxes of sodium, potassium, and barium will develop a blue tinge.

Cornwall Stone Cornwall stone is a complex mixture derived from a deposit of partially decomposed granite rock in England. It is composed of quartz (flint), feldspar, lepidolite, tourmaline, fluorspar, and small quantities of other minerals. Cornwall stone has charactistics that lie between those of kaolin and feldspar. It is a major ingredient of many English glazes and bodies and is subject to less firing strains than kaolin and feldspar. Because of the more intimate mixture of naturally occuring minerals, a smaller amount of alkali flux is necessary than would otherwise be needed. Since less bulk is required, there is less shrinkage of both the unfired and the fired glaze, thus minimizing glaze defects. Cornwall stone is roughly similar to petuntze, the feldspathic rock used for centuries by the Chinese as a major ingredient in their porcelain bodies and glazes. Like feldspar, Cornwall stone has variable composition; samples differ in the percentages of silica, potassium, sodium, and so on. If Cornwall stone is not available, a substitution of 67 parts feldspar, 22 parts flint, and 11 parts kaolin can be made for 100 units of Cornwall stone. However, as previously noted, the new glaze will not have identical characteristics. The analysis of Cornwall stone is found in the Appendix.

Cryolite Cryolite (Na_3AlF_6) is used primarily as a flux and an opacifier for enamels and glasses. It has a limited application in glazes and bodies as a source of fluxes and alumina. In some glazes, an addition of cryolite will promote crazing.

Dolomite Dolomite [$CaMg(CO_3)_2$] is a double carbonate of calcia and magnesia. Its inclusion in a glaze is a good method of introducing both calcia and magnesia, since glazes with magnesia usually have a large proportion of calcium. Dolomite contains the equivalent of 44 percent magnesium carbonate and 56 percent calcium carbonate. Dolomite will also promote a longer and lower-firing range in clay bodies. Below cone 4, the addition of a small amount of a lower-firing alkaline flux to the dolomite will greatly increase this effect.

Epsom Salts (see magnesium sulfate)

Feldspar   Feldspar is a crystalline rock composed of the aluminum silicates of potassium, sodium, and calcium. These silicates are never found in a pure state but in a mixture with one or the other predominating. For convenience in ceramic calculations, their formulas are usually given as follows:

potash feldspar (microcline) $K_2O \cdot Al_2O_3 \cdot 6SiO_2$
soda feldspar (albite) $Na_2O \cdot Al_2O_3 \cdot 6SiO_2$
lime feldspar (anorthite) $CaO \cdot Al_2O_3 \cdot 6SiO_2$

The feldspars are a major component of porcelain and whiteware bodies and are often the only source of body flux. If the feldspar content of the body is high, the substitution of soda spar for potash feldspar will reduce the vitrification point by as much as 100°F (38°C). Feldspars are a cheap source of glaze flux and have the additional advantage of being nonsoluble. Because of the presence of Al_2O_3 and SiO_2, the feldspar cannot be considered a flux at low-temperature ranges, even though some flux is contributed to the glaze. The fluxing action is increased by the fineness of the particle size. Potash forms a harder glaze than does soda and decreases the thermal expansion. Thus, unless soda is desired for color purposes, potash feldspar should be preferred in the glaze composition. (See Appendix for a comparative analysis of feldspars.)

Ferric Chloride   Ferric chloride ($FeCl_3 \cdot 6H_2O$) is more commonly called chloride of iron. It is very soluble in water and must be stored in airtight containers. Ferric chloride serves as a luster decoration on glass or glazes and produces an iridescent gold-colored film under proper conditions.

Ferric Oxide   (see iron oxide)

Ferrous Oxide   (see iron oxide)

Flint   (see silica)

Fluorspar   Fluorspar (CaF_2), also called calcium fluoride, may serve as a source of flux in glaze and body compositions. The particle size must be less than 100 mesh when used in the body, or pinholes are likely to form in the glaze. Fluorspar fluxes at a lower temperature than do other calcia compounds. When it is combined in a glaze with copper oxides, some unusual blue-green hues can be developed.

Galena   (see lead sulfide)

Gerstley Borate   Gerstley borate ($2CaO \cdot 3B_2O_3 \cdot 5H_2O$) is given the same formula as colemanite, but it usually also contains a small amount of sodium. Most dealers now supply gerstley borate when colemanite is ordered, since the latter is quite variable in quality. It is an excellent source of calcium and boron and gives a slight opalescent color to the glaze.

Ilmenite   Ilmenite ($TiO_2 \cdot FeO$) is the mineral source of titanium and its compounds. When coarsely ground into a powderlike sand, it produces dark specks in the glaze.

Iron Chromate   Iron chromate ($FeCrO_4$) combined with manganese and zinc oxide will produce underglaze brown colors; combined with cobalt it will form a black stain. Used alone, it is fugitive above cone 04.

Iron Oxides   Iron oxides have three forms: ferrous oxide (FeO), ferric oxide, or hematite (Fe_2O_3), and ferrous-ferric oxide, or magnetite (Fe_3O_4). Iron is the oxide most frequently used to produce tan or brown bodies and glazes. Were it not for its pronounced color, it could serve as a flux. It is responsible for most of the low-firing characteristics and the red color of many earthenware clays. A pink stain can be made with a smaller amount of iron, plus alumina, calcium, and flint. When reduced in a suitable glaze, iron will form gray-greens characteristic of the Chinese celadons.

Kaolin   Kaolin ($Al_2O_3 \cdot 2SiO_2 \cdot 2H_2O$) is also called china clay or pure clay. Because of its compositon and relative purity, kaolin is the highest-firing clay. It is an important ingredient of all whiteware and china bodies, since it fires to pure white. For glazes, kaolin constitutes a major source of Al_2O_3 and SiO_2. The chief residual deposits in the United States are in North Carolina, and sedimentary deposits are found in South Carolina and Georgia. For bodies, the more plastic sedimentary types are preferred. The sedimentary kaolin deposits of Florida are even more plastic and are often termed ball kaolin or EPK (see Chap. 1).

Lead Antimonate   (see antimonate of lead)

Lead Bisilicate   (see lead silicate)

Lead Carbonate   Lead carbonate [$2PbCO_3 \cdot Pb(OH)_2$], more commonly called white lead, is a major low-fire flux that imparts a lower surface tension and viscosity over a wide temperature range. This results in a smooth, brilliant glaze with few surface defects. Lead may comprise all the flux in the low-temperature range, or a lesser amount at cone 4. (See glaze recipes in the Appendix.)

Lead Oxide   Lead oxides occurs in two types: litharge, or lead monoxide (PbO), and red lead, or minium (Pb_3O_4). Litharge is a yellow powder that has a greater use in Europe than in the United States. Since litharge occasionally contains impurities and has larger particles than does the carbonate form, the latter is the preferred lead compound. Because of the greater amount of oxygen, red lead often replaces litharge. Ceramic grades of red lead are seldom pure but usually contain 75 percent red lead and about 25 percent litharge. Red lead contains more PbO by weight than does the carbonate form.

Lead Silicate   Lead silicate is a frit made of lead and silica to eliminate the toxic effects of the lead compounds. The two most common types are lead monosilicate, with a composition of 15 percent SiO_2 and 85 percent PbO; and

 Safety Caution

Unless properly compounded, lead glazes can be poisonous, because the harmful lead may be released when in contact with tea, citric-acid fruit juices, salad dressings containing vinegar, or other acids. You should handle lead only when it is fritted. Otherwise, you may absorb it into the body by inhaling the lead powder or through a cut in the skin. Copper oxide in amounts greater than 2 percent and combinations of iron oxide and manganese dioxide greater than 5 percent increase the toxic lead release. Larger amounts of alumina, silica, calcium, and zirconium increase the acid resistance of lead glazes. Additions of sodium, potassium, and barium all decrease acid resistance (see pp. 229, 278).

lead bisilicate, which has a formula of 65 percent PbO, 34 percent SiO$_2$, and 1 percent Al$_2$O$_3$.

Lead Silicate, Hydrous [2PbSiO$_2$·Pb(OH)$_2$] has a molecular weight of 807. This material is the basic silicate of white lead. It is used as a substitute for lead carbonate when the CO$_2$ released by the carbonate forms pinholes or is otherwise objectionable in the glaze.

Lead Sulfide Lead sulfide (PbS), also called galena, is the black powder that is the raw source of all lead compounds. It has a very limited use in glazes.

Lepidolite Lepidolite (LiF·KF·Al$_2$O$_3$·3SiO$_2$), also called lithium mica, contains from 3 to 6 percent lithia. It has some use as a body ingredient in chinaware and is a source of flux, Al$_2$O$_3$, and SiO$_2$ in higher-temperature glazes. It will tend to brighten most glazes, lower thermal expansions, and reduce brittleness (see lithium carbonate).

Lime (see whiting)

Litharge (see lead oxide)

Lithium Carbonate Lithium carbonate (Li$_2$CO$_3$) is a common source of lithia. With lithia, greater amounts of Al$_2$O$_3$, SiO$_2$, and CaO can be used in alkaline glazes, thus producing a more durable glaze while retaining the unusual copper blues characteristic of the alkaline glazes. It can be used in place of lead in the medium-temperature ranges when volatilization is a problem. When substituted for sodium or potassium, it reduces glaze expansion and promotes crystallization. Other sources of lithia are lepidolite and spodumene.

262 **Don M. Olstad**, U.S.A. Box. Cut from a laminated block of brown and white porcelain with black slip in the neriage technique, clear-glazed at cone 10.

Magnesium Carbonate Magnesium carbonate (MgCO$_3$), also called magnesite, acts as a refractory element at lower temperatures, changing to a flux at higher temperatures. It is valuable for slowing down the fluid qualities of crystalline and other runny glazes. It also improves glaze adhesion. Because magnesium carbonate has some solubility in water that causes drying and firing shrinkage, it is best added to glazes in the form of dolomite [CaMg(CO$_3$)$_2$]. It has a slight tendency to promote opacity in glazes.

Magnesium Sulfate Magnesium sulfate (MgSO$_4$·7H$_2$O) is better known as epsom salts. It serves to thicken glazes applied to nonporous bodies. Usually 1 percent, dissolved in hot water, will be sufficient and will have no apparent effect on the glaze.

Magnetite (see iron oxides)

Manganese Dioxide (see manganese oxide)

GLAZES: CALCULATIONS AND CHEMICALS

Plate 40 Joe Fafard, Canada. *Farley Mowat,* a colorful portrayal of a Scotsman and his dog in brilliant low-fired glazes and luster. Talc body, length 29″ (73.6 cm).

Plate 41 Nan Bangs McKinnell, U.S.A. Vase. Thrown and altered porcelain with iridescent pearl luster glazes; height 3.5″ (8.75 cm).

Plate 42 Paul Soldner, U.S.A. Slab plate with white and copper slips. Later decorated with copper and iron oxides, low-fired and lightly smoked, 10″ × 11″ (25 × 27.5 cm).

Manganese Oxide   Manganese oxide (MnO_2) is primarily a colorant. It should not be used in concentrations greater than 5 percent in either body or glaze, because blisters may develop. The usual colors produced are in the brown range. With cobalt, a black results; with the proper alkaline fluxes, purple and dark reddish hues can be produced. When it is fritted with alumina, a pink colorant will be formed.

Naples Yellow   (see antimonate of lead)

Nepheline Syenite   Nepheline syenite ($K_2O \cdot 3Na_2O \cdot 4Al_2O_3 \cdot 9SiO_2$) is a material roughly similar to feldspar (see Appendix for composition). In glazes, nepheline syenite can substitute for potash feldspar but will lower the maturing point. It also produces a greater firing range and increased thermal expansion, which in turn will reduce crazing tendencies in the glaze.

Nickel Oxide   Nickel oxide is used in two forms, green nickel oxide, or nickelous (NiO), and black nickel oxide, or nickelic (Ni_2O_3). The function of nickel in a glaze is almost solely as a colorant. Depending upon the flux used and the ratio of alumina, a variety of colors can be produced: with zinc, a blue; with lime, a tan; with barium, a brown; and with magnesia, a green. None of these hues are particularly brilliant. In general, nickel will soften and alter other coloring oxides. In addition, 5 to 10 percent nickel in a suitable glaze promotes the formation of a crystalline structure.

Ochre   Ochre is a term given to clays containing varying amounts of red iron or manganese oxides. Their primary function is in paint manufacturing. However, they can be used as glaze or slip colorants to impart tan, brown, or brick-red hues.

Opax   Opax is a standard, commercially produced opacifier with the composition listed in the table at the right.

Opax does not have the power of tin oxide, but it is considerably cheaper, and for this reason it often replaces part of the tin oxide in glaze recipes.

Opax

Oxide	Percent
ZrO_2	90.84
SiO_2	6.48
Na_2O	1.11
Al_2O_3	0.91

Pearl Ash   (see potassium carbonate)

Petalite   Petalite ($Li_2O \cdot Al_2O_3 \cdot 8SiO_2$), lithium-aluminum silicate, is chiefly used as an auxiliary body flux to reduce thermal expansions and increase shock resistance in ovenware bodies. At about cone 6 it converts into beta spodumene, which has almost no volume change when heated or cooled. It serves as a source of lithia and silica primarily for medium- and high-temperature glazes.

Plastic Vitrox   Plastic vitrox ($1RO \cdot 1.69Al_2O_3 \cdot 14.64SiO_2$) is a complex mineral mined in California that is a source of silica, alumina, and potash in both glaze and body formulas. It resembles potash feldspar and Cornwall stone in composition. (See Appendix for comparative analysis.)

Potash Feldspar   (see feldspar)

Health Hazards in the Studio

Because potassium chromate is very poisonous, you should handle it with caution.

Potassium Carbonate Potassium carbonate (K_2CO_3) is more commonly called pearl ash. It is used primarily to modify color effects. When pearl ash is substituted for lead, sodium, or calcium content in a glaze, the colors resulting from copper oxide can be changed from the usual green to either a yellow-green or a bright blue.

Potassium Dichromate Potassium dichromate ($K_2Cr_2O_7$) is used in glazes as a green colorant. When it is calcined with tin, low-fire stains developing pink and red hues are formed (see chromic oxide).

Praseodymium Oxide Praseodymium oxide (Pr_6O_{11}), a black oxide, is a rare earth compound used in ceramics as a yellow colorant. It is commonly combined with zirconium oxide and silica to form a glaze stain that is stable at all normal firing temperatures.

Pyrophyllite Pyrophyllite ($Al_2O_3 \cdot 4SiO_2 \cdot H_2O$) is used primarily in wall-tile bodies, where it decreases thermal expansions, crazing, and moisture expansions to which tile is subjected. Since it is nonplastic, it has limited use in throwing or hand-building bodies.

Red Lead (see lead oxide)

Rutile Rutile (TiO_2) is an impure oxide of titanium containing small amounts of iron and vanadium. It serves as a tan colorant in glazes and imparts a mottled or streaky effect.

Selenium Selenium (Se) is a glass colorant. It has a limited application in ceramic glazes and overglaze colors, primarily as cadmium-selenium red frits. These frits, unfortunately, are fugitive at higher temperatures.

Silica Silica (SiO_2) is called flint or, in foreign publications, quartz. It is commonly obtained from sandstone, quartz sands, or flint pebbles. True flint is obtained from England, France, and Denmark. This cryptocrystalline flint has a different specific gravity (2.33) from that prepared from quartz sand or sandstone (2.65). For glaze purposes, the silica (silicon dioxide) derived from flint is important.

When used alone, silica melts at the extremely high temperature of 3119°F (1700°C) and forms an unusually hard and stable crystal. It combines under heat, however, with a variety of fluxes at much lower temperatures to form a glass, and with the alumina compounds to form the more refractory body structure. An increase in the silica content of a glaze has the effect of raising the maturing temperature as well as increasing hardness and resistance to wear. In a glaze, in addition of silica decreases its thermal expansions; in a body it increases them.

Silicon Carbide Silicon carbide (SiC) has many industrial uses. Its value in ceramics is as the sole or major ingredient in high-temperature kiln furniture and muffles. When added to an alkaline glaze in small amounts (0.5 percent), the carbon will reduce the copper oxides to form localized copper reds.

Silver Chloride   Silver chloride (AgCl) is the major silver compound used in luster overglaze preparations (see the section on lusters later in this chapter.) When silver chloride is combined with bismuth and with a resin or fat oil as a binder, an overglaze metallic luster with greenish or yellow tints will form.

Soda Ash   (see sodium carbonate)

Sodium Aluminate   Sodium aluminate ($Na_2O \cdot Al_2O_3$) is used to prevent casting slips from settling and to increase the strength of dry ware.

Sodium Bicarbonate   Sodium bicarbonate ($NaHCO_3$), also called bicarbonate of soda, has some use in casting slips and in forming stains with cobalt sulfate. Sodium carbonate ($NaCO_3$) is the sodium form more commonly used as a flux. Many potters are experimenting with sodium bicarbonate for salt glazing, as a less toxic alternative to sodium chloride (common salt).

Sodium Carbonate   Sodium carbonate (Na_2CO_3) is commonly called soda ash. It is a very active flux, but because of its solubility it is more often used in glazes as a frit ingredient. Small quantities of soda ash, functioning as a deflocculant, will reduce the water of plasticity required in a clay body. This increases workability and strength of the plastic body and reduces shrinkage from the wet to the dry state.

Sodium Silicate   Sodium silicate is a compound that can vary from $1Na_2O \cdot 1.6SiO_2$ to $1Na_2O \cdot 3.75SiO_2$. It usually comes in liquid form and is the major deflocculant for casting slips. Like soda ash, it greatly reduces the water required to make the clay into a slip form. In doing so, it lessens the rate of shrinkage, the strains of drying, and breaking in the green and dry states.

Sodium Uranate   Sodium uranate ($Na_2O \cdot UO_3$), more commonly called uranium yellow, has not been available in the United States since World War II because of restrictions placed on uranium by the Atomic Energy Commission. Uranium yellows are still available, however, in Europe. Uranium compounds formerly were the best source of yellow colorants. When uranium compounds are combined with various fluxes or with tin and zirconium oxide, a variety of hues from bright yellow through orange to vermilion red can be developed (see uranium oxide).

Spodumene   Spodumene ($Li_2O \cdot Al_2O_3 \cdot 4SiO_2$) is an important source of lithia. The use of lithia, which is an active flux, helps to develop unusual copper-blue hues. Spodumene is also added to whiteware and porcelain bodies. As a replacement for feldspar, it will reduce the vitrification temperature as well as the shrinkage rate. Strange as it may seem, the crystalline form of spodumene expands, instead of shrinking, at about 1700°F (927°C). When a mixture of 60 percent spodumene and 40 percent lead bisilicate is used, a nonplastic, press-formed body can be made that will have zero absorption and zero shrinkage at 1970°F (1077°C).

Stannic Oxide   (see tin oxide)

Steatite Steatite, a hydrous magnesium silicate, is a massive variety of talc. Most steatite is used in powdered form for electrical insulators. It has very little shrinkage, and occasionally the rocklike nuggets are turned down on a lathe for special projects. Steatite was used by the Egyptians almost 5000 years ago for the creation of beads and small figurines. These were generally covered with a turquoise alkaline copper glaze (see talc).

Talc Talc varies from $3MgO \cdot 4SiO_2 \cdot H_2O$ to $4MgO \cdot 5SiO_2 \cdot H_2O$. In the solid and more impure form, it is also known as steatite or soapstone. Talc is occasionally used in glazes, but it is more frequently employed as a major ingredient in whiteware bodies firing at moderate temperatures (cones 4 to 6). Like dolomite, it will lower the firing temperatures of the other body ingredients, usually kaolin, ball clays, and feldspars. Talc will promote a slight opacity in glazes. (See Plate 40, p. 251).

Tin Oxide Tin oxide (SnO_2), also called stannic oxide, is the most effective of all opacifiers. From 5 to 7 percent will produce a completely opaque white glaze. An excess will create a dull surface. Tin also has wide use in stains, since it has considerable effect on the color qualities of most color-forming oxides. Because of its relatively high price, tin substitutes are frequently used.

Titanium Oxide Titanium Oxide (TiO_2), or more correctly titanium dioxide, is a major opacifier when used either alone or in a frit. Like rutile, which is an impure form containing iron, titanium will encourage a semimat surface texture.

Uranium Oxide Uranium oxide [U_3O_8(black)], is a depleted nuclear fuel that was used formerly as a yellow colorant in low-fire lead glazes. The tin-vanadium, zirconium-vanadium, and praseodymium yellow stains have greater flexibility and no radiation hazard. They are more readily available and are preferred by most potters.

Vanadium Pentoxide Vanadium pentoxide (V_2O_5) is a rather weak yellow colorant when used alone. When fritted in the proper composition with tin, it produces a strong yellow color. This stain, known commercially as tin-vana-

263 Rolf Overberg, West Germany. *Fruit.* Wheel-thrown and altered spheres, with type-impressed inserts, green and rust-ash glazes on a manganese body, wood-fired to cone 6; height 6″ (15 cm).

dium stain, has largely replaced the uranium yellows, which are no longer available. It has a wide firing range (cones 06 to 14), is transparent, and is not affected by a reduction firing.

Volcanic Ash   Volcanic ash occurs in many regions of the western United States. It was formed from the dust of volcanic glass erupted in prehistoric times. Since the material often floated through the air many miles before being deposited, it is extemely fine and can be used with little preparation. Its composition is roughly similar to that of a granite-type rock (see the formula in the Appendix). In most glazes volcanic ash can be substituted for roughly 70 parts of feldspar and 30 parts of flint. A low-fire, cone 04 glaze can be compounded of 60 percent ash and 40 percent borax and lead or just lead.

White Lead   (see lead carbonate)

Whiting   Whiting ($CaCO_3$) is a calcium carbonate produced domestically by processing marble or limestone. European whiting is generally obtained from chalk deposits, such as those at the famous cliffs of Dover. Whiting is the major high-fire flux, although it has a limited use in bodies where a small amount will lower vitrification temperatures and reduce porosity. As a flux, it produces much harder and tougher silicates than will either the lead or alkaline compounds. For this reason, small amounts of whiting are often added to lower-fire glazes, although it is most effective at cone 4 and above. As with other fluxes, calcium has an effect upon the coloring oxides, particularly chrome greens.

Wollastonite   Wollastonite ($CaSiO_3$) is a natural calcium silicate. As a replacement for flint and whiting, it reduces firing shrinkage and improves heat shock. It is used in both bodies and glazes.

Zinc Oxide   Zinc oxide (ZnO) is a difficult compound to classify. At high temperatures it is an active flux. When used to excess in a glaze low in alumina and cooled slowly, zinc will produce crystalline structures. Opacity will develop if zinc is used in a high-alumina, low-calcium glaze, with no borosilicate fluxes, at cone 1 or higher. In general, zinc increases the maturing range of a glaze and promotes a higher gloss, brighter colors, reduced expansions, and, under some conditions, an opacity.

Zirconium Oxide   Zirconium oxide (ZrO_2) is seldom used alone as an opacifier in ceramics but is generally combined with other oxides and fritted into a more stable silicate form. Below are listed a few commercial zirconium silicates. None have the strength of tin oxide, but they are considerably cheaper.

calcium zirconium silicate: 51.12 percent ZrO_2, 25.41 percent SiO_2, and 22.23 percent CaO

magnesium zirconium silicate: 53.75 percent ZrO_2, 29.92 percent SiO_2, and 18.54 percent MgO

zinc zirconium silicate: 45.78 percent ZrO_2, 23.08 percent SiO_2, and 30.52 percent ZnO

zirconium spinel: 39.94 percent ZrO_2, 25.25 percent SiO_2, 19.47 percent ZnO, and 19.41 percent Al_2O_3

Most of these compounds are used in combination with other opacifiers, such as tin or titanium compounds (see also opax and zircopax.)

Zircopax Zircopax is a standard commercially produced opacifier with the composition of 64.88 percent ZrO_2, 0.22 percent TiO_2, 34.28 percent SiO_2.

Guide to Use of Colorants

Color	Oxide	Percentage	Temperature	Atmosphere
black	cobalt	1-2	any	either
	manganese	2-4		
	cobalt	1		
	iron	8	any	either
	manganese	3		
blue	cobalt	0.5-1	any	either
turquoise	copper (alkaline flux)	3-5	low	oxidizing
slate-blue	nickel (with zinc)	1-3	low	oxidizing
brown	rutile	5	any	reducing
	chromium (with MgO, ZnO)	2-5	low	either
	iron	3-7	any	oxidizing
	manganese	5	any	either
	nickel (with ZnO)	2-4	any	either
green	copper oxide	1-5	any	oxidizing
gray-green	iron	1-4	any	reducing
	nickel-magnesia	3-5	low	oxidizing
red	copper (alkaline flux)	1	any	reducing
	iron (high SiO_2, KNaO), CaO	2-5	low	oxidizing
pink	chrome and tin (1 to 18)	5	any	oxidizing
coral	chromium (with high PbO)	5	low	oxidizing
purple	manganese (with KNaO)	4-6	any	oxidizing
tan	iron	2	any	either
	manganese	2	any	either
	rutile	2	any	either
yellow	antimony yellow stain (with high PbO)	3-5	low	either
	praseodymium yellow stain	4-6	any	either
	uranium yellow and orange (with high PbO)	5-8	low	oxidizing
	zirconium-vanadium stain	5-10	any	either
	tin-vanadium stain	4-6	any	either

Colorants for Glazes and Decoration

Coloring Oxides Most studio potters obtain their glaze colors from the oxides or carbonates of the more common metals, such as iron, copper, nickel, tin, zinc, and manganese. Other oxides, such as vanadium and cobalt, although rarer and more expensive, are extensively used because of a lack of cheaper substitutes. The accompanying list of major colorants indicates the oxide necessary and the amount generally used to produce a particular color. However, just because an oxide is listed as producing a green does not mean that it will produce a green in every situation. A study of the previous section on ceramic materials will reveal that generally the particular color that develops from an oxide depends upon the type of flux used, the proportions of alumina or silica, and the firing temperature. In some instances, even the rate of cooling will have an effect upon the glaze. Therefore, the list of oxides and colors is merely for convenience in determining color possibilities. Before using the oxide, the potter should be aware of its characteristics and the characteristics of the glaze to which it is added.

It is common practice to use two or more colorants in order to modify harsh colors and to obtain subtle variations or mottled color effects. Copper and nickel are often added to soften powerful cobalt hues. Opacifiers will brighten colors. Rutile is a frequent addition, since it contributes a runny and speckled quality as well as slightly matting a glaze.

Opacifiers Opacifiers are, for the most part, relatively insoluble in the glaze melt. Tin oxide and zirconium oxide are the chief examples of this type. As such, they remain suspended in the glaze and, if dense enough, prevent light from penetrating through to the body. Most opacifiers, and of course those of the greatest value, are white. Some, however, give a slight yellow, pink, or bluish cast to the glaze.

Opacifiers

Color	Oxide	Percentage	Temperature	Atmosphere
pure white	tin	5	any	either
weak blue white*	titanium	8-12	any	either
white	zirconium	8-12	any	either
weak yellow white	antimony	10-12	low	oxidizing
white	opax (a frit)	10	any	either
white	zircopax (a frit)	10	any	either

*a yellowish coloration with lead flux

Another type of opacifier is titanium (or zinc under some conditions), which tends to form minute crystalline structures within the glaze. Having a different index of refraction from the major portion of the glaze, it thus breaks up and prevents much light penetration. This is the type of crystal formation associated with mat glazes. It is the reason why all mats must be, necessarily, either wholly or partially opaque.

Spinel Stains Under certain circumstances, the use of a raw coloring oxide may be objectionable. For example, most metallic oxides are quite soluble in the melting glaze. The previous section noted that the fluxes and other elements of the glaze had considerable effect upon color quality. Overglaze and underglaze decoration with any degree of precision or control is impossible with colorants that diffuse into, or flow with, the glaze. In these instances, a special type of colorant known as a spinel is used.

A spinel stain is a colored crystal that is highly resistant to attack by fluxes in the glazes and to the effects of high temperatures. In strict chemical terms, *spinel* refers to the mineral magnesium aluminate ($MgOAl_2O_3$). However, manganese, iron, and chromium may be present by replacement. The crystal is an octahedron variety of extreme hardness. The ruby gem is a red spinel. By calcining certain oxides together, some very stable colored spinels can be formed. In general, these follow the formula $RO \cdot R_2O_3$. The RO member can be MgO, ZnO, NiO, CaO, MnO, or FeO, and the R_2O_3 can be Cr_2O_3, Al_2O_3, or Fe_2O_3.

Preparation of a spinel stain is a long procedure, and it is not recommended unless it is necessary for advanced experimental work. A wide range of commercial stains, expertly prepared, are available at reasonable cost. However, the general idea of the preparation should be understood. Detailed information can be found in the reference texts listed in the Bibliography.

It is extremely necessary that the chemicals involved be mixed completely and intimately. To this end the raw chemicals should first be passed through an 80-mesh sieve. It is preferable that they be in the form of soluble salts, that is, the nitrates or sulfates of the oxides listed above. These are thoroughly mixed in a liquid solution. After the water has been evaporated, the dry mixture is placed in a crucible or a kiln and calcined. The temperature will vary with the mixture. If the mixture melts into a solid mass, it should be calcined in a pot furnace so that the crucible can be removed with tongs and the contents poured into water, thus preventing the spinel from hardening into a solid crystalline block. Afterwards, the material is broken up with an iron mortar and pestle into a coarse powder, which is then ball milled. For a uniform color without specks, the particle size of the spinel must be extremely small. This may necessitate grinding in the ball mill for well over a hundred hours. When it is sufficiently fine, the stain should be washed several times with hot water to remove any remaining soluble salts. Filters may be necessary at this point in the process to prevent the loss of fine particles.

Other Colored Stains Besides the spinels, a number of other chemical compounds are calcined to produce stable colorants at certain temperatures. A discussion of a few of the better-known examples will serve to illustrate some of the numerous possibilities in the preparation of colorants.

An ultramarine blue can be formed by a silicate of cobalt. It is made by calcining cobalt oxide and flint, plus a flux such as feldspar.

Green stains can be developed by calcining fluorspar and chrominum oxide.

left: 264 **Georgette Zirbes**, U.S.A. Plate. White stoneware with colored slips, stains, and trailed-slip decoration under a clear glaze, fired to cone 9; diameter 24″ (61 cm).

right: 265 **Susanne Stephenson**, U.S.A. Vase. Cut and altered porcelain, pink, blue, brown, and yellow slips under a clear glaze; height 10″ (25.4 cm).

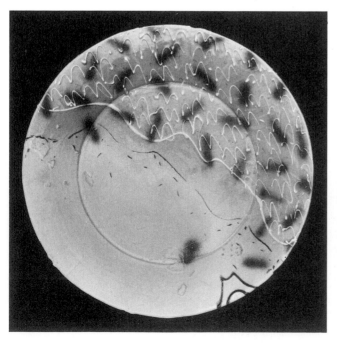

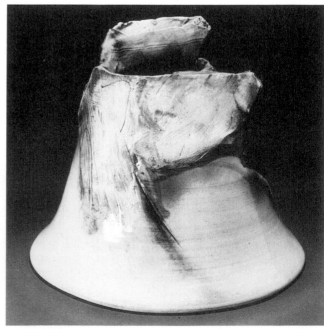

Yellow stains, such as Naples yellow and yellow base, are made from antimony, lead, and tin. Calcium and sodium uranate can also be used, when available, to form various yellow and orange colorants.

Pink and red stains are made by a number of methods. One of the most unusual is the precipitation of colloidal gold upon kaolin, which is then calcined and ground to form the stain. Other red stains are formed from a mixture of tin, calcium, flint, and chromium. (For further information and specific details, consult the reference texts by Parmelee, Norton, and Koenig and Earhart listed in the Bibliography.)

Underglaze Colors Underglaze colors were mentioned before briefly in Chapter 6 on decoration. As the term indicates, they are colors used under the glaze. Since they will eventually be fired at the same temperature as the glaze, the variety of colors available is less than for overglaze colors. For example, at the hard porcelain range of cone 14 (2548°F, 1398°C), most, if not all, of the delicate hues available in overglaze colors will burn out completely. This leaves only the blues, browns, grays, gold-pinks, reduction reds, and celadon hues available for use at these higher temperatures. It is advisable to run a series of firing tests before attempting any amount of decorative work at such temperatures. The basic reason for employing underglaze rather than overglaze colors is durability.

Underglaze colors are made up of a colorant (either a raw oxide or a spinel), a flux such as feldspar to allow the color to adhere to the body, and a diluent like silica, calcined kaolin, or ground bisque ware. The purpose of these last materials is either to lighten the color or to equalize shrinkage. It is rather important that the mixture be adjusted properly to the bisque ware and the final glaze. The glazed surface should show no change in gloss over the decoration.

Overglaze Colors The major differences between overglaze colors and underglaze colors are the use of a lower melting flux and a wider range of colors. Since the overglaze decoration is to be applied to a previously fired glaze, the final firing need be only high enough to allow the flux to melt into the glaze and seal the color. This is usually about cone 020 to cone 015, approximately 1231° to 1549°F (666°–843°C). The flux is made of varying proportions of lead, borax, and flint, depending upon the color to be used with it. The mixture is calcined lightly, ground, and washed. The colorant, and if necessary, an opacifier, is then added, and the whole mixture is ball milled to an adequate fineness. A vehicle such as gum or oil is used to help the mixture adhere to the glazed surface. In commercial production, where decoration is standardized, printing methods are used. The colors of both types of decoration are applied by decals or silk screen. (See Chap. 6 for application methods.)

Lusters Since lusters are employed more as decoration than as a glaze, they are included in this section on decorative coloring materials. As was noted earlier in the discussion of glaze types (Chap. 6), a luster is nothing more than a thin layer of metal that is deposited and fused upon the surface of the glaze. There are various methods by which this can be accomplished, some of them outlined below. Luster can give a variety of effects, depending upon the transparency or color of the composition and the type of glaze upon which it is applied. In Persian and Hispano-Moresque pieces it is very effectively combined with underglaze decoration. In fact, luster really comes into its own when it is used to enrich other types of decoration. The colors available in lusters are a transparent iridescent, a nacreous silver white, and metallic hues in a variety of yellows, greens, browns, and reds. (See Chap. 6 for methods of application and Plate 44, p. 252.)

Preparation of lusters will vary according to the specific method of firing to be employed. There are three types of preparation, the first being the most common.

1. A mixture composed of a resin, oil of lavender, and a metallic salt is brushed on the glazed ware. The ware is then fired in an oxidizing kiln to a low temperature of between 1100° and 1300°F (593°–704°C), at which point the carbon in the resin reduces the metallic salt to its metal form. Most lusters contain bismuth nitrate, an active flux, as well as the other metal salts. This is used in combination with zinc acetate, lead acetate, and alumina to produce a clear, iridescent luster. The various metal colorants are always used in the form of a salt that decomposes at the lower temperatures needed to form the luster coating. Yellows can be made with chrome alum and bismuth nitrate. Nickel nitrate, cobalt sulfate, manganese sulfate, and iron chloride will produce a variety of browns, shading from yellowish to reddish hues. Uranium nitrate, where available, develops a greenish yellow. Gold is commonly used to produce red hues and platinum to create silvery lusters. Many combinations of these colorants are used and results will be varied, depending in part upon the basic glaze and the firing schedule. In general, the luster mixture will consist of 1 part metallic salt, 3 to 5 parts resin, and 7 to 10 parts oil of lavender. The resin, usually gum dammar, is heated; when it becomes liquid, the nitrate or chloride is added. When the nitrate dissolves, the oil is slowly poured in. The solution is then filtered or cooled and decanted. The experiments in *Literature Abstracts of Ceramic Glazes* by J. H. Koenig and W. H. Earhart (see Bibliography) will help in creating formulas.

2. Another type of preparation is similar to that employed many centuries ago by Egyptian and other Middle Eastern potters, although it is seldom used today. These Islamic craftsmen developed luster and carried it to its highest level of artistic merit. The chief difference between their method and that described earlier is the use of a reduction fire to reduce the metal rather than having a reducing agent contained in the resin. The mixture, which is brushed on the glazed ware, consists of 3 parts metal, usually in a carbonate form, 7 parts red ochre, and an adhesive, such as gum tragacanth. Old recipes call for vinegar or wine, but gum is doubtless more efficient. In the firing cycle, the atmosphere is oxidizing until a low red heat is reached, whereupon reduction is started and continued to the temperature necessary to reduce the metal, usually from 1200° to 1300°F (649°–704°C).

3. The third method of developing a luster is also seldom used, but in rare instances it occurs by accident. The color is incorporated into the glaze, preferably in the form of a metallic salt. Various combinations can be used in proportions ranging from 0.5 to 8 percent of the total glaze. As in the resinate type of luster glaze, the use of bismuth, in addition to the other metallic salts, will aid luster development. The kiln is fired, oxidizing to the maturity point of the glaze, then cooled to between 1200° and 1300°F (649°–704°C). At this point the kiln is relit and fired for about fifteen minutes with a reducing atmosphere. Accurate records should be kept on reduction firings, since variations of temperature and reduction periods will produce quite different results.

Binders

Various materials can be added to either a clay body or a glaze to increase the green or dry strength of the ceramic form, to aid glaze adhesion, and to lessen injury to the fragile glaze coating during the kiln loading. The several binders and waxes used in industrial production to increase the body strength are not really needed by the studio potter, since a plastic clay body is usually adequate in this regard.

Clay   If the glaze contains an excess of 10 percent kaolin, additional binders may not be needed. However, if the clay content is low, the inclusion of about 3 percent bentonite will increase adhesion. It should be mixed with the dry ingredients. Macaloid and Veegum T are both refined colloidal magnesium aluminum silicate clays. Macaloid is similar to bentonite as a plasticizer in both clay bodies and glazes. Veegum T is useful both as a plasticizer and as an aid in suspending chemicals that tend to settle in the glaze. The addition of 2 or 3 percent to the glaze will prove helpful. Veegum T should be soaked in hot water.

Gums   Traditionally, gum arabic or gum tragacanth has been used as a glaze binder. The granular gum crystals are soaked overnight in water and stirred vigorously the following day. Heating in a double boiler will speed up the process. Straining may be necessary. About 0.25 ounces (7.5 g) will make a quart (0.95 liters) of creamlike mucilage binder. A couple of drops of carbolic acid are needed to prevent decomposition. One or two teaspoons of this solution per quart (0.95 liters) of glaze is usually adequate.

Gelatin   Gelatin, another glaze binder, is an animal glue dissolved in 4 parts water and added to the glaze in a proportion of 1 to 6. The gelatin solution may also be brushed onto either a vitreous or a very porous bisqued surface for better adhesion of the glaze.

Methocel   Methocel is a synthetic methylcellulose compound that will not deteriorate as the gums will and that also serves as an agent to prevent settling. The latter is a problem to which colemanite, in particular, is susceptible. Normally 1 to 2 percent methocel by dry weight is sufficient. The dry powder should not, however, be added to a liquid glaze. Instead, the powder should be sifted into hot water in a double boiler, the mixture soaked overnight, and then the resultant jellylike mass poured into a large container of hot water. When all the methocel is dissolved, it can be added to the glaze ingredients. An electric mixer is useful for this step, since it greatly speeds up the combining of ingredients.

Temporary Binders   In an emergency, sugar, syrup, or wheat flour can be used as a binder. Of course, all of these will ferment and therefore must not be stored without adding a few drops of formaldehyde to the glaze. The medium used in painting to produce acrylic pigments can also be used as a binder. Because it is a plastic, it does not decompose, although it may cause the glaze to settle.

Kilns and Firing

Much like the fisherman, the potter has in his work many elements of chance and failure. This is especially true of the final firing, in which pots may crack, glazes run, and other mishaps occur. It is no wonder that ancient potters were superstitious; they placed a votive figure over the kiln door and made supplications prior to firing. The following quotation is from a life of Homer purportedly by the fifth-century-B.C. Greek historian Herodotus but actually an imitation from a much later period (c. 130–80 B.C.). It is a "begging song" attributed to Homer, who, while visiting the island of Samos, was offered several pots by some potters in exchange for a song.

If you will pay me for my song, O potters,
then come, Athena, and hold thy hand above the kiln!
May the kotyloi and all the kanastra turn a good black,
may they be well fired and fetch the price asked,
many being sold in the marketplace and many on the roads,
and bring in much money, and may my song be pleasing.
But if you (potters) turn shameless and deceitful,
then do I summon the ravagers of kilns,
both Snytrips (Smasher) and Smaragos (Crasher) and
    Asbetos (Unquenchable) too, and Sabaktes
    (Shake-to-Pieces)
and Omodamos (Conqueror of the Unbaked), who makes much
    trouble for this craft.
Stamping on stoking tunnel and chambers, and may the whole kiln
be thrown into confusion, while the potters loudly wail.
As he grinds a horse's jaw so may the kiln grind
to powder all the pots within it.
[Come, too, daughter of the sun, Circe of many spells,
cast cruel spells, do evil to them and their handiwork.
Here too let Cheiron lead many Centaurs,
both those that escaped the hands of Herakles and those
    that perished.
May they hit these pots hard, and may the kiln collapse.
And may the potters wail as they see the mischief.
But I shall rejoice at the sight of their luckless craft.]
And if anyone bends over to look into the spy-hole, may
    his whole face
be scorched, so that all may learn to deal justly.*

Modern Kilns

The kiln types employed by the ancients, discussed in Chapter 2, are still in use today, but they have been modified to accommodate new fuels, new materials, and, in the ceramic industry, the need for expanded and efficient large-scale production. Perhaps the most drastic change in kiln design in recent times was caused by the development of a new source of power—electricity. Since the electric kiln needs no chimney or fuel lines and is comparatively portable, simple, and safe to operate, it has played a large part in the current popularity of ceramics. It is especially convenient for the potter

*From Joseph Veach Noble, *The Techniques of Painted Attic Pottery* (New York: Watson-Guptill, 1965), p. 107. Based on the text reproduced in Wilamowitz, *Vitae Homeri et Hesiodi*, trans. by Marjorie J. Milne (Bonn, 1916), pp. 17–18.

whose studio might be relatively temporary or for the school in which the original design provided for neither a chimney nor a source of fuel.

The increase in the 1970s in the prices of all fuels—oil, gas, and electricity—presents a real challenge to the potter. Kilns must be designed to operate as efficiently as possible. When fuel was relatively cheap, the potter building a new kiln often scrimped on materials, using inexpensive but not the most effective ones. New products now on the market are both light and convenient, as well as efficient in firing. Combined with traditional materials they promise a fuel saving. Although the price of refractory and insulating materials has risen, the most efficient materials will doubtless pay for their cost over the long run.

Fuel Kilns

Whether wood, coal, oil, or gas is used as a fuel, the basic kiln design is much the same. A combustion area is needed either below or to one side of the kiln chamber. Wood or coal requires a larger firebox area equipped with a grate and an ash pit. Saggers, which protect the glazed ware from flying ash, take up much space; they can be replaced with an inner muffle chamber that serves the same purpose. Both fuel oil and manufactured gas contain sulfur, which often causes dullness and blistering on the glaze surface. The updraft muffle kiln shown in Figure 266 was designed to eliminate this problem. The design, however, creates extra heat in the floor area, making an even firing difficult. Placing burners closer to the side wall will alleviate the problem to some extent. Most portable gas kilns are of the updraft type. They usually lack muffles and have small vertical burners spaced across the floor area.

The downdraft kiln illustrated in Figure 267 provides a more even heat distribution and has come to be the standard design preferred by most potters. This is especially true since the advent of cleaner natural gas, which has eliminated the need for a muffle. In this downdraft kiln the heat enters from multiple burners on each side, is deflected upward by the bag wall, and then is drawn down through the ware to a channel under the floor by the suction of the chimney. If the fuel supply and draft are adequate, it will ensure a heat deviation of no more than 1 cone from top to bottom.

For a smaller-size kiln, a layout such as that illustrated in Figure 268 with the burners placed to one side, may prove equally satisfactory. Numer-

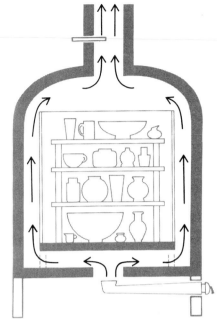

266   Gas-fired updraft muffle kiln.

left: **267**   Standard design for a gas-fired downdraft kiln.

right: **268**   Downdraft kiln with burner on one side.

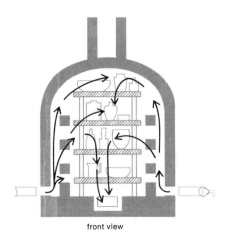

front view

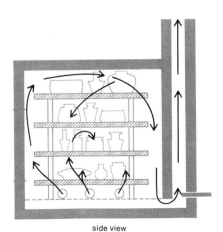

side view

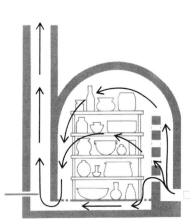

ous other burner arrangements have been tried, despite the fact that the design sketched in Figure 268 is most efficient.

A kiln fired with fuel oil requires a slightly larger combustion area than one fired with natural gas. The catenary-arch kiln shown in Figure 269 is ideal for fuel oil, since the flare at the bottom provides the extra combustion area needed. Except for the arch construction, the design is similar to that of a gas kiln. The curve is established by suspending a chain from two points, thus forming a natural self-supporting arch. A proportion in which the base equals the height is the most stable and provides excellent heat distribution. Although the arch is self-supporting, tie rods are desirable from front to back, since some movement occurs during firing. Oil is a satisfactory fuel, cheaper than gas, but it has some drawbacks. A separate shedlike installation is desirable, since the fumes that are given off, together with the noisy blowers, make an oil-burning kiln impractical for use inside the potter's studio or the classroom.

Square kilns are more likely to fire evenly, and are easier to load, if the door width is larger than the depth of the chamber. It is assumed that the chambers of the kilns discussed have a loading area of about 10 to 20 cubic feet (3.05 to 6.1 m³). However, many schools need a larger capacity. The physical strain incurred in stretching to load the heavy shelves and ware at the far end of a 30-cubic-foot (9.14–m³) chamber is too much for many people. In such situations a car kiln (Fig. 270) may be a good solution. This, again, is essentially the Figure 267 design, but the floor section is built on a steel frame and wheels, so that it can be rolled in and out of the kiln on a track. The door becomes an integral part of the car, instead of being bricked up in the usual fashion. There must be a close fit between the floor and the side walls, with a channel iron in the floor extending into a sand trough in the side wall to form a heat seal. In the car kiln the ware can be loaded from either side without undue strain.

In a large kiln, more burners may be needed than the illustrations show. As a rule, a more even firing results from several smaller burners rather than two or more extremely large units. In a long kiln, openings in the bag wall will need to be varied from front to back, because the draft, and the heat, may be greater at the rear, near the chimney.

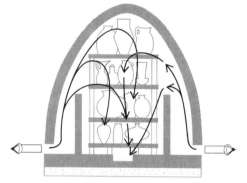

above: **269** Caternary-arch kiln.

right: **270** Downdraft car kiln design.

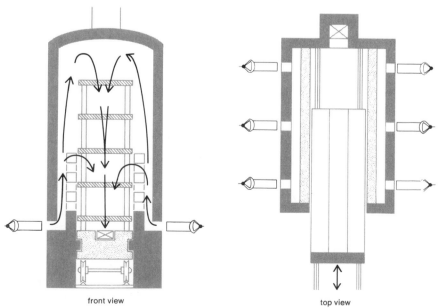

front view

top view

Electric Kilns

The gas kiln, because of its cheaper operation, greater size, and ability to maintain a reducing atmosphere, is preferred by most studio potters and university ceramics departments in the United States. In the Scandinavian countries, however, where electricity is relatively cheap and gas is not common, the electric kiln is almost universally used by the studio potter. The electric kiln has many advantages for the public school. It is almost as simple to operate as turning on a light switch, and there are no problems of burner adjustment or draft control. The small kiln, normally weighing about 300 pounds (136.08 k) can be wheeled anywhere. It requires only a 220-volt electrical outlet—a minor consideration compared to the gas kiln's demand of a high-temperature chimney and large-size gas lines. While in theory, room ventilation should not be a problem, in practice the kiln room, even for an electric kiln, should be well ventilated and if possible fitted with a hood with a fan exhaust to the outside. In firing, most clays give off carbon monoxide and sulfur. There are very few glazes that do not release some noxious fumes, all of which seep into the room atmosphere from the expanding pressure of the heated kiln chamber.

The electric kiln comes in two basic styles—the top loader and the front loader. In either type, a kiln with less than an 18-by-18-inch (45.72–by–45.72-cm) interior should not be considered, for it is too small to fire most pieces. The heat comes from radiation produced by coiled elements recessed in the side walls; therefore, a kiln chamber bigger than 24 by 24 inches (60.96 by 60.96 cm) requires a large coil or strip element, which greatly increases the cost of the kiln. Because they must have a stand and a heavy frame to carry the door, plus flexible connections to the door elements, front-loading kilns are much more expensive. The top loader is cheaper and easier to load, so it is a more logical purchase.

More recent top-loading electric kilns are made in a circular form with eight or ten insulating bricks cut at an angle to ensure a tight fit. The side wall is usually only 2.5 inches (6.35 cm) thick. The brick structure is wrapped in a thin stainless steel sheet, which holds the bricks in place. As shown in Figure 272, the usual controls are mounted on the side wall with a hinged top cover.

left: **271**   Unique front-loading electric kiln for temperatures to cone 10. Chamber 17″ × 17″ × 17″ (43.18 × 43.18 × 43.18 cm); weight 600 lbs. (270 kg).

right: **272**   Paragon octagonal top-loading electric kiln for temperatures to cone 8. Chamber 7 cu.′ (0.2 m³) with optional 4.5″ (11.25-cm) extension.

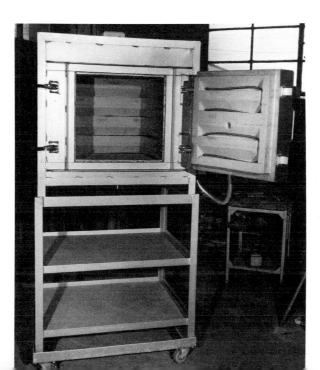

Occasionally additional sections may be added to fire unusually tall pieces. [The construction of a circular kiln is lighter as well as cheaper than that of the usual square kiln. More or heavier elements are needed to compensate for the greater heat loss. As a result the circular kiln both fires and cools off faster than the usual square kiln.] Some glazes react slightly different in a shorter firing cycle.

There are three types of electric heating elements. Suitable for a low fire (up to 2000°F or 1098°C) are those made of coiled nickel-nichrome wire. The kanthol type is constructed of a different alloy and will produce temperatures up to cone 8 (2305°F or 1263°C) although some types will go higher. Larger and higher-firing industrial kilns use carbon compounds in the form of a rod from 0.25 inches to 2 inches (0.64 to 5.08 cm) in diameter. Unfortunately, the special transformers needed are more expensive than the kiln itself, which makes the kiln more costly than gas or oil kilns.

Kiln Loading and Firing

The final step in the potter's art—the loading and firing of the kiln—is most important, for carelessness can easily ruin the potter's previous efforts. It can also do permanent damage to the kiln. With the exception of some salt-glaze ware and commercial high-fire porcelain, most pottery is fired first at a low bisque temperature. Some clay bodies can be glazed successfully in the raw state, but the fragility of unfired clay and the difficulty of glazing some shapes make a double firing desirable, especially in schools, where techniques of glazing and loading are being taught.

Pyrometric Cones and Other Temperature Gauges

Pyrometric cones provide the most accurate method of measuring the *work heat* in the kiln. The name is inaccurate, for the pyrometric "cone" is actually a tetrahedron or pyramid shape. Large cones are 1.75 inches (4.45 cm) high, with a base 0.5 inches (1.27 cm) across; small cones are 1.13 inches (2.87 cm) high and 0.25 inches (0.64 cm) wide at the base.

Cones are compounded of a material similar to a glaze. When softened by heat, they bend; when the cone forms a half circle, the temperature in the kiln is that of the cone number (see Appendix). The cone base is beveled to indicate the proper angle at which to press it into a pad of clay. A common practice is to use three cones—for example, 6, 8, and 9 if the firing is to reach cone 8. The bending of cone 6 warns that the kiln is approaching the proper temperature, and the potter should make burner or damper adjustments to stabilize the heat at this point. In a large kiln the cones are placed near both top and bottom, not too close to the door. As cone 8 bends, the burners can be cut back for a *soaking* period (holding the kiln at the same temperature). A softening of cone 9 indicates an overfiring. Kilns usually fire slightly hotter at the bottom, so a dryer glaze can be used there. If the cones are difficult to see, blowing into the peephole through a tube or inserting a metal rod near the cones will reveal them more clearly.

A slower rise in temperature, and the resulting longer period of chemical reaction, will permit a glaze to mature at a lower temperature than if the

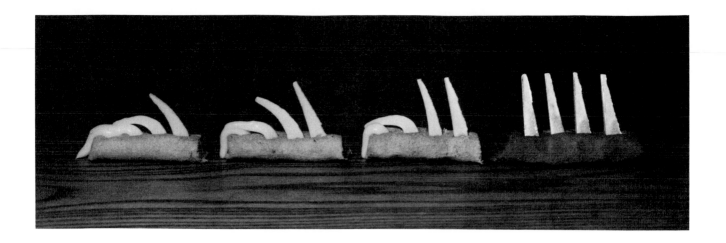

heat rise is rapid. This relationship between time and temperature is called the *work heat ratio,* and it is recorded by the pyrometric cone but not by the *pyrometer* (Figure 274). The pyrometer consists of a pair of welded wires of dissimilar metals, called a *thermocouple,* which is inserted into the kiln. When the kiln is heated, a minute electrical current indicates temperature change on a millivolt meter calibrated in degrees Fahrenheit (F) or centigrade (C). A pyrometer is convenient for making adjustments to produce the most efficient heat rise or to determine the proper time to begin a reduction. However, unless the potter has an exact and unvarying firing schedule, it is not completely accurate. In time, corrosion of the thermocouple tips affects the accuracy of the reading, but this can be adjusted to the proper cone by moving a tiny screw on the meter face.

above: **273** Pyrometric cones pressed into pads of clay; the pad at the right has not been fired, the others indicate different temperatures reached in the kiln.

274 Unique pyrometer with insulated leads and thermocouple.

Pyrometers are available in both low- and high-fire models. The rather inexpensive ones used by potters are seldom reliable over a wide range of temperatures; that is, if the cone 8 reading is correct, the cone 4 may be inaccurate. A slightly more expensive pyrometer has a thermocouple with wire tips completely enclosed in a porcelain jacket. This instrument is recommended for larger kilns in frequent use, for it is less apt to be damaged in kiln loading or by slight chemical reactions during firing. Optical pyrometers are also available; these are quite accurate, except in a reducing fire, but rather expensive. Glazed-clay draw rings, which were common before the introduction of cones, can also be used to measure kiln temperature. Such rings are the only method of determining glaze buildup in a salt kiln.

Various devices with a cone in a spring arrangement and an electrical cutoff are used in small electric kilns. They are a great convenience provided they work consistently. It must be noted that only the small-size cones, which have a different temperature range than the standard cones (see Appendix), can be used. While many potters use these cutoff devices, the author's experience has not been too satisfactory. The working parts tend to corrode and accumulate glaze from the melted cone. Although their design has doubtless improved over the years, he personally would not lock the studio and depend solely on the cutoff to turn off the kiln.

The Bisque Fire

The bisque temperature is generally between cone 010 and cone 06, depending upon the clay body used. Fired bisque ware must be hard enough to endure normal handling in the glazing operation, yet sufficiently absorbent to permit glaze adhesion. Ware bisqued below cone 012 may crack during the glaze fire if too much flux is absorbed into the porous clay body. The stacking of a bisque kiln is quite different from that required for a glaze fire. In each situation, however, at least 1 inch (2.54 cm) of free space must be left between the electrical elements and the ware. In a gas kiln 3 inches (7.62 cm) between the kiln wall and the ware is a desirable margin to allow free passage of heat and to avoid hot spots.

Raw ware must be completely dry before it is loaded in the bisque kiln. The accepted test for dryness is to hold the piece against the cheek. If it feels cold, there is still moisture in the clay.

Since there is no problem of glaze sticking, kiln wash in not needed, and pieces may touch one another. It is possible to stack one piece inside or on top of another, building to a considerable height. The potter must take care to make foot rims coincide for support and to avoid placing heavy pieces on more fragile ones. Large, shallow bowls, which might warp, can be fired upside down on their rims if the kiln shelf is even. Several smaller sizes can be placed underneath. Covers should be fired in place to prevent warping, and tall knobbed covers can often be reversed to save space.

Even though apparently dry, raw clay contains much moisture, and firing should proceed at a low heat for several hours. Kiln doors should be left ajar or peepholes left open for an hour or so to allow this moisture to escape. Large, heavy pots or sculptural pieces must be fired slowly to prevent the moisture contained in hidden air pockets from being converted into steam, which would cause the piece to explode. Figure 275 shows a pot, containing excess organic matter, that bloated in a too-rapid bisque fire.

275 Pottery shard with a bloated base from a too-rapid bisque fire.

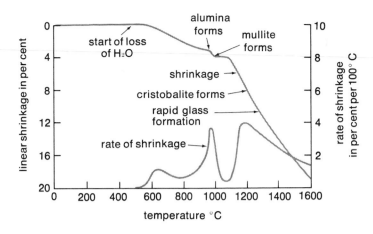

276 Linear shrinkage and rate of shrinkage for kaolin (F. H. Norton, *Elements of Ceramics*, Addison-Wesley, 1952).

Chemical Changes

Chemical changes in the body during firing are slight at first (Fig. 276). When the temperature reaches 350° to 400°F (178°-204°C), all atmospheric moisture should have left the ware, causing little or no shrinkage. Most of the chemically combined water will leave the ware at temperatures between 950° and 1300°F (510°-705°C). During this "water smoking" period considerable shrinkage occurs as both the chemically combined water and gases from organic material leave the body. The firing should not be too rapid, for the body is very weak. As the temperature approaches 1750°F (955°C) and continues to 1850°F (1010°C) tough, needlelike crystals of alumina-silica ($3Al_2O_3 \cdot SiO_2$), called *mullite,* begin to form, but they are not fully developed until stoneware temperatures are reached. These crystals give toughness to the body, and as the temperature increases, additional free silica forms a glass around them. Because of impurities and varying composition, clay bodies achieve maximum hardness at different temperatures. Earthenware clay matures at about 2000°F (1090°C), stoneware at about 2350°F (1290°C), and pure clay (kaolin) at about 3000°F (1650°C). Porcelain fires in the same range as stoneware, normally between cones 8 and 10, although higher temperatures are possible.

Quartz Inversion

A major problem in the successful compounding of ceramics bodies is quartz inversion. During the firing of a ceramic body, silica (quartz) changes its crystalline structure several times. This is especially true of free silica that is not in a chemical bond with other body components. The most pronounced change occurs when the firing temperature reaches 1063°F (575°C). At this point the quartz crystals change from alpha to beta quartz, with a resultant expansion. At about 1850°F (1010°C) tough, interlocking mullite crystals composed of alumina and silica begin to form, and this chemical combination gives the fired body its strength. In the cooling process the situation is reversed. When the kiln temperature drops at 1063°F, the free silica in the body contracts. Quartz inversion is one of the reasons why a slow cycle of firing and cooling is essential. If a ceramic piece is heated or cooled too quickly, or if the distribution of heat is uneven, the piece will crack. Special precautions are required for ovenware, which must be able to withstand, with minimal thermal expansion, the heat to which it will be exposed in use.

Cooling Procedures

Cooling procedures are important to the maintenance of kilns. When the correct temperature has been reached, the electric kiln can simply be turned off and allowed to cool. In the fuel-burning kiln, the chimney damper must be closed immediately to prevent a cold draft of air from being sucked into the burner pots, which might crack both the ware and the shelves. Just as the kiln must be fired slowly, so must it be allowed to cool naturally. The damper can be opened after cooling overnight, and the peephole plugs can be removed, but the door must not be opened more than a crack until the temperature has dropped to 400°F (204°C). Even slower cooling may be desirable for extremely large or heavy pieces. An expensive kiln, which should give at least ten years' service before repairs are needed, may be ruined after a short time by careless firing and cooling.

277 Loading a double shuttle car kiln at Bennington Potters.

KILNS AND FIRING

The Glaze Fire

The glaze fire differs in several respects from the bisque fire: the loading is different, the kiln atmosphere may be varied, and the final temperature must be controlled carefully. Since mishaps may occur from runny glazes, all kiln shelves must be scraped and coated with a *kiln wash*. Kiln wash consists of equal parts of silica (flint) and kaolin in a creamy mixture. Several coats may be needed, each coat applied before the last is completely dry. A new shelf can be sprayed or brushed with aluminum paint before the kiln wash is applied. Dusting on a thin layer of coarse silica sand gives additional protection. The shelf edges must be cleaned to prevent this sand from sifting down on the ware below. All glazed ware should be *dry footed*—that is, all glaze cleaned off the base and about 0.25 inches (0.64 cm) up the foot rim. Glazes that are runny, such as crystalline and copper-reds, can be placed on a pedestal made from high-firing insulating brick coated with kiln wash. This will facilitate any later grinding of the excess glaze.

A uniform load without tight spots will produce an even firing. The potter should never try to fire a half load, since uneven temperatures are almost certain to occur. Staggering the shelves in a large kiln will create a more even heat flow. In the typical electric kiln, shelves should not be placed close to the bottom or the top, for a cold spot will develop in the center area. Test tiles must always be stacked near the middle, since there is usually some temperature variation from top to bottom. A center support is desirable for larger shelves. Damp clay pads used to level uneven posts should be dusted first with dry flint to avoid sticking. If the shelves are of moderate size, three posts will eliminate leveling problems. As in the bisque fire, covers are best fired in place, but the potter must make certain that the contact areas are clear of glaze. Placing glazed ware too close to the upper bag wall often results in shiny spots, although gaps in the bricks may even out the heat in this area. Glazed pieces should be at least 0.25 inches (0.64 cm) apart because heat radiation can also cause shininess. This may not be necessary with high-shrinkage bodies.

Reduction Firing

Reduction firing, or reducing, means that part of the firing cycle is conducted with an inadequate amount of oxygen to burn up all the fuel. As a result, the free carbon in the kiln atmosphere unites with, and thus reduces, the oxygen content of the metallic oxides in both the body and the glaze, thereby altering their color. In a forced-draft burner this process is accomplished by cutting down on the air supply, while in a natural-draft burner the flue damper is cut back slightly, so that less air will be sucked into the kiln.

Excessive reduction is undesirable. Not only does the temperature drop rapidly, but the body may erupt with blisters or even crack, and the glaze becomes a dirty gray. In a natural-draft kiln a slight backing up of the flame at the burner ports will occur. This is all that is necessary for a reduction, not the belching of flame and smoke that some people seem to enjoy—until the blistered pots are unloaded.

The atmosphere should be an oxidizing one during the first part of the firing cycle, in order to ensure the most efficient heat rise. The reduction needed to produce a rich body color is effective only at the temperatures below which the glaze begins to melt. When the maximum temperature has

 Safety Caution

Because of atmospheric pressure built up during reduction, you should pull out the peep plugs cautiously, with your face turned away, for the flame will shoot out at least a foot (30.05 cm). In a tall bricked-up door, inserting a section of curved sheet metal under the tie rod and pressing against the top bricks is helpful, since the door bricks may lean outward due to the pressure of the expanding gases in the kiln.

been reached, the damper can be adjusted to provide a neutral or slightly reducing fire. The usual practice is to cut back the burners slightly after the cones begin to bend to allow a half hour or so of an oxidizing *soaking heat* during which temperatures can stabilize and glazes become smoother.

The term *reduction fire* must not be confused with *reduction glazes*. The latter are glazes especially compounded to produce copper-red and celadon colors (see Chap. 6). In the firing of these glazes there may be little change in body color but rather a reduction of the coloring oxides in the glaze from an oxidic to a metallic form. Thus, copper-green becomes a rich red, and the iron brown-red is transformed into a gray-green or even a pale shade of blue. In a reduction glaze fire the reduction begins later than for a body reduction, but it must occur before the glaze begins to melt. Since the reduction causes the heat rise to diminish, there is usually an alternation of reduction and oxidation. Too much oxidation will bleach out the color. Copper-red color variations range from a mottled blue, green, and red to a deep purple-red or a pale pink, depending upon the reduction sequence, the glaze thickness, and the body color. In both copper-red and celadon glazes the body should be porcelain. However, the celadon body may have 1 or 2 percent iron. This slightly gray body usually improves the celadon color.

A *localized reduction* can be obtained by adding 0.5 percent of silicon carbide (carborundum, 40-mesh or finer) to a suitable copper-alkaline glaze. The result is usually a speckled red-and-purple color. Its only real advantage is its adaptability to the electric kiln. The atmosphere in an electric kiln can be reduced by popping a few mothballs through the peephole. The kiln should have heavy elements, which have a good oxidized coating from many previous firings. Continuous reductions will eat away the elements and corrode and eventually destroy the electrical connections, but an occasional one will do little harm to the kiln.

Raku Firing

In the last twenty years raku ware has developed in an entirely different direction from its Japanese origin (see Chap. 3). While it still requires a low-temperature (usually below cone 4) rapid-fire process, the infusion of contemporary images and the availability of lightweight insulating materials for kilns has directed the attention of potters away from the Japanese tea ware tradition. As a demonstration technique raku firing can be very useful because it compresses the amount of time needed to take a pot through the entire ceramic process. As a medium of expression it allows a variety of glaze and surface techniques. At first it would seem that most of the raku firing results are accidental, but in time the experienced potter can learn to control the effects, which seem so unpredictable, and still be rewarded with some unexpected results. The potter should look for variations in the clay body formula that might affect the fired density and crackle patterns. The range of glaze and engobe possibilities are immense and affect the ability of the ware to form lusters and accept reduction. The cooling cycle and related reduction smoking affect body color (see Plates 43 and 44, p. 285) and luster and crackle formation.

The raku body is usually formulated as a white body, which remains porous after both bisque and glaze firing. Fireclay with from 10 percent to 30 percent grog is a good place to begin. Additions of more plastic clays or shock-resistant materials such as kyanite may be tried to facilitate larger pots.

Safety Caution

Safety is an important consideration when handling hot raku pots. Equipment such as tongs, asbestos mittens, a face shield, cap, leather jacket, and leather shoes should all be available as protection from heat, flame, and smoke.

KILNS AND FIRING

Even low-temperature talc bodies have been used successfully for intricate forms.

Raku pots should be glazed a day in advance of firing to allow all glaze water to evaporate. Prior to placing them into the hot kiln they should be preheated to about 400°F (204.44°C). The glaze can be observed through a small peephole in the kiln, and as it nears the proper melt an area should be prepared for "working" the pot during the cooling cycle.

Reduction generally takes place outside the kiln in a separate metal container using combustibles such as sawdust, shredded paper, excelsior, or dry leaves (Fig. 278). The alternate cooling and smoking of the pot produces color patterns in the open clay, crackle in the glaze, and lusters from certain metallic oxides (copper being the most common). See Plate 35, p. 216.

The raku kiln need not be a complex piece of equipment. A mortarless construction of #26 insulation firebrick with a corbeled arch and portable door will work well. The introduction of ceramic-fiber blanket has made simple, lightweight kilns possible. The interior of a metal drum can be lined with a fiber blanket 1 inch (2.54 cm) thick, using a special cement provided by the manufacturer. The resulting kiln will be easy to handle and heat up quickly for repeat firing. Whichever approach to kiln construction is used, the interior should be designed just slightly larger than the largest pot to be fired. Empty space does not heat up efficiently. The burner should be aimed in such a way as to use the space under the shelf as a firebox to avoid playing the flame directly on the pot.

left: **278**   After the glowing pot is placed in shavings to obtain a reduction the container is momentarily removed to induce a crackle.

right: **279**   Peach Valley Pottery raku kiln with ceramic fiber insulation; chamber 12″ × 14″ (40 × 60 cm), weight 12 lbs. (5.4 kg).

Firing Lead Glazes

Lead glazes require extra care in formulation (see Chap. 7) and also precautions in firing. Lead melts at a relatively low temperature, so a portion of the lead volatilizes into the kiln atmosphere. In cooling, this free lead settles back onto the glaze surface. This unstable lead film easily breaks down under normal use, thus increasing the danger of lead poisoning. The problem is limited to electric kilns because in a fuel kiln all gaseous impurities are drawn off by the chimney draft. A small hole drilled in the lower and upper peephole plugs will allow the lead particles to be drawn off by the natural movement of the heated air. This need be done only during the end of the firing cycle. A hood with an exhaust fan must be installed over the electric kiln, for otherwise the potter will inhale the lead-bearing air. The same is true of the gas kiln. There are always cracks that open up in the firing and allow gaseous impurities to escape into the studio, especially during reduction cycles.

Salt-Glaze Firing

Salt glazes are unusual from several standpoints. Decorative pieces, or those glazed raw on the inside, can be fired in a single firing. Salt (sodium chloride) is not applied directly to the ware to form the glaze but is inserted in the kiln when the maturity of the clay body has been reached. This procedure causes the salt to volatilize and combine with the silica in the clay body to form the glaze. The clay body should have a high silica content. If silica is added to the body, it should be finely ground, because coarse silica particles will not unite with the vaporous sodium to form a glaze.

The interior of any kiln used for salt glazing must be lined with either a hard refractory firebrick or a castable, because insulating firebrick will soak up the sodium and deteriorate rapidly. Traditionally, salt kilns were made of hard firebrick. The salt was permitted to build up in a coating on the brick surface. During the first firings in a new kiln a great deal of salt was needed. In effect, the kiln was being glazed along with the ware. After a while, when the glaze coating had built up, much less salt was needed. The kiln used in this manner is unsuitable for normal glaze firings. And, in time, the interior surfaces deteriorate as the salt reacts with the silica contained in the refractory firebrick and literally eats into it.

Some potters try to prevent this corrosion by either coating the interior of the kiln with alumina compounds or using a high-alumina cement to cast the interior and the kiln roof. ALCOA's calcium-aluminate cement (#CA-25) and tabular-aluminate (grog) will produce a refractory wall that can withstand temperatures higher than 3000°F (1650°C). The usual mixture for this refractory material is 15 parts cement, 85 parts tabular-aluminate, plus 10 percent water. Larger amounts of water will result in a weaker bond. Since the mixture sets up in an hour, all forms must be ready. It is possible to pour in sections if the joints are left rough. The roof arch, however, must be completed at once.

Salting begins when the body has matured. (Cones are not completely accurate in determining the body maturation temperature because the sodium vapor from the kiln walls will react on the cones.) Coarse rock salt is the preferred material; about 5 ounces per cubic foot (141.75 g per 30.48 cm^3) of kiln space will be needed, less if the salt kiln is well coated. The salt should be moistened with water and divided into eight portions. These portions can be placed in small paper condiment cups (purchased from a restaurant supply house). By means of a ring formed from a wire coat hanger, the salt packets can be inserted through the salting ports into the firebox area. In a Rhineland downdraft salt kiln the ports are located in the arch of the roof; in an open-draft design, salting can be done through the burner ports. A closed, forced-draft kiln design will have to be modified to allow for special salting ports.

The draft must be cut back slightly when the salting begins in order to prevent the salt from being drawn out the stack. The coarse, damp rock salt will explode and scatter through the kiln. At this point deadly fumes of chlorine gas are given off, so the kiln room must be well ventilated. Many salt kilns are constructed in outside sheds that can be opened during salting to discharge the fumes harmlessly.

A recommended salting procedure requires two hours, with the eight portions of salt introduced at fifteen-minute intervals. Because the draft is cut back, a slight reduction will occur. After about five minutes the draft can be adjusted to a neutral fire so that the heat loss during reduction can build up again. The potter may want to develop a slightly different salting procedure to account for variations in kiln design, materials, and clay body, but the two-hour sequence is recommended as a starting point. Too short a salting sequence will not allow for a proper buildup of the glaze.

Instead of the cones normally used to gauge the firing, several draw rings or clay doughnuts should be placed in the areas of the kiln where cones would usually be placed. After about half the salt has been used, one or more test clay rings should be hooked out of the kiln so that the potter can observe the glaze buildup. Care should be taken in placing and removing the clay rings, or they may be knocked down into the kiln.

A characteristic of the salt glaze is its pebbly appearance. Potters who prefer a smoother glaze surface sometimes add about 5 percent borax. Feldspar and other semifluxes can be used in slip decoration to obtain sections of still glossier glaze. As in normal kiln firings, the body must be reduction-fired, if desired, before any appreciable glaze buildup occurs.

Because of the toxic effects of chlorine gas given off by rock salt, many potters have experimented with sodium bicarbonate ($NaHCO_3$) instead of sodium chloride ($NaCl$). The bicarbonate form does not disperse so readily in the kiln as does the rock salt when inserted through the burner ports, so it is helpful to use a small, low-powered electric blower. Some potters have found that sodium bicarbonate mixed with water and sprayed into the kiln works better than the dry form. The atmosphere can be neutral or slightly reducing. As in the customary salting procedure, the glaze buildup will take several hours.

Salt glazes generally fire in the cone 8 to cone 10 range and can be used on either a stoneware or a porcelain body. Lower-fire salt glazes (as low as cone 04) are possible with additions of borax.

Since the salt glaze alone is colorless, any color in the glaze must come from the body or from coloring oxides applied in engobes on the raw ware. Soluble forms of oxides, such as nitrates or chlorides, can also be brushed onto the ware. Deep forms must be glazed inside, for little vaporous salt will reach the interior. The kiln load must be uniform and not too tight, or else the glaze coating will be uneven. Incised or pressed designs will be accentuated by uneven amounts of glaze buildup, a factor that adds to the interest of the salt glaze.

Some potters fume their ware to produce an iridescent sheen on portions of the glaze. The general technique is to cool the salted kiln to a low red heat. Then, water-soluble colorants (such as chlorides or nitrates) are sprayed into the kiln in a thin mist. Often the sole chemical used is the chloride form of tin. This will react with the other colors in the clay and engobes to form varied iridescent hues. Dry colorants that volatilize under the heat can also be used.

Kiln Materials

Thanks to the industrial market, most kiln materials are available in any large city, but prices may vary. Even in a small town a building-supply dealer can generally provide firebrick and other basic supplies.

Firebrick

Firebrick is made in a number of special compositions, but the common alumina-silica *hard refractory firebrick* is satisfactory for most purposes. Different grades are produced for operating temperatures of 1600°, 2000°, 2300°, 2600°, and 2800°F (870°, 1093°, 1260°, 1427°, and 1538°C), and some can be used at temperatures as high as 3000° and 3200°F (1650° and 1760°C).

The bricks used for higher operating temperatures are denser and lose much of their insulating ability. They are also more expensive. Therefore, a potter should not purchase a higher-grade brick than is needed. A 2600°F (1427°C) brick is generally used for kilns firing from cone 8 to cone 10. Special arch- and wedge-shape bricks can be ordered for the curve of the kiln

280 Alpine updraft gas car kiln with standard insulating firebrick for temperatures to cone 14. Capacity 90 cubic feet (2.7 m³), shipping weight 14,000 lbs. (6300 kg).

roof. A kiln constructed entirely of hard firebrick will consume a great deal of fuel, since the bricks absorb and conduct a considerable amount of heat. Fortunately, porous insulating firebrick is also made, which has an insulating value from three to five times as great as that of the hard brick. Insulating firebricks are available in a temperature range similar to that of hard brick, but the cost is much higher. They are most often used as a backup layer next to the hard brick, although kilns made entirely of insulating bricks are common. Insulating firebricks require less fuel and can be cut easily with a coarse-tooth saw, such as an inexpensive pruning or bow-saw.

Ceramic-Fiber Insulation

Research in new, lightweight, high-temperature insulating materials for the space program resulted in the development of ceramic-fiber insulation. These new materials are, for the most part, extruded, fine-dimension fibers of alumina and silica. They have a purer composition than the denser, heavier firebrick. Ceramic-fiber insulation comes in several forms: 0.75- and 1-inch (1.91- and 2.54-cm) rigid panels, 24 by 36 inches (60.96 by 91.44 cm) in area; 1-inch (2.54-cm) lightweight, ceramic-fiber blankets, in a roll 2 feet wide by 25 feet (0.61 by 7.62 m) long; loose granular materials; and a lightweight, ceramic-fiber castable mixture. These materials are compounded for operating temperatures between 2300° and 2600°F (1260°–1427°C). Ceramic-fiber cements are available for joining sections and filling cracks. Ceramic studs can be used to tie inner rigid panels to the outer kiln structure. When these products first appeared on the market, they had a number of flaws. Considerable shrinkage occurred in the rigid panels, and cracks appeared in the castable mixture when it was exposed to long firing cycles. However, improvements have been made in recent years.

281 Westwood updraft gas kiln with ceramic fiber insulation for temperatures to cone 10. Capacity 12 cubic feet (0.36 m³), weight 725 lbs. (326 kg).

The fiber insulation, although costlier than firebrick, is much lighter, and the size of the panels speeds up construction time. The Peach Valley raku kiln (Fig. 280) could not have its convenient lift-up feature without the lightweight blanket insulation. The Westwood kiln (Fig. 281), made of lightweight ceramic-fiber material, is one-third the weight of similar-size models using traditional construction. The new fibers can also serve as a sandwich layer or a backup layer to the conventional firebrick.

Castable Refractories

Castable refractories of varying compositions for several operating temperatures are also available. These can be mixed and poured like concrete. Although more expensive than brick, castable refractories are useful for forming odd shapes, such as burner ports or small arches. They are dense and conduct heat much as hard brick does. A castable calcium-alumina refractory can serve as liner for a dual-purpose salt kiln, so that salt will not accumulate on the firebrick interior. With this arrangement a bisque or glaze kiln can safely be used for the occasional salt-glaze firing. Over a long period the door bricks will have to be replaced several times, and the combustion area near the burner ports will require chipping out and recasting as a result of the salt action, but the rest of the kiln will remain largely unaltered.

Other Insulating Materials

Insulating materials of a lower heat tolerance but with great insulating value can also be used for a backup layer. Even common soft red brick will serve this purpose. Kilns of more than 30 cubic feet (9.14 m^3) are commonly built with a hard firebrick core, a middle portion of insulating firebrick, and an outer layer of red brick.

Asbestos sheets and blocks of various sizes provide good insulation. When the outer walls rise to a height of several courses, loose granular vermiculite poured to a depth of 6 to 8 inches (15.24 to 20.32 cm) will give further insulation to the roof crown, which in most situations tends to be rather cool. To insulate further a high curved brick roof, such as a catenary arch, vermiculite can be mixed with plaster of paris and troweled on. Chicken wire embedded in the mixture will provide additional support, as expansions and cracks occur during firing. Commercial block insulation made of vermiculite, asbestos fibers, and cement is available in slabs 2 by 6 by 24 inches (5.08 by 15.24 by 60.96 cm). This will serve as a backup insulation at temperatures below 1800°F (980°C).

Safety Caution

Asbestos fibers are dangerous if inhaled and should be sealed if exposed.

Transite

A rigid cement-asbestos sheet material, transite, comes in 4-by-8-foot (1.22-by-2.44-m) panels, in 0.25- and 0.39-inch (0.64- and 0.99-cm) thicknesses. It is useful for the outer wall of a small kiln having an angle iron frame, since it protects and dresses up the brickwork and serves as a retainer for loose insulation poured between the brick wall and the transite. Transite is also available in tubular form, and in this guise it makes a quite satisfactory chimney or flue duct, provided sufficient air space surrounds the pipe. A thickness of 0.5 inches (1.27 cm) is usually sufficient; thicker sections tend to chip and flake off because of the great difference in the heats to which the inner and outer surfaces are exposed. Sometimes a bad mixture of materials or dampness in the flue will cause transite to explode. It is safer to use a fireclay-lined, steel-encased chimney section or a heavy sheet-metal chimney, provided it is kept at a proper distance from any flammable material.

Kiln Furniture

The shelves, posts, and other props used in the kiln comprise the kiln furniture. Heavy fireclay shelves have been replaced by newer materials. Mullite shelves are suitable for earthenware temperatures, but the more expensive silicon carbide shelves give longer service and are compounded for higher temperatures. A 0.75-inch (1.91-cm) inch thickness is adequate for standard loads. To avoid sagging and possible breakage in spans of 24 inches (60.96 cm) or more, a center post is necessary. Rectangular shelves are less subject to strain in cooling and heating, so they give longer service than square ones. A slow heating and cooling cycle not only minimizes damage to the pots but will prolong the life of the kiln furniture, especially the shelves. Salt glazes eat away the normal kiln shelves. Coating all surfaces with alumina hydrate mixed with a binder will help. The best solution is to use an especially compounded high-alumina shelf, but these are usually expensive.

Posts made of fireclay are available in various sizes. They often have a center opening to promote a more even expansion. High-temperature insulating bricks can be cut to make satisfactory posts. Dipping the ends of the fireclay posts into aluminum paint will lessen their tendency to stick to silicon carbide shelves. This problem does not arise with triangular slip-cast posts made of porcelainlike material. Triangular porcelain stilts having pointed contact areas, and often a nickel-nichrome wire insert can be used for some covers or for small pieces that must be glazed overall. The small contact blemishes are not noticeable.

Kiln Construction

Twenty-five years ago few potters were building their own kilns, but with the burgeoning interest in ceramics and with increased knowledge this practice is now quite common. The beginner, who has little experience in the principles of kiln design, would be advised to duplicate a proven design, rather than to experiment. Not counting the value of labor, the potter may save 50 percent over the cost of a prefabricated model. Moreover, larger heavy-duty downdraft kilns are seldom available readymade.

Electric Kilns

The electric kiln, which needs no chimney or gas lines, presents the least challenge to the novice (Fig. 282). Unless the student potter is technically inclined, he or she will best forego the problems of calculating length of element wire, size, resistance, and ohms necessary to obtain the desired heat in the kiln chamber. It is easier to purchase replacement elements for a standard kiln made by a reputable manufacturer. The electrical switches may be quite difficult to locate, for the best type is not commonly available. Kiln manufacturers carry replacements.

282 Cross section of a square electric kiln.

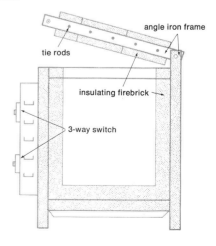

The angle-iron frame with supporting angles can be fabricated easily, but it must be square and accurate. Transite in 0.25-inch (0.64-cm) thickness, cut a bit small to allow for heat expansion, can make the floor base and outer walls. Standard insulating firebrick straight (9 by 4.5 by 2.5 inches, or 22.86 by 11.43 by 6.35 cm) laid "on the flat," is used for the side walls—the 2300°F (1260°C) grade for a cone 4 kiln, 2600°F (1427°C) for a cone 6 to 8 kiln. No cutting of the bricks is required for an 18-by-18-inch (45.72- by 45.72-cm) interior. The bricks must be staggered as the courses are built up. To prevent them from shifting, long finishing nails can be driven through the bricks or a thin coat of fireclay and sodium silicate moistened with water, can be applied. No cement should be used within 1.5 inches (3.81 cm) of the elements, in case the elements are placed in the joint between bricks.

The element recess can be cut with a coarse saw (a Swedish pruning saw, for example) and a round rasp, or with a simple cutting tool in a drill press. To retard possible contamination the recesses can be coated with aluminum paint or with a thin coat of kiln wash before inserting the elements. Low-fire nickel-nichrome replacement elements come in a coil like a screen-door spring. They can be stretched to fit the kiln by driving four nails into a section of plywood at a distance comparable to the size of the element recess and a fifth at the point where the element end enters the kiln from the control box. Most elements go twice around the kiln and need a diagonal slot to complete the circle. The coils must not touch at any point, or a hot spot will develop.

Unless the potter has some electrical experience, it is advisable to hire an electrician to hook up the wiring. Bolts in the transite to hold the control panel should be inserted before the bricks are laid in place. A piece of transite can serve as the base. Brass bolts should be used as connecting posts between the elements and the insulated switch wires (Fig. 283). The usual switch has three positions—low, medium, and high—hooked up on 110 volts, 210 volts in series, and 210 volts in parallel to give the needed current. After repeated firings the nickel-nichrome elements will contract, but they can be removed, carefully stretched again, and put back in place. A ventilated cover with adequate clearance must enclose the exposed connections.

283 Detail of electric kiln showing brick, element, and wiring placement.

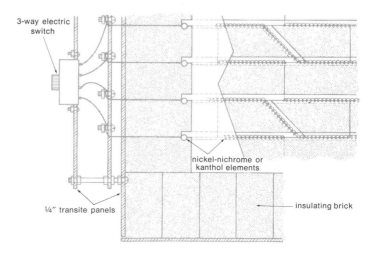

3-way electric switch

nickel-nichrome or kanthol elements

¼" transite panels

insulating brick

above: **Plate 43** **Wayne Higby**, U.S.A. *Tidesands Inlet.* Wheel-thrown and altered earthenware. White slip with iron and cobalt stains. Raku fired, diameter 19″ (47.5 cm).

right: **Plate 44** **Barbara Segal**, U.S.A. *Eroded Sun.* Raku plate with mat glaze border and golden luster, 15″ (37.5 cm) square.

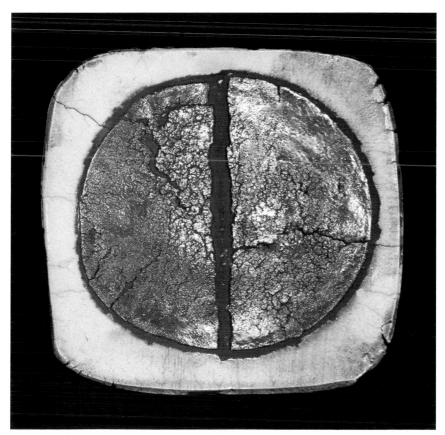

285

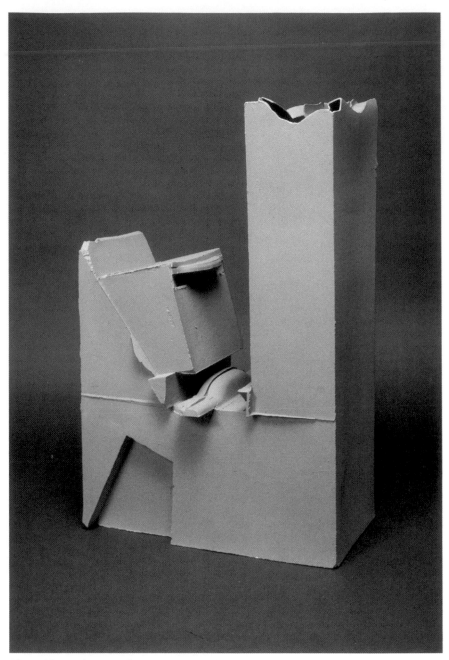

Plate 45   Robert Sedestrom, U.S.A. Slip-cast form of vitreous china; 25″ × 13″ × 7″ (63.5 × 33 × 17.7 cm).

The cover on a top-loading kiln presents little problem, for 0.25-inch (0.63-cm) bolts—two in each brick, running through an angle iron on each side—will provide adequate support. If the angle is continued to the rear and the back frame angle is elevated 2 inches (5.08 cm), a hinge can be contrived by drilling a hole and inserting a rod. Similarly, an extension in front and a rod inserted in a pipe will provide a lifting handle.

The high-fire (cone 8) electric kiln can also use bricks 4.5 inches (11.4 cm) thick. In this situation, however, an extra 1-inch (2.54-cm) backing of asbestos or ceramic fiber would be desirable. Unless a porcelain insert channel is used, the potter must take greater care in selecting firebricks. Because of the higher heat, any iron impurities in the firebricks will melt and cause the element to flux and burn out. It is extremely important to obtain the proper bricks before attempting any construction. The hard kanthol elements become brittle after use, but their tendency to contract is diminished if they are first fired to cone 8, even though subsequent firings are lower.

Gas Kilns

Thanks to the uniformity of insulating firebricks, a small gas kiln can be built with no cement. This is particularly true of raku kilns, which are small and temporary in nature. A single burner can be placed in a simple box, with the pots set on a few bricks. A flat roof with a small hole for exhaust is sufficient. Either a bolted top or a similar side section can be used, since the ware is inserted and removed from the hot kiln with tongs.

A portable raku kiln can be constructed by cutting a 55-gallon (208.2-liter) steel drum about 3 inches (7.62 cm) from the top to make a cover. The remaining drum is too deep to load conveniently, so an additional 10 inches (25.4 cm) can be cut off and discarded. A 4-inch (10.16-cm) hole is cut in the cover section to serve as an exhaust; a 3-inch (7.62-cm) hole is cut into the base section about 4 inches (10.16 cm) from the bottom to serve as the burner inlet.

Since raku kilns fire at a low heat, the usual high-temperature castables are not necessary and can be replaced by a calcium-aluminate cement, with vermiculite substituting for a large part of the grog. A 3-inch (7.62-cm) layer is poured in both cover and base, and, using a fiberboard drum as a mold, a 3-inch (7.62-cm) side wall is poured. A portion of a plastic container is used as a mold for the firing and exhaust ports. Iron rods shaped and welded to the cover and base facilitate loading and make the kiln portable. A ceramic-fiber blanket can be used in place of the castable, as in the kiln shown in Figure 280. A few firebrick posts and a small kiln shelf form the combustion chamber and loading floor. Since the heat can be raised quickly, a small burner and fan unit works well, although a regular Bunsen burner can also be used.

For a small gas kiln a single 4.5-inch (11.43-cm) wall of insulating brick may be adequate, as in the single-bag-wall design illustrated in Figure 268. A 4- or 5-cubic-foot (1.21- or 1.52-m^3) kiln can be fired easily with two atmospheric burners. The square kiln is most likely to have a uniform heat. Deep kilns are hard to load, and a tall chamber will often cause a temperature variation from top to bottom. Insulating bricks are not hard to cut, but it is easier to plan a design based on the uncut unit.

After the desired size has been established (as close to a cube form as possible), a calculation should be made to determine the burner capacity needed. Manufacturers supply information on the Btu (British thermal units) of their various burners. Unless the kiln is quite small, several burners are preferable to one large unit, in order to avoid a concentration of heat. Generally about 6000 to 7000 Btu are required in a stoneware kiln for each cubic foot ($0.31 \ m^3$) of capacity, including the combustion area. For the average Bunsen or aspirating burner, a 3-inch (7.62-cm) opening is sufficient. The chimney size should be at least equal to the area of all burner ports, even slightly larger if possible, especially if there are angles in the flue connection or if the chimney is unusually high (both of which circumstances result in friction loss).

The opening through which the depressed flue in the floor sends exhaust into the chimney should be smaller than the chimney itself to prevent a too-rapid heat loss. It should be constructed in such a way, however, as to allow easy enlargement, if necessary. Unless the kiln is unusually large, a bag wall constructed of firebrick laid on edge is sufficient. Only the first few courses of bricks need be permanent. The function of the bag wall is to force the flames and heat upward in the kiln. Its height will depend upon the kiln size, the chimney draft, and other factors. Additional bricks can be laid without cement if more heat is needed in the upper kiln area. Openings may be desirable in the upper wall. About 4 or 5 inches (10.16 or 12.7 cm) of combustion area between the kiln and the bag wall is sufficient in the average gas kiln. A slightly larger area is needed if oil is used for fuel.

Refractory mortar cements, in either dry or wet form, are available for bonding the bricks. A cheaper and essentially similar material can be mixed from 2 parts fireclay and 1 part fine grog. An even stronger bond can be made by adding 1 gallon (3.79 liters) of sodium silicate of 100 pounds (45.36 kg) of the dry mix. Unless the bricks are first moistened, they will soak up too much mortar, so it is best to immerse them in water and then allow them to drain. Only the thinnest layer of mortar is needed, since the bricks are very uniform and do not require a thick layer of cement for leveling purposes. The best method is to dip the edges of the bricks in a soupy mortar and tap them into place immediately with a hammer on a wood block. Because of their porosity, insulating bricks expand very little in heating and can be placed very close together. The dense firebricks, however, expand considerably under heat; therefore, about 0.25 inches (0.64 cm) of space with no mortar should be left in every third or fourth space between bricks, for otherwise the outside layer of cooler brick will be forced open in firing.

It is especially advisable to plan on a unit brick size when using hard bricks. They can be cut by tapping a groove on each side with a mason's hammer, then hitting a solid blow on a mason's chisel with a heavy hammer. No such procedure is possible with the wedge-shape bricks needed for the kiln arch. The usual arch rises at the rate of 1.5 inches per foot (3.81 cm per 30.48 cm). Placing the bricks on edge for a 4.5-inch (11.43-cm) thickness provides sufficient strength for the average-size kiln. The #1 arch brick tapers from 2.5 to 2.13 inches (6.35 to 5.41 cm). By drawing two curves 4.5 inches (11.43 cm) apart on a large board and using a 1.5-inch rise per foot (3.81 cm per 30.48 cm) over the desired span, the potter can calculate the required number of #1 arch bricks. Some straight bricks will be needed, but they should be kept to a minimum, as should the mortar.

These calculations present no problem in an insulating brick arch, since the softer bricks can be trimmed to a wooden pattern using a coarse rasp. A sharply angled skewback brick is needed where the arch meets the side wall.

The kiln will require a 2.5-inch (6.35-cm) angle-iron support at each corner, with 0.5-inch (1.27-cm) take-up rods at top and bottom. While these give a slight rigidity to the kiln, their main purpose is to hold the heavy angle-iron brace, which is needed on the outer wall to take up the thrust of the kiln arch. A very heavy spring (such as a valve lifter spring from a car motor) is sometimes used under the nut, since some expansion takes place while firing.

A supporting form to hold the arch can be made easily by cutting several boards to the arch curve and covering them with a Masonite sheet. It is wise to leave a bit of slack and to place wedges under the uprights so that the form can be removed easily after the steel angles and rods are in place. The catenary-arch kiln is self-supporting and needs no metal bracing for the arch, but angle irons across the front and rear secured with a tie rod are still desirable. Its curve can be established by suspending a chain from two nails at the desired floor width. The result will be a rather pointed curve. The structure will be most stable if the height approximates the width of the base. This design is perhaps best suited to an oil-burning kiln, since the flare at the base provides the extra combustion area needed for oil fuel.

The weight of a kiln is considerable, and it requires at least a 4-inch (10.16-cm) concrete base. In order to avoid leaning over and bumping the head in loading, it is a good idea to build the kiln on a reinforced concrete slab elevated to the necessary height with concrete blocks. Such a kiln can be moved later, if necessary, with little or no damage. The brick structure should always be arranged so that the joints are staggered and there is an occasional tie brick to bind two courses together. The corner bricks should be laid first, after it is certain that the plan is perfectly square. A level and a guide line are essential, since the eye is not dependable. Common red bricks can be used as backup for that part of the floor area not depressed for the exhaust channel. The kind of brick to be used and the wall thickness are determined by the size and general use of kiln. For the salt kiln or oil-fueled kiln an inner course of 4.5-inch (11.43-cm) hard firebrick is necessary, backed up by 2000°F (1090°C) insulating firebrick. If the size reaches 30 cubic feet (9.14 m^3), an extra outer layer of red brick is desirable.

A properly constructed kiln will give many years of service and require few repairs. A stoneware kiln with a 15- to 25-cubic-foot (4.57- to 7.62-m^3) capacity can be built with 2600°F (1427°C) insulating brick on edge and 2000°F (1090°C) brick on the flat, thus creating a 7-inch (17.78-cm) wall. Although the initial cost is high, the construction is easier and the fuel cost lower. However, insulating bricks retain little heat and cool more rapidly; therefore it may be desirable to use a hard inner liner for a 30-cubic-foot (9.14-m^3) or larger kiln. The kiln door jambs should be built of the same brick as the inner liner, whatever the type used. Kilns that are covered by only a simple roof are often used in summer schools and camps. These should be covered with plastic during the winter to keep out moisture that can freeze and cause severe damage.

It should be obvious from all these examples that there is no one way to build a kiln. The illustrations show a variety of burner placements. Most potters find the downdraft layout (Fig. 284, p. 290) to be the most satisfactory for the 15- to 30-cubic-foot (4.57- to 9.14-m^3) size. Although the updraft muffle (Fig. 266) is a common design for commercial kilns, neither this nor the open-flame updraft is recommended for construction by the potter, because the downdraft design usually fires more uniformly and reduces more efficiently.

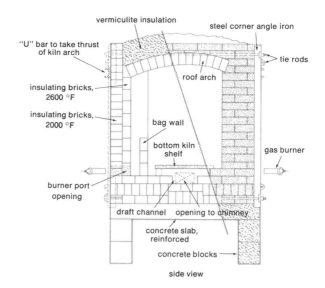

vermiculite insulation

steel corner angle iron

"U" bar to take thrust of kiln arch

tie rods

roof arch

insulating bricks, 2600 °F

insulating bricks, 2000 °F

bag wall

bottom kiln shelf

gas burner

burner port opening

draft channel   opening to chimney

concrete slab, reinforced

concrete blocks

side view

Oil Kilns

In locations where natural gas is not available or propane (L.P.G., liquid petroleum gas) is difficult to obtain, the potter should consider the use of #2 fuel oil. Oil is slightly cheaper than gas, and it produces a hotter flame. However, there are several disadvantages. Except with the most sophisticated and expensive burner types, fuel oil tends to be very smoky in the early stages of firing. This will be objectionable to neighbors, unless the potter lives in an isolated location. Some potters have solved this problem by preheating the kiln with portable gas burners before starting the oil fire. During the early stages of firing an oil burner, there is a greater chance of soot building up and causing a malfunction, so the firing must be carefully supervised.

Since fuel oil contains many impurities not found in natural or propane gas, the inner lining of the kiln must be made of hard refractory brick or a castable. The usual soft insulating firebrick will deteriorate under these conditions. There is also a greater volume expansion of volatilized oil gases, and this mandates a slightly larger combustion chamber such as found in the catenary-arch kiln illustrated in Figure 285, on page 292. Otherwise, the basic design of the oil-burning kiln is little different from the gas kiln illustrated in Figure 284. Oil-burning units, especially those with forced air, are often placed in the front of the kiln, where the flame can run down the length of the combustion area without immediately impinging against the bag wall.

Wood Kilns

The increasing cost of electricity, gas, and oil fuels has stimulated much interest in the wood-burning kiln. Many potters are especially attracted to the accidental effects that may result from ashes settling on the pots in a random fashion. Delicate glazes can also be fired in wood-burning kilns if the pots are placed in saggers.

There are, however, several drawbacks to the wood kiln. For one thing, the actual process of stoking the kiln is a long and arduous affair. There is no such thing as taking a dinner break or trimming pots while the kiln automatically goes up to temperature. The usual firing cycle of the wood kiln takes about 24 hours. It begins with a small amount of split wood in the ash pit. The fire is deliberately kept at a low heat for several hours as moisture leaves the ware and the kiln gradually warms up. Then wood is placed on the grate, and the actual firing begins. Relatively large pieces of wood are needed in this beginning stage because they burn slowly.

Although hard woods—oak, maple, birch, or ash—have potentially more heat value, soft woods such as pine, fir, and hemlock burn faster. The resin in soft woods volatilizes and produces a long flame that extends throughout the kiln. It is essential that the wood be perfectly dry—cut, split, and placed under cover for a period of about two years. Damp wood will expend a large proportion of its heat value in the process of drying out. The firing progresses from a stoking of relatively large split pieces every hour or so, to a rate of several 1- or 2-inch-by-2-foot (2.54- or 5.08-by-60.97-cm) sticks every five minutes. These thin pieces explode in the heat of the firebox and send a long flame through the kiln and up the chimney. The stoke and ash pit holes remain closed so that excessive drafts will not cool the chamber. Air vents in the ash pit and the grate area must be regulated carefully as the firing progresses. The ashes should not be disturbed unless it is absolutely necessary to level them out, because this will also cause a heat loss. Usually, wood is added only when the previous load has burned down to a bed of coals. The grate must not be overloaded, for if there is not enough oxygen to keep the wood burning brightly, there will be a drop in temperature. Normally, there is a slight reduction after stoking, which changes to an oxidation firing as the fuel is consumed.

A somewhat remote location is also desirable for wood firing. The white smoke given off is largely water vapor, the black smoke carbon. Neither is as harmful as the sulfur fumes of the oil kiln, but they will disturb neighbors, as will the flames that shoot out of the chimney when higher temperatures are reached. A screen is necessary on the chimney to contain the larger wood sparks. An open, well-ventilated kiln shed set a safe distance from buildings or trees would be a good solution.

The average wood kiln of 30 to 60 cubic feet (9.14 to 18.29 m^3) will use from 1 to 2 cords of wood for each firing (a cord is a stack of split wood 4 by 4 by 8 feet, or 1.22 by 1.22 by 2.44 m), so a good source of fuel is essential. Woodworking factories often have a quantity of kiln-dried wood scraps available. Slabs from a sawmill (bark-covered first cuts from a log) are another good prospect. The considerable labor of cutting timber with a chain saw, then hauling and splitting it into small sizes, may not be justified. To eliminate part of the arduous firing schedule, some potters fire their kilns overnight to a low red heat on portable gas burners and then complete the firing with wood during daylight hours.

The catenary-arch design is especially well suited to the wood kiln because the expanded base can contain a large portion of the firebox (Fig. 285). For the typical well-insulated stoneware kiln about 1 square foot (0.30 m^2) of grate space is needed for each 6 square feet (1.82 m^2) of floor area. A firing chamber on each side of the kiln generally provides a more even heat, but successful designs have also utilized a single firebox opposite the chimney. The single firebox design saves space, because only one bag wall is needed and a single grate need not be as wide as the combined width of two grates.

The floor and firebox area must be of hard refractory firebricks, while the inner kiln lining is usually of 2800°F (1538°C) firebrick backed up by 2300°F (1260°C) insulating firebrick (Fig. 286). Wood ash does not do great damage to insulating brick, and the upper kiln area can be of such brick for

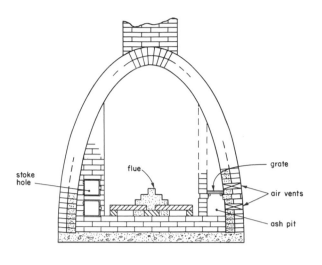

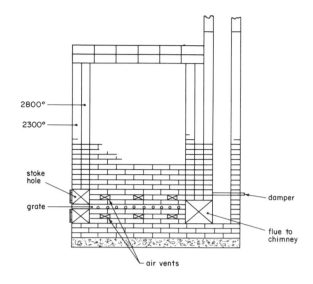

285 Front and side views of a catenary-arch wood-burning kiln.

greater insulating value. Plastic refractory coatings are available to coat the porous surface, if that is desired.

Various materials have been used for the fire grates, ranging from old cast-iron sash weights to scrap iron rods. The most durable—although expensive—choice would be 1-inch (2.54-cm) stainless-steel rods. These can be placed at 1.5- to 2-inch (3.81- to 5.08-cm) intervals. A greater width between rods is possible if a second grate of 0.5-inch (1.27-cm) rods is used below to catch the smaller embers. The bricks should be laid to form an indentation of 0.5 inches (1.27 cm) at the grate level, to provide a supporting ledge. The grate rods should be cut 0.25 inches (0.64 cm) shorter to allow for heat expansion. Two 0.5-inch (1.28-cm) rods welded to the heavier grates will prevent shifting. The ash pit should be 8 or 9 inches (20.32 or 22.86 cm) deep with three air intakes each 2.5 by 4.5 inches (6.35 by 11.43 cm) in the ash pit area and three more intakes immediately above the grate. Doors for the ash pit and stoke holes should be made of sheet steel on heavy hinges, because the chore of removing firebricks is too time-consuming.

As mentioned before, the curve of the catenary-arch kiln is determined by suspending a light chain between two points after the size of the floor has been decided. The height of the arch is normally chosen to equal its base width. The result is a somewhat pointed, completely self-supporting arch. Templates cut to this curve and faced with 0.13-inch (0.33-cm) Masonite will form a mold for the brick construction.

For convenience in loading, the reinforced slab foundation can be raised and cast on a foundation of concrete blocks. The outer 9 inches (22.86 cm) of slab floor should incline inward at a pitch of 1 inch to 10 inches (2.54 to 25.4 cm). Otherwise, a #1 arch brick must be used for the base brick in order to obtain the proper angle between the foundation and the rising side wall. Afterward, the usual 2800°F (1538°C) hard firebrick straights can be used for the inner wall until the approach to the crown of the arch, where several rows of #1 arch brick will be needed. A thin mortar of one-half fireclay and one-half grog can be used. A 0.25-inch (0.64-cm) space with no mortar should be left between brick at three- or four-brick intervals to allow for heat expansion. Because the brick courses must be staggered, a number of half bricks will also be necessary.

The large volume of hot gases in a wood kiln means that the opening from the chamber to the chimney must be about twice that for the usual gas kiln, and the chimney itself must be larger—about 12 by 12 inches (30.48 by 30.48 cm) for a 30- to 40-cubic-foot (9.14- to 12.19-m^3) kiln. A rule of thumb is to have 1 foot (0.30 m) of height for each inch (2.54 cm) in diameter, and more if there is any horizontal run from the kiln to the chimney. A kiln shelf that slides into a slot at the base makes a suitable damper. A firebrick and red-brick combination is suitable for the lower chimney section with fireclay tile and red brick for the upper chimney.

Chimneys

Because of the extreme temperatures involved, a kiln cannot emit exhaust into an ordinary household chimney. For a shedlike studio a simple transite pipe may be sufficient to carry the exhaust. In the classroom, however, an insulated fireclay Van Packer unit may be necessary, especially for the portion within the building. The exterior section can have the usual fireclay liner and brick construction. Small kilns can emit exhaust into a metal hood above the kiln, thus sucking the cooler room air into the stack and eliminating some of the temperature problem. Stainless steel sections with an inner core of fiberglass are commonly available. They should be used with a hood to reduce the stack temperature.

A short, direct connection from kiln to chimney is just as important for a proper draft as is the height of the stack. If needed, overhead connections can be made with a metal fireclay-lined pipe. Undue length or angles in this connection will require a much higher and larger stack size than normal. Tall stacks with unusual connections will probably need a burner or a fan in the stack base to induce an initial draft. If there are no surrounding buildings to cause a downdraft, a 15- to 20-foot (4.57- to 6.1-m) chimney should be sufficient. A 6-by-6-inch (15.24-by-15.24-cm) flue is usually adequate for a 10-cubic-foot (3.05-m^3) kiln, and a 9-by-9-inch (22.86-by-22.86-m^3) flue for a 20-cubic-foot (6.1-m^3) gas kiln. However, an even larger size is recommended, especially in a taller stack, which has some friction loss. A slot for a damper must be left in the draft flue at the point where it leaves the kiln. The damper can be a small or broken kiln shelf.

Burners

The proper burner size and type are of critical importance to the success or failure of a kiln. In the past many potters were forced to construct their own burners because the small sizes they needed were not always available on the market. Increased interest in kilns has changed this situation. The manufacturers listed in the Appendix produce a wide variety of burners and will recommend the type most suitable to individual kilns. Although burners can be improvised to duplicate commercial designs, the anticipated savings are not worth the potentially unsatisfactory firings.

Gas Burners Natural-draft gas burners are easy to install and quiet in operation. The Bunsen-type burner pictured in Figure 286 (p. 294) has a rating of 26,000 Btu. Six of these burners are needed for a downdraft gas kiln with a loading area of about 30 cubic feet (9.14 m^3). The burner ports should be about 3 inches (7.62 cm) in diameter, with the burner installed about 1 inch (2.54 cm) behind the opening to allow additional air to be sucked into the

286 Simple Bunsen-type burner, 26,000 B.T.U. Length 10.44″ (26.5 cm). Johnson Gas Appliance Company, Cedar Rapids, Iowa.

287 Venturi-type gas burner, 75,000 B.T.U. Length 14.75″ (37.5 cm).

***right*: 288** Forced-draft gas burner, ⅓ horsepower blower motor. 200,000–800,000 B.T.U. Johnson Gas Appliance Company, Cedar Rapids, Iowa.

kiln. The burner has a brass valve to control the flow of gas, as well as an adjustment on the tip to regulate the length of the flame during firing. An average kiln will need a 2-inch (5.08-cm) gas line direct from the natural gas main. If propane gas is used, a 500-gallon (1892.71-liter) tank is recommended. Several smaller tanks can be hooked up together but will need frequent filling. The amount of gas generated by the liquid propane decreases in cold weather and when the tank is less than a quarter full. There should be 10 pounds (4.54 kg) of pressure from the tank to a regulator at the kiln that reduces the pressure to 6 to 8 ounces (170.1 to 226.8 g). A T-fitting at the rear of the kiln will distribute equal pressure to the burners on each side. A thermocouple unit and a solenoid safety valve should be installed on at least the first burner on each side. School safety regulations may require a solenoid valve on each burner.

Larger kilns, such as car kilns (Fig. 280), will need the large Venturi-type burner unit pictured in Figure 287, which has a Btu rating of 75,000. Large car kilns require five to six such burners for a uniform heat distribution. The units can be installed sideways with 90-degree elbows to conserve space.

The forced-draft gas burner illustrated in Figure 288 provides from 200,000 to 800,000 Btu per hour. A large kiln will require two of these units. The burners can be located at either the front or the rear of the kiln; the blower will cause the flame to travel the length of the firing chamber. The blower unit can be fitted with a T-joint to service two units placed on the same side of the kiln.

Smaller forced-draft units, although expensive, provide a quick and portable means for a raku firing. Many potters have also used discarded vacuum cleaner fans in conjunction with a straight pipe containing a gas aperture. Such improvised units are satisfactory for the relatively short span of the raku firing but are not capable of standing up under longer firings at higher temperatures.

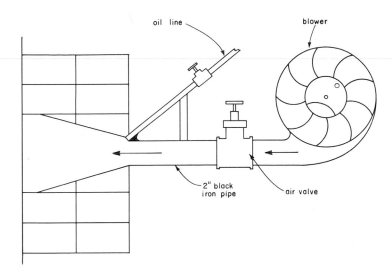

oil line

blower

2" black iron pipe

air valve

289 Oil burner unit with an oil drip feed and blower.

Oil Burners Oil burners range from simple to very complex devices. A rudimentary burner consists of a cast-iron pan placed beneath a 4-inch (10.16-cm) hole leading into a chamber below the kiln floor. A small metal pipe running from a 55-gallon (208.2-liter) drum to the pan should have a valve to control the flow of oil. To begin firing, an oily rag is placed in the pan and ignited. The valve is adjusted so that oil drips slowly into the pan, resulting in a very smoky flame. When a red heat is reached, the oil will volatilize sufficiently to produce an efficient use of the oil. A slightly more practical device consists of a square steel port with a series of ladderlike angled plates. The oil drips down these plates and is volatilized with a better air mixture. Both these methods produce a very sooty chimney exhaust until a red heat develops.

A forced-air unit that disperses the oil and provides a greater amount of oxygen for oil combustion is a more desirable solution. Many potters have used the simple arrangement pictured in Figure 289. The blower must be a heavy-duty type capable of continuous operation with a ⅓–horsepower motor. Two burners can be run from a single blower. The burner should be preheated before the blower is started. This can be done by igniting some oily rags as mentioned earlier. When a good blaze develops, a little oil should be allowed to trickle in to maintain the fire. To elminate this smoky period some potters preheat with a small portable gas unit or a gas line connected to the oil line. It is preferable to begin the firing with a light oil (such as kerosene), which has a lower flash point. Later, the oil can be switched to #2 fuel oil or strained and filtered crank case oil.

Even more efficient are the commercial burners that inject oil under pressure into a mixing chamber and blow it into the kiln in a gaseous mixture. This provides a cleaner and more complete combustion. Some burners are even equipped with ignition and safety cutoff devices. In view of the increasing cost of all fuels, the expensive but efficient burner may be a bargain in the long run.

The operation of an oil burner is not automatic, since the oil and air supply must be monitored constantly. Too much air will cool the kiln, while excessive oil will result in incomplete combustion, reduction, and a lowering of temperature. Air and oil input both will be smaller in the early stages of firing and must be increased gradually as higher temperatures are reached.

10

The
Professional
Potter

In centuries past, children usually followed the craft of their father, helping from an early age and gradually learning the basic skills. The Industrial Revolution of the early nineteenth century suddenly changed these age-old patterns as the potter became an hourly wage earner rather than an independent craftsman. A strange contradiction of modern life is that the average potter today is likely to be a college graduate, one who more or less accidentally came upon ceramics as a diversion from a more academic field of study. In the present impersonal world, dominated by big government and big business, it is no wonder that many students are attracted to a life-style and profession in which the daily routine is a matter of individual decision.

Forty years ago there was little public interest in the crafts in the United States, and the few opportunities for the studio potter to earn a living lay largely in teaching. In time the graduate programs in universities expanded to the point where there is today a surplus of teachers. Fortunately public interest in the crafts has grown at the same time. The many craft exhibitions and fairs are but one indication that an increasing number of the public prefers the more individual expression of the craftsman to the mass-produced plastic gadgets of industrial America. Consequently, many pottery students are seriously considering the profession of the studio potter.

Perhaps the most difficult task for potters dreaming of their own studios is to develop a realistic dollars-and-cents approach. The few pots sold during student days seem to represent a great profit. Would-be potters must calculate, however, the cost of the kiln, fuel, and chemicals and clay. All these items, plus the rental of studio space, the expense of utilities, and such miscellaneous expenditures as advertising and mailing, add immeasurably to overhead.

Paradoxical as it may seem, the Internal Revenue Service, with its insistence upon accurate records, may well provide the prospective potter with the best means of judging a venture's chances of success. When sales are finally made and cash is in the till, the potter too often considers this to be profit. Many people starting out in business disregard items of overhead and incidental expenses, so they are unaware that they are working at less than a living wage. A glance at the tax laws governing self-employed persons will provide a checklist of deductible items—and thus a list of expenses to be calculated in determining profitability.

The first item to be considered is the studio and in some instances a sales room. Such quarters will involve a yearly rental or lease and the accompanying insurance. If, by good fortune, the potter owns the property, then a proper return on the investment must be allowed, plus any taxes, mortgage payments, and insurance. Depreciation should be calculated upon the building and major equipment items, such as kilns, pug mill, wheels, and fixtures. Additional costs may be incurred in installing gas lines, propane tanks, or heavy electrical wiring. After the initial outlay, there will be continual small maintenance expenses.

Too often the above items are disregarded and the potter only considers the costs of clay, glaze chemicals, and fuel. Beyond these are the usual overhead items such as light, heat, and the telephone. Under some circumstances, paid newspaper announcements, business cards, brochures, stationery, and postage may be necessary. Wrapping paper, twine, tape, packing material, and boxes will be needed to send pottery to customers. Mailing will involve shipping fees, insurance, breakage losses, and perhaps a bad debt or two. Mileage costs should be determined in the transport of materials and merchandise. Travel and living expenses are usually involved in attending craft fairs. Membership in professional organizations, magazines, books, and attendance at meetings and exhibitions are also tax deductible.

Only when potters keep an accurate record of such varied items can they determine how their operation is actually progressing. Unnecessary expenses should be eliminated and the more profitable items and outlets expanded. The workshop must be laid out for the greatest efficiency. Shortcuts made in the forming and decorating processes will enable them to create an interesting and pleasing product in less time.

If a potter plans to have a sales outlet in connection with a studio, location becomes very important. The expense and restrictions of a metropolitan area often make such a situation impractical, and, moreover, many potters prefer to live in the country. Setting up shop near a major highway is not really necessary. True pot lovers will seek out an excellent craftsman and bring their friends.

Some potters sell mainly through outside shops, but since the usual markup in these outlets is 100 percent, it is easy to price themselves out of sales, unless they can produce an attractive line that can be thrown and decorated quickly. Items placed on consignment traditionally have a 50 percent markup. Unfortunately, shops that carry consignment goods often have commercial lines as well and use the consignment pieces primarily as window dressing, without making much effort to sell them. For some years craft fairs have been popular in many parts of the country. Many potters have found these to be an important source of summer sales, with orders taken for winter. One potter operating in a rural location near a large city has had good results by holding a "kiln opening" periodically during the summer. Postcards sent to a list of interested customers ensure a good turnout over the weekend.

What to make is perhaps more important than the details of the selling procedure. It is usually a great shock for beginning potters to realize that the public does not always have the same preferences that they do. While the craftsman may like the mottled brown-glazed bowl, it could sell twice as fast if it were blue. It is not that treasured show pieces will not sell, for indeed they will. But new customers are more likely to buy, for example, a set of mugs. As they grow to enjoy the feel of the handle and the slight irregularity of form and glaze, they may become interested in something that is more exciting to the potter. Unlike the usual retail operation, a very personal relationship develops between studio potters and their customers. Buyers greet a kiln opening with the same degree of anticipation as does the potter.

While ceramics teachers to some degree are subsidized to allow freedom of design, the professional studio potter must sell consistently. This does not mean a lowering of standards but rather an orientation toward salable items, because the market for the large show piece is limited. Although the average home may have room for a few decorative vases, its capacity for mugs, sugarbowls and creamers, casseroles, pitchers, planters, and so forth, is almost unlimited, and these objects will constitute the major area of sales. To idealistic beginners the ash-tray-and-candy-dish line may seem like the lowest form of ceramics, and most talented potters would agree. But upon opening a shop, beginners will discover that the customer who will pay $30 for a vase also wants a hand-made ash tray and will buy anything that could remotely serve this purpose. After refusing to make ash trays for several years, I finally gave up.

THE PROFESSIONAL POTTER   299

In a callous and practically anti-aesthetic world, which often seems to pander to the lowest taste, the high standards of the craftsman are refreshing. However, to make what one pleases and insist that the public take it or leave it can be self-defeating. For example, it is not logical to have only one teapot on the shelf, no matter how attractive it may be. Rather, it is essential to have several styles, colors, and so forth in different price ranges. Some customers will want the most expensive, the best in the house! Others will be bargain hunters. It really makes no difference that all the teapots may represent the same amount of effort on the part of the craftsman. Just as the customer in a clothing store would be distressed to find that all the suits were brown and bore the same price, so the potential buyer of ceramics will hope to find a wide selection.

Studio Potters

On the following pages are brief personal statements by several successful studio potters. It is hoped that their experiences will prove helpful to the student who is considering pottery as a profession. One must caution against excessive optimism, however. Considering the many tasks, costs, and requirements mentioned above, it is not surprising that a large proportion of new small businesses fail every year.

Robert Eckels
Bayfield, Wisconsin

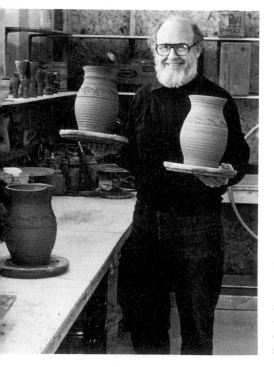

290 Robert Eckels at the Pot Shop, Bayfield, Wisconsin.

When I first began my shop, my goal was to produce fine handmade ceramics and make them available to the public at reasonable prices; I subscribed to the concept that the masterpiece emerges from an abundance of production. This principle still prevails.

For a number of reasons, I found that I could not achieve my goal alone. Others may need isolation, but it did not suit my work habits because I am much more productive when other people are working around me. It was also soon evident that by myself I could not make and sell enough pots to cover my production and overhead costs. Therefore, I gathered a small staff. At about that time the University of Wisconsin Extension did a free analysis of our business, pointing out that it usually takes a minimum sale of $3.00 worth of goods to make a profit of $1.00—if you are lucky. The final evaluation was that we needed to double either our production or our prices. What a shock! Following this advice, we added two more apprentices to our work staff, and our work area was enlarged. Later I discovered (in self-defense) that recognized potters such as Leach and Hamada had many people working for them. Even they did not do it alone!

Perhaps the most important thing that I have learned is that it takes continuous diligence, consistent long hours, and much hard work to produce quality handmade pots in the volume needed to earn a living. Though hard work is a prerequisite of success in any field, the artist potter must have extreme self-discipline and face his or her work with a dedication almost to the point of obsession for what turns out to be a very low hourly wage. We average eight to ten hours of work per day, six days a week year round, and in the summer we are open from 9:00 A.M. to 9:00 P.M. seven days a week.

Almost without exception our new apprentices have to be convinced of a stronger work ethic. It still surprises them—and me—that the actual time of throwing is only a small part of our day's activities. Other requirements such as trimming, mixing clay and glazes, glazing, decorating, loading and unloading kilns, arranging displays, selling, and cleaning the shop (there are no school janitors around) absorbs about three-quarters of our time.

The starting assignment given to newcomers is very simple and practical. They are asked to design and throw 60 to 80 mugs that match. Never have they been able to complete this assignment in the first week. Eventually we get to the bread-and-butter items—those that sell regularly and pay the bills. These are usually functional and sell at competitive prices. Quantities of mugs, bowls, sugar bowls and creamers, casseroles, baking dishes, lamps, lanterns, and a multitude of specialty items have to be made. These must have spouts that do not drip, lids that fit, and handles that handle. Apprentices must usually be reprogrammed toward a salable final product without sacrificing quality for quantity. Though we repeat forms when necessary— when we do sets of things—no two dinnerware sets are alike. In a sense we do many one-of-a-kind objects, which keeps our work interesting for us and our products engaging for the buyer.

The most painful thing I have learned is that accurate bookkeeping is essential. I hate doing the books, but what do you do when the I.R.S. person comes around? Also, when you are selling your work you may think you are making a profit when you really are not. The simple distinction, among cost of production, overhead, and profit must be understood and applied seriously.

There are many pleasures and advantages in selling directly to the public. We avoid all of the hassles of wholesale and consignment business. It is fun to know and talk to the people who are buying your work. This allows the craftsman to observe first-hand reactions to his or her efforts. Both positive and negative attitudes can be reacted to quickly. You would be surprised how many good suggestions we have received from our visitors. Adjustments to product and market that might otherwise take months can easily be made. Our gallery has an open view of our studio. This seems to be good public relations because people enjoy watching and talking to us as we work. We are authentic! Over the years we have made many good friends who return to see us year after year, even though they probably have enough pots to start a shop of their own.

291 Clary Illian with examples of her functional ware.

Clary Illian
Garrison, Iowa

I live in Garrison, Iowa, a town of 450. My pottery is modest in size and minimally equipped. The studio is in a 24-by-40-foot barn with a double-chambered, cross-draft, drip-feed oil kiln; a vertical clay mixer that handles 50-pound batches; a Leach wheel; and lots of racks and ware boards. I market solely from a showroom in the barn loft (24 by 24 feet), depending upon drop-in trade and the sales announced via a large mailing list accumulated over the years. This system of marketing works because I am near several large towns. When I began in 1966 with a $2000.00 loan, the economic picture was quite different from that of the present. Real estate, supplies, and fuel were cheap. I also lived and continue to live simply, without dependents.

I can speak, however, about attitudes that I think apply beyond the circumstances of the times. The core of these attitudes is respect—respect for the craft and respect for the public. To begin at the beginning, this respect means that the aspiring potter should obtain the best training possible. Anything less suggests that there is no realization of the profound aesthetic and technical content of the craft nor of the potential ability of every pot owner to discern excellence. In other words, learning should not be at the expense of the consumer.

For many years my pottery was in the Garrison Brick and Tile Works, a turn-of-the-century charmer of a site complete with steam engine and beehive kilns. This experience taught me that potters need a context that calls attention to their work. That context may be an interesting location or an unusual working arrangement, or it may have to do with the content of the pots themselves. This is a public-relations compromise, if you will, which will not prostitute the work itself.

I cannot overstate how important it is to be consistently available to potential buyers. Convenient business hours, a plentiful and diverse selection of pots, and surroundings that show pride in the work and consideration for visitors are all necessary aspects of professional potting. Although these suggestions come from my experience with retailing, they could also be translated to a wholesale situation.

There is another sense in which consistent availability is a necessity. The process of making pottery demands constant and total attention—an awareness of every single aspect from the mundane fact that crud on ware boards makes crud on pot bottoms to the elusive fact that a certain curve makes a form sing. For the professional this awareness must be as focused upon the pottery studio as upon the pots since the one produces the other. I often observe that ceramists who do not work full time sabotage their work by sloppiness or the absence of a system.

The perennial cry of small-business owners is that the business begins to run them rather than their running it. This is a particularly poignant danger for the potter, and it takes vigilance not to let the work you love become poisoned by stress. Although I often suffer from this complaint, I have never seriously considered my life in pottery to be anything less than meaningful and a privilege.

292 Richard and **Marj Peeler** in the doorway of their studio.

Richard and Marj Peeler
Reelsville, Indiana

My wife and I do not write about our experiences in operating a ceramics studio in the spirit of giving advice or with the feeling that ours is the best or the only way to operate. Rather we describe some of the things that work for us and seem right for us, given our location, circumstances, and background. We realize that there are many different circumstances, attitudes, and methods for making a living. In school, we specialized in ceramics within the context of an art major. We have always been involved in art and feel that we have a good background of art education and experience. We think that a good foundation in art fundamentals is pretty important.

Marj and I live way out in the country—thirteen miles from a small university town in Indiana, hardly the ideal location. I taught for 21 years and made pottery and sculptures all that time, so we gradually worked into full-time pottery making. In 1972 I quit teaching altogether, and I have not done any teaching since then with the exception of a few short-term workshops. As far as studio layout goes, ours is far from perfect. It just grew over the years with no long-range planning. Ideally, I think, the display area should be out front, then the packing area, then the work area, and finally the kilns in back.

Since our location is so remote, people who take the time and trouble to find us and drive out here are generally knowledgeable about what we do and are interested in making purchases; so, we have very few drop-ins and browsers. Approximately 90 percent of our visitors purchase something, so this situation has worked out well. We value our customers and try to learn their names and interests. We offer them a cup of tea, coffee, or whatever, and we have a toybox for the kids. We've found that friends bring friends to our pottery. And word of mouth is the very best kind of advertising. We never wanted to run a store. We like to do the work—to make the pots, fire, and glaze them. It has worked out that nothing we can do is more profitable than making pots—more profitable than teaching, doing art fairs, giving workshops or lectures, writing a book, or whatever.

Most of our production is utilitarian pottery. That is what sells most readily. We think that lots of little pieces to work into the spaces around the larger pots is important. I've always thought that the smaller the piece, the more profitable. We make each firing count. We stack tightly. I attach a great deal of importance to firing space in the kiln, and I want to get a certain amount of income from each firing.

We sell wholesale to about eighteen shops; but more than half our total income comes from sales at the pottery. Presently we do not sell at art fairs. We find them strenuous. Our work is priced lower than practically everyone else's. We produce a large quantity of work; and our nonsalable or failure rate has been less than 1 percent (knock wood!). We don't resent or "hate" any phase of the work. We don't allow ourselves to think this way. When we pack pots for United Parcel Service we turn on the TV, throw our minds in neutral, and just do it.

We've never had to suffer through a really bad period. We have always had orders to fill, and with the excellent market for handmade pottery of the last fifteen to twenty years, we've always made a good living. We are thankful that we are able to live where we want, set our own schedule, and make a nice living doing something that we love to do.

293 John Glick in his Plum Tree Pottery.

John Glick
Farmington, Michigan

I trace my technical training to Bill Pitney at Wayne State University and my artistic roots from exposure to Maija Grotell at Cranbrook Academy. Observing German studio potters in the Rhineland area near Hohr-Grenzhausen during an army tour (1962–1964) was another influence. The concept of a small-scale studio pottery as described in Leach's *A Potters Book* also encouraged me to set up my own studio.

I'm glad, however, that I didn't have an apprenticeship in the usual Leach or Hamada tradition. This is not to criticize the role of the apprenticeship concept; it is just that I feel that many masters who would give opportunities are just not open enough or versatile enough to give wide expression and exposure to their apprentices. It is a rare apprenticeship opportunity that includes both the technical training and that rare infusion of philosophy that will leave the apprentice still open and absorbing and resilient enough to be able to proceed as a unique and vital person on his or her own.

I am very concerned about the words *production potter*. I do not like the term applied to myself. I say "productivity" but not "production pottery," when I speak of myself. I define productivity in terms of motivation. I do not define it in terms of numbers of product. So "productive" is a word that comes from a drive to find out what will be next in a series of ideas. Out of that comes earning a living, because when one is driven, one is productive.

By the second year of full-time studio work, I had developed a catalogue, beautifully designed by a friend, informing architects that I made planters for buildings and offices. I simply could not answer all the requests for these large planters, with the net result that attempting to do so squashed my ability to work on the many ideas that were developing. I had a showroom from the very beginning, and it certainly influenced me because I received a great deal of direct contact with customers. I enjoyed their praise and also accepted and used their criticisms—all of them formed together in a way to help build my own trust in my ideas and my willingness to risk and take the consequences.

A basic premise in my philosophy is smallness. I don't want one, two, three, or four people to come between me and a finished piece. And that smallness is really a key to my basic approach—approximately two thousand pots a year is an average from my pottery. That implies a certain pricing structure to yield a livable income, although I have never set out and calculated pieces, time, and costs. In the end, all the satisfactions built into the making of pots are a major source of return for me. The pots are sold after I have had the satisfaction, the enjoyment, of making each piece. Fortunately, earning a living has fallen in place around my enthusiasm for studio work. It is a happy balance.

Potting begins and ends in the studio. What comes after that in selling the work or in receiving recognition is a wonderful addition. It is great to earn your living and to be respected by your peers, but really the deepest satisfaction occurs during the making of the pots at any stage. I love it all, including cleaning and maintaining the studio. There is another sense of obligation that I feel relates to the general field of pottery. I write, give workshops, and trade information with other potters primarily because that network of people has been good to me and continues to be that way. I sense a feeling of community with other potters and artists in general and with those that work with them—gallery owners, writers, teachers. I, therefore, feel that I want to contribute in any way I can and when I can—ideas, techniques, and philosophy.

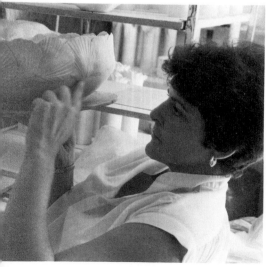

294 Carol Jeanne Abraham at work in her studio.

Carol Jeanne Abraham
Ojai, California

The most important thing when you are working is that whatever you create, you are doing it because you believe in it. Whether you are solving a problem for a specific commission or spontaneously creating an object, your work must be fulfilling to yourself. It must come from within you, and you must feel you have done the best you can. Compromise is never easy, so when you must compromise be sure that it is in an area that does not compromise your ethics. Whatever you create, there will be people who value what you do, and there will always be people who abhore what you do. None of it makes any difference if you are doing what you believe in. You will find a buyer for whatever you want to make, whether it is monumental sculpture or a tea bowl. Say something with your work; communicate anything that you feel is important. Technology and good design are essential to each work, but the work will be empty if it does not express its creator.

I've always felt that it was important to have a solid foundation for one's actions. Therefore, I found further training desirable and obtained a master's degree in clay. The importance of seeking a degree is threefold: the accreditation, the contact with other creative individuals, and the equipment that is available for experimentation. When I was in graduate school, I became aware of the small number of teaching jobs in relationship to the large number of qualified teachers. That disparity directed me towards pursuing art as my career rather than teaching.

Communication with others is important and stimulating to me and has been satisfied by part-time teaching, giving or taking workshops, and attending international symposiums. These three areas have enabled me to fulfill a need and maintain an excellent income from my studio. I have supported myself and, from time to time, others since graduation. The reality of the situation is that you have to make money to live. There are two ways of going about it: *either you support yourself with your art, or you find a way to support your art.* My choice was to support myself with my art. Then there are more choices: design something inexpensive to sell in quantity, or design a unique item difficult for others to reproduce. Personally I prefer to make one $1,000.00 item than two hundred $5.00 items, the latter being much more labor-intensive. This is not for everyone, but I would rather spend the one hundred hours designing instead of loading kilns.

My studio has always been part of my living situation. Either I have lived in my studio or my studio has been with my home. The organization of my studio is dependent upon the processes used to make my one-of-a-kind sculpture and/or production work. The total studio space is divided into two parts. One half is for the prefired clay work and the other half is for postfired assemblage. The choice of my kiln was made by considering my mobile life-style ("Have kiln will travel,") and the cost of the kiln and its cost-effectiveness. I chose the least expensive kiln for the most amount of firing space; also taking into consideration the cost per firing and the value of the pieces in the kiln. In 1982 the ratio has been approximately $8.00 in firing costs with a minimum of $1,000.00 worth of work per load.

I changed all clay and glaze formulas so that I could use a single firing, thus cutting my labor and costs in half. Single firing also reduced breakage and handling time. My kiln is round, 8 cubic feet of firing space, and electric, and it holds all I can make in one day so that by myself, in full production, I can fire all my work every day. It is essential to spare your energy and mechanize the process of clay preparation. Take it from one who must (because of the nature of the material) hand mix all the thixotropic clay she uses. For making my slips I have a 1-horse-power motor attached to two pulleys with a rubber belt on a shaft and four propellors in a 50-gallon plastic drum. The total cost was $73.00 (one nice pot). My glazing is done with a $150.00 airless spray gun. No spray booth is necessary, no compressor either.

Craft fairs have been a valuable source of income for many people. There are several every weekend across the country. Talk to other crafts people about the various fairs to find out which are the most profitable. As in most things, the cost of the show is an indication of its value, *but not always*. Try a variety of fairs, mall shows, weekends in resort towns, annual city shows, juried shows, gift shows. Vary the type of buyer your work is exposed to and elminate the least profitable. If you do set up a circuit across the country, be sure you love to travel, research the show, have lightweight and easy-to-dismantle booths, and love to answer stupid questions. Keep a mailing list of everyone who has bought from you and notify people when you are showing in their area. Advance mailings work and so do notices in the publications listing galleries and shops across the country. Notify anyone who may be interested; one or two additional sales will cover the mailing costs. Buyers like the personal touch; make them feel you remember them. The more you show your work the more it will sell. The more your name comes up the more likely you are to be chosen. Keep in mind that galleries are looking for people whose work they can show. They need at least twelve a year. Don't waste your time sending slides in the mail or walking in off the street. Galleries seldom look at your work or your slides. Have someone recommend your work. Read all the periodicals cover to cover to keep informed. It is amazing how much you can learn from them.

Having a good business sense is important. When working with mail-order catalogues be very careful that contracts are specific. Get paid for your work up front. Do not let them hold your stock and pay you as they sell; your payments will be delayed for months and you will not get your unsold stock back without going to court. Selling on consignment requires a lot of paperwork for relatively little money. Take that into consideration when pricing your work. Be specific with these contacts, also, and always clarify when your pieces are insured. Return shipping needs careful attention. Determine who packs the work and shipment time; check insurance coverage and decide who pays for all the costs of returning the work. Sources of income I have used include the following: open houses or kiln openings; gallery exhibitions; craft fairs; gift shows; mail-order catalogs; competititions; juried exhibitions; grants; gift shops; department stores; commissions; interior decorators.

William Daley
Philadelphia, Pennsylvania

Every potter's work progresses in a different fashion. Over the years it has been my tendency to work larger and larger, first in slab forms and finally in styrofoam-molded garden vessels. Since the pottery process is somewhat related, it was only natural that I should eventually try larger, segmented mural forms, [See Fig. 172, p. 130].

As a large ceramic mural may take from six months to a year to complete, my situation is quite unlike that of the usual studio potter. To me it is important to behave like a professional and make the client feel comfortable. First, you won't make anything that your client doesn't like or that you don't like. Second, you will work on the idea until everyone is pleased, provided that you are the only one working on it. I will not enter a competition unless I am paid for design time at a satisfactory hourly rate. If I am awarded the job, this fee becomes part of the overall cost.

THE PROFESSIONAL POTTER

295 **William Daley** with one of his large planters.

After the design is accepted we make a contract, which states what I will do and at what time. It outlines a schedule of payment and makes provision for at least one visit by the client when the project is in progress. I reserve the right to change anything in process but only after consultation with the client or his representative. Payment is usually made in thirds—the first third on signing the contract (for materials and help if necessary), the second third usually after the client's visit to determine satisfactory progress, and the final third after the successful installation. A last consideration is who pays for shipping and installation, particularly when you are not doing it yourself. I keep a day book for records of work hours, materials, etc. It is a great help in costing out future commissions. Otherwise one can very well be working for little or nothing.

I usually make about 20 percent more units than are actually needed, as in firing, pieces may warp or vary in color. When all is finished I make a mock-up on the side of my house, change units if necessary, and work out the details of the fastenings needed and any problems of installation. If union help is used in the installation, any delays can be very costly. An opinion in writing should be obtained from the client's architect as to the suitability of the fastening system and installation procedures in case mishaps and insurance problems occur in the future.

As an aid to future commissions, newspaper publicity should be obtained on the initial award and photos taken of the work in progress and finally at the unveiling of the mural. Letters from the client attesting to his satisfaction are also desirable. We assume that the craftsman has talent and motivation. But, unless the business aspects are attended to, a mural award can end up as an unfortunate experience.

Apprenticeships in Pottery

In Europe where many aspects of the old craft-guild system survive, young potters learn the trade by becoming apprentices, starting in the early teens and continuing about five years. A specific contract is drawn up, which usually requires the master potter to provide living expenses, but little salary is paid apprentices until the later years when they become productive enough to make a contribution to the pottery.

In the United States, federal laws, influenced by large trade unions and industry, make no provision for the training of apprentices and, in fact, discourage it. American public trade schools merely teach a skill and not the blend of art and technique needed by the craftsman. Since fledgling potters in the United States are likely to be older and often are college graduates, the traditional long apprenticeship is out of the question. If new graduates have some financial resources and are highly motivated they can learn the craft by trial and error as they gradually become more efficient and gain the business insights to market their work.

Many would-be potters, however, will find apprenticeship a quicker way to gain experience. It may be a mistake for a novice to seek out the most famous potter in the area; personal compatibility is likely to be the most important ingredient in a relationship, assuming the master potter is competent. Tensions can easily arise in the close confines of the studio. A one- or two-week probationary period is desirable for the benefit of both parties.

The compensation pattern for apprentices is quite varied. New college graduates often have an exaggerated idea of their worth, yet it may be several months before their efforts reach the value of the minimum wage scale. Thus a summer apprenticeship is usually a losing proposition for the potter since a great deal of his or her time is needed for instruction. The usual period is for a year, although a longer stay may be desirable.

In rare instances apprentices pay the potter in what is essentially a teaching situation in which the students perfect their skills and learn the routine of a producing studio and the various aspects of marketing. At the other extreme, apprentices become hourly employees, receiving at first only a minimum wage. The potter is then saddled with withholding taxes and workmen's compensation. Since the employment period is temporary, with apprentices likely to leave at just the time they become of some value, many potters throw up their hands and say, forget about it!

In other arrangements the potter provides apprentices with room and board and pays them a commission on work produced beyond a certain amount. A few potters pay the apprentice entirely on a piece-work basis. A full understanding by both parties should be reached at the very beginning.

The studio should be large enough for all to work conveniently. Apprentices should receive instruction and criticism and have a wheel and adequate work space. They should be allowed to work at some period independently on their own projects. To be successful each party must have some empathy for the other's concerns; the apprentices need a working knowledge of the craft, and the master potter needs a relationship that does not become so time-consuming that his or her own work suffers and the relationship becomes both an emotional and a financial drain. (For further material see *Apprenticeship in Craft,* edited by Gerry Williams [Daniel Clark Books, 1980] available from Box 65, Goffstown, New York 03045.)

Pottery for Industry

While it is most unlikely that pottery students will ever design for industrial production, it might be of interest for them to understand factory procedures. They might even find the need to use molds or the slip-casting process in a limited way. The techniques of today's potters are basically not very different from those of potters a thousand or even two thousand years ago. It is true that gas and oil are more convenient fuels than wood and coal. The electric wheel is a great advance, and the availability of pulverized clay and glaze chemicals saves a lot of hand labor. But a glance at the historical chapters reveals that more primitive equipment did not prevent potters from producing a variety of quality ware that potters today find difficult to equal, let alone surpass.

Labor-saving devices were used by the ancients. The Etruscans used bisque molds as early as the fifth century B.C., and slip casting was practised in a limited way in T'ang China (618–906). The imperial kilns at Ching-Te-Chên, established in the fifteenth century, produced an immense amount of porcelain and were really factories. All labor, however, was by hand with each worker endlessly repeating a small part of the process. The coming of steam-powered factories in eighteenth-century England relieved workers of many onerous tasks, but it also meant the end of handcrafts, as noted in Chapter 3. The development of plaster of paris in 1745 made possible the casting of ornate forms and decorations having little relation to the natural qualities of clay. Transfer decorations from engraved plates led to a rigid and mechanical treatment of the glazed surface. The only advantage was that ordinary tableware could be purchased at a reasonable cost. But even this ware was susceptible to inappropriate decoration.

Designing

Industrial production need not mean poor design, but the design must take the industrial process into account. While the prototype for a mass-produced piece may evolve on the potter's wheel, it is essential that the ceramic designer have a working knowledge of the techniques of slip casting and jiggering. The long process that finally results in placing a pattern in production requires close cooperation among the designer, the mold maker, the glaze chemist, and the production engineer. The prototype is usually thrown on the wheel, but the mold maker most often works from a scale drawing.

The designer first works up a variety of designs and then gradually eliminates those that are obviously nonfunctional, too commonplace, or too difficult to reproduce. Since the cup is the most-used item in a dinner set, it is often the starting point. When its shape has been roughly determined, other pieces are designed to relate to it. It is essential that the designer have a feeling for the clay form and a knowledge of how it can be deformed in firing. Heavy dinnerware is not very popular. Therefore, the foot-rim and wall thickness must be of a dimension only sufficient to support the form.

After the cross sections are determined, a plaster model is made. A metal template made from the profile drawing is placed on the turning jig. Plaster is poured around the pin in small amounts until the form is completed. A circular movement of the template trims off the excess and develops a solid plaster study model (Figs. 296C and D, p. 310).

A

B

C

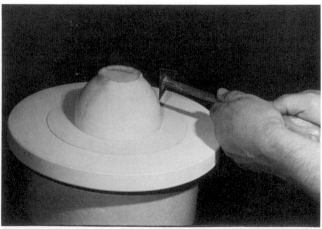

D

E

F

G

Designing Forms for Production from Sketches to Completed Product

296

Courtesy Peter A. Slusarski

A and **B** Initial sketches and cross sections of dinnerware set.

C A solid plaster cup is formed with a template.

D Trimming refines the form of the plaster model.

E The reverse of the cup mold is shaped to fit the jigger wheel.

F Top and bottom sections of the case mold.

G Steel template is ground to the contour of the cup mold.

continued

296, *continued*

H Half section of cup handle.

I Two sections of a plaster mold for the cup handle.

J A steel template to shape the bottom surface of a saucer.

K The completed place settings.

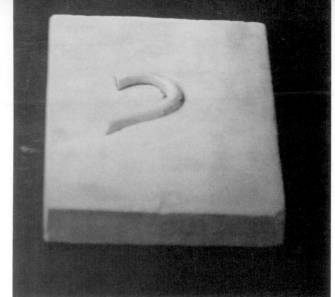

H

I

J

K

312   THE PROFESSIONAL POTTER

Because of shrinkage that will occur in firing, the final model is oversize. Minor refinements in form can be made with cutting tools. After the plaster model of the cup is complete, it is coated with a plaster separator. A retaining collar is put in place, and fresh plaster is poured over the model to form the original jigger mold. Figure 296E shows the trimming of the mold to fit the wheel head of the jigger machine. It is necessary to have a mold for each cup to be made in the day's production, which may be thousands. Figure 296F illustrates the top and bottom sections of the case mold used to make the jigger block mold. The ball-and-socket projections allow for an accurate positioning of the sections prior to pouring the block mold. The case molds are made of a harder and denser plaster mix than that used for the jigger mold, which must readily absorb water from the clay after it is jiggered.

In jiggered ware, only one surface is shaped by the plaster form. The inner cup surface is formed by the jigger template. Figure 296G shows the steel template being checked for clearance. Figure 296H illustrates a half section of the cup handle on a plaster or marble base. After the retaining walls are in place and the surface has been shaped, a layer of plaster is poured in, forming one half of the mold. Keys are carved out of the fresh plaster, and the complete handle section is put in place. English Crown soap commonly serves as a mold separator. If the plaster mold is dry, it must be moistened before soaping and casting, for otherwise the soap would be drawn into the dry cast, causing the two sections to stick (Fig. 296I). After the cast is finished, it is a simple matter to carve pouring openings into the damp plaster. Before a clay handle is poured, however, the mold sections must be dry. For the pilot design project, a single handle mold is adequate; in production, a dozen handles normally are cast at one time.

Designing a plate or saucer is a somewhat different operation from designing a cup. The plaster mold is shaped to form the inside, or upper contour, of the plate. The template is cut to form the bottom surface (Fig. 296J).

The process from the initial sketches to the finished product is long, and several years may elapse before marketing can begin (Fig. 296K).

Mixing Plaster

There are available a variety of plasters of different hardnesses and setting rates for use in model making, block molds, or case molds. Theoretically, 18.6 pounds (8.37 kg) of water will set up 100 pounds (45.36 kg) of plaster; in practice, at least 60 pounds (27.22 kg) of water will be needed to achieve the proper flow. The less water used, the stronger the cured plaster will be. Plaster normally sets in about twenty minutes, but it must be poured before it hardens. This time will depend upon the amount of mixing. The plaster must be sieved into the water (to avoid large lumps) until the water will absorb no more. It is then allowed to set from three to four minutes until it is thoroughly wet. Small batches can be mixed by hand or larger ones with a power mixer. After a few minutes of mixing, the plaster will begin to thicken. It must be poured at this point. Once it begins to set, it is useless and must be discarded. (It cannot be poured down the sink, for it will clog the drains.) Plaster manufacturers furnish tables giving strength and porosity for various mixtures. For production it is most important that all molds have a similar porosity.

297 Removing a slip-cast teapot from a three-piece mold.

Slip-Casting Techniques

Slip casting is a method of making ceramics in which liquid clay is poured into a hollow, absorbent mold. Within a few minutes after pouring, a film of firm clay appears on the inner surface of the mold. As water is absorbed into the plaster, the clay becomes thicker. When the desired thickness develops, the mold is upended and the excess clay, which is still liquid, is poured out. The remaining clay coating continues to harden and eventually shrinks away from the mold. Simple cup forms can be made in a single-piece mold, while undercut and more complicated shapes require two, three, or occasionally more pieces in the mold.

When multiple sections are used, they are keyed together with ball-and-socket projections and are held together during pouring with heavy rubber bands, such as one might cut from an automobile inner tube. As the water soaks into the plaster mold, the level of slip in the cavity falls, and a small amount must be added. To avoid frequent slip additions during casting, a collar is added to the top of the original model to serve both as a funnel for the slip and as a clay reservoir. The angle of the collar is used as a guide in trimming the top edge of the formed piece. This is done with a fettling knife when the cast piece has hardened sufficiently. At this stage the mold sections are carefully removed, and the casting seams on the piece are scraped off and sponged to create a smooth surface.

In order to avoid uneven shrinkage or air pockets, some pieces must be cast in sections and joined together with slip. This is particularly true of small handles, which are cast solid rather than drain cast. Depending upon the character of the clay, this type of joining can be done at either the leather-hard or the dry stage. The procedure is quite different from that used for thrown objects, in which sections should be joined as soon as they can be handled without distortion. (See Plate 45, p. 286.)

Casting Slips

Unlike a clay used in throwing, a clay body for jiggering and casting need not be very plastic. In fact, the plastic clays are often avoided, since their greater water absorption means more shrinkage, which is usually accompanied by warping. Various types of binders are used to impart greater green and dry strength to the ware. This more than compensates for the substitution of less-plastic ingredients.

Of great importance in a casting slip is the use of *deflocculants*, such as sodium silicate and soda ash. The addition of about 1 percent of either of these chemicals to the dry weight of the clay will reduce considerably the amount of water needed to make a fluid slip. A properly deflocculated casting slip is easily pourable but has a clinging, syrupy consistency that substantially retards the settling of the heavier slip particles. Georgia kaolin, which has a uniform particle size, is the major porcelain clay used in casting slips. One negative feature of the slip body is that its bland smoothness is relatively uninteresting when compared to the color and texture of a throwing clay. Some typical casting slips for various temperatures are listed in the Appendix.

A common name for sodium silicate is water glass. It is, in fact, a solution of sodium silicate in water. The sodium silicate is made by fusing a mixture of soda ash and silica sand. The term is a general one, since the proportion of sodium to silica may vary greatly. N-brand solution is the trade name given to the type commonly used as a deflocculant in ceramics. Soda ash (sodium carbonate), either alone or in combination with sodium silicate, is a more effective deflocculant than sodium silicate alone in casting slips containing organic matter, such as is found in ball clay. Slip should not be stored for long periods, especially in warm weather, because fermentation occurs, and this may cause pinholes in the cast ware.

A standard practice is to use about 3 parts N-brand sodium silicate by weight to 1 part soda ash. The proportions depend on the body formula. If it includes a large amount of clay, a 1-to-1 mixture of soda ash and N-brand silicate solution may prove more satisfactory. After weighing, the soda ash should be dissolved in hot water and then both deflocculants added to the water. As a beginning one might take 100 pounds (45.36 kg) of slip body and slowly add it to a large crock containing 50 pounds (22.68 kg) of water, which is about 6 gallons (22.71 liters). More or less of the slip body may be needed, depending upon the ingredients and the deflocculant action. The resulting slip should have a thick, syrupy consistency. A blunger is helpful in mixing the ingredients, although a large wire whisk can be used for test batches. Slip should always be screened before using, for any lumpy particles will settle and give a poor casting. Care must be taken in screening and filling the mold in order not to trap air bubbles in the slip. Jarring the mold may help the air rise to the surface.

It is better to use not more than 1 percent deflocculant, even less if possible, in relation to the dry ingredients' weight, since an excess will sometimes cause the slip to become pasty and nonpourable. It will also gradually seal the pores of the plaster mold with an insoluble film of calcium silicate, making removal of the casting difficult and eventually spoiling the mold completely. Soda ash is more troublesome in this regard than silicate. Drying the molds from the outside by inverting them or covering the mouths will help to prevent this accumulation on the inner mold surface.

298 A metal template trims off excess clay from the bottom profile of a dinner plate as the plate revolves on the jigger.

Jiggering Methods

As every novice potter soon learns, it is impractical to throw large, flat shapes on the potter's wheel. Countless generations of potters have used bisque molds to shape one surface of flat dishes and to support the soft clay in drying. With the use of plaster molds, the forming process is quite rapid and accurate. In addition, the plaster mold produces a smoother surface than would be possible with a bisque mold.

The composition of the clay used for jiggering is different from that of throwing clay. Since the ware is supported by the mold during the initial drying period, the clay need not be so plastic. In fact, since plastic clay shrinks more in drying, thus increasing the likelihood of warpage, it is used in limited amounts. To compensate for this loss in green and dry strength, various binders—such as lignin extract and methocel—are frequently added to the clay body.

Sections of clay can be extruded from the pug mill in different diameters, depending on the use to which they will be put. The size used for the plate shown in the jigger machine (Fig.9.17) would be 6 to 8 inches (15.24 to 20.32 cm). A slice about 1 inch (2.54 cm) thick is cut off the pugged clay with a wire and placed over a square of canvas on the bench. The clay slice is then hit with a malletlike weight that compresses it to half this thickness. The resulting clay bat is in turn slapped down over a plaster plate mold resting on the jigger head. The next step is to force out any air remaining between the clay and the plaster mold. This is usually done with the moistened hand as the jigger head revolves slowly. The operator then brings the steel template down toward the mold, further compressing the clay and cutting away the excess to form the bottom contours of the plate and the foot rim. The mold bat and plate are placed on a conveyor belt that carries them through a dryer. Finally, the plate is removed from the mold, and the seam created where the template and mold meet is trimmed away.

THE PROFESSIONAL POTTER

It is difficult to obtain a perfectly uniform thickness in slip casting. Heavy cups with attached handles are often slip cast, but thinner porcelain cups are jiggered, since even the slightest variation would be noticeable. The procedure in jiggering cups and bowls is slightly different: the mold is a hollow form, and the template is shaped to the inside surface of the piece. One method of jiggering cups is to throw a wad of clay into the mold and allow the template to force the clay downward and outward to form the walls of the cup. Another way begins with the throwing of a rough cup form on a potter's wheel. This form is placed into the mold and jiggered. The particular method used depends largely upon the characteristics of the clay body and to some extent upon the shape desired. The latest machines are completely automatic and produce a fantastic hourly output.

Press Forming

Certain forms can be duplicated very economically by the use of molds in hydraulic presses. Most electrical insulators are made in this fashion, using a nearly dry body with wax as a forming lubricant. The process illustrated is more adaptable to pottery production, provided the shapes are simple and have no undercuts.

The body ingredients are weighed and mixed in a blunger as in the preparation of a casting slip. The resultant liquid is screened and pumped into a *filter press,* an accordionlike machine of metal and canvas that squeezes excess water from the slip, leaving plastic clay. Clay comes from the filter press in slabs about 1 to 1.5 inches (2.54 to 3.81 cm) thick and 16 to 24 inches (40.64 to 60.96 cm) square. These slabs are then placed in the hopper of a *pug mill,* which operates much like a meat grinder. At one end is a vacuum attachment, which, combined with the compressing action of the screw blades, removes even the smallest air pockets from the clay. This feature not only eliminates possible body defects but also makes the clay more plastic. Though not as crucial as in throwing, the absence of air bubbles in clay used for jiggering and press forming is still important. Male and female (positive and negative) dies shape the form and, under great pressure, squeeze out the excess clay. An unusual feature is that the hard but porous gypsum plaster die has a tubular grid embedded in the plaster. Compressed air flowing from the tubes into the die allows the clay form to be released immediately after pressing. The pressing operation is very rapid. Compressed air released into the lower die breaks the clay suction, and the press rises.

Appendices

Reference Tables

Atomic Weights of Common Elements

Element	Symbol	Atomic Number	Atomic Weight	Element	Symbol	Atomic Number	Atomic Weight
aluminum	Al	13	26.97	manganese	Mn	25	54.93
antimony	Sb	51	121.76	molybdenum	Mo	42	95.98
barium	Ba	56	137.36	neon	Ne	10	20.183
bismuth	Bi	83	209.00	nickel	Ni	28	58.69
boron	B	5	10.82	nitrogen	N	7	14.008
cadmium	Cd	48	112.41	oxygen	O	8	16.00
calcium	Ca	20	40.08	palladium	Pd	46	106.70
carbon	C	6	12.01	phosphorus	P	15	30.98
chlorine	Cl	17	35.457	platinum	Pt	78	195.23
chromium	Cr	24	52.01	potassium	P	19	39.096
cobalt	Co	27	58.94	silicon	Si	14	28.06
copper	Cu	29	63.54	silver	Ag	47	107.88
fluorine	F	9	19.00	sodium	Na	11	22.997
gold	Au	79	197.20	sulfur	S	16	32.066
hydrogen	H	1	1.008	tin	Sn	50	118.70
iridium	Ir	77	193.10	titanium	Ti	22	47.90
iron	Fe	26	55.84	uranium	U	92	238.07
lead	Pb	82	207.21	vanadium	V	23	50.95
lithium	Li	3	6.94	zinc	Zn	30	65.38
magnesium	Mg	12	24.32	zirconium	Zr	40	91.22

Common Ceramic Raw Materials

Material	Raw Formula	Compound Molecular Weight	Equivalent Weight	Fired Formula
aluminum hydroxide	$Al_2(OH)_6$	156	156	Al_2O_3
antimony oxide	Sb_2O_3	292	292	Sb_2O_3
barium carbonate	$BaCO_3$	197	197	BaO
bone ash (calcium phosphate)	$Ca_3(PO_4)_2$	310	103	CaO
boric acid	$B_2O_3 \cdot 3\,H_2O$	124	124	B_2O_3
borax	$Na_2O \cdot 2\,B_2O_3 \cdot 10\,H_2O$	382	382	$Na_2O \cdot 2\,B_2O_3$
calcium borate (colemanite, gerstley borate)	$2\,CaO \cdot 3\,B_2O_3 \cdot 5\,H_2O$	412	206	$2\,CaO \cdot 3\,B_2O_3$
calcium carbonate (whiting)	$CaCO_3$	100	100	CaO
chromic oxide	Cr_2O_3	152	152	Cr_2O_3
cobalt carbonate	$CoCO_3$	119	119	CoO
cobalt oxide, black	Co_3O_4	241	80	CoO
copper carbonate	$CuCO_3$	124	124	CuO
copper oxide, green (cupric)	CuO	80	80	CuO
copper oxide, red (cuprous)	Cu_2O	143	80	CuO
Cornwall stone[a]	$(1\,RO \cdot 1.16\,Al_2O_3 \cdot 8.95\,SiO_2)$	652	652	same

Material	Raw Formula	Compound Molecular Weight	Equivalent Weight	Fired Formula
cryolite	$Na_3 \cdot AlF_6$	210	420	$3\ Na_2O \cdot Al_2O_3$
dolomite	$CaCO_3 \cdot MgCO_3$	184	184	$CaO \cdot MgO$
feldspar, potash	$K_2O \cdot Al_2O_3 \cdot 6\ SiO_2$	557	557	same
feldspar, soda	$Na_2O \cdot Al_2O_3 \cdot 6\ SiO_2$	524	524	same
kaolin (china clay)	$Al_2O_3 \cdot 2\ SiO_2 \cdot 2\ H_2O$	258	258	$Al_2O_3 \cdot 2\ SiO_2$
kaolin (calcined)	$Al_2O_3 \cdot 2\ SiO_2$	222	222	$Al_2O_3 \cdot 2\ SiO_2$
iron chromate	$FeCrO_4$	172	172	$FeCrO_4$
iron, oxide, red (ferric)	Fe_2O_3	160	160	Fe_2O_3
iron oxide, black (ferrous)	FeO	72	72	FeO
flint (quartz, silica)	SiO_2	60	60	SiO_2
fluorspar (calcium fluoride)	CaF_2	78	78	CaO
lead carbonate (white lead)	$2\ PbCO_3 \cdot Pb(OH)_2$	775	258	PbO
lead monosilicate	$3\ PbO \cdot 2\ SiO_2$	789	263	same
lead oxide (litharge)	PbO	223	223	PbO
lead oxide, red	Pb_3O_4	685	228	PbO
lepidolite	$LiF \cdot KF \cdot Al_2O_3 \cdot 3\ SiO_2$	356	356	same
lithium carbonate	Li_2CO_3	74	74	Li_2O
magnesium carbonate	$MgCO_3$	84	84	MgO
manganese carbonate	$MnCO_3$	115	115	MnO
manganese dioxide (black)	MnO_2	87	87	MnO
manganese oxide (greenish)	MnO	71	71	MnO
nepheline syenite[b]	$1\ RO \cdot 1.04\ Al_2O_3 \cdot 4.53\ SiO_2$	447	447	same
nickel oxide, green	NiO	75	75	NiO
nickel oxide, black	Ni_2O_3	166	83	NiO
petalite	$Li_2O \cdot Al_2O_3 \cdot 8\ SiO_2$	197	197	same
plastic vitrox[c]	$1\ RO \cdot 1.69\ Al_2O_3 \cdot 14.64\ SiO_2$	1139	1139	same
potassium carbonate (pearl ash)	K_2CO_3	138	138	K_2O
pyrophyllite	$Al_2O_3 \cdot 4\ SiO_2 \cdot H_2O$	360	360	$Al_2O_3 \cdot 4\ SiO_2$
sodium bicarbonate	$NaHCO_3$	84	168	Na_2O
sodium carbonate (soda ash)	Na_2CO_3	106	106	Na_2O
spodumene	$Li_2O \cdot Al_2O_3 \cdot 4\ SiO_2$	372	372	same
talc (steatite)	$3\ MgO \cdot 4\ SiO_2 \cdot H_2O$	379	126	$3\ MgO \cdot 4\ SiO_2$
tin oxide (stannic oxide)	SnO_2	151	151	SnO_2
titanium dioxide (rutile impure TiO_2)	TiO_2	80	80	TiO_2
wollastonite	$Ca \cdot SiO_3$	116	116	same
zinc oxide	ZnO	81	81	ZnO
zirconium oxide	ZrO_2	123	123	ZrO_2

[a]formula for Cornwall stone	K_2O	0.4453	Al_2O_3	1.0847	SiO_2	7.796
	Na_2O	0.2427	Fe_2O_3	0.0065		
	CaO	0.1873				
	MgO	0.0821		*Mol. weight* 652		
	CaF_2	0.0421				
[b]formula for nepheline syenite	Na_2O	0.713	Al_2O_3	1.04	SiO_3	4.53
	K_2O	0.220				
	CaO	0.056		*Mol. weight* 447		
	MgO	0.011				
[c]formula for plastic vitrox	CaO	0.045	Al_2O_3	1.693	SiO_2	14.634
	MgO	0.058	Fe_2O_3	0.005		
	Na_2O	0.054				
	K_2O	0.842		*Mol. weight* 1139.40		

Analysis of Common Clays and Chemicals

Material	SiO$_2$	Al$_2$O$_3$	Fe$_2$O$_3$	TiO$_2$	CaO	MgO	K$_2$O	Na$_2$O	Li$_2$O	Ignition Loss
red Dalton clay	63.2	18.3	6.3	1.3	0.3	0.5	1.6	1.2		6.4
Barnard clay	41.4	6.7	29.9	0.2	0.5	0.6	1.0	0.5		8.4
Monmouth stoneware	56.8	28.5			0.3	0.3	0.3	1.3		12.2
Jordan stoneware	69.4	17.7	1.6	1.3	0.1	0.5	1.5	1.39		6.4
Albany slip	57.6	14.6	5.2	0.4	5.8	2.7	3.2	0.8		9.5
ball clay	51.9	31.7	0.8	1.5	0.2	0.2	0.9	0.4		12.3
sagger clay	59.4	27.2	0.7	1.6	0.6	0.2	0.7	0.3		9.4
fireclay	58.1	23.1	2.4	1.4	0.8	1.1	1.9	0.3		10.5
Georgia kaolin	44.9	38.9	0.4	1.3	0.1	0.1	0.2	0.2		14.21
English kaolin	47.25	37.29	0.84	0.05	0.03	0.28	1.8	0.04		12.21
petalite	77.0	17.5					(0.5)		4.3	0.7
pyrophyllite	73.5	20.0	0.5		0.1		1.4	1.2		3.3
bentonite	64.32	20.7	3.47	0.11	0.46	2.26	2.9			5.15
volcanic ash	72.51	11.55	1.21	0.54	0.68	0.07	7.87	1.79		3.81
plastic vitrox	75.56	14.87	0.09		0.22	0.20	6.81	0.29		2.04
feldspar, potash	68.3	17.9	0.08		0.4		10.1	3.1		0.32
feldspar, soda	66.8	19.6	0.04		1.7	trace	4.8	6.9		0.2
Cornwall stone	72.6	16.1	0.23	0.06	1.4	0.1	4.56	3.67		2.54
nepheline syenite	60.4	23.6	0.08		0.7	0.1	9.8	4.6		0.7
lepidolite	55.0	25.0	0.08				9.0	1.0	4.0	0.92[a]
spodumene	62.91	28.42	0.53		0.11	0.13	0.69	0.46	6.78	0.28

[a]plus 5 percent fluorine.

Analysis of Several Standard Feldspars[a]

Material	SiO$_2$	Al$_2$O$_3$	Fe$_2$O$_3$	CaO	MgO	K$_2$O	Na$_2$O	Ignition Loss
Spruce Pine #4	67.9	19.01	0.05	1.54	trace	4.98	6.22	0.08
Bell	68.3	17.9	0.08	0.4	trace	10.1	3.1	0.32
Eureka	69.8	17.11	0.1	trace		9.4	3.5	0.2
Kingman	66.0	18.7	0.1	0.1		12.0	2.8	0.2
Oxford	69.4	17.04	0.09	0.38		7.92	3.22	0.3
Chesterfield	70.6	16.33	0.08	0.3		8.5	3.75	0.4
Buckingham	65.58	19.54	trace	0.16	0.2	12.44	2.56	0.32
Kona F-4	66.8	19.6	0.04	1.7	trace	4.8	6.9	0.2
Kona A-3	71.5	16.3	0.08	0.4	trace	7.5	4.0	0.2

[a]The variable quality of the feldspar fluxes is a major reason why glaze recipes may need alteration unless materials are identical.

Water of Plasticity of Various Clays

washed kaolin	44.48–47.50
white sedimentary kaolin	28.60–56.25
ball clays	25.00–53.30
plastic fireclays	12.90–37.40
flint fireclays	8.89–19.04
sagger clays	18.40–28.56
stoneware clays	19.16–34.80
brick clays	13.20–40.70

$$\text{water of plasticity} = \frac{\text{weight of plastic sample} - \text{weight of dry sample}}{\text{weight of dry sample}} \times 100$$

REFERENCE TABLES

Oxide Equivalents of Selected Commercial Frits[a]

Supplier	Supplier's Frit No.	K₂O	Na₂O	CaO	PbO	Al₂O₃	B₂O₃	SiO₂	Formula Weight
Pemco	54		0.32	0.68			0.64	1.47	191
	67	0.12	0.19	0.69		0.37	1.16	2.17	311
	926	0.01	0.31	0.68		0.11	0.61	1.90	225
	83		0.28		0.72	0.20	0.26	2.43	276
	316[b]				1.00	0.25		1.92	364
	349	0.09	0.09	0.58	0.24	0.19	0.36	2.80	313
Ferro	3124	0.02	0.28	0.70		0.27	0.55	2.56	279
	3134		0.32	0.68			0.63	1.47	210
	3211			1.00			1.11		133
	3223		1.00				2.00	5.00	502
	3419		0.28		0.72		0.57	0.89	276
	3386	0.02	0.08		0.90	0.13	1.77	4.42	499
	3396		0.50		0.50		1.00	2.00	332
Hommel	285	0.10	0.90			0.21	0.94	2.72	315
	267	0.13	0.31	0.56		0.29	1.24	2.05	301
	266		0.32	0.68		0.32	1.10	1.31	245
	22			0.47	0.53		0.98	2.88	385
	240		0.28		0.72		0.56	0.90	271
	13		0.30		0.70		0.39	0.41	227

[a]In most cases the above frits will constitute a complete glaze at cone 06.
[b]Cone deformation eutectic for PbO·Al₂O₃·SiO₂ system.

Average Temperatures to Which Various Ceramic Products Are Fired

Products	Degrees F	Degrees C
Heavy clay products		
common brick—surface clay	1600–1800	870–982
common brick—shale	1800–2000	982–1093
face brick—fireclay	2100–2300	1150–1260
enamel brick	2100–2300	1150–1260
drain tile	1700–1900	927–1038
sewer pipe	2030–2320	1110–1271
roofing tile	1960–2140	1071–1171
terra cotta	2070–2320	1021–1271
Pottery		
flowerpots	1580–1850	860–1010
stoneware (chemical)	2650–2700	1455–1482
stoneware (once fired)	2318–2426	1270–1330
semivitreous ware	2282–2354	1250–1290
pottery decalcomanias	1400–1500	760–816
Refractories		
firebrick—clay	2300–2500	1260–1371
firebrick—silica	2650–2750	1455–1510
silicon carbide	3236–3992	1769–2200
Whitewares		
electrical porcelain	2390–2500	1310–1371
hotel china—bisque	2390–2436	1310–1336
hotel china—glaze	2210–2282	1210–1250
floor tile	2318–2498	1270–1370
wall tile—bisque	1886–2354	1030–1290
wall tile—glaze	1186–2246	641–1230

Color Scale for Temperatures

Color	Degrees C	Degrees F
lowest visible red	475	885
lowest visible red to dark red	475–650	885–1200
dark red to cherry red	650–750	1200–1380
cherry red to bright cherry red	750–815	1380–1500
bright cherry red to orange	815–900	1500–1650
orange to yellow	900–1090	1650–2000
yellow to light yellow	1090–1315	2000–2400
light yellow to white	1315–1540	2400–2804
white to dazzling white	1540 and higher	2804 and higher

Melting Points of Selected Compounds and Minerals

Material	Degrees C	Degrees F
alumina	2050	3722
barium carbonate	1360	2480
bauxite	2035	3695
borax	741	1365
calcium oxide	2570	4658
cobaltic oxide	905	1661
copper oxide (CuO)	1064	1947
corundum	2035	3695
cryolite	998	1830
dolomite	2570–2800	4658–5072
ferric oxide	1548	2818
fireclay	1660–1720	3020–3128
fluorspar	1300	2372
kaolin	1740–1785	3164–3245
lead oxide (litharge)	880	1616
magnesium carbonate (dissociates)	350	662
magnesium oxide (approx.)	2800	5072
mullite	1810	3290
nepheline syenite	1223	2232
nickel oxide	400	752
orthoclase feldspar (potash)	1220	2228
potassium oxide	red heat	
rutile	1900	3452
silica	1715	3119
silicon carbide (decomposed)	2220	3992
sillimanite	1816	3301
sodium oxide	red heat	
tin oxide	1130	2066
titanium oxide	1900	3452
whiting (dissociates)	825	1517
zircon	2550	4622

Temperature Equivalents—Orton Standard Pyrometric Cones[a]

Cone Number	Large Cones 150°C[b]	270°F[b]	Small Cones 300°C[b]	540°F[b]	Seger Cones (used in Europe) Degrees C
020	635	1175	666	1231	670
019	683	1261	723	1333	690
018	717	1323	752	1386	710
017	747	1377	784	1443	730
016	792	1458	825	1517	750
015	804	1479	843	1549	790
014	838	1540			815
013	852	1566			835
012	884	1623			855
011	894	1641			880
010	894	1641	919	1686	900
09	923	1693	955	1751	920
08	955	1751	983	1801	940
07	984	1803	1008	1846	960
06	999	1830	1023	1873	980
05	1046	1915	1062	1944	1000
04	1060	1940	1098	2008	1020
03	1101	2014	1131	2068	1040
02	1120	2048	1148	2098	1060
01	1137	2079	1178	2152	1080
1	1154	2109	1179	2154	1100
2	1162	2124	1179	2154	1120
3	1168	2134	1196	2185	1140
4	1186	2167	1209	2208	1160
5	1196	2185	1221	2230	1180
6	1222	2232	1255	2291	1200
7	1240	2264	1264	2307	1230
8	1263	2305	1300	2372	1250
9	1280	2336	1317	2403	1280
10	1305	2381	1330	2426	1300
11	1315	2399	1336	2437	1320
12	1326	2419	1335	2471	1350
13	1346	2455			1380
14	1366	2491			1410
15	1431	2608			1430

[a]From the Edward Orton, Jr., Ceramic Foundation, Columbus, Ohio
[b]Temperature rise per hour

Temperature Conversion Formula

Centigrade to Fahrenheit

example: $100°C \times \dfrac{9}{5} = 180 \quad 180 + 32 = 212°F$

Fahrenheit to Centrigrade

example: $212°F - 32 = 180 \quad 180 \times \dfrac{5}{9} = 100°C$

When dealing with foreign suppliers or consulting references printed abroad, the potter should be able to convert readily from the American system of weights and measures to the metric system, employed by virtually every country outside the United States. The following tables provide multipliers for converting from metric to U.S. and the reverse; the multipliers have been rounded to the third decimal place and thus yield an approximate equivalent.

Metric to U.S.			U.S. to Metric		
to convert from	to	multiply the metric unit by	to convert from	to	multiply the U.S. unit by
Length:					
meters	yards	1.093	yards	meters	.914
meters	feet	3.280	feet	meters	.305
meters	inches	39.370	inches	meters	.025
centimeters	inches	.394	inches	centimeters	2.540
millimeters	inches	.039	inches	millimeters	25.400
Area and volume:					
square meters	square yards	1.196	square yards	square meters	.836
square meters	square feet	10.764	square feet	square meters	.093
square centimeters	square inches	.155	square inches	square centimeters	6.451
cubic centimeters	cubic inches	.061	cubic inches	cubic centimeters	16.387
Liquid measure:					
liters	cubic inches	61.020	cubic inches	liters	.016
liters	cubic feet	.035	cubic feet	liters	28.339
liters	*U.S. gallons	.264	*U.S. gallons	liters	3.785
liters	*U.S. quarts	1.057	*U.S. quarts	liters	.946
Weight and mass:					
kilograms	pounds	2.205	pounds	kilograms	.453
grams	ounces	.035	ounces	grams	28.349
grams	grains	15.430	grains	grams	.065
grams per meter	ounces per yard	.032	ounces per yard	grams per meter	31.250
grams per square meter	ounces per square yard	.030	ounces per square yard	grams per square meter	33.333

*The British imperial gallon equals approximately 1.2 U.S. gallons or 4.54 liters. Similarly, the British imperial quart equals 1.2 U.S. quarts, and so on.

Glaze and Stain Recipes

The glaze recipes listed here are intended to supplement the previous chapters on glazes and chemicals. Why so many, one might ask? The answer is that the various fluxes, alone or in combination, and even the proportion of alumina and silica contribute different qualities to a glaze. Some are transparent and others opaque, shiny and mat, runny and viscous. As mentioned before, the type of flux has a great effect upon the colorants.

But before using these or any other new glazes the potter should run some tests. The variability of the feldspars has been noted before. Other chemicals may contain impurities and vary from mine to mine. The fineness to which chemicals are ground often lowers slightly the maturity of the glaze. The rate of heat rise or fall, as a result of kiln construction or of its size, also plays a part. A difference will usually be found if the same glaze is fired in a gas or an electric kiln. Some reaction also occurs between the body and the glaze, more pronounced at the higher temperatures and especially under reducing conditions. Some glazes must be fired to a very exact temperature (see the discussion and eu-

tectics in the section on variables of glaze formulation in Chap. 8), while others can tolerate a couple of cones difference but with usually some change in surface appearance and often in color.

While it is important for the potter to have an understanding of glazes and chemicals, this knowledge is not a panacea. Many potters use only a few glazes with which they are completely familiar. Underlying slips and even thickness of application can produce quite varied results. But a potter's student years should be a period of experimentation. It takes a lot of trial and error to discover that certain forms, glazes, and decoration have an affinity and seem to naturally go together.

Low-Fire Lead* and Alkaline Glazes, Cones 08–04

Cones 05–03, Lithium Blue

27.0	lithium carbonate
14.1	kaolin
55.9	flint
3.0	bentonite
4.0	copper carbonate

Cones 04–02, Barium Mat Glaze

6.4	whiting
41.6	white lead
21.0	potash feldspar
12.5	barium carbonate
6.7	calcined kaolin
11.8	flint

Cones 08–09, Chromium Red

70.04	red lead
18.80	flint
2.13	soda ash
9.03	kaolin
5.00	potassium bichromate

Cones 04–02, Alumina Mat

48.0	white lead
12.0	whiting
21.8	potash feldspar
13.7	calcined kaolin
4.1	kaolin

Cone 04, Lithium Semiopaque

(from K. Green)

18.5	lithium carbonate
17.6	white lead
8.2	bone ash
6.0	soda feldspar
10.7	kaolin
37.1	flint
1.9	bentonite

Cone 04, Semimate

5.8	barium carbonate
10.0	lithium carbonate
9.8	whiting
9.8	zinc oxide
22.4	kaolin
42.2	flint

*In substituting red for white lead, approximately 11.5 percent less material is needed for the same PbO.

Cone 06, Lead Glaze, Resistant to Food Acids

36.78	white lead
18.95	soda feldspar
9.78	gerstley borate
4.90	boric acid
6.80	kaolin
21.70	silica
0.83	zirconium oxide

Cone 04, Volcanic-Ash Mat

(from A. Garzio)

22.7	colemanite
5.8	whiting
3.0	barium carbonate
7.0	white lead
5.0	borax
30.0	volcanic ash
20.0	kaolin
3.5	zinc oxide
6.8	tin oxide

Cone 04, Semigloss Rutile

(from K. Green)

66.00	white lead
5.03	plastic vitrox
15.68	kaolin
13.29	flint
5.70	rutile

Cone 04, Lead-Borax Turquoise, Fluid

12.0	whiting
26.0	borax
1.5	soda ash
19.5	white lead
27.5	potash feldspar
13.0	flint
0.5	kaolin
10.5	tin oxide
2.8	copper carbonate

Cone 04, Burnt-Red Glaze

48.2	white lead
7.3	whiting
11.5	kaolin
3.0	zinc oxide
30.0	flint
6.0	tin oxide
4.0	red iron oxide

Cones 08–06, Raku Glaze

33.5	gerstley borate
50.0	kaolin
16.5	flint

Medium-Fire Glazes Cones 2–4

Cones 1–2, Clear Glaze

52.60	white lead
15.70	soda feldspar
3.36	whiting
2.84	zinc oxide
9.90	flint
15.60	Cornwall stone
0.2	gum tragacanth

Cone 2, Plastic Vitrox

29.0	white lead
16.7	potash feldspar
44.3	plastic vitrox
10.0	whiting

Cone 2, Colemanite

8.20	calcined zinc oxide
38.50	potash feldspar
17.55	colemanite
6.80	barium carbonate
6.45	talc
22.50	flint

Cone 4, Dinnerware Glaze*

51.5	Ferro frit #3124
25.1	Pemco frit #316
4.0	whiting
4.7	kaolin
14.7	flint

Medium-Fire Glazes, Cones 5–6

Cone 6, Barium Blue

55.5	potash feldspar
41.5	barium carbonate
3.0	zinc oxide
2.0	copper carbonate
1.0	methocel or gum

*Acid-resistant commercial glaze, containing 0.233 equivalents of PbO.

Cone 6, Mat

63.6	potash feldspar
18.3	whiting
9.1	kaolin
4.5	talc
4.5	zinc oxide

Cone 6, Ash

38	wood ashes
20	potash feldspar
20	whiting
13	talc
9	kaolin

Cone 6, Mat

46.15	nepheline syenite
17.70	kaolin
10.60	talc
3.55	whiting
18.45	flint
3.55	zinc oxide

Cones 5–6, Wood Ash

(from A. Garzio)

23	Wood ash (mixed)
23	Nepheline Syenite
18	Whiting
13	Colemanite
9	Barium carbonate
2	Kaolin
2	Bentonite

Cone 6, Black Mat, Oxidation

40	Albany slip
25	kaolin
20	wollastonite
15	nepheline syenite
	plus
2.0	red iron oxide
0.75	cobalt oxide
0.25	chrome oxide

Cone 6, Opaque Semimat, Oxidization

38	nepheline syenite
10	gerstley borate
15	wollastonite
15	barium carbonate
10	kaolin
5	flint
7	tin oxide

Cone 6, Clear Glaze

4.8	lithium carbonate
4.5	whiting
11.0	zinc oxide
49.2	potash feldspar
14.4	kaolin
16.1	flint

Cone 6, Barium Mat

31.0	barium carbonate
3.2	whiting
7.8	zinc oxide
26.8	potash feldspar
9.5	kaolin
21.7	flint

Cone 5–7 Stoney Mat

(from A. Garzio)

59	nepheline syenite
23	barium carbonate
5	lithium carbonate
6	kaolin
5	flint
2	bentonite

Porcelain and Stoneware Glazes, Cone 8

Cone 8, Semimat

36.5	potash feldspar
25.7	kaolin
17.5	whiting
12.0	flint
8.2	rutile

Cone 8, Lepidolite (Crackle Glaze)

18.8	lepidolite
43.4	potash feldspar
6.3	cryolite
6.3	bone ash
12.6	whiting
12.6	colemanite

Cone 8, Mottled Blue

27.0	barium carbonate
50.0	potash feldspar
4.0	dolomite
9.0	kaolin
9.0	flint
3.9	copper carbonate

Cone 8, Feldspar

44.5	soda feldspar
12.0	whiting
7.3	kaolin
36.2	flint

Cones 7–8, Semimat Volcanic-Ash Glaze

(from A. Garzio)

26.7	volcanic ash
7.5	colemanite
19.7	nepheline syenite
6.1	whiting
7.5	magnesium carbonate
7.2	kaolin
5.3	flint

Cone 8, Dolomite Mat

35	potash feldspar
20	dolomite
10	whiting
5	kaolin
30	flint
3	bentonite

Porcelain and Stoneware Glazes, Cones 8–13

Cones 9–10, White Mat

(from R. Eckels)

43.0	potash feldspar
18.3	whiting
11.2	flint
22.8	kaolin
4.7	zinc oxide
3.0	rutile
2.0	tin oxide

Cones 8–9, Satin Blue-Green Mat

(from A. Garzio)

48.0	Custer feldspar
10.0	whiting
8.0	dolomite
2.0	pearl ash
30.0	flint
2.0	bentonite
2.0	chrome oxide
1.5	cobalt oxide

GLAZE AND STAIN RECIPES

Cones 8–10, Wood Ash

(from C. Ringel)

39.0	wood ash (mixed)
29.5	kona F4 feldspar
10.0	whiting
19.5	kaolin
2.0	bentonite

Cones 8–9, Portland Cement (Dry)

(from A. Garzio)

85.0	portland cement
13.0	Cornwall stone
2.0	bentonite
2.5	vanadium pentoxide

Cone 9, Oil-Spot Temmoku

46.5	Albany slip
37.2	potash feldspar
9.3	Kentucky ball clay
4.7	red iron oxide
2.3	borax

Cone 9, Opaque

10	gerstley borate
15	talc
5	dolomite
50	potash feldspar
5	kaolin
15	flint

Cone 9, Red Oxidation

11.5	bone ash
7.7	whiting
4.9	barium carbonate
6.0	talc
54.6	potash feldspar
15.3	flint

(plus 7–11% red iron oxide)

Cone 9, Mottled Blue-Brown

18	whiting
42	potash feldspar
13	kaolin
27	flint

(plus 4% each of rutile and red iron oxide)

Cones 9–10, Barium Blue Mat

(from A. Garzio)

64.0	Custer feldspar
34.0	barium carbonate
2.0	bentonite
8.5	copper carbonate

Cones 10–13,

(from A. Garzio)

53.8	potash feldspar
19.2	whiting
19.2	ball clay
4.6	kaolin
3.2	zinc oxide

Cones 8–11, White Opaque

45.35	potash feldspar
12.85	kaolin (Florida)
17.50	whiting
1.45	borax
20.50	flint
2.35	zinc oxide
30.20	zircopax

Cones 10–12, Mat

40.0	potash feldspar
22.3	whiting
21.0	kaolin
16.7	silica
4.4	titanium oxide

Reduction Glazes

Cone 04, Celadon

20.5	white lead
1.6	whiting
52.5	soda feldspar
25.4	soda ash
1.5	red iron oxide
2.5	tin oxide

(Grind dry, use immediately if wet. Fire: reduction, cone 012–07; oxidizing, cone 07–04.)

Cone 04, Copper Luster

66.30	white lead
24.50	Cornwall stone
9.20	flint
1.94	cobalt oxide
1.15	copper oxide
9.60	manganese oxide

(Black when thin, copper when thick. Fire: reduction cone 012–07; oxidizing cone 07–04.)

Cone 2, Local Copper-Red Reduction

(from Harder)

34.00	soda feldspar
28.40	borax
0.75	soda ash
6.60	fluorspar
12.45	kaolin
17.80	flint
2.00	tin oxide
0.50	copper carbonate [plus 0.5 percent silicon carbide (180 mesh carborundum)

Cone 6, Copper-Red Reduction

11.8	white lead
11.8	red lead
5.9	whiting
2.9	kaolin
29.4	flint
29.4	borax
4.4	boric acid
4.4	soda ash
1.7	tin oxide
0.5	copper oxide

Cones 7–8, Flambé, Semigloss

(from A. Garzio)

49.0	Custer feldspar
29.0	colemanite
20.0	flint
2.0	bentonite
3.0	copper carbonate
0.5	cobalt carbonate

Cone 8, Copper-Red Reduction

27.9	Cornwall stone
32.5	flint
4.0	zinc oxide
9.3	barium carbonate
4.3	soda ash
22.0	borax
2.0	copper carbonate
2.0	tin oxide

Cones 6–8, Celadon Reduction

62.2	potash feldspar
7.6	whiting
5.0	kaolin
25.2	flint
1.5	red iron oxide

Cones 8–10, Celadon

79.5 potash feldspar
6.2 whiting
14.3 flint
2.0 red iron oxide

Cone 8, Local Copper reduction
(from Baggs)

32.8 soda feldspar
1.9 soda ash
28.0 borax
7.3 whiting
12.3 kaolin
17.7 flint
1.8 tin oxide
0.3 copper carbonate
0.65 silicon carbide

Cones 9–11, Celadon

26.55 whiting
25.50 Cornwall stone
25.50 kaolin (EPK)
20.40 flint
2.05 red iron oxide

Cones 9–10, Copper Red

13.0 Ferro frit #3191
44.0 soda feldspar
14.0 whiting
3.0 kaolin (EPK)
25.0 flint
1.0 tin oxide
0.2 copper carbonate

(Add 0.2 silicon carbide for local reduction.)

Cones 9–11, Celadon

27.05 potash feldspar
19.45 whiting
19.80 kaolin
32.70 flint
1.00 red iron oxide

Cone 10, Rutile Blue
(from P. Shrope)

15.8 dolomite
30.0 Custer feldspar
11.1 whiting
16.8 edgar plastic kaolin
26.3 flint

(Add 8.0 rutile.)

Cone 11, Rutile Blue
(from P. Shrope)

28.9 Custer feldspar
20.6 whiting
18.9 edgar plastic kaolin
31.6 flint

(Add 7.0 rutile.)

Ovenware and Flameware Glazes

Cones 9-10, Flameware Glaze
(from R. Propst)

32.0 lepidolite
25.0 dolomite
3.0 whiting
3.0 talc
2.5 gerstley borate
25.0 Kaolin
9.5 flint

Cone 9, Ovenware Glaze

21.5 dolomite
18.0 spodumene
3.0 whiting
26.5 potash feldspar
22.0 kaolin
9.0 magnesium zirconium silicate

Crystalline Glazes

Cones 07–05, Aventurine

45.7 borax
2.6 borium carbonate
3.3 boric acid
1.7 kaolin
46.7 flint
17.7 red iron oxide

(Grind and use immediately or frit without the clay.)

Cones 3–4, Zinc Crystal

13.4 soda ash
15.5 boric acid
22.2 zinc oxide
42.8 flint
6.1 ball clay
6.7 rutile

(Grind and use immediately or frit without the clay.)

Cone 11, Zinc Crystal

45.5 feldspar
15.9 whiting
15.9 flint
22.7 zinc oxide

Cones 03–04, Aventurine

94 Ferro frit #3304
19 red iron oxide
6 kaolin (EPK)

Cone 8, Zinc Crystal (Pale Green)

11.6 sodium carbonate
6.6 whiting
18.2 kaolin (EPK)
42.2 silica
21.4 zinc oxide
3.1 copper carbonate
5.3 titanium (rutile)

(Grind and use immediately or frit without the clay.)

Cone 11, Titanium Crystal

25 soda ash
50 flint
25 zinc oxide
10 titanium oxide

Cones 9–10, Zinc Crystal
(from M. Hansen)

74	Pemco frit #283	
21.5	zinc oxide	
4.5	flint	
1.0	bentonite #1	
plus	MnO_2	5 percent
	$CuCo_3$	5 percent
	rutile	4 percent
	#2	
	$CuCO_3$	3 percent
	rutile	5 percent
	#3	
	NiO	1 percent
	$CuCO_3$	3 percent

Ceramic Stains*

(For preparation, see Chap. 8.)

#1 Pink Stain

50	tin oxide
25	whiting
18	flint
4	borax
3	potassium dichromate

(Calcine to cone 8; stain is lumpy and must first be broken up in iron mortar, then ground.)

#2 Pink Stain

50.5	tin oxide
19.0	whiting
7.5	fluorspar
20.5	flint
7.5	potassium dichromate

(Calcine to cone 8 and grind.)

#3 Crimson Stain

22.9	whiting
6.6	calcium sulfate
4.4	fluorspar
20.8	flint
43.7	tin oxide
1.6	potassium dichromate

(Calcine to cone 8 and grind.)

#4 Ultramarine Stain

50	chromium oxide
12	flint
38	cobalt oxide

(Calcine to cone 8 and grind.)

#5 Blue-Green Stain

41.8	cobalt oxide
19.3	chromium oxide
39.0	aluminium oxide

(Calcine to cone 8 and grind.)

#6 Orange Stain

29.8	antimony oxide
12.8	tin oxide
14.9	red iron oxide
42.5	red lead

(Calcine to cone 6 and grind.)

*These stains must be finely ground to obtain the desired color.

#7 Black Stain

43	chromium oxide
43	red iron oxide
10	manganese dioxide
4	cobalt oxide

(Calcine to cone 8 and grind.)

#8 Turquoise Stain

56	copper phosphate
44	tin oxide

(Calcine to cone 6 and grind.)

#9 Red-Brown Stain

22	chromium oxide
23	red iron oxide
55	zinc oxide

(Calcine to cone 8 and grind.)

#10 Brown Stain

64.6	zinc oxide
9.7	chrome oxide
9.7	red iron oxide
8.0	red lead
8.0	boric acid

(Calcine to cone 8 and grind.)

#11 Yellow Stain

33.3	antimony oxide
50.0	red lead
16.7	tin oxide

(Calcine to cone 6 and grind.)

#12 Black Stain

65	chromium oxide
35	red iron oxide

(Calcine to cone 8 and grind.)

Clay Bodies

The clay body preferred by the studio potter is quite different from that used by a commercial pottery. For slip casting or jiggering, a uniformity of texture is necessary, for obvious technical reasons. Similarly, any impurities imparting color to the body are undesirable. Therefore, bodies used in commercial production are carefully selected, ground, and refined. Plasticity is of minor importance, and, since it is associated with high shrinkage rates, it is avoided.

Local supplies of earthenware and plastic fireclays are available in the United States, particularly in the Midwest. Since they are widely used in cement, plaster, and mortar mixtures, they are competitively priced and generally quite reasonable.

Because the volume of clay used in the school studio will normally be measured in tons (metric tons) per year, both the initial cost and the shipping charges are important. Thus, clay that can be bought locally has a decided advantage, even if it needs a certain amount of sieving or small additions. Occasionally, a truckload of raw clay can be purchased reasonably from a local brick or tile works.

Earthenware Bodies

Earthenware bodies present no real problem of supply in the Midwest, since there are many brick and tile factories that also sell bagged clay. Shale clays with coarse particles will cause trouble unless they are run through a sieve of from 15 to 20 meshes per inch (2.54 cm). Some earthenware clays contain soluble sulfates, which will form a whitish scum on the fired ware; however, the addition of 0.25 to 2 percent barium will eliminate this fault. Many such clays will not be very plastic unless they are aged. Adding about 5 percent bentonite, which is extremely plastic, will usually render a short clay workable. Often two clays that alone are not suitable can be mixed together to form a good body. Only experimentation will indicate the necessary changes.

Occasionally, the body will lack sufficient flint to fuse with the fluxes it contains. Cream-colored clays can be rendered more plastic by the addition of ball clays. Talc has some plasticity and is often used in low-fire whiteware bodies as a source of both flux and silica. Feldspar, nepheline syenite, and plastic vitrox are also added to various bodies to contribute fluxing qualities.

Stoneware and Porcelain Bodies

Stoneware and porcelain bodies are usually compounded from several ingredients. In fact, it is quite rare for a single clay to satisfy all throwing and firing requirements. There is no clay that, by itself, will make a porcelain body. Oriental porcelain is made from one or two clay-like minerals that are fairly plastic. Since nothing in the Western world compares with petuntze, porcelain bodies must be compounded from clay and various minerals.

Both stoneware and porcelain will form hard, vitrified bodies at cone 10. The major difference between the two is that stoneware contains some impurities, chiefly iron, which give it a gray or tan color. Both stoneware and porcelain bodies are compounded for varying temperatures and, in the case of porcelain, for different degrees of translucency. Greater translucency is usually obtained by increasing the feldspar ratio, which has the accompanying disadvantage of an increase in warpage when the ware is fired.

Fireclay and stoneware clays differ from pure clay (kaolin) chiefly in that they contain various fluxes and impurities that lower the fusion point and impart a gray, tan, or buff color. Fireclays, which have a more universal industrial use, can be substituted for stoneware. Some fireclays are very plastic and fine enough for throwing. They often contain some iron impurities, which give the body a flecked appearance. Depending upon the firing temperature and the effect desired, it may be necessary to blend in an earthenware or stoneware clay or ingredients such as feldspar, talc, or silica.

The following recipes for clay bodies are included merely as suggestions, since it usually will be necessary to vary these recipes depending upon the raw materials available locally.

Engobes

Engobes are essentially clay slips, with the significant difference that some engobes are intended for use on either dry or bisque ware, thus necessitating additions of flint, feldspar, and occasionally a flux to the slip in order to adjust the varying shrinkage rates. The general purpose of an engobe is to provide a smoother surface and usually a different-colored base for glaze or brushed decoration.

If the engobe is to be used on a damp piece, a sieved slip of the throwing body can be used, provided the color is not objectionable. The usual colorants can be added, except for the chrome oxides, which react unfavorably with tin. One percent of a strong oxide, such as cobalt, is sufficient, although from 5 to 7 percent of iron or vanadium may be needed. Blistering will result if over 7 percent manganese is used. Five percent of an opacifier is often needed to lighten the color.

Engobes used on leather-hard ware must be adjusted to reduce shrinkage by calcining part of the clay and by additions of flint and feldspar. On dry ware the clay content of the engobe can rarely be more than 40 percent, with the balance composed of flint and feldspar. A 5-percent addition of borax will toughen the surface and aid adhesion.

When used on bisque ware, an engobe must have a clay content of less than 25 percent, or it will shrink excessively and flake off the pot. Furthermore, it must contain sufficient fluxes to fuse with the bisque surface. Its characteristics resemble those of an underfired glaze. In view of the low clay content, a binder may be necessary.

Too thick an application of an engobe on any surface, whether leather-hard clay or bisque ware, will crack or flake off. On the other hand, a thin coating will allow the body color to show through. In addition to the usual finely ground coloring oxides, coarsely ground ores, ilmenite, rust chips, chopped copper scouring pads, and other materials can be added to the engobe. Such additions melt out into the covering glaze with interesting effects limited to the area of the applied engobe.

Suggested Clay Bodies

Cone 08, Egyptian Paste (Self-Glazing Body)

40	Buckingham spar
20	flint
15	kaolin
6	bicarbonate of soda
6	soda ash
5	ball clay
5	dolomite
3	bentonite

Colorants for Egyptian Paste

purple-blue	0.75%	cobalt carbonate
light green	0.50%	copper carbonate
turquoise	2.50%	copper carbonate
yellow	7.00%	vanadium stain

Cones 08–06, Raku Body

48	stoneware clay
12	Cedar Heights Redart clay
12	ball clay
20	grog

Cone 04, Black Basalt Body

61	Kentucky ball clay
10	Pemco frit #25
5	nepheline syenite
2	bentonite
3	red iron oxide
2	cobalt oxide
2	manganese dioxide

Cone 6, Black Basalt Body

40	red clay
18	kaolin
15	Kentucky ball clay
16	red iron oxide
6	manganese dioxide
3	bentonite
2	nepheline syenite

Cones 2–8, Stoneware Body

20	Jordan or Monmouth clay
25	ball clay
30	plastic fireclay
10	nepheline syenite
5	flint
12	grog (fine mesh for wheel work)

Cones 8–10, Stoneware Body

50	Cedar Heights clay (or Goldart, Jordan, Monmouth)
25	fireclay (APG)
10	Kentucky ball clay
5	flint
5	Cedar Heights Redart

Cone 9, White Stoneware Body

10	potash feldspar
25	kaolin (EPK)
30	sagger clay
20	Kentucky ball clay
15	flint

Cone 9, Porcelain Body

50	grolleg (English kaolin)
25	potash feldspar
25	flint (finely ground)

Cones 9–11, Porcelain Body

27	potash feldspar
45	grolleg (English kaolin)
6	bentonite
26	flint

Cone 9 Porcelain
(from T. Turner)

75	#6 tile kaolin
38	kaopaque-20
60	F-4 feldspar
60	silica (200 mesh)
12	O.M. #4 ball clay
4	Vee Gum T
4	Ceramitalc 10AC

Cones 8–12, Porcelain Body

27	ball clay
27	kaolin
27	potash feldspar
19	flint

Cones 10–15, Porcelain Body

25	ball clay
25	kaolin
25	potash feldspar
25	flint

Cones 9–10, Flameware Body
(from R. Propst)

30	spodumene (Kings Mt., 200 mesh)
10	pyrophyllite (Pyrotrol, 200 mesh)
10	feldspar (Kings Mt., 200 mesh)
20	Kentucky ball clay
30	fireclay (A. P. Green)
2	bentonite
1	macaloid

Cone 9, Ovenware Body

40	spodumene
30	fireclay (A. P. Green)
20	Kentucky ball clay
10	Cedar Heights Redart

Cone 9, Ovenware Body

30	spodumene
30	sagger clay
20	fireclay (A. P. Green)
10	bonding clay (Cedar Heights)
10	grog (fine mesh)

Thixotropic Clay Body

Cone 5	Cone 9	
25	25	Kentucky ball clay
15	15	spodumene
15	15	kona F-A
15	15	kaolin (EPK)
10	25	flint
20	5	Ferro Frit #3110

Cone 5 glaze for above body
(Crazes at cone 9)

16	kaolin (EPK)
24	nepheline cyenite
60	Ferro frit #3124

Casting Slips

Cones 06–05, Talc Body

16	plastic vitrox
35	ball clay
49	talc

Cones 3–4, Parian Body

60	feldspar
30	kaolin
10	ball clay

Cones 8–9, Porcelain Body

20	flint
36	feldspar
30	kaolin
14	ball clay

Colorants for Clay Bodies

The oxides should be added to dry white stoneware or porcelain body ingredients, the mixture seived, and enough water added to make a muddy consistency. After the mixture has set up it should be wedged very well. As with other formulas, these should be tested in small batches.

pink	8.0%	commercial pink stain
yellow	8.0%	commercial yellow stain
yellow	8.0%	rutile
black	0.5%	cobalt oxide,
	7.0%	iron chromate
green	0.5%	green chrome oxide
lavender	5.0%	commercial pink stain,
	0.5%	cobalt carbonate
blue	0.5% to 1.0	cobalt carbonate
brown	3.0%	red iron oxide

Sources of Equipment and Materials

The cost of kilns, wheels, clay, and glaze materials has increased at such a rapid rate in recent years that the potter and the teacher should develop a cost-efficient approach to purchasing. In the college program, a course in kiln building will be of benefit to both the department and the students, and the cost of materials will be much less than that of a manufactured kiln. Wheels, kilns, pug mills, and so forth available through local ceramic-supply houses, as well as from their manufacturers. Quite frequently a discount will be allowed by the dealers to schools. In case of damage or needed repairs, a local dealer will be of more as-sistance than a more distant source.

The price of clay, which seems so cheap by the pound (kilogram) mounts alarmingly for the enormous quantities used in the classroom. The shipping costs often total as much as three times the actual cost of the clay at the mine. Considerable savings result from quantity purchases. Several potters or even nearby schools can share in a large shipment, since the relative shipping cost for a single ton is much more than for twenty tons (18.04 metric tons). Fireclays have many industrial applications and are available at building-supply houses. Plastic fireclay is a suitable base for a stoneware body. Earthenware clays are often used commercially to make concrete more dense and waterproof. They may be sold under a trade name, but they are essentially clays suitable for both earthenware and stoneware bodies. Many are of a shale origin and need sieving, but they are relatively inexpensive and therefore worth the bother.

The public school teacher, often limited by time, cannot arrange the usual studio procedures, especially complex glaze formulation. It is wasteful to buy the expensive little 1-pound (0.45-kg) glaze packets, when frits in 100-pound (45.36-kg) lots are much more economical. Most fire to cone 06, but the addition of 10 percent kaolin will increase adhesive properties and lower the maturing temperature to cone 04. Coloring oxides can be purchased in 1- to 10-pound (0.45- to 4.54-kg) lots. Since these are used in relatively small amounts, the total cost per pound (kilogram) of glaze will be small. Because of the dangers resulting from improper compounding of lead glazes, the borosilicate frits are recommended.

Sources of Equipment and Materials in the United States

Manufacturers

Kilns

A. & A. Potters Warehouse, 2100 North Wilmot Road, Units 201-202, Tucson, Ariz. 85712

American Art Clay Co. (electric), 4717 West 16th Street, Indianapolis, Ind. 46222

A.D. Alpine, Inc., 3051 Fujita Street, Torrance, Calif. 90505

California Kiln Co., 8375 Los Osos Rd., Atascadero, Calif. 43422

Ceramic Fiber Fabrication, Inc., 878 South Rose Place, Anaheim, Calif. 92805

Contemporary Kiln Co., P.O. Box 573 Novato, Calif. 94947

Cress Mfg. Co. (electric), 1718 Floradale Avenue, South, El Monte, Calif. 91733 or 201 Bradshaw Pike Ext., Hopkinsville, Ky. 44240

Crusader Ceramic Equipment, 417 West 16th Street, Indianapolis, Ind. 46222

Geil Kilns (gas), 1601 Rosecrans Avenue, Gardena, Calif. 90249

L. & L. Mfg. Co., Box 348, 144 Conchester Road, Twin Oaks, Pa. 19104

Marathon Kilns (gas), 128 Mile Street, Healdsburg, Calif. 95448

Olsen Kilns, Box 205 P.C., Mt. Center, Calif. 92361

Olympic Kilns, 8660 Willows Road, Redmond, Wash. 98052

Paragon Industries (electric), Box 10133, Dallas, Tex. 75207

Peach Valley Pottery, 317 West 3rd, Carthage, Mo. 64836

Shutt Ceramic Products, Inc. (electric), 2618 Southeast Steele Street, Portland, Oreg. 97202

Unique Kilns, P.O. Box 246, Ringoes, N.J. 08551

Westby Ceramic Supply & Mfg. (electric), Box 422 Clinton, Wash. 98236

West Coast Kiln Co., P.O. Box 6374, Orange, Calif. 92667

Westwood Ceramic Supply Co. (gas), 14400 Lomitas Avenue, City of Industry, Calif. 91744

Clay Mixers and Pug Mills

A. D. Alpine, Inc., 3051 Fujita Street, Torrance, Calif. 90505

Bluebird Manufacturing, P.O. Box 2307, Fort Collins, Colo. 80522

Walker Jamar Co., Inc., 365 First Avenue, East, Duluth, Minn. 55802

Peter Pugger, 9460 Carmel Road, Atascadero, Calif. 93422

Randall Pottery, Inc., Box 774, Alfred, N.Y., 14802

Soldner Pottery Equipment Co., P.O. Box 428, Silt, Co. 81652

Slab Rollers

Bailey Pottery Equipment Corp., C.P.O. 1577, Kingston, N.Y. 12401

Robert Brent Corp., 128 Mill Street, Healdsburg, Calif. 95448

Estrin Manufacturing, Ltd., 1916 Fir Street, Vancouver, B.C., Canada

Menco Engineers, Inc., 4525 Industrial Street, Simi Valley, Calif. 93063

Potter's Wheels

A. D. Alpine, Inc. (kick & electric), 3051 Fujita Street, Torrance, Calif. 90505

American Art Clay Co. (kick & electric), 4717 West 16th Street, Indianapolis, Ind. 46222

Robert Brent Corp. (kick & electric), 128 Mill Street,

Gilmor Campbell (electric), 2700 Erskine, Detroit, Mich. 48213

Creative Industries (electric), 5366 Jackson Drive, La Mesa, Calif. 92041

Arch T. Flowers (electric), Queen Lt. and Ivy Hill Road, Philadelphia, Pa. 19118

Holmgren C. Corp, (kick) P.O. Box E-816, 102 Wamsulta, New Bedford, Mass. 02742

Menco Engineers, Inc. (electric), 4525 Industrial Street, Simi Valley, Calif. 93063

Oak Tree Pottery (electric), Box 635, Las Gatos, Calif. 95030

Pacifica Wheels (kick & electric), P.O. Box 1407,
  Ferndale, Wash. 98248
Paoli Clay Co. (kick) Rt. #1, Belleville, Wis. 53508
Randall Wheel (kick & electric), Box 774, Alfred, N.Y. 14802
Shempo-West (electric), 14400 Lometas Avenue, City of Industry,
  Calif. 91746
Skutt Ceramic Products (electric), 2618 Southeast Steele Street,
  Portland, Oreg. 97202
Soldner Pottery & Equipment, Inc. (kick & electric),
  P.O. Box 428, Silt, Co. 81652

Clay Extruders

A & A Potters' Warehouse, 2100 North Wilmot Road #201,
  Tucson, Ariz. 85712
Bailey Pottery Equipment Corp., C.P.O. 1577, Kingston, N.Y. 12401
Robert Brent Corp., 128 Mill Street, Healdsburg, Calif. 95448
Clay Pacific, Inc., Box 151, Willamina, Oreg. 93396
Halvorsen Kiln Co. (small-size coils) 8025½ Greenleaf
  Avenue, Whittier, Calif. 90602
Kemper Manufacturing Inc. (miniature coils) Box 545,
  Chino, Calif. 91710
Randall Pottery, Inc., Box 774, Alfred, N.Y. 14802
Scott Creek Pottery, 482 Swanton Road, Davenport, Calif. 95017

Miscellaneous Equipment

Bluebird Manufacturing (hammermill), P.O. Box 2307, Fort Collins,
  Calif. 80522
Big Joe Manufacturing Co. (forklift) 7225 North Koster Avenue,
  Chicago, Ill. 60646
Brocton Machine & Foundry Co., Inc. (jiggers) Brocton, N.Y. 14716
Mid-America Casting Equipment Co. (slip casting)
  834 Central Avenue, Kansas City, Kans. 66101
Ram, Inc. (clay presses), 25 Snyder Street, Springfield, Ohio 45504

Kiln Burners

A. D. Alpine, Inc., 3051 Fujita Street, Torrance, Calif. 90505
California Kiln Co., Inc., 8375 Los Osos Road, Atascadero, Calif. 43422
Berman Kilns, 5622 Cahuenga Boulevard, North Hollywood,
  Calif. 91601
Eclipse Engineering, 1105 Buchanan, Rockland, Ill. 61101
Flynn Burner Corp., 432 Fifth Ave., New Rochelle, N.Y. 10802
Johnson Gas & Appliance Co., 1950 O'Donnell Street,
  Cedar Rapids, Iowa 52400
Surface Combustion Co. (Din Midland Rosa)
  2389 Dorr Street, Toledo, Ohio 53601

Refractory Materials

Many large building-supply dealers carry firebrick, insulating brick,
  and castables. The following manufacturers will supply addresses
  of regional sources.
Aluminium Co. of America, 1501 Alcoa Building, Pittsburgh, Pa. 15219
Babcock & Wilcox (Refractories Div.), 1288 Merry Street,
  Augusta, Ga. 30903
Chicago-Wellsville Firebrick Co., 1467 North Elston Street,
  Chicago, Ill. 60622
Johns-Manville, 22 East 40th Street, New York, N.Y. 10016
A. P. Green Refractories Co., Mexico, Mo. 65265
Kaiser Refractories, Kaiser Center, Oakland, Calif. 94604

Kiln Shelves

Shelves may be obtained from all kiln companies; however, for large
  quantities, a better price may often be obtained from the following manufacturers.

Carborundum Co. (Refractories Div.), Box 337, Niagara Falls,
  N.Y. 14302
Ferro Corp. (Electric Div.) 2000 Harvey Avenue, East Liverpool,
  Ohio. 43920; 416 Maple Avenue, Box 151, Crooksville,
  Ohio, 43731
New Castle Refractories, Box 471, New Castle, Pa. 16103

Clays

Bell Operations, 157 Virginia Avenue, Chester, W. Va. 26034
Burns Brick Works, P.O. Box 4787, Macon, Ga. 31208
L. H. Butcher Co., 15th & Vermont Streets, San Francisco
  Calif. 94107
Cedar Heights Clay Co., 50 Portsmouth Road, Oak Hill, Ohio 45656
Columbus Clay Co., 1205 17th Avenue, Columbus, Ohio, 43211
Edgar Plastic Kaolin Co., Edgar, Fla. 32009
Georgia Kaolin Co., 433 North Broad Street, Elizabeth, N.J. 07207
Hammill & Gillespie, Inc., P.O. Box 104, South Livingston
  Avenue, Livingston, N.J. 07039
J. M. Huber Corp., Huber, Ga. 31040
Industrial Minerals Co., 7268 Frasinetti Road, Florin, Calif. 95828
Interpace Corp., 2901 Los Feliz Boulevard, Los Angeles, Calif. 90039

Ceramic Chemicals and Colors

L. H. Butcher Co., 15th & Vermont Streets, San
  Francisco, Calif. 94107
Ceramic Color and Chemical Manufacturing Co., P.O. Box
  297, New Brighton, Pa. 15066
Ferro Corp (Color Div.), 4150 East 56th Street,
  Cleveland, Ohio 44105
General Color & Chemical Co., Inc., Box 7, Minerva, Ohio 44657
Harshaw Chemical Co., 1945 East 97th Street, Cleveland, Ohio 44106
Hercules, Inc. (Drakenfeld Div.), Box 519, Washington, Pa. 15301
Industrial Minerals, 7263 Frasinetti Road, Florin, Calif. 95828
O. Hommel Co., Box 475, Pittsburgh, Pa. 15230
Kraft Chemical Co., 917 West 18th Street, Chicago Ill. 60608
Mason Color & Chemical Works, Inc., Box 76,
  206 Broadway, East Liverpool, Ohio 43920
Pfizer Minerals (Pigments & Metals Div.),
  235 East 42nd Street, New York, N.Y. 10017
Trinity Ceramic Supply, Inc., 9016 Diplomacy Row,
  Dallas, Tex., 75247
Whittaker, Clark & Daniels, 100 Church Street, New York, N.Y. 10017

Local Supply Houses

Clay, Chemicals, Kilns,
Wheels, Etc.

East Coast

Amherst Potters Supply, 44 McCallan Street, Amherst, Mass. 01002
Bennett Pottery Supply, Inc., 707 Nicolet Avenue,
  Winter Park, Fla. 32789
Ceramic Supply of New York & New Jersey (formerly Baldwin
  Pottery) 534 LaGuardia Place, New York, N.Y. 10012
  and 87 Dell Glen Avenue, Lodi, N.J. 07644
Clay Art Center, 40 Beech Street, Port Chester, N.Y. 10573
  or 342 Western Avenue, Brighton, Mass. 02135
Clay Factory, Inc., 804 South Dale Mabry Avenue, Tampa, Fla. 33609
Creek-Turn Ceramic Supply, Route #38, Hainesport, N.J., 08036
Cutter Ceramics, 47 Athletic Field, Waltham, Mass. 02154
  or 700 Federal Road., Brookfield, Conn. 06804
Del Val Potters Supply Co., Queen Street & Ivy
  Hill Road, Philadelphia, Pa. 19118

Eagle Ceramics, 8 Colonial Avenue, Wilmington, Del. 19805
  or Route #2, Box 287, Wendell, N.C. 27591
Florida Potters, Supply, Inc., 675 Industrial
  Drive, Tallahassee, Fla. 32304
Kickwheel Pottery Supply, 1428 Mayson Street, Northeast,
  Atlanta, Ga. 30324
Miami Clay Co., 18954 Northeast 4th Court, Miami, Fla. 33179
  or 4446 Southwest 74th Avenue, Miami, Fla. 33155
Miller Ceramics, 4022 Mill Road., Skaneateles, N.Y. 13152
Salem Craftsmen's Guild, 3 Alvin Place, Upper Montclair, N.J. 07043
Seeleys Ceramic Service, Inc., 9 River Street, Oneonta, N.Y. 13820
Jack D. Wolfe Co., 724 Meeker Avenue, Brooklyn, N.Y. 11222

Midwest and South

American Art Clay Co. Inc., 4717 West 16th Street,
  Indianapolis, Ind. 46222
A.R.T. Studio, 921 Oakton Street, Elk Grove, Ill. 60007
Boekm Ceramic Supply, 916 Post Oak Road, Sulphur, La. 70663
The Clay Hand, P.O. Box 7213, Columbia, Mo. 65205
Eagle Ceramics, 1300 West 9th Street, Cleveland, Ohio, 44113
House of Ceramics, Inc., 1011 North Hollywood,
  Memphis, Tenn. 38108
L. & R. Specialties, P.O. Box 309, 202 East
  Mt. Vernon, Nixa, Mo. 65714
Minnesota Clay Co., 8001 Grand Avenue, South
  Bloomington, Minn. 55420
Newell Ceramic Supply, 4916 North State Street, Jackson, Miss. 39206
Ohio Ceramic Supply, P.O. Box 630, Kent, Ohio 44240
Owl Creek Pottery, 11416 Shelbyville Road, Louisville, Ky. 40243
Paramount Ceramics, 220 North State Street, Fairmont, Minn. 56031
Posterity Studio, 2687 Osceola Avenue, Columbus, Ohio 43211
Robbins Clay Co., 1021 West Lill Street, Chicago, Ill. 60614
Rovin Ceramics, 6912 Schaefer Road, Dearborn, Mich. 48126
Willmars Ceramic Supply, 1121 Bolton Avenue, Alexandria, La. 71301
  or 9526 South Choctaw, Baton Rouge, La. 70815

West and Pacific Coast

Anhowe Ceramic Supply Co., 3825 Commercial, North East
  Albuquerque, N. Mex. 87107
Armadillo Clay & Supplies, 3307 East 4th Street, Austin, Tex. 78702
Bateman Ceramic Supply, 718 Pierce Street, Dallas, Tex. 75211
Bay-Shore Ceramic Supply, Inc., 590 Aldo Avenue,
  Santa Clara, Calif. 95050
Capitol Ceramics, Inc., 2174 South Main Street, Salt Lake City,
  Utah, 84115
Ceramics, Hawaii Ltd., 543 South Street, Honolulu,
  Hawaii, 96813
Conville Ceramic Supply, 4566 30th Street, San Diego,
  Calif. 92116
Leslie Ceramics Supply Co., 1212 San Pablo Avenue, Berkeley,
  Calif. 94706
Marjon Ceramics, Inc., 3434 West Earl Drive, Phoenix, Ariz.
  85017, also 420 West Alturas, Tuscon, Ariz. 85705
Montana Ceramic Supply Co., 2016 Alderson Avenue,
  Billings, Mont. 59101
Portland Pottery Supply, 1117 Northwest Flanders, Portland,
  Oreg. 97209
N. W. Ceramic Supply, Inc., 1916 Southeast 50, Portland,
  Oreg. 9725
Seattle Ceramics Supply Co., 400 East Pine Street, Seattle,
  Wash. 98122

Trinity Ceramic Supply Co., Inc., 9016 Diplomacy Row,
  Dallas, Tex. 75247
Van Howe Ceramic Supply, 11975 East 40th Street, Denver,
  Colo. 80239
Way-Craft, 394 Delaware Street, Imperial Beach, Calif. 92032
Webco Supply Co., Inc., P.O. Box 6054, Tyler, Tex. 75711
Westby Ceramics, Box 422, Clinton, Wash. 98236
Western Ceramic Supply Co., 1601 Howard Street,
  San Francisco, Calif. 94103
Westwood Ceramic Supply Co., 14400 Lomitas Avenue,
  City of Industry, Calif. 91746

Sources of Materials and Equipment in Canada
Suppliers
Clays

A. P. Green Firebrick Co., Rosemount Avenue, Weston, Ont.
Baroid of Canada, Ltd., 5108 Eighth Avenue, Southwest, Calgary, Alta.
Jean Cartier, 1029 Bleury Street, Montreal, P.Q.
Clayburn Harbison, Ltd., 1690 West Broadway, Vancouver, B.C.
Maycobac Mining Co., 510 Fifth Street, Southwest, Calgary, Alta.
Pembena Mountain Clay, 945 Logan, Winnipeg, Man.
Plainsman Clays, Box 1266, Medicine Hat, Alta.
Saskatchewan Clay Products, P.O. Box 970, Estevan, Sask.
Stratford Clay Supply, Ltd., P.O. Box 344, Stratford, Ont.

Glaze Materials

Barrett Co., Ltd., 1155 Dorchester Boulevard, West Montreal, P.Q.
Blyth Colors, Ltd., Toronto, Ont.
Ferro Enamels, P.O. Box 370, 26 Davis Road, Oakville, Ont.
E. Harris & Co. of Toronto Ltd., 73 King Street, East Toronto, Ont.

Clay Mixers

Estrin Manufacturing Ltd., 1916 Fir Street, Vancouver, B.C.

Local Supply Houses

Clay, Chemicals, Wheels, Kilns, etc.
Alberta Ceramic Supplies, Ltd., 11565 149th Street, Edmonton, Alta.
Ceramic Supply Depot, 837B 50th Street, East,
  Saskatoon, Sask. 57K 3Y5
Cobequid Ceramics, Ltd., 43 Forrester Street, Truro, N.S.
Greater Toronto Ceramic Center, 167 Lakeshore Road,
  Toronto, Ont.
Island Ceramic Supplies, Island Highway, Box 351
  Nanaimo, B.C.
Jonasson Ceramic Supply Ltd., 267 Maryland Street,
  Winnipeg, Man.
Lewiscraft Supply House, 28 King Street, West
  Toronto, Ont.
Mercedes Ceramic Supply, 13 Wallace Street,
  Woodbridge, Ont.
Pottery Supply House, 2070 Speers Road, Oakville,
  Ont.
Regina Ceramics, Ltd., 1733 McAra Street, Regina,
  Sask.
Terra Ceramic Supplies, Ltd., 518 42nd Avenue,
  Southeast Calgary, Alta.
Tucker's Pottery Supplies, 111 Esna Park Drive,
  Unite #9, Markham, Ont.
Uniceram, Inc. 1356 Newton Street, Boucherville,
  P.Q.

Glossary

absorbency The ability of a material (clay, plaster of paris, and so forth) to soak up water.

acid One of three types of chemicals that constitute a glaze, the other two being the bases and the intermediates, or neutrals. The acid group is symbolized by the radical RO_2. The most important acid is silica (SiO_2).

Albany slip A natural clay containing sufficient fluxes to melt and function as a glaze. It develops a dark brown-black glaze at cones 8 to 10 without any additions. Since it is mined in several localities in the vicinity of Albany, N. Y., its composition may vary slightly from time to time. Similar clays, found in various sections of the United States, were much used by early American stoneware potteries.

alkali Generally, the base compounds of sodium and potassium but also the alkaline earth compounds lime and magnesia. They function as fluxes, combining easily with silica at relatively low temperatures.

alumina (Al_2O_3) A major ingredient found in all clays and glazes. It is the chief oxide in the neutral group (R_2O_3) and imparts greater strength and higher firing temperatures to the body and glaze. When added to a glaze, it will assist in the formation of mat textures, inhibit devitrification, and increase the viscosity of the glaze during firing.

ash Generally, the ashes of trees, straw, leaves, and so forth. It is commonly used to provide from 40 to 60 percent of high-temperature glaze ingredients. Depending upon the type, ash will contain from 40 to 75 percent silica, from 5 to 15 percent alumina, and smaller amounts of iron, phosphorus, lime, potash, and magnesia.

aventurine A type of glaze in which single, often small, crystals are suspended in the glaze surface. The glaze usually contains soda, lead, or boric oxide flux often with an excess of iron oxide (more than 6 percent).

bag wall A baffle wall in a kiln, separating the chamber from the combustion area.

ball clay An extremely fine-grained, plastic, sedimentary clay. Although ball clay contains much organic matter, it fires white or near white in color. It is usually added to porcelain and whiteware bodies to increase plasticity.

ball mill A porcelain jar filled with flint pebbles and rotated with either a wet or dry charge of chemicals. It is used to blend and to grind glaze and body ingredients.

barium carbonate ($BaCO_3$) A chemical used in combination with other fluxes to form mats in the low-temperature range. A very small percentage (0.25 to 2) added to a clay body will prevent discoloration caused by soluble sulfates, such as the whitish blotches often seen on red bricks and earthenware bodies.

basalt ware A hard, black, unglazed stoneware body developed about 1775 by the Wedgwood pottery in England in an effort to imitate classical wares.

bat A disk or slab of plaster of paris on which pottery is formed or dried. It is also used to remove excess moisture from plastic clay.

batch Raw chemicals comprising a ceramic glaze that have been weighed out in a specific proportion designed to melt at a predetermined temperature.

bentonite An extremely plastic clay, formed by decomposed volcanic ash and glaze, which is used to render short clays workable and to aid glaze suspensions.

binders Various materials—gums, polyvinyl alcohol, and methylcellulose—that increase glaze adherence or impart strength to a cast or pressed clay body.

bisque or biscuit Unglazed ware fired to a temperature sufficient to harden but not mature the body.

bisque fire Preliminary firing to harden the body, usually at about cone 010, prior to glazing and subsequent glaze firing.

bistone Coarse crushed quartz used in saggers to support thin porcelain in the bisque.

blowing (bloating) The bursting or warping of pots in a kiln caused by a too-rapid temperature rise. The water content of the clay turns into steam and forces the body to distort or expand and explode.

blunger A mixing machine with revolving paddles used to prepare large quantities of clay slip or glaze.

bone china A hard, translucent whiteware produced chiefly in England. The body contains a large amount of bone ash (calcium phosphate), which allows it to mature at cone 6. It is not very plastic and is therefore difficult to form; it also tends to warp.

calcine To heat a ceramic material or mixture to the temperature necessary to drive off the chemical water, carbon dioxide, and other volatile gases. Some fusion may occur, in which case the material must be ground. This is the process used in the production of plaster of paris, portland cement, and ceramic stains.

casting (or slip casting) A reproductive process of forming clay objects by pouring a clay slip into a hollow plaster mold and allowing it to remain long enough for a layer of clay to thicken on the mold wall. After hardening, the clay object is removed.

celadon A glaze characterized by a soft gray-green color that results from firing iron oxide in a reduction atmosphere. Because of the likeness to jade, celadon glazes were much favored by the ancient Chinese.

chemical water Water (H_2O) chemically combined in the glaze and body compounds. At approximately 842°F (450°C) during the firing cycle this water will begin to leave the body and glaze as water vapor. Little shrinkage occurs at this point, although there is a loss in weight.

china A loosely applied term referring to whiteware bodies fired at low porcelain temperatures. They are generally vitreous, with an absorbency of less than 2 percent, and may be translucent.

china clay *See* kaolin.

clay A decomposed granite-type rock. To be classed as a clay the decomposed rock must have fine particles so that it will be plastic. Clays should be free of vegetable matter but will often contain other impurities, which affect their color and firing temperatures. They are classified into various types, such as ball clays, fireclays, and slip clays. Pure clay is expressed chemically as $Al_2O_3 \cdot 2SiO_2 \cdot 2H_2O$.

coefficient of expansion The ratio of change between the length of a material mass and the temperature to which it is subjected.

coiling A hand method of forming pottery by building up the walls with ropelike rolls of clay and then smoothing over the joints.

combing A method of decoration developed by dragging a coarse comb or tip of a feather over two contrasting layers of wet clay slip or glaze.

Cornwall stone (also Cornish stone) A feldspathic material found in England and widely used there for porcelainlike bodies and glazes. Compared to American feldspar, it contains more silica and a small amount, though a greater variety, of fluxes. It comes closest to approximating the Chinese petuntze, which is a major ingredient of Oriental porcelain bodies and glazes.

crackle glaze A glaze containing minute cracks in the surface. The cracks are decorative and are often accentuated by coloring matter that is rubbed in. They are caused in cooling by the different rates at which the body and the glaze contract after firing.

crawling Separation of a glaze coating from the clay body during firing, caused by too heavy application, resulting in exposed areas of unglazed clay.

crazing An undesirable and excessive crackle in the glaze, which penetrates through the glaze to the clay body. It should be remedied by adjusting the glaze or body composition to obtain a more uniform contraction ratio.

crocus martis Purple-red oxide of iron, used as a red-brown glaze colorant.

crystal glazes Glazes characterized by crystalline clusters of various shapes and colors embedded in a more uniform and opaque glaze. Macrocrystals are larger than aventurine and may on occasion cover the entire surface. The glaze ingredients generally used are iron, lime, zinc, or rutile with an alkaline flux, high silica, and low alumina ratio. A slow cooling cycle is necessary for the development of the crystals.

cupric and cuprous oxides Copper oxides (CuO, Cu_2O), the major green colorants. They will also produce red under reducing conditions, with an alkaline flux.

damp box A lined metal cabinet in which unfinished clay objects are stored to prevent them from drying.

decals Designs produced on thin sheets of paper and transferred to a glazed surface after being soaked in water. When fired to cones 020 to 018, the designs become permanent.

deflocculant Sodium carbonate or sodium silicate used in a casting slip to reduce the amount of water necessary and to maintain a better suspension.

Delft ware A light-colored pottery body covered with a tin-lead glaze, with overglaze decoration in cobalt on the unfired glaze. Delft was first made in Holland in imitation of Chinese blue-and-white porcelain.

della Robbia ware Ceramic sculpture of glazed terra cotta, generally in relief, produced in Florence by Lucca della Robbia or his family during the fifteenth century. The glaze used was the tin-lead majolica type developed in Spain.

dipping Glazing pottery by immersing it in a large pan or vat of glaze.

dryfoot To clean the bottom of a glazed piece before firing.

dunting Cracking of fired ware in a cooling kiln, the result of opening the flues and cooling too rapidly.

earthenware Low-fire pottery (below cone 03), usually red or tan in color

with an absorbency of from 5 to 20 percent.

eggshell porcelain Translucent, thin-walled porcelain.

Egyptian paste A clay body that has glaze-forming ingredients and colorants incorporated into the body in a soluble form. The body is nonplastic and fires to between cones 08 and 05. First developed by the Egyptians before 3000 B.C., this paste was the earliest form of glaze known. A term often used today for Egyptian faience.

empirical formula A glaze formula expressed in molecular proportions.

engobe A prepared slip that is halfway between a glaze and a clay; contains clay, feldspar, flint, a flux, plus colorants. It is usually applied to damp ware although it may be used on bisque ware.

equivalent weight A weight that will yield one unit of a component (RO or R_2O_3 or RO_2) in a compound. This is usually the same as the molecular weight of the chemical compound in question. In ceramic calculations, equivalent weights are also assigned to the RO, R_2O_3, and RO_2 oxide groups that make up the compound. If one of these oxide groups contains more than one unit of the oxide, its equivalent weight would be found by dividing the compound molecular weight by this unit number. (*See* Chap. 8).

eutectic The lowest melting point of the mixture of materials composing a glaze. This is always lower than the melting points of the individual materials.

faience Earthenware covered with a tin-lead glaze; a French term for earthenware derived from the Italian pottery center at Faenza, which, during the Renaissance, produced this ware partially in imitation of Spanish majolica. (*See* also majolica and Delft ware.)

fat clay A plastic clay such as ball clay.

ferric and ferrous oxides (Fe_2O_3 and FeO) Red and black iron oxide. As impurities in clay, the lower the firing temperature. They are the chief source of tan and brown ceramic colors and, under reducing conditions, the various celadon greens.

fire box Combustion chamber of a gas, oil, or wood-fired kiln, usually directly below the kiln chamber.

fireclay A clay having a slightly higher percentage of fluxes than pure clay (kaolin). It fires tan or gray in color and is used in the manufacture of refractory materials, such as bricks and muffles for industrial glass and steel furnaces. It is often quite plastic and may be used by the studio potter as an ingredient of stoneware bodies.

flint *See* silica.

flocculation Thickening or settling of a glaze or slip.

flues Passageways around the kiln chamber through which the heating gases pass from the firebox to the chimney.

flux Lowest-melting compound in a glaze, such as lead, borax, soda ash, or lime, and including the potash or soda contained in the feldspar. The flux combines easily with silica and thereby helps higher-melting alumina-silica compounds to form a glass.

foot The ringlike base of a ceramic piece, usually formed by tooling the excess clay.

frit A partial or complete glaze that is melted and then reground for the purpose of eliminating the toxic effects of lead or the solubility of such compounds as borax or soda ash.

frit china A glossy, partly translucent chinaware produced by adding a glass frit to the body.

galena Lead sulfide, used as a flux for earthenware glazes; more common in Europe than in the United States.

glaze A liquid suspension of finely ground minerals that is applied by brushing, pouring, or spraying on the surface of bisque-fired ceramic ware. After drying the ware is fired to the temperature at which the glaze ingredients will melt together to form a glassy surface coating.

glaze fire A firing cycle to the temperature at which the glaze materials will melt to form a glasslike surface coating. This is usually at the point of maximum body maturity, and it is considerably higher than the bisque fire.

glost fire Another term for a glaze firing.

greenware Pottery that has not been bisque fired.

grog Hard-fired clay that has been crushed or ground to various particle sizes. It is used to open up a raku body or to reduce shrinkage in such ceramic products as sculpture and architectural terra-cotta tiles, which, because of their thickness, have drying and shrinkage problems. From 20 to 40 percent grog may be used, depending upon the amount of detail desired and whether the pieces are free standing or pressed in molds. Finely crushed grog is also used in throwing bodies to help the clay stand up.

grolleg A refined English kaolin that is relatively plastic.

gum arabic or gum tragacanth Natural gums used in glazes as binders to promote better glaze adhesion to the body. Binders are necessary for fritted glazes containing little or no raw clay. They are also useful when a bisque fire accidentally goes too high, or in reglazing. The gum, of course, burns out completely during the fire.

hard paste True porcelain that is fired to cone 12 or above; also called hard porcelain.

ilmenite ($TiO_2 \cdot FeO$) An important source of titanium. In the granular form it is used to give dark flecks to the glaze. It is often sprinkled upon the wet glaze without previous mixing.

iron oxide *See* ferric oxide.

jiggering, jollying An industrial method of producing pottery. A slab of soft clay is placed upon a revolving plaster mold of the object to be formed. As the wheel head turns, a metal template on a moving arm trims off the excess clay and forms the reverse side of the piece.

kanthol A special metal alloy produced in Sweden for wire or strip elements in electric kilns firing from cones 03 to 12.

kaolin ($Al_2O_3 \cdot 2SiO_2 \cdot 2H_2O$) Pure clay, also known as china clay. It is used in glaze and porcelain bodies and fires to a pure white. Sedimentary kaolins found in Florida are more plastic than the residual types found in the Carolinas and Georgia.

kiln A furnace made of refractory clay materials for firing ceramic products.

kiln furniture Refractory shelves and posts upon which ceramic ware is placed while being fired in the kiln.

kiln wash A protective coating of refractory materials applied to the surface of the shelves and the kiln floor to prevent excess glaze from fusing the ware to the shelves. An inexpensive and effective wash can be made from equal parts of flint and kaolin.

lead White lead [basic lead carbonates $2PbCO_3 \cdot Pb(OH)_2$], red lead (Pb_3O_4), and galena (lead sulfide, PbS) are among the most common low-fire fluxes.

leather hard The condition of the raw ware when most of the moisture has left the body but when it is still plastic enough to be carved or joined.

limestone A major flux in the medium- and high-fire temperature ranges when it is powdered in the form of whiting (calcium carbonate). If a coarse sand is used as a grog, it should not contain limestone particles.

luster A type of metallic decoration thought to have been discovered in Egypt and further developed in Iran during the ninth and fourteenth centuries. A mixture of a metallic salt, resin, and bismuth nitrate is applied to a glazed piece and then refired at a lower temperature. The temperature, however, must be sufficient to melt the metal and leave a thin layer on the decorated portions.

luting A method of joining together two pieces of dry or leather-hard clay with a slip.

macaloid A refined magnesium montmorillonite clay. It is used as a flocculating agent in glazes or a plasticizer in clay bodies.

majolica Earthenware covered with a soft tin-lead glaze, often with a luster decoration. The ware originally came from Spain and derived its name from the island of Majorca, which lay on the trade route to Italy. Faenza ware was greatly influenced by these Spanish imports. All Renaissance pottery of this type is now generally called majolica ware.

mat glaze A dull-surfaced glaze with no gloss but pleasant to the touch, not to be confused with an incompletely fired glaze. Mat surfaces can be developed by the addition of barium carbonate or alumina and by a slow cooling cycle.

maturity The temperature or time at which a clay or clay body develops the desirable characteristics of maximum nonporosity and hardness; or the point at which the glaze ingredients enter into complete fusion, developing a strong bond with the body, a stable structure, maximum resistance to abrasion, and a pleasant surface texture.

mold A form or box, usually made of plaster of paris, containing a hollow negative shape. The positive form is made by pouring either wet plaster or slip into this hollow. (*See* casting.)

muffle A lining, made of refractory materials, forming the kiln chamber, around which the hot gases pass from the firebox to the chimney. The purpose is to protect the ware from the direct flames of the fire and the resulting combustion impurities. Some of these panels may be removed for a reduction fire.

muffle kiln A kiln with muffle features as opposed to a kiln using saggers. (*See* saggers.)

mullite A mineral with interlocking needlelike crystals of aluminum silicate ($3Al_2O_3 \cdot 2SiO_2$) that begin to form in high-temperature bodies between cones 06 and 6. This formation is responsible for much of the greater toughness and hardness of stoneware and porcelain, and in particular for the closer union developed between the glaze and the body.

neutral fire A fire that is neither oxidizing nor reducing. Actually, this fire can be obtained in practice only by a slight alternation between oxidation and reduction.

opacifier A chemical whose crystals are relatively insoluble in the glaze, thereby preventing light from penetrating the glass formation. Tin oxide is by far the best opacifier. Zirconium and titanium oxides are also used. Many other oxides are effective in certain combinations and within limited firing ranges. These are commercially available in frit forms under trade names, such as Zircopax, Opax, and Ultrox.

overglaze Decoration applied with overglaze colors on glazed and fired ware. The firing of the overglaze decoration is at a lower temperature than that of the glaze fire.

overglaze colors Colors applied on top of other glazes and containing coloring oxides or ceramic stains, a flux, and some type of binder. The fluxes are necessary to allow the colors to melt into the harder glaze beneath. The lower temperatures at which most overglazes are fired (about cones 016–013) allow the use of colorants that are unstable at higher temperatures.

oxidizing fire A fire during which the kiln chamber retains an ample supply of oxygen. This means that the combustion in the firebox must be perfectly adjusted. An electric kiln always gives an oxidizing fire.

paste The compounded bodies of European-type porcelains.

peach bloom A Chinese copper-red reduction glaze with a peachlike pink color.

peeling Separation of the glaze or slip from the body. Peeling may be caused when slip is applied to a body that is too dry or when a glaze is applied too thickly or to a dusty surface.

peephole A hole placed in the firebox, kiln chamber, or muffle flues of a kiln, through which one can observe the cones or the process of combustion.

petuntze A partially decomposed feldspathic rock found in China, roughly similar in composition to Cornwall stone. With kaolin it forms the body of Oriental porcelains.

plaster of paris Hydrate of calcium sulfate, made by calcining gypsum. It hardens after being mixed with water. Because it absorbs moisture and it can be cut and shaped easily; it is used in ceramics for drying and throwing bats, as well as for molds and casting work.

plasticity The quality of clay that allows it to be manipulated and still maintain its shape without cracking or sagging.

porcelain (Chinese) A hard, nonabsorbent clay body, white or gray in color, that rings when struck.

porcelain (hard) A hard, nonabsorbent clay body that is white and translucent. In both types of porcelain the bisque is low-fired and the glaze is very high-fired (generally cones 14–16).

press-forming A commercial production method for forming clay objects by pressing soft clay between two plaster molds.

pug mill A machine for mixing plastic clay.

pyrometer An instrument for measuring heat at high temperatures. It consists of a calibrated dial connected to wires made of two different alloys, the welded tips of which protrude into the kiln chamber. When heated, this welded junction sets up a minute electrical current, which registers on the indicating dial.

pyrometric cones Small triangular cones (1.13 and 2.63 inches, or 2.87 and 6.68 cm in height) made of ceramic materials that are compounded to bend and melt at specific temperatures, thus enabling the potter to determine when the firing is complete.

quartz Flint or silica (SiO_2).

quartz inversion The changing of the crystalline structure of quartz (silica) during firing. The resultant expansion and contraction necessitates a slow cycle of heating and cooling.

raku Glazed, groggy earthenware originated in Japan and associated with the tea ceremony. Raku ware is unique in that the glazed preheated bisque is placed in the red-hot kiln with long-handled tongs. The glaze matures in 15 to 30 minutes, and the ware is then withdrawn and cooled immediately.

reducing agent Glaze or body material such as silicon carbide, which combines with oxygen to form carbon monoxide during the firing.

reduction fire A firing using insufficient oxygen; carbon monoxide thus formed unites with oxygen from the body and glaze to form carbon dioxide, producing color changes in coloring oxides.

refractory The quality of resisting the effects of high temperatures; also materials, high in alumina and silica, that are used for making kiln insulation, muffles, and kiln furniture.

rib A tool of wood, bone, or metal that is held in the hand while throwing to assist in shaping the pot or to compact the clay.

RO, R_2O_3, RO_2 The symbols, or radicals, for the three major groups of chemicals that make up a ceramic glaze. The RO radical refers to the base chemicals, such as the oxides of sodium, potassium, calcium, and lead, which function in the glaze as fluxing agents. The R_2O_3 radical refers to the neutral or amphoteric oxides, some of which may on occasion function either as bases or acids. The chief oxide in this group is alumina (Al_2O_3), which always reacts as a refractory element. The third radical, RO_2, stands for the acid group, the glass formers, such as silica (SiO_2).

rouge flambé A type of Chinese copper-red reduction glaze (*sang de boeuf*) that is a mottled deep red with green and blue hues, also called a transmutation glaze.

rutile An impure form of titanium dioxide (TiO_2) containing much iron. It will give a light yellow or tan color to the glaze, with a streaked and runny effect. Used in large amounts, it will raise the maturing temperature.

sagger Round boxlike container of fireclay used in kilns lacking muffles. The glazed ware is placed in a sagger to protect the glaze from the combustion gases.

sagger clay A refractory clay able to withstand the thermal shock of the repeated firings of saggers. Often plastic and suitable for inclusion in a stoneware body.

salt glaze A glaze developed by throwing salt (NaCl) into a hot kiln. The salt vaporizes and combines with the silica in the body to form sodium silicate, a hard glassy glaze. A salt kiln is of a slightly different construction and is limited in use to the salt glaze.

sang de boeuf The French term for oxblood, which describes the rich, deep-red hues produced by the Chinese in their copper-red reduction glazes.

sgraffito Decoration achieved by scratching through a colored slip or a glaze to show the contrasting body color beneath.

shard A broken fragment of pottery.

short Descriptive of a body or clay lacking in plasticity.

shrinkage Contraction of the clay in either drying or firing. In the firing cycle the major body shrinkage for stoneware clays begins at approximately cone 09. Earthenware clays will begin to fuse and shrink at slightly lower temperatures.

silica Flint (SiO_2) produced in the United States by grinding almost pure flint sand.

silicate of soda A deflocculant. A standard solution of sodium silicate (commercial N brand); has the ratio of 1 part soda to 3.3 parts silica. Specific gravity 1.395.

single fire A firing cycle in which the normal bisque and glaze firings are combined. The advantages are a great saving of fuel and labor and development of a stronger bond between the body and the glaze. These are partially offset by the need for greater care in handling the ware, plus the danger of cracking if in glazing the raw pieces absorb too much moisture. In a salt glaze, however, these disadvantages do not occur.

sintering A firing process in which ceramic compounds fuse sufficiently to form a solid mass upon cooling but are not vitrified. An example is low-fire earthenware.

slab construction A hand-building method in which forms are created by joining flat pieces of clay. The pieces are thinned and flattened with a rolling pin or slab roller.

slip A clay in liquid suspension.

slip casting *See* casting.

slip clay A clay such as Albany or Michigan containing sufficient fluxes to function as a glaze with little or no additions.

spinel Chemically, magnesium aluminate ($MgO \cdot Al_2O_3$), an extremely hard crystal arranged in an octahedron atomic structure. In ceramics, a spinel is a crystal used as a colorant in place of the metallic oxides because of its greater resistance to change by either the fluxing action of the glaze or the effects of higher temperatures.

spray booth A boxlike booth equipped with a ventilating fan to remove spray dust, which, whether toxic or not, is harmful when inhaled.

spraying Applying glazes with a compressed-air spray machine, the chief commercial method.

sprigging Applying clay in a plastic state to form a relief decoration.

stain Sometimes a single coloring oxide, but usually a combination of oxides, plus alumina, flint, and a fluxing compound. This mixture is calcined and then finely ground and washed. The purpose is to form a stable coloring agent not likely to be altered by the action of the glaze or heat. While stains are employed as glaze colorants, their chief use is as overglaze and underglaze decorations and body colorants.

stilt A ceramic tripod upon which glazed ware is placed in the kiln. Tripods with nickel-nichrome wire points are often used to minimize blemishes in the glaze.

stoneware A high-fire ware (above cone 6) with slight or no absorbency. It is usually gray in color but may be tan or slightly reddish. Stoneware is similar in many respects to porcelain, the chief difference being increased plasticity and the color, which is the result of iron and other impurities in the clay.

talc ($3MgO \cdot 4SiO_2 \cdot H_2O$) A compound used in most whiteware bodies in the low to moderate firing ranges as a source of silica and flux. It is slightly plastic and can be used to lower the firing range, if need be, of a stoneware or fireclay body.

temmoku A Japanese term for a stoneware glaze high in iron that creates a streaked surface (*hare's fur*) or a mottled appearance (*oil spot*).

terra-cotta An earthenware body, generally red in color and containing grog. It is the common body type used for ceramic sculpture.

terra sigillata The red slip glaze used by the Romans, similar to the Etruscan bucchero and Greek black varnish ware and made of fine decanted particles of red clay.

thixotropic clay A body containing alkaline electrolytes, which permit it to change to a fluid state when shaken. When allowed to rest, it returns to a plastic gel form.

throwing Forming plastic clay on a potter's wheel.

tin enamel A term used incorrectly to describe the tin-lead majolica-type glaze. An enamel is a very low-fire glaze used as an overglaze decoration. It was extensively used by the Turks and the late Ming and Ch'ing potters.

tin-vanadium stain A major yellow colorant produced by a calcined mixture of tin and vanadium oxides.

trailing A method of decorating by applying slip with a rubber syringe.

translucency The ability of a thin porcelain or whiteware body to transmit a diffused light.

turning or tooling Trimming the walls and foot of a pot on the wheel while the clay is leather hard.

underglaze Colored decoration applied to the raw or bisque ware before the glaze coating.

Veegum T Trade name for a refined magnesium silicate used as a flocculant in glazes and plasticizer in clay bodies.

viscosity The nonrunning quality of a glaze, caused by glaze chemicals that resist the flowing action of the glaze flux.

vitreous Pertaining to the hard, glassy, and nonabsorbent quality of a body or glaze.

volatilization Action under influence of extreme heat of the kiln in which some glaze elements turn successively from a solid to a liquid, and finally into a gaseous state.

ware Pottery or porcelain in the raw, bisque, or glazed state.

warping Distortion of a pot in drying because of uneven wall thickness or a warm draft of air, or in firing when a kiln does not heat uniformly.

water glass Another term for a liquid solution of sodium silicate that is used as a deflocculant.

water smoking The initial phase of the firing cycle up to a dull red heat (1000°–1100°F, 537°–594°C). Depending upon the thickness of the ware, this may take from two or three hours for thin pottery, up to twelve hours for sculpture. The heat rise must be gradual to allow atmospheric and chemical water to escape. In some situations there will be organic impurities which will also burn out, releasing carbon monoxide.

wax resist A method of decorating pottery by brushing on a design with a hot melted wax solution or a wax emulsion. This will prevent an applied stain or glaze from adhering to the decorated portions. The wax may be applied to either the raw or bisque ware, over or between two layers of glaze.

weathering The exposure of raw clay to the action of rain, sun, and freezing weather, which breaks down the particle size and renders the clay more plastic.

wedging Kneading plastic clay with the fingers and heels of the hands in a rocking spiral motion, which forces out trapped air pockets and develops a uniform texture.

whiteware Pottery or china ware with a white or light cream-colored body.

whiting Calcium carbonate ($CaCO_3$), similar chemically to limestone and marble; a major high-fire flux.

zircopax Trade name of a commercial frit used as an opacifier. It is composed primarily of zirconium oxide and silica. It is about half as strong as tin oxide, but its price is much lower regardless of the quantity used.

Bibliography

References on Technique

Chapell, James. *The Potter's Complete Book of Clay and Glazes.* New York: Watson-Guptill, 1977. Detailed material on a wide range of bodies and glazes.

Colson, Frank. *Kiln Building with Space Age Materials.* New York: Van Nostrand Reinhold, 1975.

Conrad, John W.: *Contemporary Ceramic Formulas.* New York: Macmillan, 1980. Chemicals, glazes, and other ceramic materials, toxic qualities.

Cooper, Emmanuel, and Royle, Derek. *Glazes for the Potter.* New York: Scribner, 1978. Glaze types, formulas, and their historical development.

Greabnier, Joseph. *Chinese Stoneware Glazes.* New York: Watson-Guptill, 1975. An excellent treatment of Chinese glazes with formulas.

Hamilton, David. *Architectural Ceramics.* New York: Thames & Hudson, 1977. Techniques of forming and decorating ceramic elements used in architecture. Historical and modern examples.

Koenig, J.H., and Earhart, W.H. *Literature Abstracts of Ceramic Glazes.* Ellenton, Fla., College Institute, 1951. Formulas from many technical sources, although somewhat dated at present.

Lawrence, W.G. *Ceramic Science for the Potter.* New York: Chilton, 1982.

Leach, Bernard. *A Potter's Book.* Levitton, N.Y.: Transatlantic Arts, 1965. Now in its eighteenth edition, continues to be the "bible" of the potter interested in functional ware.

Paak, Carl E. *The Decorative Touch.* Englewood Cliffs, N.J.: Prentice-Hall, 1981. A variety of decorative techniques, glazing, and glaze formulas.

Parks, Dennis. *A Potters Guide to Raw Glazing and Oil Firing.* New York: Scribner, 1979. Single-fire glazing and oil-fired kilns.

Parmalee, Cullen W., and Harman, Cameron G. *Ceramic Glazes.* Boston: Cahners, 1973. A revised edition of the standard text on chemicals and glazes.

Reigger, Hal. *Raku: Art and Technique.* New York: Van Nostrand Reinhold, 1970. A short but fairly complete treatment of raku procedures and kilns.

Rhodes, Daniel. *Clay and Glazes for the Potter.* Rev. ed. Radnor, Pa.: Chilton, 1973. A complete and well-illustrated treatment of clay, glazes, and calculations.

————. *Kilns, Design, Construction and Operation.* Rev. ed. Radnor, Pa.: Chilton, 1980. A standard text on kilns, their operation, and their historical development.

————. *Pottery Form.* Radnor, Pa.: Chilton, 1977. Ceramic form as it evolves from imagination and tradition, as well as technique.

————. *Stoneware and Porcelain: The Art of High-Fired Pottery.* Radnor, Pa.: Chilton, 1959. A companion book to *Clay and Glazes for the Potter* with an emphasis on high-fire glazes and bodies.

Sanders, Herbert H. *How to Make Pottery.* New York: Watson-Guptill, 1974. A short but complete and well-illustrated text on forming techniques.

————. *Glazes for Special Effects.* New York: Watson-Guptill, 1974. A beautifully illustrated text dealing primarily with iron and copper reduction, crystalline, luster, and raku glazes.

————. *The World of Japanese Ceramics.* Palo Alto, Calif.: Kodansha International, 1967. The many techniques shown will be of interest to all potters, as will the many illustrations.

Storr-Britz, Hildegard. *Ornaments and Surfaces on Ceramics.* Dortmund, West Germany: Verlagsanstalt Handberk GMBH, 1977. An international selection of works displaying a wide range of decorative techniques.

Troy, Jack. *Salt Glazed Ceramics.* New York: Watson-Guptill, 1977. Origin, kilns, and methods of salt glazing.

Williams, Gerry; Sabin, Peter; and Bodine, Sarah, eds. *Studio Potters Book.* Warner, N.H.: Daniel Clark Books, 1978. Major articles selected from six years of the *Studio Potter* magazine.

Zakin, Richard. *Electric Kiln Ceramics.* Radnor, Pa.: Chilton, 1980. Clays, glazes, and decorative techniques in oxidation.

Supplemental Texts

Birks, Tony. *The Art of the Modern Potter.* New York: Van Nostrand Reinhold, 1977. Some of the experimental British potters.

Campbell, James Edward. *Pottery and Ceramics: A Guide to Information Sources.* Detroit: Gale Research, 1978. Reference books (in English) covering all historical periods, including materials and processes.

Cardew, Michael. *Pioneer Pottery.* New York: St. Martin's, 1976. Use of simple materials, local clays, wood kilns.

Garth, Clark. *Ceramic Art Comment and Review 1882–1977.* New York: E. P. Dutton, 1978. Anthology by fourteen potters and craftsmen covering the Victorian era, Japanese crafts, and modern influences.

Casson, Michael. *Pottery in Britain Today.* New York: Transatlantic Arts, 1967.

Charleston, Robert L. *World Ceramics.* New York: McGraw-Hill, 1968. A historical survey of the ceramics of the major world cultures.

Coyne, John, ed. *The Penland School of Crafts Book of Pottery.* New York: Bobbs-Merrill, 1975. The step-by-step process of the hand-building, throwing, and glazing techniques of eight of Penland's potters.

Cox, Warren E. *The Book of Pottery and Porcelain.* New York: Crown, 1953. A historical survey of world ceramics.

Donhauser, Paul. *History of American Ceramics.* Dubuque, Iowa: Kendall/Hunt, 1977. A survey of the work and social outlook of American potters from the Colonial era to the present.

Storr-Britz, Hildegard. *Contemporary International Ceramics.* Cologne, West Germany: DuMont, 1980. Survey of recent work by the potters of 26 countries.

Hetts, Karel, and Pravoslav, Rada. *Modern Ceramics.* London: Drury House, 1965.

Lewenstein Eileen, and Cooper, Emmanuel. *New Ceramics.* New York: Van Nostrand Reinhold, 1974.

Ramie, Georges. *Picasso's Ceramics.* New York: Viking, 1976.

Woodhouse, Charles P. *The World's Master Potters.* New York: Pitman, 1975. Discussion of historical ceramics with an emphasis on the evolution of materials and techniques.

Magazines

American Ceramics, 15 West 44 Street, New York, N.Y. 10036. A quarterly with critical essays and reviews of American clay work.

Ceramics Monthly, 1609 Northwest Boulevard, P.O. Box 12448, Columbus, Ohio 43212. The North American ceramic scene, with many illustrations and useful articles for the student potter.

Craft American, 22 West 55th St., New York, N.Y. 10022. Contemporary, historical, and related craft fields as featured in this publication of the American Crafts Council.

Studio Potter, Box 172, Warner, N.H. 03278. A well-illustrated semiannual publication with many practical articles on all aspects of ceramics. Especially recommended for the serious potter.

Foreign Publications

Dansk Kunstaandvaerk, Palaegade 4, Copenhagen, Denmark. The entire Danish design field; well illustrated. Many sections in English.

Designed in Finland, Finnish Foreign Trade Association, E. Esplanaadik 18, Helsinki. Illustrated booklet on Finnish design published each year with English text.

Domus, via Monte di Pieta 15, Milan, Italy. Covers the decorative arts fields, emphasizing architecture; beautifully illustrated.

Form, Svenska Slöjdföreningen, Nybrogatan 7, Stockholm, Sweden. Journal of the Swedish Design Society covering all design fields; well illustrated; including a short English section.

Kontur, Svenska Slöjdföreningen, Nybrogatan 7, Stockholm, Sweden. Beautifully illustrated booklet on Swedish design and crafts, published once a year. Text in English.

Kunst + Handwerk, Arnold-Heise Strasse 23, Hamburg 20, West Germany. Industrial design and handcrafts in Germany and Europe. Well illustrated, with German text.

La Ceramica, via F. Corridoni 3, Milan, Italy. An industrial publication but many articles on studio potters and sculptors. English summary very short.

Pottery Quarterly, Northfields, Tring, Herts., England. A variety of articles, both historical and contemporary, as well as critiques. Well illustrated.

Pottery in Australia, 30 Turramurra Avenue, Turramurra, N.S.W. Biannual journal of the Potters' Society, well illustrated.

Tactile, 100 Avenue Road, Toronto, Canada. Bimonthly publication of the Canadian Guild of Potters, with coverage of exhibitions, technical articles, and Guild news.

Selected Historical Texts

Ancient Middle Eastern and Ancient Mediterranean Ceramics

Alexion, Styliaros; Platon, Nicolaos; and Gunanella, Hanni. *Ancient Crete.* New York: Praeger, 1968.

Arias, P. E. *Greek Vase Painting.* New York: Abrams, 1961.

Boardman, John. *Pre-Classical, from Crete to Archaic Greek.* Baltimore: Penguin, 1967.

Chamoux, Francois. *Greek Art.* Greenwich, Conn.: New York Graphic Society, 1966.

Hambridge, Jay. *Dynamic Symmetry: The Greek Vase.* New York: Dover, 1967. Reprint of the 1920 edition.

Hutchinson, R. W. *Prehistoric Crete.* Baltimore: Penguin, 1962.

Martinatos, Spyridon. *Crete and Mycenae.* New York: Abrams, 1960.

Noble, Joseph Veach. *The Techniques of Painted Attic Pottery.* New York: Watson-Guptill, 1965.

Petrie, Flinders. *The Making of Egypt.* London: Sheldon Press, 1939.

Platon, Nicolaos. *Crete.* Cleveland, Ohio: World Publishing, 1966.

Raphael, Max. *Civilization in Egypt.* New York: Pantheon, 1947.

————. *Prehistoric Pottery.* New York: Pantheon, 1947.

Richardson, Emeline Hill. *The Etruscans.* Chicago: University of Chicago Press, 1964.

Richter, Gisela M., and Milne, Marjorie. *Shapes and Names of Greek Vases.* New York: Metropolitan Museum of Art, 1935.

Swedish Institute in Rome. *Etruscan Culture.* New York: Columbia University Press, 1962.

Oriental Ceramics

Beurdeley, Michel. *Chinese Trade Porcelain.* Rutland, Vt.: Tuttle, 1966.

Bushell, Stephen W. *Chinese Pottery and Porcelain.* 1910. Reprint. New York Oxford University Press. A translation f *T'ao Shuo,* written by Chu Yen in 1774.

Chang, K.C. *The Archaeology of Ancient China.* New Haven: Yale University Press, 1977.

Egami, Namio. *The Beginnings of Japanese Art.* New York: Weatherhill/Heibonsha, 1973.

Griffing, Robert P. *The Art of the Korean Potter.* New York: Asia Society, 1968.

Hayashiya, Seizo, and Hasebe, Gakuji. *Chinese Ceramics.* Rutland, Vt.: Tuttle, 1966.

Ho, Ping-Ti. *The Cradle of the East.* Chicago: University of Chicago Press, 1975.

Hobson, R. L. *Chinese Pottery and Porcelain.* 1915. Reprint. New York: Dover, 1976.

Honey, William Bowyer. *The Ceramic Art of China.* London: Faber and Faber, 1944.

————. *Japanese Pottery.* New York: Praeger, 1970.

Jenyns, Soame. *Later Chinese Porcelain.* New York: Yoseloff, 1965.

Kidder, J. Edward. *Prehistoric Japanese Arts: Jomon Pottery.* New York: Kodansha International, 1969.

Kim, Chewon, and Kim, Won-Yong. *Treasures of Korean Art.* New York: Abrams, 1966.

Koyama, Fugio, and Figgess, John. *Two Thousand Years of Oriental Ceramics.* New York: Abrams, 1960.

Leach, Bernard. *Hamada, Potter*. New York: Kodansha International, 1975.

————. *Kenzan and His Tradition*. London: Faber and Faber, 1966.

Medley, Margaret. *Yuan Porcelain and Stoneware*. London: Pitman, 1974.

Mikami, Tsugio. *The Art of Japanese Ceramics*. New York: Weatherhill/ Heibonsha, 1972.

Miki, Fumio. *Haniwa*. New York: Weatherhill/Shibundo, 1974.

Munsterberg, Hugo. *The Ceramic Art of Japan*. Rutland, Vt.: Tuttle, 1964.

Peterson, Susan Harnly. *Shoji Hamada: His Way and Work*. New York: Kodansha International, 1974.

Prodan, Mario. *The Art of the T'ang Potter*. London: Thames & Hudson, 1960.

Islamic, Hispano-Moresque, and African Ceramics

Frothingham, Alice Wilson. *Lusterware of Spain*. New York: Hispanic Society of America, 1951.

Grube, Ernest J. *The World of Islam*. London: Hamlyn, 1966.

Lane, Arthur. *Early Islamic Pottery*. New York: Van Nostrand, 1948.

————. *Later Islamic Pottery*. London: Faber and Faber, 1957.

Meauzé, Pierre. *African Art*. Cleveland: World Publishing, 1967.

Mellaart, James. *The Neolithic of the Near East*. New York: Scribner, 1976.

Newman, Thelma. *Contemporary African Arts and Crafts: On-Site Working with Forms and Processes*. New York: Crown, 1974.

Wassing, René S. *African Art*. New York: Abrams, 1968.

Wilkinson, Charles K. *Iranian Ceramics*. New York: Abrams, 1963.

Wilson, Ralph Pinder. *Islamic Art*. New York: Macmillan, 1957.

Yoshida, Mitsukuni. *In Search of Persian Pottery*. New York: Weatherhill/Tankosha, 1972.

Medieval Through Nineteenth-Century Western Ceramics

Barrett, Richard Carter. *Bennington Pottery and Porcelain*. New York: Bonanza, 1958.

Berendson, Anne. *Tiles, General History*. New York: Viking, 1967.

Evans, Paul. *Art and Pottery of the United States*. New York: Scribner, 1974.

Quilland, Harold. *Early American Folk Pottery*. Radnor, Pa.: Chilton, 1971.

Hiller, Bevis. *Pottery and Porcelain, 1700–1914*. New York: Meredith, 1968.

Honey, William B. *European Ceramic Art*. London: Faber and Faber, 1949.

Ketchum, William C., Jr. Early *Potters and Potteries of New York State*. New York: Funk and Wagnalls, 1970.

Lane, Arthur. *Italian Porcelain*. London: Faber and Faber, 1954.

Liverani, Giuseppe. *Five Centuries of Italian Majolica*. New York: McGraw-Hill, 1960.

Mountford, Arnold R. *Staffordshire Salt-Glazed Stoneware*. London: Barrie & Jenkins, 1971.

Rackham, Bernard. *Medieval English Pottery*. New York: Van Nostrand, 1949.

Ramsay, John. *American Potters and Pottery*. New York: Tudor, 1947.

Savage, George. *Eighteenth Century German Porcelain*. New York: Tudor, 1968.

Spargo, John. *Early American Pottery and China*. New York: Century Library of American Antiques, 1926.

Watkins, Jura W. *Early New England Potters and Their Wares*. Hamden, Conn.: Anchron, 1968.

Webster, Donald Blake. *Decorated Stoneware Pottery of North America*. Rutland, Vt.: Tuttle, 1970.

Pre-Columbian Ceramics

Anton, Ferdinand, and Dockstader, Frederick J. *Pre-Columbian Art*. New York: Abrams, 1968.

Bushnell, G. H. S. *Ancient American Pottery*. New York: Pitman, 1955.

Disselhoff H.D., and Linne, S. *The Art of Ancient America*. New York: Crown, 1960.

Dockstader, Frederick J. *Indian Art in South America*. Greenwich, Conn.: New York Graphic Society, 1967.

Haberland, Wolfgang. *The Art of North America*. New York: Crown, 1964.

Kubler, George. *The Art and Architecture of Ancient America*. Baltimore: Penguin, 1962.

Lehmann, Henri. *Pre-Columbian Ceramics*. New York: Viking, 1962.

Lehmann, Henri. *Pre-Columbian Ceramics*. New York: Viking, 1962.

Litto, Gergrude. *South American Folk Pottery*. New York: Watson-Guptill, 1976.

Peterson, Susan. *The Living Tradition of Maria Martinez*. New York: Kodansha International, 1977.

von Hagen, Victor W. *The Desert Kingdoms of Peru*. Greenwich, Conn.: New York Graphic Society, 1964.

Willey, Gordon R. *An Introduction to American Archaeology*. Englewood Cliffs, N.J.: Prentice-Hall, 1966.

Index

Abraham, Carol Jeanne, covered jar, 127, Fig. 167 G; personal statement, 304–306, Fig. 294; steps in thixotropic forming, 124–127, Fig. 167A–F

acid oxides, 229, 230, 243

Africa, 69–70; Benin terra-cotta, 70, Fig. 99; Ife bronze figure, 69, Fig. 97; Ife, head, 70, Fig. 98; Mangbetu bottle, 71, Fig. 100

Albany slip, 243, 322

Alfonso, Leoni, construction 212, Fig. 243

alkaline fluxes, 229–230

alkaline glazes, 211, 327

alumina compounds, 242, 244

American pottery, early, 78–79; jug, 79, Fig. 114; pie plate, 78, Fig. 113; pitcher 79, Fig. 115

Ancient Middle East, 40–43; Egypt, 43, vase, Fig. 55; storage vessel, 43, Fig. 56; Ushabti, 43, Fig. 57; Iran, cup, 41, Fig. 52; cup, 42, Fig. 53; Mesopotamia, lion wall, 42, Fig. 54.

antimonious oxides, 242, 244

appendages: handles, 164–165; lids, 167–170, Fig. 204; spouts 166–167, Fig. 199

apprenticeships in pottery, 308

architectural ceramics, 128–131, Figs. 168–173

Art Nouveau vase, 80, Fig. 116

Arneson, Robert, *Samuel Gompers,* 125, Pl. 12

asbestos, 282

ash glazes, 213–214, 328

atomic weights, common elements, 320; in glaze formulation, 228

aventurine glazes, 223, 330

Baggs, Arthur E., jar, 82, Fig. 120

ball clay, 4–5; analysis of, 322

barium compounds, 239, 244

basalt body, 78, 332

base oxides, 239–241

batch recipe, 230–235

Bennington Potters, 79

bentonite, 6, 244, 322

binders, 263

bismuth, 244

bisque fire, 272–274, Fig. 275

Blain, Sandra J., planter 97, Fig. 132

bone ash, 78, 245

borax, 245

boric oxide, 242, 245

bottle form, 142; throwing of, 147, Fig. 184A–F

bowl form 142; throwing of, 145, Fig. 183A–H

Bristol glaze, 224, 225, Fig. 251

Buonagurio, Toby, *Super Duesie,* 126, Pl. 13

burners, 293–295, 335, Figs. 286–289

cadmium, 245

calcium-aluminate cement, 278

calcium compounds, 240, 245

Cardew, Michael, jar, 85, Fig. 125

Chinese ceramics, 24–28, 54–56; Chin, horse and rider, 27, Fig. 30; Ch'ing, 56; teapot, 55, Fig. 76; Han vase, 28, Fig. 31; Ming, 55; cup, 55, Fig. 75; jar, 54, Fig. 74; Neolithic, 24–26, bowl, 25, Fig. 27; jar, 26, Fig. 28; Shang, 26, vase, 27, Fig. 29; Sung, 28, camel, 39, Pl. 1; vase, 29, Fig. 33; vase and incense burner, 39, Pl. 2; T'ang, 28, horse and rider, 29, Fig. 32; Yüan 55, bottle, 54, Fig. 73

Caruso, Nino, modular sculpture, 113, Fig. 152, 153; slip casting, 111–112, Figs. 149–151

casting, 111, 112, Figs. 149, 150, 151

casting slips, 110; recipes for, 333

celadon, 220; historical, 28, 39, 55, Pl. 2

centering, 138, 139, Figs. 180A–D

chemicals, ceramic, 239–258; analysis of, 320, 321

chimney, 293

chinaware, 10

Cicansky, Victor, *Working,* 126, Pl. 14

chrome oxide, 243, 245

clay, analysis of common types, 322; firing changes 273, Fig. 276; formation of, 2, 3, Fig. 1; mixers, 334; plasticity of, 3–6; preparation of, 14, 88; tests for, 12–13; prospecting, 14, 15, Figs. 15, 16; tests for, 12–13; safety caution, 14; types of 3–6; wedging, 88, Fig. 126; 89, Fig. 89; 90, Fig. 127; 93, Fig. 128

clay bodies, absorption of, 13; aging of, 13, 89; defects, 201; recipes for, 331–333; tests, 12, 13; types of, 7–11

cobalt oxides, 246

coil and paddle, 98

coil construction, 95–99, Figs. 131A–E

colemanite, 246

colorants, 12, 258, 333

combed slipware, 76, 186, Fig. 220

cones, temperature table, 325; use of, 270, 271, Fig. 273

conversion tables, 326

Coper, Hans, bottle, 188, Fig. 225

copper oxides, 247

copper-red glazes, 221, 329, 330, Fig. 247; historical, 55, Fig. 75

Cornwall stone, 247; analysis of, 321

Cournoyer, Georgette, tool bag, 12, Fig. 13

covers, 170, Fig. 204

crackle glazes, 221, Figs. 248, 249

crawling, 202

crazing, 203, 209

Crumbiegel, Dieter, bottle, 235, Fig. 256

cryolite, 247

crystalline glazes, vase, 81, Fig. 118; 222–223, Fig. 240; 330

Currier, Ann, teapot, 110, Fig. 148

cylinder, throwing of, 139–141, Figs. 182A–H

Cypriote pottery, 46, Fig. 62

Daley, William, forming a mural unit, 130, Figs. 172A–D; mural, 131, Fig. 173; personal statement, 306–307, Fig. 295

David, Willis Bing, *Ancestrial Ritual Vessel,* 114, Fig. 155

decals, 200–201, Fig. 241

decoration, 178–189; on bisque ware, 188–189; on clay, 181–183; on dry ware, 187–188; incising 183, Fig. 213; on leather-hard clay, 183–187; in plastic state, 181–183, Figs. 209, 212, 213, 217

deflocculants, 315

De Larios, Dora, wall sculpture, 3, Fig. 2; head, 11, Fig. 11

della Robbia, Luca, *Madonna and Child,* 75, Fig. 107

de Jong, Hans, vase, 184, Fig. 216

de Rooden, Jan, *Pressure,* 233, Fig. 255

designing for production, 309–313

Dillon, Allester, vase, 7, Fig. 6

Dixon, Bob, 152, Fig. 185

Dresang, Paul A., raku teapot, 162, Pl. 22; jar, 216, Pl. 33

Duckworth, Ruth, *Clowds over Chicago,* 126, Pl. 15; garden sculpture, 116, Fig. 157; vase, 98, Fig. 134

earthenware clay, 5–6, 311

Eckels, Robert, bottle, 134, Fig. 174; personal statement, 300, 301, Fig. 290

Egyptian ceramics, storage vessel, 43, Fig. 56; Ushabti, 43, Fig. 57; vase, 43, Fig. 55

Egyptian paste, 42–43, 182–183, 322; hippopotamus, 40, Pl. 4

elements, (kiln), 270

empirical glaze formula, 230

English ceramics, historical, 76; dish, 76, Fig. 108; jug, 200, Fig. 241; platter, 186, Fig. 220

engobes, 187, 188, 332

Photographic Sources

Cover and title page   William Hunt Company and *Ceramics Monthly*

Color plates   5: John King, New Canaan, Ct. 7: Joe Schopplein 11: Frank J. Thomas, Los Angeles 14: Don Hall 15: Hedrich-Blessing, Chicago 18: Joe Schopplein 23: Leslie Bellavance 24: James O. Milmoe 25: Bob Barrett 28: Mark Schwartz 29: Lester Bergman 30: Roger Schricber 31: Leslie Bellavance 38: John Morser 41: James O. Milmoe 44: Leslie Segal, New York 45: Bob Barrett

Black-and-white photographs   1: Kenneth M. Towe, Smithsonian Institution, Washington, D.C. 6: Robin Collier 8: Dennis R. O'Hoy, Bendigo C.A.E., Australia 14: Charles Frizzell 16: Amoco Minerals Company, Denver Pages 16–17: Ashmolean Museum, Oxford 17: Yan/Toulouse, France 27: Robert Harding Associates, London 40: Peter Moore, New York 43: Helga Photo Studios, New York 45, 47: Carmelo Guadagno, New York 58: Tap Service, Athens 61: Department of Antiquities, Cyprus 67: Sporintendenza Archeologica, Rome Pages 52–53: Bettmann Archive, New York 97: Eliot Elisofon, Life Magazine, © Time Inc. 122: Japanese Embassy, Washington, D.C. 128: George Gardner, Belle Harbor, N.Y. 130: F. W. Parks 133: Jim Lindsey 137: George Gardner, Belle Harbor, N.Y. 139: John T. Ferrari, Brooklyn, N.Y. 142–143F: © Evon Streetman 147A–C: Bing & Grøndahl Copenhagen Porcelain, Ltd. 154: Roger Schreiber, Seattle 155: Bifocal Photography 160: M. Barling 161: Arts Council of Great Britain, London; John Webb, Cheam, Surrey 162: Jarvis Grant 164–165I: R. Vigiletti 176–177: from "Dona Rosa, Mexican Potter" by Mollie Poupeney (*Ceramics Monthly,* May 1974); photos by Mollie Poupeney 181: Joshua Schreier 198: R. Vigiletti 201: Marissa Burton, Office of Public Relations, Ferrum College, Ferrum, Va. 202: Neil Saver 207A–D: Leslie Bellavance 216: Dick Wolters, Ovezande, Holland 226: Joe Laval 229: Bing & Grøndahl Copenhagen Porcelain, Ltd. 242: Pat Probst Gilman 249: Al Schoenborn 250: John Morser 252: Carmelo Guadagno, New York 255: Olivier Pictures, Amsterdam 261: Joshua Schreier 271: Leigh Photograph, Trenton, N. J. 273: George Gardner, Belle Harbor, N.Y. 274: Leigh Photograph, Trenton, N. J. 293: R. Vigiletti 297–298: Syracuse China Corporation, Syracuse, N.Y.

Photographs by Peter Dommermuth: 126A–B, 131A–E, 180A–D, 182A–H, 183A–H, 184A–F, 186A–F, 191–192, 206A–H, 213, 222